D1401453

FUNDAMENTAL CONCEPTS OF PROGRAMMING SYSTEMS

JEFFREY D. ULLMAN
Princeton University

ADDISON-WESLEY PUBLISHING COMPANY
Reading, Massachusetts
Menlo Park, California · London · Amsterdam · Don Mills, Ontario · Sydney

This book is in the
ADDISON-WESLEY SERIES IN
COMPUTER SCIENCE AND INFORMATION PROCESSING

Michael A. Harrison
Consulting Editor

Copyright © 1976 by Addison-Wesley Publishing Company, Inc. Philippines copyright 1976 by Addison-Wesley Publishing Company, Inc.

All rights reserved. No part of this publication may be reproduced, stored in a retrieval system, or transmitted, in any form or by any means, electronic, mechanical, photocopying, recording, or otherwise, without the prior written permission of the publisher. Printed in the United States of America. Published simultaneously in Canada. Library of Congress Catalog Card No. 75-374.

ISBN 0-201-07654-3
GHIJKLMNO-MA-8987654321

Preface

This book evolved from class notes developed at Princeton University for a course, Eng217, entitled "Introduction to Programming Systems." Nominally at the sophomore level, the course presumed only the freshman programming course in which FORTRAN and SNOBOL were taught.

We found that Eng217 was taken by two roughly equinumerous groups. The first group consists of students intending to specialize in computer science, many of whom took the course in their freshman year. The second consists of nonspecialists—mostly mathematicians and engineers of various stripes—who took the course for a survey of computer science. In attempting to serve both groups, the course covered much material, hitting the highlights of many separate fields of computer science. PL/I (and also IBM 360 assembly language) was covered in the laboratory, assuring that by the time the lectures covered programming-language concepts, the students had experience with at least three such languages.

Use of the Book

Early versions of the Eng217 course included three topics—structured programming, binary computer arithmetic, and elementary computer organization. At the time of this writing, these have largely filtered down to the freshman year. I have retained Chapters 0, 1, and 2 on these subjects because I regard them as essential for what follows and suspect that they are not universally included in a first course in programming. The middle chapters of the book, covering machine-level data-structure implementation, assemblers, loaders, link editors, and programming-language concepts, appear here essentially at the same level as they were covered in the course. The later chapters, on context-free grammars, parsers, and compiling were covered more briefly in class. The final chapter, on proving programs correct, was covered in a series of optional lectures after the formal end of the course. My feeling is that this topic stimulates interest and deserves some mention in the Computer Science curriculum, if only for what it says about how to document programs.

Notes on the Exercises

The exercises are grouped into three levels of difficulty. Unstarred exercises should
be within the ability of all students; singly starred exercises are more difficult; and
doubly starred ones are the most difficult. This last group is probably unsuitable for
homework problems, but might provide an occasional challenge. The exercises also
include a set of programming problems. These could be used either as a vehicle for
learning a language such as PL/I, or simply to reinforce understanding of the concepts covered in the book.

Acknowledgments

I have profited greatly from critical readings of the manuscript by Al Aho, Mike
Harrison, and Tom Szymanski. The students in Eng217 deserve thanks for wading
through the bugs in the manuscript: the comments of Steve Horowitz should be
mentioned as especially helpful. Discussions with Bruce Arden and Doug McIlroy
are also acknowledged. An excellent job of typing the many iterations of the manuscript was done by Hannah Kresse.

Princeton, N.J.   J. D. U.
August 1975

Contents

Chapter 0

Structured Programs

Throughout this book we assume that the reader has knowledge of a scientific programming language—most likely FORTRAN, but possibly ALGOL 60 or that part of PL/I appropriate for scientific computing. Nothing else in the way of computer science knowledge is assumed. Therefore we shall treat in turn the various aspects of programming systems—the computer itself, machine and assembly languages, assemblers, loaders, programming languages, and compilers. Our starting point is "structured programming"—a subject which pertains not to the way in which programs are run on the computer but to the design of the programs themselves. The goal of structured-programming is to make programs easy to design, debug, and be understood by persons other than the writer of the program.

The importance of structured programming is only one of the reasons we have chosen to begin with this topic. The notation of structured programming is an excellent method of describing algorithms informally, and we shall use it throughout the book.

0.1 THE SYSTEMS APPROACH TO LIFE

When small pieces are connected to form a whole, the conglomeration is called a *system*. The concept of a system pervades all walks of life from the organization of the economy of a nation to the building of "computer systems" from hardware and software components. As we shall see, a program can likewise be regarded as a system.

From the systems point of view:

1. Components of a system should have minimal interaction with other pieces of the system and that only through a well-defined *interface* which provides rigid control of the data, signals, goods, or other interactions that pass through it.

2. A second aspect of the systems point of view is that there must be a *hierarchy* of systems components. Components at any given level are themselves systems of components at the next lower level; this proceeds downward to progressively lower

1

levels, until the components at the "lowest level" are so elementary that they can be considered indivisible. Thus in the simple system shown in Fig. 0.1, the design of component A, which is itself a system of more elementary components, can be undertaken with the designer having knowledge only of what is expected at the $A-B$ and $A-C$ interfaces. The designer of A does not need to know about the design of B, and more important, he cannot base his own design on the presumed design of B or C.

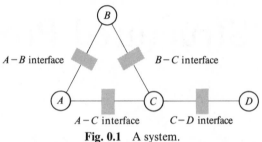

Fig. 0.1   A system.

This approach has the advantage that should modification of A be desired at some future time (and in long-lasting systems, modification of components is the rule rather than the exception), there would be no need to worry about what effect the new A would have on B. It would be sufficient to make A conform to the rules governing the $A-B$ and $A-C$ interfaces, in order to ensure that the whole system would continue to work.

Example 0.1.   A factory producing glassware may be regarded as part of an economic system, as can the railroad that ships the output of the factory. The rules of the interface are that the factory's output must be delivered to the railroad depot packed in cartons in such a way that the glasses will not break if the carton is subjected to shocks of up to a certain severity. The factory is responsible for packing the glassware sufficiently well to meet the interface condition, and the railroad must maintain its equipment such that shocks exceeding the specified tolerance will not be administered.

It might be tempting for the factory manager to attempt to determine the particular car in which his goods would be shipped each day and to save money by packing in flimsier cartons on those days when the railroad was providing a car with particularly good shock absorbers. This strategy would, however, lead to chaos should a car breakdown necessitate either a last-minute or an en-route substitution. Thus it is usually cheaper in the long run to maintain the discipline of a fixed interface than to attempt to take advantage of interactions between system components, even if malfunctions caused by these interactions are extremely rare.   ∎

The hierarchical view of a system permits thinking about different issues at different levels, while screening out the problems arising at other levels.

Example 0.2.   We can regard an economic system as composed of industries and consumers. At this, the highest level, the most important interactions are those of supply and demand. At the next level, industries may be regarded as composed of companies.† The interactions between companies chiefly concern competitive actions or the lack thereof. At the third level, we might regard companies as composed of factories and concern ourselves with which factory should be closed down or take on an additional shift were a change in production warranted. We could worry about issues on the level of interactions between factories without being concerned with what on a higher or lower level caused the problem. For example, the need to close a factory could be caused by a change in demand, by a strengthening of the company's competitors, or by a number of other factors. The root cause is of minor importance on the factory level. The important issues can be described on the factory level alone, e.g., which factory is least efficient.

Going further down the hierarchy, factories are composed of departments, which, in turn, are composed of people. At this point, while the systems component, the "person," could certainly be subdivided still further, there is no value in doing so as far as the understanding of an economic system is concerned. ∎

0.2 STRUCTURED PROGRAMMING

A program can be regarded as a system whose components are smaller programs. These component programs can, in turn, be regarded as systems composed of still smaller programs, and so on, down to some reasonable level, where the components tend to consist of a few statements each. It is generally believed that programmers should be strongly encouraged to write their programs with the systems point of view in mind, and that programming languages should even be redesigned from this point of view if necessary. Programs written in this way are often referred to as *structured.*

As previously mentioned, the intended advantages of structured programming include ease of writing, understanding, and debugging. Writing is made easier because programs are written "top down." Initially we write the program as an interconnection of a few routines (components) described informally. Hopefully, the interactions between these components are few, and each can be designed in relative isolation. Each component is designed by writing it as a system of smaller components, down to the level of a single programming language statement, a group of a few statements, or a subroutine.

Example 0.3.   The true virtues of structured programming can be demonstrated only by the design of a very large program—one that is too large for the typical programmer to write easily. However, the methodology can be illustrated by a comparatively short example such as that of multiplying two 10×10 matrices.

For introduction, a matrix is a two-dimensional array. We can denote the element in the ith row and jth column of matrix M by M_{ij} mathematically or by $M(I, J)$ using

---

† Let us assume for simplicity that each company is engaged in only one industry. In reality, the fact that companies often operate in many industries complicates the system by introducing additional interfaces between industries.

the style of FORTRAN or almost any programming language. The product of two $n \times n$ matrices A and B is that matrix C such that for all i and j between 1 and n,

$$C_{ij} = \sum_{k=1}^{n} A_{ik} B_{kj}.$$

Put another way, the *dot product* of two vectors (one-dimensional arrays), say $(v_1, v_2, \ldots, v_n)$ and $(w_1, w_2, \ldots, w_n)$ is the sum of the products of corresponding elements, that is

$$\sum_{i=1}^{n} v_i \, w_i.$$

Then the element in row i, column j of the product of matrices A and B is the dot product of the ith row of A with the jth column of B.

Now let us design a FORTRAN program to read two 10×10 matrices, multiply them, and print the result. On the broadest level, the program consists of the three components indicated by the flowchart of Fig. 0.2(a). We have specified neither the details of the computation nor the way in which data is to be represented in the computer, on the input or on the printed output. At this, the highest level of the hierarchy, we have simply noted that the program will consist of three pieces which are executed in series.

We must now refine each of the boxes of Fig. 0.2(a) if necessary. Boxes 1 and 3 require little work. For box 1 we need only decide on a format for the input. Let us say that the elements of the matrices are integers, and that complete columns are punched on cards in a 10I8 format, those of A preceding those of B. The obvious choice for representation inside the computer is as a two-dimensional array. Then, after suitable DIMENSION and INTEGER statements, we could refine box 1 directly into two simple FORTRAN statements, a read statement and a format statement:

```
          READ (5,100) A,B
     100  FORMAT (10I8)
```

Similarly, box 3 becomes

```
          WRITE (6,200) C
     200  FORMAT (10I12)
```

assuming we wish to print C column by column.

In this simple example, only box 2 is truly a system of smaller components. We can easily recognize that to compute C we must compute the dot product of row I of A and column J of B for all I and J in any order we choose. A convenient approach is to use an iterator for J inside an iterator for I. The resulting system is shown in Fig. 0.2(b).

Boxes 2.1 and 2.2 are easily implemented by DO loops, but box 2.3 can profit from further refinement. The approach used is a system consisting of an initialization of $C(I, J)$ to 0, followed by iteratively adding to it the product $A(I, K) * B(K, J)$ as K ranges from 1 to 10. This refinement is shown in Fig. 0.2(c).

Now that we have refined each component sufficiently, we can write our program directly. The final program is shown in Fig. 0.3. ∎

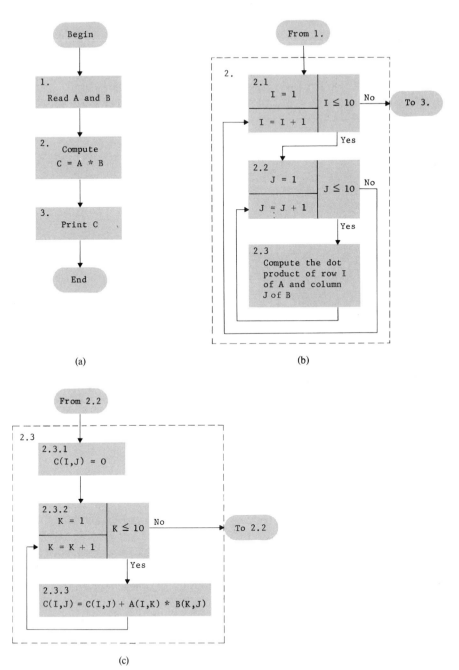

Fig. 0.2 Top-down design of a program to multiply matrices.

From box		Statement
		DIMENSION A(10, 10), B(10, 10), C(10, 10)
		INTEGER A, B, C
1		READ (5, 100) A, B
1	100	FORMAT (10I8)
2.1		DO 10 I = 1, 10
2.2		DO 10 J = 1, 10
2.3.1		C(I, J) = 0
2.3.2		DO 10 K = 1, 10
2.3.3	10	C(I, J) = C(I, J) + A(I, K) * B(K, J)
3		WRITE (6,200) C
3	200	FORMAT (10I12)
		STOP
		END

Fig. 0.3   Program to multiply matrices.

Another important advantage of structured programming is ease of understanding by a person other than the program writer. The importance of this understanding should not be minimized by a person who has programmed only "student jobs." Industrial programs are often modified and run for years by a succession of programmers after the original writer has gone elsewhere.

Understanding is achieved "bottom up." First the smallest portions are grasped; then they are fitted together to make larger systems, which are grasped; and so on. For example, given the program of Fig. 0.3, it is not hard to understand the action of the code written for the flowchart of Fig. 0.2(c). It sets

$$C_{ij} = \sum_{k=1}^{10} A_{ik}B_{kj}.$$

Having grasped this fact, one should then easily understand the code written for all of Fig. 0.2 (b); it computes C_{ij} for all i and j between 1 and 10. Finally, the entire program should become clear.

In FORTRAN, it is hard to tell just by looking at the program that the 7th through 9th lines form a major component corresponding to box 2.3 in Fig. 0.2. Subsequently, we shall see ways that certain languages can be used to make structure more apparent to the reader of a program.

Regarding debugging: it is a useful technique to debug small components in isolation, using test data appropriate to the problem. Once small components have been debugged, they can be put together to form the next level of component, which can be debugged in turn. Any errors introduced at this level can be attributed with some assurance to the interface between component pieces. With the source of error narrowed down in this way, debugging of the larger components is simplified.

If we debug in this manner, it is often useful to make components be subroutines wherever feasible. In addition to the usual benefits of subroutines, it is particularly easy to try out a subroutine on a variety of test data.

0.3   METHODS OF PRODUCING STRUCTURED PROGRAMS

Let us now consider some of the programming techniques that lead to programs having "structure." In essence, we want methods of writing programs in which a program can be broken into a hierarchy of components, with any one section of code interacting with other portions of the program in two possible ways. First, control can flow either in or out of the section of code in question. To limit such interaction, then, we may wish to limit the number of ways control enters or leaves those sections of code which can reasonably be regarded as components of the system.

Interaction also occurs when a variable has a value assigned to it outside a section of code and that value is used within, or vice-versa. Thus if a section of code is a system component, it would be useful to know that only a few program variables carried data in or out of the section. Even more important is the need to know *exactly* which variables *do* transmit values in or out of the section; that is, we need to determine the exact interface between this component and the outside world. With these considerations in mind, let us list a few suggestions to help lend structure to programs.

1. Avoid, wherever possible, goto statements and conditional jumps or branches, such as FORTRAN arithmetic IF statements[†] or IF statements containing GOTO. Such statements make it difficult to tell what the components of a program should logically be, since many sections of code might have several ways in which they could jump in or out. Moreover, there is no way short of eyeballing the entire program to determine from whence control can reach a given point.

To affect the flow of control in a program, we prefer those types of control statements that tend to form system components; that is, we try to construct sections of code that begin at one particular point and end at another. A FORTRAN DO loop is a reasonable choice for a system component. Since jumps into a DO loop are forbidden, we know each DO loop begins at its DO statement. Many DO loops are written so the only way to get out of the loop is by reaching the statement following the loop after the loop index has exceeded its maximum value. However, jumps out of the DO loop to other parts of the program are, of course, permitted.

Other loop-forming statements which tend to create loops that may naturally be regarded as system components are the PL/I DO WHILE ... END statement and the ALGOL **for** statement.

Certain types of branching statements also help form components, since they cause control to wind up at a single place, independent of which branch is actually taken. For example, the FORTRAN logical IF[‡] ultimately causes the statement on the next line to be executed independent of whether the logical expression is true or not (provided of course that the statement following the logical expression is not a GOTO statement). Similarly, the IF ... THEN ... and IF ... THEN ... ELSE ... constructs from PL/I or ALGOL will return control to a unique point provided the

---

† That is, statements of the form IF (arithmetic expression) label1, label2, label3.

‡ That is, IF (logical expression) statement.

pieces of code following THEN and ELSE do not contain a goto statement or conditional jump to a place outside these pieces of code.

2. Use subroutines. A subroutine is a natural component of a system. The interface between the subroutine and the rest of the program is its parameters. There is a "hidden" interface, however, if the subroutine uses data that is neither local to itself nor a parameter, e.g., COMMON data in FORTRAN programs. Such manipulations, called *side effects*, must also be regarded as crossing the interface and tend to work against the idea of isolating system components. Thus our third technique for increasing program structure is:

3. Avoid side effects as far as possible.

4. Try to limit the scope[†] of variables. The goal is to make clear when a variable really does pass information between two places in a program (i.e., is part of an interface). For example, in FORTRAN, a DO loop index should not be assumed to take on any particular value after the loop, so its scope can be regarded as limited to the DO loop. Thus if we see two nonnested DO loops using the same index, say I, we know at once that I does not form part of the interface between the loops.

Many programming languages, including ALGOL and PL/I but not FORTRAN, have *blocks*,—sequences of statements preceded by the keyword BEGIN and followed by END—which are used to limit the scope of variables. That is, the scope of any variable declared between a matching BEGIN and END is limited to the block between that BEGIN and that END. Blocks may be nested within one another, and a variable, say X, declared in one block is distinct from any other variable X declared in another block.

Example 0.4.   Consider the block structure of Fig. 0.4, which might have been taken from an ALGOL program. An identifier I is declared in block 1, which contains two blocks, 2 and 3, nested within it. It is possible that blocks 2 and 3 each use I, but in essentially independent ways, such as for the index of two different loops. Since I is still declared in the region between blocks 2 and 3, we must be concerned with the possibility that the value held by I when block 2 ends could have some effect on block 3. That is, I forms part of the apparent interface between blocks 2 and 3,[‡] even though the two blocks may have no actual effect upon one another.

A better approach, from the structured programming viewpoint, would be to declare I twice, once inside block 2 and once inside block 3, if in fact the value of I when block 2 ends has no effect upon block 3. Then, since I would not even be declared in the gap between these blocks, the absence of interaction would be immediately obvious to a person trying to understand the program.   ∎

[†] The *scope* of a variable is the program region over which it is defined. For example, in FORTRAN a variable other than a parameter or COMMON variable mentioned in a subroutine has scope contained within that subroutine. That is, its value cannot be used or modified outside the subroutine, even if another routine has a variable with the same name.

[‡] Of course, with effort, a person reading this program could discover that I really conveyed no information between blocks 2 and 3. However, one goal of structured programming is to make things easy for the reader of the program. The situation being described works counter to that goal.

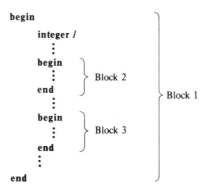

Fig. 0.4   A block structure.

0.4   A GOTOLESS LANGUAGE

While it is far from obvious, all the varieties of control flow—branches, loops and so on—can be obtained by a very simple language with only three control structures to influence the sequencing of statements. Moreover, these control structures naturally induce a hierarchical structure on every program, and they limit interactions between "system components" from which a program is built. We shall give an example based on FORTRAN for the elementary kinds of statements. The reader can easily substitute another style for elementary statements, say PL/I or ALGOL, if he desires.

Our *gotoless language* will be based on the notion of a "statement," which will be effectively synonymous with "program." That is, any statement can be a program. The rules for constructing statements are the following.

1. Any FORTRAN declaration, assignment, input/output statement, or subroutine call or return is a statement in the language. Thus we have eliminated all the "FORTRAN-style" control statements, IF, DO, GOTO, and computed and assigned GOTO's.

2. Our first control construct is used to form loops. If $\mathscr{E}$ is a FORTRAN logical expression and $\mathscr{S}$ is any statement, then

while $\mathscr{E}$ do $\mathscr{S}$

is a legal statement in our language and has the meaning indicated by the flowchart of Fig. 0.5(a). That is, we test whether $\mathscr{E}$ is true, and if so, do $\mathscr{S}$. Then, we test $\mathscr{E}$ again and so on.

Note that the only way for this loop to terminate is for $\mathscr{E}$ to be false initially, in which case the loop is never entered, or for repeated execution of $\mathscr{S}$ to eventually make $\mathscr{E}$ false. For example, $\mathscr{E}$ might be $I \cdot LT \cdot 100$ and $\mathscr{S}$ might be a large program which each time through sets $I = I + 1$.

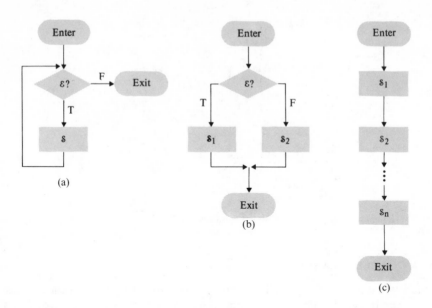

Fig. 0.5 Flow charts for compound statements: a) **while** . . . **do**; b) **if** . . . **then** . . . **else**; c) **begin** . . . **end**.

3. Our second construct is used for branching. If $\mathscr{E}$ is a FORTRAN logical expression, and $\mathscr{S}_1$ and $\mathscr{S}_2$ are any two statements, then

$$\textbf{if } \mathscr{E} \textbf{ then } \mathscr{S}_1 \textbf{ else } \mathscr{S}_2$$

is a legal statement. The meaning of this statement is indicated in Fig. 0.5(b). We may omit **else** $\mathscr{S}_2$ occasionally. In that case, we do nothing at all if $\mathscr{E}$ is false.

4. If $\mathscr{S}_1, \mathscr{S}_2, \ldots, \mathscr{S}_n$ are statements, then

$$\textbf{begin } \mathscr{S}_1; \mathscr{S}_2; \ldots; \mathscr{S}_n \textbf{ end}$$

is a statement. This type of statement enables us to sequence actions, as shown in Fig. 0.5(c).

It should be apparent that the $\mathscr{S}$'s which we have referred to as "statements" can actually be lengthy collections of the simple statements described in rule (1), with structure put on the collection by the constructs of rules (2) through (4). To ensure that the structure is more apparent when programs are written, we shall exhibit the constructs of rules (2) through (4) in nested fashion on the page as shown in Fig. 0.6.

It is beyond the scope of this book to prove that every FORTRAN program can be converted to a program in our gotoless language. It should be observed that the construction whereby we can convert from FORTRAN to our language has certain

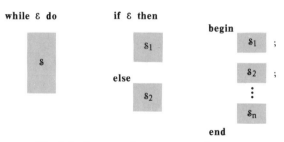

Fig. 0.6   Layout of structures on the page.

undesirable features. We may be forced to introduce new Boolean-valued identifiers and/or duplicate large blocks of code. Nevertheless, our ability to write efficient structured programs is guaranteed by the introduction of certain new structures as discussed in the next section. Two examples of structured programming using the gotoless language follow.

Example 0.5.   Let us write a program (statement) in the gotoless language to compute $M = N!$ if $N \geqslant 0$ and set $M = 0$ if $N < 0$.[†] Our basic strategy will be to read N from the input and initialize M to 1 if $N \geqslant 1$. We repeatedly multiply M by N and decrement N by 1. When N reaches 1, the initial value of M (i.e., 1) will have been multiplied by each number between 1 and the initial value of N.

Having described our strategy "top down," we may then begin to write a code for the smallest components by first designing a compound statement to do the multiplication of M by N and decrementing of N. The **begin** . . . **end** construct enables us to sequence them thusly.

$$\begin{array}{l} \textbf{begin} \\ \quad M = M * N; \\ \quad N = N - 1 \\ \textbf{end} \end{array}$$

We must perform the above operation until N reaches 1. Thus, the loop forming **while** . . . **do** . . . construct can be used to build the loop as follows.

$$\begin{array}{l} \textbf{while } N . GE . 1 \textbf{ do} \\ \quad \textbf{begin} \\ \quad\quad M = M * N; \\ \quad\quad N = N - 1 \\ \quad \textbf{end} \end{array}$$

Next, we must string the above code together with a statement that initializes M to 1 as shown in Fig. 0.7.

[†] $N! = N(N - 1)(N - 2) \ldots (2)(1).$ 0! is taken to be 1.

```
begin
    M = 1;
    while N . GE . 1 do
        begin
            M = M * N;
            N = N - 1
        end
end
```

Fig. 0.7   Program to compute $M = N!$ for $N \geqslant 0$.

Finally, we must include the reading of N and the printing of M. However, if $N < 0$, the above code will not set $M = 0$ as intended. Thus we must introduce an **if** ... **then** ... **else** ... construct and make the above code the alternative only if $N \geqslant 0$. The entire program is the statement shown in Fig. 0.8. ▌


```
begin
    READ, N;
    if N . LT . 0 then
        M = 0
    else
        begin
            M = 1;
            while N . GE . 1 do
                begin
                    M = M * N;
                    N = N - 1
                end
        end;
    PRINT, M
end
```

Fig. 0.8   Completed factorial program. In this program we use simple READ and PRINT statements not universally implemented in FORTRAN. Note that since only one elementary statement is executed when $N . LT . 0$ is true, it need not be surrounded by **begin** ... **end**. The semicolon after "**end**" marks the end of the statement that began with **if**.

It should not be deduced from the above example that things always fit nicely into place when constructing programs in our gotoless language. The following is an example of one way in which awkwardness can be introduced—the case where we wish to build a loop which makes its test at the end rather than at the beginning.

Example 0.6.   A FORTRAN DO loop is always executed once, even if the lower limit exceeds the upper limit. For example, the DO loop:

```
        DO 10 I = 4, N
    10   A(I) = B(I)
```

is executed once if $N \leqslant 4$ and $(N - 3)$ times if $N \geqslant 5$. Thus, the gotoless statement of Fig. 0.9. is wrong, since the statement $A(I) = B(I)$ will not be executed at all if $N \leqslant 3$. The "solution," in this case, is to first precede the **while** . . . **do** . . . loop by the body of the FORTRAN DO loop for the initial value of I, that is, $I = 4$. Then initialize I to 5 and follow it with the **while** . . . **do** . . . loop. The statement of Fig. 0.10 correctly simulates the above DO loop. ∎

> **begin**
>   I = 4;
>   **while** I . LE . N **do**
>   **begin**
>   A(I) = B(I);
>   I = I + 1
>   **end**
> **end**

Fig. 0.9   Gotoless program not identical to DO loop.

> **begin**
>   A(4) = B(4);
>   I = 5;
>   **while** I . LE . N **do**
>   **begin**
>   A(I) = B(I);
>   I = I + 1
>   **end**
> **end**

Fig. 0.10   Correct simulation of DO loop.

0.5   ADDITIONAL CONTROL CONSTRUCTS FOR STRUCTURED PROGRAMMING

One way to improve our language and decrease the frequency of such problems as that shown in Example 0.6 is to introduce other constructs to provide alternative structures. For example, the construct

repeat 𝒮 until ℰ

with the flowchart of Fig. 0.11 can help with DO loop problems.

Example 0.7.   The DO loop of Example 0.6 could be programmed as in Fig. 0.12 using **repeat** . . . **until** . . . . ∎

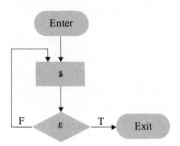

Fig. 0.11   Flow chart of **repeat** . . . **until**.

```
begin
    I = 4;
    repeat
        begin
            A(I) = B(I);
            I = I + 1
        end
    until
        I · GT · N
end
```

Fig. 0.12   Another structured program for DO loop.

A more direct approach is to introduce a control structure similar to the DO loop or the ALGOL **for** statement. For simplicity, we shall use a syntax that is considerably less general than the ALGOL **for**.

If INITIAL and FINAL are any integer or integer-valued variables, STEP is an integer, INDEX is an integer-valued variable, and $\mathscr{S}$ is any statement of our gotoless language, then

$$\text{\textbf{for} INDEX = INITIAL \textbf{by} STEP}^\dagger \text{ \textbf{to} FINAL \textbf{do} } \mathscr{S}$$

is a statement. If STEP is a positive integer, the flowchart of this statement is shown in Fig. 0.13(a). If STEP is a negative integer, the flowchart is that of Fig. 0.13(b).

Example 0.8.   We could write the DO loop of Example 0.6 as

$$\text{\textbf{for}   I = 4 \textbf{to} N \textbf{do}}$$
$$A(I) = B(I)   \blacksquare$$

In a sense, our **for** statement is a slightly generalized DO loop. There is one impor-

---

† If STEP is 1, we may omit **by** STEP.

tant difference, however. Unlike the DO loop, we can leave a **for** statement at only one place, its end. Jumps out of a **for** statement are impossible. Thus we know exactly where control will go after the **for** statement finishes. We feel, therefore, that the **for** statement induces structure in programs because its interaction with other statements due to variations in control flow are limited. Incidentally, all the above applies equally well to the **while** . . . **do** . . . and **repeat** . . . **until** . . . loops.

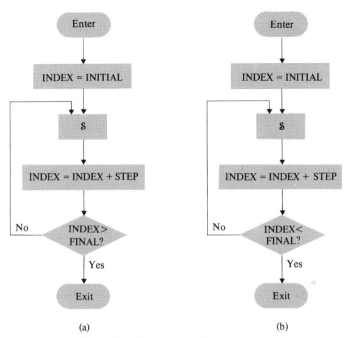

Fig. 0.13   Flow chart of **for** statement.

A final, and even more versatile augmentation of our structured language is the introduction of the **break** statement. To use this feature, we need to label certain loops, by prefixing an identifier (the label) and a colon to **while**, **repeat** or **for**, whichever type of statement formed the loop. If a loop has been labeled LOOP1, then the statement **break** LOOP1 anywhere within the loop causes the loop to terminate. Control passes to whatever statement normally follows the loop. Thus although **break** can cause loop termination to occur for various reasons, control winds up at the same point independent of whether the loop terminated normally or whether one or another **break** caused its termination.

Example 0.9.   The DO loop of Example 0.6 can be written yet another way, as shown in Fig. 0.14.   ∎

```
                    begin
                       I = 4;
           LOOP:  while . TRUE . do
                       begin
                          A(ı) = B(I);
                          if I . GE . N then
                             break LOOP
                          else
                             I = I + 1
                       end
           end
```

Fig. 0.14   DO loop simulated using **break** statement.

It should be noted that a loop may be broken from inside a nested loop, so one **break** statement may actually break several loops at once.

Example 0.10.   The program of Fig. 0.15 tests whether some entry in a 10×10 integer array A is 0, setting FOUND to $+1$ if so, and to -1 otherwise. If the **break** statement is executed, the loop named OUTER is terminated, which causes a jump to the statement PRINT FOUND. ∎

Note that the loop INNER (the name is superfluous) has two possible exits. If the break is made, control goes from INNER to WRITE FOUND, and if INNER terminates normally, by J exceeding 10, control goes to code which increments I. Thus in a sense, by allowing the **break** statement, we have decreased structure by increasing the interaction between the loop INNER and its surroundings.

```
                begin
                    DIMENSION A(10, 10);
                    INTEGER A;
                    READ, A;†
                    FOUND = -1;
          OUTER: for I = 1 to 10 do
          INNER: for J = 1 to 10 do
                    if A(I, J) = 0 then‡
                    begin
                        FOUND = 1;
                        break OUTER
                    end;
                    PRINT, FOUND
                end
```

Fig. 0.15   Program with a **break** statement that terminates two loops.

---

† Take this statement to read the entire matrix A.

‡ Note that this **if** statement has no **else** clause.

The motivation for using the **break** in the gotoless language is that the penalty for not doing so—occasional programs that are much longer or more awkward than necessary—is more severe than the penalty for using **break**, namely an occasional increased interaction between components of a program.

```
begin
      read A and B;
      compute A * B;
      print C
end
(a) first refinement
```

```
begin
      DIMENSION A(10, 10), B(10, 10), C(10, 10);
      INTEGER A, B, C;
      READ (5,100) A, B;
100 FORMAT(10I8);
      for I = 1 to 10 do
        for J = 1 to 10 do
            compute the dot product of row I of A
                  and column J of B;
        WRITE (6,200) C;
200 FORMAT (10I12)
end
(b) second refinement
```

```
begin
      DIMENSION A(10, 10), B(10, 10), C(10, 10);
      INTEGER A, B, C;
      READ (5,100) A, B;
100 FORMAT (10I8);
      for I = 1 to 10 do
        for J = 1 to 10 do
            begin
                  C(I, J) = 0;
                  for K = 1 to 10 do
                      C(I, J) = C(I, J) + A(I, K) * B(K, J)
            end
        WRITE (6,200) C;
200 FORMAT (10I12)
end
(c) final refinement
```

Fig. 0.16 Top down design using a pseudo-language.

0.6   USE OF OUR GOTOLESS LANGUAGE IN TOP-DOWN DESIGN

The language described in the two previous sections forms a reasonable "structured-programming" version of FORTRAN. We shall use it throughout the book when appropriate. Often, when informally describing algorithms, we shall use informal English, rather than FORTRAN to express the basic computational steps such as assignment statements.

In fact, our gotoless language together with some intelligible statements in informal English serve as a desirable alternative to flowcharts as a way of designing programs from the top down. The general idea is to first sketch out the program using the precise statements we have introduced for control flow, but specifying the computational steps informally where appropriate. Such a means of specification—half formal programming language and half informal English—is termed a *pseudo-language*. As the top-down refinement proceeds, the informal statements are replaced by more-detailed, but possibly still partially informal pseudo-language programs. Finally, at the last level of refinement, all informality disappears, and the pseudo-language program becomes a program in a real programming language.

Of course, many languages, in particular FORTRAN, do not have the control statements such as **while** . . . **do** that we introduced in our gotoless language. However, these control structures can be easily translated into FORTRAN or any other language the programmer chooses. For example, the **while** . . . **do** construct can be simulated by IF and GOTO statements in FORTRAN. If the programmer's chosen language has adequate control structures, he would be wise to retain those structures in his pseudo-language, rather than incorporating the particular control structures we have selected for our gotoless language.

Example 0.11.   Let us reconsider Example 0.3 (p. 3), where we did the top down design of a matrix multiplication routine. The three levels of refinement suggested by Fig. 0.2(a), (b), and (c) can be reflected in the pseudo-language programs of Fig. 0.16(a), (b), and (c), respectively. A straightforward translation of the **for** statements into DO loops results in the program of Fig. 0.3.   ∎

EXERCISES

0.1 Write programs in our gotoless language that are equivalent to the following FORTRAN programs.

a)
```
              DIMENSION J(20)
              DO 10 I = 1,20
        10    J(I) = I * (I-1)/2
              K = 0
              DO 20 I = 1,20
        20    K = K + J(I)
              PRINT, K
              STOP
              END
```

* b)

```
                    READ, N
          30    M = N -2*(N/2)†
                IF(M ·EQ· 0) GOTO 10
                IF(N ·EQ· 1) GOTO 20
                N = 3*N + 1
                GOTO 30
          20    PRINT, N
                STOP
          10    N = N/2
                GOTO 30
                END
```

0.2 Design programs "top down" to do the following tasks.

a) Determine which of the numbers from 1 to 10,000 are primes. (A *prime* is a positive integer such that no other positive integer except 1 divides it evenly.)

b) Compute SIN(X) by summing terms of the series $X - X^3/3! + X^5/5! - X^7/7! + \ldots$ until the last term added or subtracted has magnitude less than 10^{-5}. This sum will be SIN(X) with an error of no more than 10^{-5}.

Show how your flowcharts or pseudo-language programs are successively refined until each box of the lowest-level charts corresponds to a single program statement.

0.3 Convert the program of Fig. 0.15 into the basic gotoless language of Section 0.4, that is, using only **while** . . . **do** . . . , **if** . . . **then** . . . **else** . . . and **begin** . . . **end**.

0.4 Write the following DO loops:

```
              DO 10 I = 1,100
              DO 20 J = 2,I
          20  A(I,J-1) = B(I,J)
          10  A(I,I) = B(I,I)
```

a) using **while** . . . **do** . . . statements without **break**;

b) using **repeat** . . . **until** . . . statements;

c) using **for** . . . statements;

d) using **while** . . . **do** . . . statements with **break**.

0.5 a) Write programs in our gotoless language for the problems of Exercise 0.2.

b) Indicate the relationship between the hierarchy of flowchart boxes produced in Exercise 0.2 and the hierarchy of nested statements produced in part (a) of this exercise.

** **0.6** Show that for every FORTRAN program there is a gotoless program that does the same thing. *Hint:* Create a new variable L which indicates which line of the FORTRAN program is

---

† M is set to the remainder of $N/2$.

being executed. Then simulate the FORTRAN program by repeatedly determining the value of L, executing one FORTRAN statement, and simulating goto's and other jumps by assigning a new value to L.

FURTHER READING

The serious study of structured programming can be traced to Dijkstra [1968]. Hoare, Dahl, and Dijkstra [1972] gives an extensive treatment of the subject, and Kernighan and Plauger [1974] presents structured programming as well as a number of other program design ideas. The reader might also wish to examine the design of various programming languages that induce structure in their programs such as: BCPL (Richards [1969]), BLISS (Wulf, Russell, and Habermann [1971]) and PASCAL (Wirth [1973]).

A solution to Exercise 0.6 and an explanation of how arbitrary programs can be written in a highly structured language such as the one we introduced in Section 0.4 can be found in Bohm and Jacopini [1966] or Bruno and Steiglitz [1972].

Chapter 1

Data and Its Representation

We now make an abrupt change in our level of discourse; we leave the programming-language level to examine the computer at the most-detailed level relevant to programming systems. In this chapter we shall consider the representation of data as strings of 0's and 1's. Primarily, we shall be concerned with representing numerical data as fixed- or floating-point numbers, but the representation of nonnumeric data will also be briefly treated here.

In subsequent chapters we shall discuss the organization of a simple computer, and machine and assembly languages, and gradually work our way up to a second, more-comprehensive study of programming languages.

1.1 NUMBER SYSTEMS

The reader is probably aware that there are abstract objects (integers) which denote quantity (e.g, "six") and that there are many ways of representing the same abstract quantity (for example: 6 (decimal), VI (Roman), 110 (binary)). Often the distinction between the abstract quantity and its representation is not made, and we shall not bother to make that distinction here either. However, when dealing with computers, systems of representation other than decimal (notably binary, octal, and hexadecimal) are more convenient, and we must be able to switch our thinking among these number systems easily. Let us therefore proceed to the general notion of a "radix" or "base" for integers.

Let r be any integer equal to or greater than 2. We can represent any nonnegative integer as a string of digits chosen from $0, 1, \ldots, r - 1$. This string is the *radix* (or *base*) *r representation* of the integer.

Example 1.1. The decimal system uses radix $r = 10$, and integers are represented by strings of the digits $0, 1, \ldots, 9$. The number of eggs in two boxes is represented by the string 24.

In the binary system, $r = 2$. In this case, only the digits 0 and 1 may be used. The number of eggs in two boxes is then represented by 11000. We shall see why subsequently. ∎

Suppose we have a base r number $a_1 a_2 \ldots a_k$, where each of the a's is one of the digits $0, 1, \ldots, r - 1$. We can compute the integer represented by $a_1 a_2 \ldots a_k$ in the following manner. First, let us assume that we know what integer each of the digits represents, and that we know how to add and multiply integers.[†] Then the integer represented by $a_1 a_2 \ldots a_k$ is

$$a_1 r^{k-1} + a_2 r^{k-2} + \cdots + a_{k-1} r + a_k. \tag{1.1}$$

If we wish to convert from one base to another we can evaluate Expression (1.1) as if it were a polynomial whose unknown had the value r. The evaluation is performed using arithmetic in the base to which we are converting. This method is a good one if we are converting to a base system whose arithmetic we are familiar with. For most of us, this means base 10.

Example 1.2. Let us convert the binary (base 2) number 11001 to decimal. We have $a_1 = 1$, $a_2 = 1$, $a_3 = 0$, $a_4 = 0$, $a_5 = 1$, $k = 5$ and $r = 2$. Thus 11001 in binary is $1 \times 2^4 + 1 \times 2^3 + 0 \times 2^2 + 0 \times 2^1 + 1 \times 2^0 = 16 + 8 + 1 = 25$ in base 10. ∎

A more efficient method of evaluating the Expression (1.1) is to use the algorithm shown in Fig. 1.1, which is really Horner's rule for the evaluation of polynomials. Arithmetic is done in the base being converted to, and the final value of NUMBER is the desired answer. The reader may check that after the ith iteration of the loop, NUMBER has the value $a_1 r^{i-1} + a_2 r^{i-2} + \cdots + a_{i-1} r + a_i$. Thus after the kth pass, NUMBER has the value of Expression (1.1), as desired.

```
begin
    NUMBER = 0;
    for i = 1 to k do
        NUMBER = NUMBER * r + aᵢ
end
```

Fig. 1.1   Algorithm for base conversion by polynomial evaluation.

When we must indicate in what base a string of digits is to be interpreted, we shall surround the string by parentheses and subscript it with the base. Thus, Example 1.2 showed that $(11001)_2 = (25)_{10}$. An omitted subscript implies base 10.

When we wish to convert from a base whose arithmetic we are familiar with to another less familiar base, there is a second method which is more convenient than the "polynomial evaluation" method first mentioned. Suppose we have a base r number x, whose representation is $a_1 a_2 \ldots a_k$, and we wish to find the equivalent base s number. We may do the following steps.

[†] Here it is well to recall that integers are abstract, and that their sums and products are defined independently of any number system. The usual method of computing sums and products in base r reflects the accepted meanings of these operations, but the algorithm for doing arithmetic in base r is not the definition of sum or product.

1. Divide x by s. Let the quotient be q and the remainder p. If $q = 0$, end. The answer is the sequence of remainders generated, with the first remainder rightmost and the last leftmost.

2. If $q \neq 0$, set $x = q$ and return to step (1).
This algorithm is expressed in our gotoless language in Fig. 1.2.

```
repeat
    begin
        q = [x/s];
        p = x - q * s;
        comment q is the quotient of x/s and p its remainder;
        WRITE p to the left of any digits previously written;
        x = q
    end
until q = 0
```

Fig. 1.2   Algorithm for base conversion by repeated division. $[a]$ is the *floor* or *integer part* of a, that is, the greatest integer equal to or less than a. Thus $[x/s]$ is just the integer quotient of integers x and s as in FORTRAN.

To see that the algorithm of Fig. 1.2 works, we need only observe by induction on i that after the ith repetition of the loop, the original value of x (the number being converted) is equal to the number so far printed out (treated as a base s integer) plus s^i times the value of x after that repetition. When x finally becomes 0 and the repetition ends, the base s integer printed is the original value of x.

Example 1.3.   Let us convert $(13)_{10}$ to binary. We begin with $x = 13$ and divide by 2. The quotient is 6 and the remainder is 1. Thus 1 is the rightmost digit of the answer. We set $x = 6$ and return to step (1). Then, we divide 6 by 2, getting a quotient of 3 and remainder of 0. Thus, the last two digits of the answer are 01. Next we divide 3 by 2, obtaining 1 with a remainder of 1. The answer ends in 101, and we divide 1 by 2. Here we get quotient 0 and remainder 1. Since the quotient is 0, we end with answer 1101. Thus $(13)_{10} = (1101)_2$.

A convenient way to represent this calculation is shown in Fig. 1.3.

$$
\begin{array}{r|l}
2 & 13 \\
\hline
2 & 6 \quad \text{remainder 1} \\
\hline
2 & 3 \quad \text{remainder 0} \\
\hline
2 & 1 \quad \text{remainder 1} \\
\hline
 & 0 \quad \text{remainder 1}
\end{array}
$$

Fig. 1.3   Display of base conversion calculation.

The answer can be then read from the righthand column, with the bottommost remainder at the left.   ∎

If we desire to convert between two unfamiliar bases, either of the above methods may be used, but arithmetic in an unfamiliar base will have to be performed. Perhaps a better method is to use the first (polynomial evaluation) method to convert to base 10 and then the second (repeated division) method to convert to the desired base.

1.2   REPRESENTATION OF FRACTIONS

We can use the decimal point in base systems other than the decimal system.[†] The value of the decimal fraction $.b_1 b_2 \ldots b_m$ in base r is

$$b_1 r^{-1} + b_2 r^{-2} + \cdots + b_m r^{-m} \tag{1.2}$$

If we wish to convert to a familiar base, we can use Expression (1.2) in a way analogous to Expression (1.1). An algorithm for this purpose is shown in Fig. 1.4.

```
begin
        NUMBER = 0;
        for i = m by −1 to 1 do
                NUMBER = (NUMBER + bᵢ)/r
end
```

Fig. 1.4   Base conversion of fractions by "polynomial evaluation."

If we have a string with digits to both the left and right of the decimal point, we can use Expression (1.1) for the digits to the left and Expression (1.2) for those to the right.

Example 1.4.   Let us convert $(12.34)_5$ to decimal. Using the algorithm of Fig. 1.1, we see that $(12)_5 = 1 \times 5 + 2 = (7)_{10}$. Using Fig. 1.4, we find that $(.34)_5$ is $(4/5 + 3)/5 = 19/25$, or $(.76)_{10}$. Thus $(12.34)_5 = (7.76)_{10}$.   ∎

There is a repeated-multiplication method of converting fractions analogous to the repeated-division method for converting integers. Before discussing this method, we should first briefly discuss rational numbers and repeating decimals. A *rational number* is the ratio of two integers. For example $3\ 1/7 = 22/7$ is rational; π and $\sqrt{2}$ are not (although we shall not prove this fact). An *infinite fraction* in base r is an infinite sequence of digits 0 through $r - 1$, say $.b_1 b_2 \ldots$, preceded by a decimal point. An infinite fraction is *repeating* if we can write it as $.b_1 b_2 \ldots b_m c_1 c_2 \ldots c_k c_1 c_2 \ldots c_k \ldots$; that is, after a certain point (b_m in this case) a finite sequence of digits repeats ($c_1 c_2 \ldots c_k$ here). We represent this infinite sequence by $.b_1 b_2 \ldots b_m \overline{c_1 c_2 \ldots c_k}$.

The value of an infinite fraction $.b_1 b_2 \ldots$ is

$$b_1 r^{-1} + b_2 r^{-2} + \cdots \tag{1.3}$$

Note that Expression (1.2) for a finite-length (*truncated*) fraction agrees with Expression (1.3) if we take $b_{m+1} = b_{m+2} = \cdots = 0$.

---

† We shall continue to call it a "decimal" point, however.

It is known that every rational number less than 1 has a repeating fraction representing it in any base. Note that a truncated fraction is a special case of a repeating fraction where $c_1 c_2 \ldots c_k$ is 0. Conversely, for every repeating fraction we can find an equivalent rational number, using the formula for the sum of a geometric series.

Example 1.5. Let us consider the ternary (base 3) fraction $.1\overline{12} = .1121212\ldots$. The value of this fraction using Expression (1.3) is $1 \times \frac{1}{3} + 1 \times \frac{1}{9} + 2 \times \frac{1}{27} + 1 \times \frac{1}{81} + 2 \times \frac{1}{243} + \cdots$. We can rewrite this expression by grouping the second and third terms, the fourth and fifth terms, and so on, as $\frac{1}{3} + \frac{5}{27} + \frac{5}{243} + \cdots$. All but the first of these terms form a geometric series with first term $\frac{5}{27}$ and ratio $\frac{1}{9}$. The sum of this series is $\frac{5}{27}/(1 - \frac{1}{9}) = \frac{5}{24}$. When we add the first term, $\frac{1}{3}$, we find that $(.1\overline{12})_3 = (\frac{13}{24})_{10}$. ∎

In general, to find the rational equivalent of the repeating fraction $b_1 b_2 \ldots b_m \overline{c_1 c_2 \ldots c_k}$, write the expansion

$$\frac{b_1}{r} + \frac{b_2}{r^2} + \cdots + \frac{b_m}{r^m} + \frac{c_1}{r^{m+1}} + \frac{c_2}{r^{m+2}} + \cdots + \frac{c_k}{r^{m+k}} + \frac{c_1}{r^{m+k+1}} + \cdots$$

Then treat the first m terms separately, and form a geometric series whose first term is the sum of

$$\frac{c_1}{r^{m+1}} + \frac{c_2}{r^{m+2}} + \cdots + \frac{c_k}{r^{m+k}},$$

whose second term is

$$\frac{c_1}{r^{m+k+1}} + \frac{c_2}{r^{m+k+2}} + \cdots + \frac{c_k}{r^{m+2k}},$$

and so on. Thus, the ratio for the geometric series is r^{-k}, and its sum is

$$\frac{1}{1 - r^{-k}} \left(\frac{c_1}{r^{m+1}} + \frac{c_2}{r^{m+2}} + \cdots + \frac{c_k}{r^{m+k}} \right).$$

It happens that some rational numbers have truncated fractions in one base and repeating (nontruncated) fractions in another. When converting between bases, we cannot therefore expect that we will always obtain a truncated fraction, even when we begin with one. We shall therefore give an algorithm which takes a number x, $0 \leqslant x < 1$ represented in some base r[†] and produces the first m places of its fraction in base s.

The algorithm works by repeatedly multiplying x by s, listing the integer part of the product so formed, and then deleting the integer part of the product. The algorithm is shown in Fig. 1.5. Index i is used simply to count from 1 to m.

[†] If x is an infinite repeating fraction in base r, then the representation of x must be a quotient of base r integers.

```
for i = 1 to m do
    begin
        x = x * s;
        y = [x];
        write y (a base s digit) to the right of any digits printed so far;
        x = x − y;
        comment x − y is the fractional part of x * s
    end
```

Fig. 1.5   Base conversion of fractions by repeated multiplication.

To see that the algorithm of Fig. 1.5 works, we note that, after the ith iteration of the loop, the original value of x is equal to the current value of x divided by s^i plus the value of the number printed so far (treated as a base s fraction with the decimal point at the left end). Thus after m iterations, the number printed will be the original minus a proper fraction (the current x divided by s^m); the error in the result is less than s^{-m}, and we have the correct answer truncated to m places.

Example 1.6.   Let us convert $(.1)_{10}$ to octal (base 8). We shall produce three places. The first time through the loop of Fig. 1.5, we compute $x = .1 \times 8 = .8$. Thus $y = 0$ and $x - y = .8$. We set $x = .8$ and repeat. Since $.8 \times 8 = 6.4$, we have $y = 6$ and $x = .4$ after the second iteration. At the third iteration we compute $.4 \times 8 = 3.2$, so $y = 3$ and $x = .2$. The first three places of the octal fraction equivalent to $(.1)_{10}$ are thus $(.063)_8$. If we continue the process "forever," we see that $(.1)_{10} = (.0\overline{6314})_8$. A convenient representation for the process is shown in Fig. 1.6.

$$
\begin{array}{r}
0.1 \\
\times 8 \\
\hline
0.8 \\
\times 8 \\
\hline
6.4 \\
\times 8 \\
\hline
3.2 \\
\times 8 \\
\hline
1.6 \\
\times 8 \\
\hline
4.8
\end{array}
$$

Fig. 1.6   Representation of repeated multiplication.

Since the fifth iteration of the loop leaves x having the same value (0.8) as the first iteration, the second through fifth digits will repeat indefinitely.   ∎

When dealing with computers, the bases most often used (other than decimal) are binary (base 2), octal (base 8) and hexadecimal (base 16). Computers themselves are generally oriented toward base 2, but numbers in base 2 are often too long for convenience. The reason bases 8 and 16 have come into use is that there are simple conversion algorithms between these bases and base 2. Octal or hexadecimal numbers represent the binary numbers used by the computer, but the representation of an integer in these systems is roughly as long as in decimal.

To convert a binary number to octal, we do the following.

1. Group the digits to the left of the decimal point in threes, starting from the decimal point. Add one or two leading 0's, if necessary.

2. Group the digits to the right of the decimal point in threes, again starting at the decimal point. Add one or two trailing 0's if necessary.

3. Replace each group of three binary digits by their equivalent octal digit.

Example 1.7. Consider $(10111.0111)_2$. We add a leading 0 and two trailing 0's, so the numbers of places to the left and to the right of the decimal point are both divisible by 3. The grouping is 010 111 . 011 100. The octal equivalent is thus $(27.34)_8$. ▋

To convert from octal to binary, we replace each octal digit by the three binary digits having the same value. Note that 2, for example, must be replaced by 010, not 10.

Example 1.8. We convert $(31.56)_8$ to binary by replacing 3 by 011, 1 by 001, 5 by 101 and 6 by 110. We obtain 011001.101110. A zero can be deleted from both ends for obvious reasons, yielding $(11001.10111)_2$. ▋

Conversion between binary and hexadecimal proceeds in the analogous fashion, but binary digits are grouped in fours, and hexadecimal digits are replaced by four 0's and 1's. It should be observed that in hexadecimal, or any base above 10, we need new symbols for the digits higher than 9. The usual course is to use $A, B, \ldots, F$ for "ten," "eleven," ..., "fifteen," respectively. For example, $(B3E)_{16} = (2878)_{10}$.

1.3 ARITHMETIC IN VARIOUS BASES

There is very little surprising in the algorithms used to perform arithmetic in base systems other than decimal. Perhaps the only new idea is that when working in base r, one carries and borrows r's, rather than tens. We shall spell out the base r addition algorithm for integers and illustrate subtraction, multiplication and division by example. The algorithm in Fig. 1.7 adds $a_1a_2 \ldots a_k$ to $b_1b_2 \ldots b_k$ in base r. The answer is $d_0d_1 \ldots d_k$. We use i to indicate the current place at which we are performing the addition and c to hold the carry out of the previous place.

Example 1.9. Let us perform the sum

$$
\begin{array}{r}
637 \\
+\ 412 \\
\end{array}
$$

in octal. We have $k = 3$ and $r = 8$ in this case. We begin at the rightmost place, with $c = 0$, $a_3 = 7$ and $b_3 = 2$. We find $x = 9$ at line (3). Since $x \geqslant r$, we set $d_3 = 9 - 8 = 1$ and $c = 1$ at lines (7) and (8). We repeat the loop to consider the middle place. There, $x = 1 + 3 + 1 = 5$. Thus we set $d_2 = 5$ and $c = 0$. For the leftmost place, we compute $x = 0 + 6 + 4 = 10$, so $d_1 = 2$ and $c = 1$. Then we set $d_0 = 1$ at line 9, and the answer is $d_0d_1d_2d_3 = 1251$. ▋

```
      begin
(1)       c = 0;
          comment There is no carry into the rightmost place;
(2)       for i = k by −1 to 1 do
              begin
(3)               x = c + aᵢ + bᵢ;
                  comment c = 0 or 1 always, so since 0 ≤ aᵢ ≤ r − 1,
                      and 0 ≤ bᵢ ≤ r − 1, we have 0 ≤ x ≤ 2r − 1;
(4)               if x < r then
                      begin
(5)                       dᵢ = x;
(6)                       c = 0
                      end
                  else
                      begin
(7)                       dᵢ = x − r;
(8)                       c = 1
                      end
              end;
(9)       d₀ = c
      end
```

Fig. 1.7   Base r addition algorithm.

Let us now consider subtraction of $b_1 b_2 \ldots b_k$ from $a_1 a_2 \ldots a_k$ in base r. The important consideration is how to borrow. If we find we cannot subtract b_i from a_i (because $b_i > a_i$), we find the first digit to the left of a_i, say a_j, which is not zero. We "borrow" by subtracting one from a_j, changing all digits between a_j and a_i (but excluding a_j and a_i themselves) to $r - 1$ and replacing a_i by $a_i + r$.

Example 1.10.   Let us subtract 221 from 2100 in base 3. We show the sequence of steps in Fig. 1.8, with comments as to the computation occurring at each step. Thus $(2100)_3 - (221)_3 = (1102)_3$.   ∎

```
    2100
 −   221            Begin.
    202(10)
 −  22 1            Borrow from the third place from the right.
    202(10)
 −  22 1            Subtract (1)₃ from (10)₃ and then (2)₃ from
     0 2            (2)₃ to compute the last two places.
    1(10)2(10)
 −   2 2 1          Borrow from the leftmost place.
     0 2
    1(10)2(10)
 −   2 2 1          Complete the subtraction
    1 1 0 2
```

Fig. 1.8   Base 3 subtraction.

To multiply we form partial products as in decimal multiplication. We must have handy, or memorize, a multiplication table for the digits of the radix in which we are working.

Example 1.11. Let us multiply B7 by A4 in hexadecimal. Recall that A stands for "ten" and B for "eleven." The product is written below.

$$
\begin{array}{r}
\text{B7} \\
\times\,\text{4A} \\
\hline
726 \\
\text{2DC} \\
\hline
\text{34E6}
\end{array}
$$

We may think as follows. $7 \times A = (70)_{10} = (46)_{16}$.

Write down a 6 in the first partial product and carry the 4. Then $B \times A + 4 = (114)_{10} = (72)_{16}$. Thus the first partial product is 726. For the second row, $7 \times 4 = (28)_{10} = (1C)_{16}$. Write down C and carry 1. Next $B \times 4 + 1 = (45)_{10} = (2D)_{16}$. The second partial product is 2DC. The sum $(726)_{16} + (2DC0)_{16}$ is $(34E6)_{16}$. ∎

Multiplication in binary is particularly simple. Each partial product is either all 0's or the multiplicand itself.

Example 1.12. Let us multiply 10.11 by 110.1. The calculation is shown below.

$$
\begin{array}{r}
1011 \\
1101 \\
\hline
1011 \\
1011 \\
1011 \\
\hline
10001111
\end{array}
$$

The number of decimal places in the product is sum of number in the multiplier and multiplicand, three places in this case. Thus the result is 10001.111. ∎

Lastly, we perform division in base r by the usual method of trial subtraction. The following example should illustrate the method.

Example 1.13. The following shows the initial stages of the division of 34.1 by 2.04 in base 5.

$$
\begin{array}{r}
134\ldots \\
204\,\overline{)\,341000\ldots} \\
\underline{204} \\
1320 \\
\underline{1122} \\
1430 \\
\underline{1331} \\
440
\end{array}
$$

The usual rule for handling the decimal point places it after the 13 in the quotient. ∎

1.4 COMPUTER WORDS AND NUMBER REPRESENTATION

The typical computer can be thought of as having a large number of places in which sequences of *bits* (digits 0 or 1) are stored. These sequences are of fixed length, called the *word length* for the computer. Word lengths are generally in the range 8–64, with the low end, say 16 or less, common for small computers and 32 or more common for medium and large computers. It is possible to interpret a string of 0's and 1's in various ways, and we shall discuss some of these in the remainder of this chapter as well as in Chapters 2 and 3. We begin by considering the interpretation of strings of 0's and 1's as integers.

It should be plainly obvious that one interpretation of a string of 0's and 1's is as a binary integer. However, computer words normally have some method for indicating the sign of the number.

We shall discuss three methods of treating the sign. Each of these methods is a variety of what is called *fixed-point* number representation. The term fixed point refers to the fact that the decimal point may be regarded as having a fixed position in the computer word. If we regard this position as the right end, all numbers are positive or negative integers. However, we are free to imagine that the decimal point is at any fixed place we choose when computing with these numbers. The three representations we consider are:

1. *Sign-and-Magnitude Notation.* Here the leftmost bit is the sign. Usually, 0 denotes + and 1 denotes −, and this is the convention we choose. The bits other than the leftmost (sign) bit are called the *magnitude*.

Example 1.14. Let computer words be six bits long. Then in sign and magnitude notation, $(+13)_{10}$ is represented by 001101 and $(-13)_{10}$ is represented by 101101. Zero is represented by both 000000 and 100000, but all other numbers between -31 (represented by 111111) and $+31$ (represented by 011111) have a unique representation. ∎

2. *Twos'-Complement Notation.* Suppose we have k bit computer words. In twos'-complement notation, nonnegative integers less than 2^{k-1} are represented by their binary equivalent with leading 0's where necessary. Note that all nonnegative numbers begin with 0, since the largest representable number, $2^{k-1} - 1$, has $011 \ldots 1$ as a representation. Negative numbers between -2^{k-1} and -1 are represented by first adding 2^k and then writing down the binary representation for the sum. Note that each such sum is between $+2^{k-1}$ and $+(2^k - 1)$, so the k bit representation has a 1 as the leftmost bit. Thus the leftmost bit represents the sign, just as in sign and magnitude notation. In fact, nonnegative numbers have the same representation in either notation, but the representation of negative numbers is different.

Example 1.15. Again assume computer words to be six bits long. In twos'-complement notation, $(+13)_{10}$ is represented by 001101. Let us find the representation of $(-13)_{10}$. Since $k = 6$, we must compute $2^k - 13 = 64 - 13 = 51$. The binary representation of $(51)_{10}$ is 110011, so that is the representation of -13 in twos'-complement. ∎

In twos'-complement, unlike sign and magnitude, zero has only one representation, all zeros. In fact, all numbers between -2^{k-1} and $+(2^{k-1}-1)$ have a unique representation in twos'-complement. Notice, however, the lack of symmetry; -2^{k-1} is representable, but $+2^{k-1}$ is not.

3. *Ones'-Complement Notation.* In this notation, nonnegative numbers are represented exactly as in the other two notations. Numbers between $-(2^{k-1}-1)$ and 0 may be represented by adding 2^k-1 and then converting to a k-bit binary number.

Again, negative numbers are distinguished by having a leading 1, but zero now has two representations, all zeros and all ones. The range of numbers representable is between $-(2^{k-1}-1)$ and $+(2^{k-1}-1)$, as for sign and magnitude.

Example 1.16. We can compute the six-bit ones'-complement representation of $(-13)_{10}$ by computing $(2^k-1)-13=63-13=50$. Converting $(50)_{10}$ to binary, we have representation 110010. ∎

The reader may sense that sign-and-magnitude notation is quite "natural," while ones'- and twos'-complement notations are not. However, when in Section 1.5 we consider arithmetic in these notations, we shall see how the complement notations yield a savings in the amount of circuitry needed in a computer using these notations. Thus the complement notations are actually quite prevalent. Twos'-complement is used on major lines of Digital Equipment Corp. and IBM computers, for example, while ones'-complement is used on various CDC machines.

1.5 FIXED-POINT ARITHMETIC

We can perform the usual arithmetic operations on fixed-point computer words in any of the three notations mentioned in the last section. However, at the outset we should note a distinction between "ordinary" arithmetic and arithmetic dealing with computer words. In ordinary arithmetic, we expect always to get an answer (except if we divide by zero). In computer arithmetic, the answer, if we get one, will agree with our expectations. However, we may get no answer (an *overflow*), should the result not fit in a computer word of the fixed length chosen.

As a result, many of the algebraic laws that we are accustomed to using do not really hold in computer arithmetic[†].

Example 1.17. The *associative law of addition* states that $(X + Y) + Z = X + (Y + Z)$. That is, to add X, Y and Z, we may either add X and Y first, or Y and Z first; the result will be the same. However, let us consider 6-bit computer words in sign-and-magnitude notation, and suppose

$$X = 011111 = (+31)_{10}$$
$$Y = 101100 = (-12)_{10}$$
$$Z = 111000 = (-24)_{10}$$

[†] The reader should be aware of this fact, but should not take it overly seriously. To a "first approximation" the usual laws do hold.

If we add X and Y first, we get $010011 = (+19)_{10}$. Adding Z gives $100101 = (-5)_{10}$, which is correct. However, should we add Y and Z first, we get no answer, since their sum, $(-36)_{10}$ has no representation. Recall $(-31)_{10}$ is the smallest number representable in 6-bit sign-and-magnitude notation.

Various other algebraic laws can be shown not to hold, and we leave some of these for exercises. ∎

We shall now consider various arithmetic operations and algorithms for their implementation in the three fixed-point notations.

1. Negation

In sign-and-magnitude, we may negate simply by changing the sign (leftmost) bit.

In twos'-complement, we change every bit except the rightmost 1 and any 0's to its right. It is important to observe that this method does not apply to -2^{k-1}, which has no negation representable in k-bit twos'-complement notation.

In ones'-complement, we change every bit.

Example 1.18. Let us negate the number $(24)_{10}$, again using six-bit numbers. In each representation, 24 is represented by 011000. In sign-and-magnitude notation, the negation of 011000 is 111000. In twos'-complement, we change only the first two bits, since the third bit is the rightmost 1. Thus, the negation of 011000 is 101000. In ones'-complement, we change every bit to obtain 100111. ∎

2. Addition and Subtraction

In sign-and-magnitude, we add numbers by the following rules.

i) If the signs are the same, add the magnitudes. The sign of the result is the sign of the addends and the magnitude is the sum of the magnitudes. However, if the sum of the magnitudes is too large to fit in the space allotted, we get no answer, and call the result an overflow.

ii) If the signs are different, subtract the smaller magnitude from the larger. The difference is the magnitude of the answer. The sign of the result is the sign of the larger. If the magnitudes are the same, however, it is not clear whether the sign should be positive or negative, that is, which representation of zero should be chosen. A good idea is to insist that all 0's represent zero.

When we consider two's-complement addition, we see one of the chief reasons for use of this rather unintuitive system in some computers. We may add twos'-complement numbers as if they were unsigned binary integers.

If there is a carry out of the leftmost place, it is dropped and does not form part of the answer. However, if there is a carry out of the leftmost place, there must also be a carry into that place. If there is no carry out of the leftmost place, there must not be a carry into that place. If these conditions are violated, the answer will be incorrect and in fact, the correct answer is not representable in the number of bits allowed (an overflow).

Example 1.19. Let us use 6-bit twos'-complement notation to add $(-6)_{10}$ and $(+17)_{10}$. We perform the binary addition:

$$
\begin{array}{r}
111010 \\
+\,010001 \\
\hline
1001011
\end{array}
$$

There is a carry both into and out of the leftmost place.[†] We neglect the leading place of the answer to obtain the sum 001011; which represents $(+11)_{10}$.

Let us add $(15)_{10}$ and $(19)_{10}$. We perform the sum:

$$
\begin{array}{r}
001111 \\
+\,010011 \\
\hline
0100010
\end{array}
$$

There is a carry from the fifth place into the leftmost place, but there is no carry out of the leftmost place, so the answer is wrong. That is, 100010 does not represent $(34)_{10}$, which in fact has no representation here. An overflow is detected. ∎

In ones'-complement addition, we may again ignore the sign of the addends. The rule stated for twos'-complement regarding carries into and out of the leftmost place applies here as well. However, if a carry out occurs, it is an *end-around carry* and must be added to the result in the rightmost place. Note that we may have a carry out of the leftmost place but not obtain a carry into that place until the end-around carry is added in.

Example 1.20. Let us add $(-10)_{10}$ and $(-21)_{10}$ in 6-bit ones'-complement notation. We perform the sum:

$$
\begin{array}{r}
110101 \\
+\,101010 \\
\hline
1011111
\end{array}
$$

There is a carry out of the leftmost place, so we must delete it and add 1 to our answer. The final step is:

$$
\begin{array}{r}
011111 \\
+\qquad 1 \\
\hline
100000
\end{array}
$$

to give the answer $(-31)_{10}$. Note that the carry into the leftmost place did not occur until the final step. ∎

To perform subtraction in any of the three systems we may complement the subtrahend and add. An exception occurs in twos'-complement notation where $-2^{k-1} = 100\ldots0$ has no complement. We may compute $a - (-2^{k-1})$ by simply

---

[†] By "leftmost place," we are referring to the sixth place from the right, not the seventh, which only represents the carry out of the sixth place.

changing the first bit of the representation for a. Note that a must be negative (first bit 1) for the result to be valid. If a has first bit 0, then $a - (-2^{k-1})$ results in an overflow.

3. Multiplication and Division

The way to perform these operations in sign-and-magnitude notation should be obvious. Magnitudes are multiplied or divided, and signs are handled by the familiar laws (minus times minus equals plus, etc.).

However, we run greater risks of overflow with multiplication, since the product of two computer words in sign-and magnitude-notation could yield enough bits for two words. Thus, many computers arrange that when two k-bit computer words are multiplied, two words are used to hold the answer. Typically, one word contains the $k - 1$ least-significant bits of the product preceded by the sign of the result. The other word holds the most-significant bits, filled out with 0's at the left if necessary, and the sign.

Example 1.21. If we multiply 010101 by 110011 in sign-and-magnitude notation, the computation is as shown below.

$$
\begin{array}{r}
10101 \\
\times\,10011 \\
\hline
10101 \\
10101 \\
10101 \\
\hline
110001111
\end{array}
$$

If two words are available for the answer, one word will hold the rightmost five bits of the answer preceded by the sign, 1, that is, 101111. The remaining bits of the answer appear in the other word. In this case, the answer has only 9 bits, while 10 bits are possible when two 5-bit numbers are multiplied. We must therefore take 1100, and precede it by a leading 0, then by the sign, to get 101100. Thus if we use two words for the answer, the product of 010101 and 110011 in sign and magnitude is the pair (101100, 101111).

If only one word is available for the product, then the result of the above calculation is an overflow.   ∎

When we perform fixed-point division, another problem enters the picture. The quotient of integers may well not be an integer. Naturally we expect the answer produced to be the integer part of the true result.

However, we are constrained regarding the sizes of the divisor and quotient. Roughly, if k-bit words are used, we cannot expect that the sum of the significant places of the divisor and of the quotient will total more than k.

One scheme allows both the divisor and quotient to have as many significant places as the computer word will allow. We use two words for the dividend. Each word has the sign of the dividend, and we imagine that the decimal point is at the right end of the word holding the least-significant digits.

Example 1.22. Let us divide $(235)_{10}$ by $(9)_{10}$. Now $(235)_{10} = (11101011)_2$. We can use two six-bit computer words to represent 11101011 as (000111, 001011). That is, the rightmost five bits are preceded by the sign 0 to form the second word, and the remaining bits are filled out with leading 0's and the sign. We then perform the division:

$$
\begin{array}{r}
11010. \\
01001. \overline{)0011101011.} \\
-1001 \\
\hline
1011 \\
-1001 \\
\hline
1001 \\
-1001 \\
\hline
01
\end{array}
$$

Thus, the quotient is 011010. ∎

It should be noted that if the magnitude of the divisor does not exceed the magnitude of the first word of the dividend, an overflow will result, as the quotient will have a magnitude too large to represent in one computer word.

In ones'- or twos'-complement notation, there are special algorithms to perform multiplication and division. However, we recommend the simple process of converting to sign-and-magnitude notation (for positive numbers, no conversion is needed; for negative ones, the conversion is similar to a negation), multiplying or dividing as described above, and then reconverting the result.

1.6 FLOATING-POINT NUMBERS

There is a second common way to interpret computer words as numbers. This method is called *floating-point* and is similar to scientific notation. The advantage of floating-point notation is that k-bit computer words can be used to represent numbers much larger than 2^{k-1}. The disadvantage of floating-point is that we do not get as many as $k - 1$ significant bits in one word.

One bit of the word is reserved for the sign. Some bits, usually a small fraction of the word, are reserved for an *exponent*, and the remaining bits form the *mantissa*. Suppose the exponent bits "represent" the integer E and the mantissa bits "represent" the fraction M, where $0 \leqslant M < 1$. (We shall explain these representations subsequently.) In one common scheme, the value of the computer word is $\pm 2^E \times M$, depending on the sign bit. In other schemes, the value is taken to be $\pm c^E \times M$ for some constant c other than 2. For example the IBM 360/370 computers use $c = 16$. We shall consider only the scheme with $c = 2$ in examples.

The general format of a computer word treated as a floating-point number is shown in Fig. 1.9.

The m bits of the mantissa are considered to represent a fraction with the decimal point at the left end. Thus M, the value of the mantissa, is always a number between 0 and 1, but excluding 1 itself.

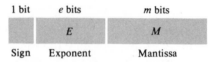

Fig. 1.9   Floating-point number.

The usual interpretation of E, the value of the exponent, is more exotic. We code E in an "excess-2^{e-1} code." In general, we can give integers an *excess-k code* by adding k and converting to binary. In the particular case of an e-bit exponent, we add 2^{e-1} to E. Since e bits can represent the integers from zero to $2^e - 1$, values of E between -2^{e-1} and $+(2^{e-1} - 1)$ can be represented. For an exercise we ask the reader to perceive a simple relation between the excess-2^{e-1} code and twos'-complement notation for e-bit computer words.

Example 1.23.   Let us consider twelve-bit computer words with $e = 4$ and $m = 7$.[†] Then $0\!\char`\^101\!\char`\^11100000$[‡] has positive sign 0, exponent 1011 and mantissa 1100000. Since $e = 4$, and $2^{e-1} = 8$, we must interpret 1011 in excess-8 code. Subtracting 8, which is $(1000)_2$, we are left with $(11)_2$. Thus, $E = 3$. We may evaluate M by evaluating $(.1100000)_2$, that is, $M = \frac{3}{4}$. The number represented is $+2^3 \times \frac{3}{4} = 6$.   ∎

Example 1.24.   Let us convert $(1.79)_{10}$ to a floating-point number in the format of Example 1.23, that is, $e = 4$ and $m = 7$. Actually, there is no 12-bit computer word that represents 1.79 exactly in that format, so we shall try to approximate it as closely as possible. Our strategy is to have seven significant bits in the mantissa, as many as is possible. This significance can be achieved only if we make the leading bit 1, that is, choose M such that $\frac{1}{2} \leqslant M < 1$.

It is easy to see that the only way $2^E \times M$ could be 1.79, with $\frac{1}{2} \leqslant M < 1$ and E an integer is if $E = 1$ and $M = .895$. Thus, we shall choose $E = 1$. In excess-8 code, 1 is represented by 1001. The mantissa must be made to approximate $(.895)_{10}$ as closely as possible. Using the conversion algorithm of Fig. 1.5 (p. 26), we find $(.895)_{10} = (.11100101\overline{0001111})_2$. This number rounded to seven places is $(.1110011)_2$. An approximate floating-point representation for $(1.79)_{10}$ is thus $0\!\char`\^1001\!\char`\^1110011$.   ∎

It is desirable in a computer that each number have a unique fixed-point and a unique floating-point representation. For example, if we have a computer word which we know is being used to represent a number in floating-point format, we may wish to test if the number represented is zero. Now zero has many representations in floating-point, in particular, any computer word whose mantissa bits are all 0's

---

[†] This choice of e and m is convenient, in that it enables us to deal with rather small words. However, it should be noted that with this choice we are quite limited in the size of numbers we may represent. It is even possible to represent larger numbers in 12-bit fixed-point notation. To get a feel for the power of floating-point notation, the reader should compare the ranges of fixed and floating point numbers for words of length 40, with $e = 9$ and $m = 30$.

[‡] We use carats to mark the separation between sign, exponent and mantissa. They are not part of the word itself.

represents zero. It would be awkward if we had to test whether a computer word was any of the various representations for zero.

For this reason, computers are usually constructed so that any arithmetic performed gives an answer which is a specific one of the possible computer words having the same value, or at least, it is a frequently exercised option of the programmer that the computer do this. Words in the "proper" format are called *normalized*.

We have already met this problem in a rudimentary form when we considered sign-and-magnitude notation and ones'-complement notation. In the first case, $00 \ldots 0$ and $10 \ldots 0$ each represent zero and in the second case, $00 \ldots 0$ and $11 \ldots 1$ represent zero. All other numbers that are representable at all in these notations have unique representations. We could therefore define a normalized sign-and-magnitude number to be any word but $10 \ldots 0$, and a normalized ones'-complement number to be any word but $11 \ldots 1$. In twos'-complement, no number has two representations, so we may regard any word as normalized in twos'-complement.

The usual strategy for normalizing floating-point numbers is to call a word normalized if and only if it satisfies the following.

1. If the mantissa is all 0's, then the word is all 0's. This rule guarantees that zero has but one representation.

2. If the mantissa is not all 0's, then either the leftmost bit of the mantissa is 1 or the exponent is all 0's. That is, to normalize a nonzero number, repeatedly shift the mantissa left one place and simultaneously subtract 1 from the exponent (it is easy to see that this action does not change the value of the number represented) until either the leading one of the mantissa reaches the leftmost place or the exponent E reaches its smallest (most negative) value.

Example 1.25. Let us again consider 12-bit computer words with $e = 4$ and $m = 7$. The word 001100011000 has $E = -2$ and $M = \frac{3}{16}$. The value of the word is $2^{-2} \times \frac{3}{16} = \frac{3}{64}$. The mantissa is 0011000. It has two leading 0's, so we normalize the word by shifting the mantissa two places left, bringing 0's in from the right, and subtracting 2 from the exponent. The resulting word is 001001100000. This word has $E = -4$ and $M = \frac{3}{4}$, so its value is $2^{-4} \times \frac{3}{4} = \frac{3}{64}$.

1.7 FLOATING-POINT ARITHMETIC

In this section we shall give algorithms to perform the usual arithmetic operations on floating-point numbers. As a general rule, whenever we operate on floating-point data we run the risk of "losing significance" in our answer.

For example, in pencil-and-paper arithmetic, if we add

$$
\begin{array}{r}
12.3 \\
+ \quad .0456 \\
\hline
12.3456
\end{array}
$$

the last three places are not significant. The usual reasoning is that 12.3 measures something whose "true" value is between 12.25 and 12.35. Thus the true sum is between 12.2956 and 12.3956. The last three places tell us nothing, and might as well not be there. Moreover, in floating-point representation, we are limited in the number of places we can carry in the mantissa. Even if we knew that 12.3 were 12.3$\overline{0}$, we might not have room to store the equivalent of six decimal places in the mantissa, and we would have to store the result as 12.3456 rounded or truncated to some number of places.

We shall now consider the various arithmetic operations. Throughout, we assume e-bit exponents and m-bit mantissas.

1. Addition

Let us add $X_1 = \pm 2^{E_1} \times M_1$ and $X_2 = \pm 2^{E_2} \times M_2$. The first job is to "line up" the mantissas, by shifting the mantissa corresponding to the smaller of E_1 and E_2 enough places right that we may make the exponents equal. Let us assume that $E_1 \geqslant E_2$. We do the following.

i) Shift the mantissa of X_2 to the right $E_1 - E_2$ places, bringing 0's from the left, and replace E_2 by E_1 in X_2.[†]

ii) If the signs of X_1 and X_2 are the same, add M_1 and the shifted M_2 to obtain M_3. If the signs of X_1 and X_2 are different, subtract the smaller of M_1 and the shifted M_2 from the other and call the result M_3.

iii) It is possible that there are as many as $m + 1$ bits in M_3. If so, shift M_3 one place right and add one to E_1 (an overflow will occur here if E_1 was initially all 1's).

iv) The answer has the sign of either X_1 or X_2, whichever has the larger magnitude, exponent E_1 (possibly incremented in (iii)) and mantissa M_3 (possibly shifted in (iii)). Normalization at this point is optional, but desirable.

Remember that the shifting of mantissas right in steps (i) and (iii) causes bits to be "lost" at the right end, since all mantissas have m bits.

A flowchart of the above algorithm is shown in Fig. 1.10. It assumes that the two numbers have been read, that they have signs S_1 and S_2, exponents E_1 and E_2, and mantissas M_1 and M_2, respectively. Also, we assume $E_1 \geqslant E_2$. Otherwise, we could interchange the roles of the two arguments. We also assume that all arithmetic on mantissas is truncated m bits to the right of the decimal point.

Example 1.26. Let us use $e = 4$ and $m = 7$ and add 0110011101010 to 0101111110111. We have $E_1 = 4$, $M_1 = (.1101010)_2$, $E_2 = 3$ and $M_2 = (.1110111)_2$. If E_2 had turned out larger than E_1, we would have reversed the roles of the numbers. Since $E_1 - E_2 = 1$, we shift M_2 one place right to obtain $M_2 = (.0111011)_2$, and since

---

[†] The last $E_1 - E_2$ places of the mantissa are lost. An alternative algorithm would *round* at this step and at other steps where bits are shifted out the right end of the mantissa. To round when k places are shifted, add 1 to what remains if the most significant bit lost is 1. For example, if we shift 101100 three places right and then round, we get 110 because the third place from the right is 1. Rounding does not ensure accuracy, but on the average will result in less deviation from the "true" answer.

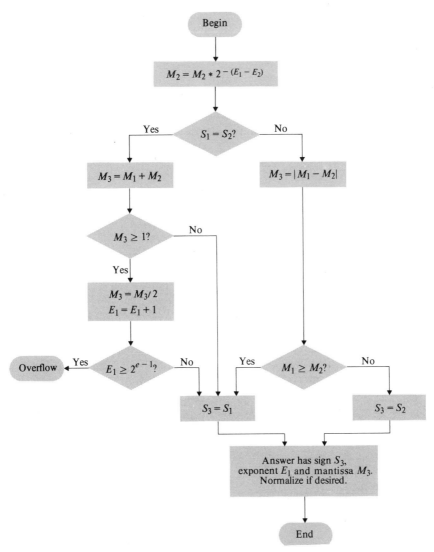

Fig. 1.10   Floating-point addition algorithm. $|x|$ stands for x if $x \geq 0$ and $-x$ if $x < 0$; that is, $|x|$ is the magnitude of x.

the signs are both $+$, we add $M_1 + M_2$ to obtain $M_3 = (1.0100101)_2$. As we have generated an eighth place, we must shift M_3 one place right, yielding $(.1010010)_2$. We then add one to E_1, which becomes 1101 in excess-8 notation. The answer is 0.1101.1010010.

Note that floating-point addition introduces some inaccuracy, as we have added $13\frac{1}{4}$ to $7\frac{7}{16}$ and obtained $20\frac{1}{2}$ as a result. Had we rounded instead of truncating, we would have obtained $20\frac{3}{4}$ instead, still not correct, but closer.   ∎

2. Subtraction

To subtract in floating-point, change the sign of the subtrahend and proceed as for addition.

3. Multiplication

When multiplying, we have options, depending chiefly on whether we wish to normalize the result (a good idea) and whether we wish to construct one or two words for an answer. We shall give an algorithm that incorporates these options. Suppose we wish to form the product of $X_1 = \pm 2^{E_1} \times M_1$ and $X_2 = \pm 2^{E_2} \times M_2$.

i) Form the product $M_3 = M_1 \times M_2$, a fraction with $2m$ places.

ii) Let $E_3 = E_1 + E_2$. We can form the sum of two e-bit exponents in excess-2^{e-1} code by adding them in the normal fashion and then subtracting 2^{e-1}. Note that E_3 may temporarily be too large or small to be represented in e-bits in excess-2^{e-1} code. An overflow may result, but we shall not discover this for a while.

iii) a) If $E_3 < -2^{e-1}$, shift M_3 right $|E_3| - 2^{e-1}$ places and set E_3 to -2^{e-1}.

b) (optional, but a good idea to avoid loosing significant bits, if possible). If $E_3 \geqslant -2^{e-1}$, normalize the answer by repeatedly shifting M_3 a place left and subtracting one from E_3, until either M_3 has a 1 in the leftmost place, or E_3 becomes -2^{e-1}.

iv) Let the rightmost m bits of M_3 be M_5 and the remaining m bits be M_4. The answer has exponent E_3 and mantissa M_4. The sign of the answer is determined from the sign of X_1 and X_2 in the obvious way. If it is desired to have a second word hold the less-significant bits of the answer, we may represent that word in floating-point by giving it exponent $E_3 - m$ and mantissa M_5, with the obvious sign.

Example 1.27. Let us multiply the computer words 010011010101 and 010100101010 as floating-point numbers with $e = 4$ and $m = 7$. We have $E_1 = 1$, $M_1 = (.1010101)_2$, $E_2 = 2$ and $M_2 = (.0101010)_2$. The product $M_1 \times M_2$ is $M_3 = (.00110111110010)_2$. We compute $E_3 = E_1 + E_2 = 3$. This calculation can be done in excess-8 code as follows

$$
\begin{array}{rr}
E_1 & 1001 \\
+E_2 & +1010 \\
\hline
& 10011 \\
-8 & -1000 \\
\hline
& 1011
\end{array}
$$

Since $E_3 \geqslant -8$, rule (iiib) applies. We shift M_3 two places left and subtract two from E_3 to obtain $M_3 = (.11011111001000)_2$ and $E_3 = 1$. In step (iv) we split M_3 into $M_4 = (.1101111)_2$ and $M_5 = (.1001000)_2$. Note that $M_4 + 2^{-m}M_5 = M_3$. The answer has exponent E_3, mantissa M_4, and sign 0. That is, the answer is $Y =$

0̱10011101111. If we wished to form another computer word with the less-significant bits, we would give it exponent $E_3 - 7 = -6$, mantissa M_5 and sign 0. This word is $Z = 0̱00101001000$.

Note that $X_1 = 1\frac{21}{64}$, $X_2 = 1\frac{5}{16}$, $Y = 1\frac{47}{64}$ and $Z = \frac{19}{1024}$. Thus, $X_1 \times X_2 = Y + Z$. This equality holds in general, unless $E_3 < -2^{e-1}$ and rule (iiia) causes the loss of significant places. If we took Y alone as the product $X_1 \times X_2$, there would be a small error introduced. ∎

4. Division

It is a possible, although not frequently exercised, option to represent the dividend of a floating-point division problem by two words, just as in fixed-point division. We shall therefore couch our algorithm as though two words were available for the quotient. If only one is used, take the second (M_2' in what follows) to be zero.

Let the divisor be $X_1 = \pm 2^{E_1} \times M_1$ and let the dividend X_2 be represented by two words $\pm 2^{E_2} \times M_2$ and $\pm 2^{E_2 - m} \times M_2'$ where $X_2 = \pm 2^{E_2} \times (M_2 + 2^{-m} \times M_2')$. Assume $M_1 \neq 0$. Do the following.

i) Divide $M_2 + 2^{-m} \times M_2'$ by M_1. Produce enough bits so that there are m bits including and to the right of the leftmost 1. Call the result M_3. Since we are not assuming our numbers normalized, the decimal point may be either to the left or right of the leftmost 1.

ii) Compute $E_3 = E_2 - E_1$. We may subtract numbers in excess-2^{e-1} code by subtracting normally, then adding 2^{e-1}. Note that E_3 may not currently be representable in e bits.

iii) a) If the decimal point of M_3 is D places to the right of the leftmost 1, move the decimal point to the left of that 1 and add D to E_3.

   b) (optional) If the decimal point is to the left of the leading 1 in M_3, normalize by repeatedly shifting M_3 a place left and subtracting one from E_3, until either $E_3 = -2^{e-1}$ or the leftmost 1 reaches the decimal point.

iv) Compute the sign of the quotient in the obvious way. The exponent of the quotient is the current value of E_3 and its mantissa is the m bits currently to the right of the decimal point.

Example 1.28. Using the same floating-point format as the previous examples, let us divide 0̱11001011000 into 0̱01101110000. That is, $E_1 = 4$, $M_1 = (.1011000)_2$, $E_2 = -2$, and $M_2 = (.1110000)_2$. Since no second word for the quotient is specified, take it to be zero. Thus $M_2' = 0$ and $M_2 + 2^{-m} \times M_2' = M_2$. We divide M_2 by M_1, producing $M_3 = (1.010001)_2$. We compute $E_3 = E_2 - E_1 = -6$. Step (iiia) applies, with $D = 1$. We change M_3 to $(.1010001)_2$ and add D to E_3, making $E_3 = -5$. The quotient is therefore 0̱00111010001 in floating-point notation. That is, we have divided 11 into $\frac{7}{32}$ and obtained $\frac{81}{4096}$ as a result. There has been an error due to inexactitude of the division M_2/M_1 amounting to about 0.6%. ∎

1.8 MULTIPLE-PRECISION ARITHMETIC

Computer words are usually long enough to make everyday calculations to sufficient precision, even though, as we have seen, errors are regularly introduced into the least significant places in floating-point arithmetic.[†] Nevertheless, there are applications in which numbers need to be expressed to such precision that more than one computer word is necessary. Therefore, many computers have "built in" the ability to do *double-precision* arithmetic, using two computer words to represent numbers, in either fixed- or floating-point. In addition, it is possible to use any number of computer words to represent one quantity if we are willing to write programs to perform arithmetic on such *multiple-precision* numbers correctly.

There are two common styles of representing multiple-precision numbers.

1. Treat r computer words of length k as if it were one computer word of length rk. For example, for floating-point arithmetic, the second and subsequent words could be treated as an extension of the mantissa of the first. This scheme is useful if the computer has been given the ability to operate on such sequences of words automatically. However, if we must simulate the effect of arithmetic operations on r-precision words by performing a sequence of operations on single words, we run into trouble. The chief problem is that the leftmost bit of a computer word represents the sign when single-precision is used, while this scheme uses it as another bit of the mantissa in the second and subsequent words.

2. Use a sequence of single words to represent their weighted sum. For example, a common scheme for fixed-point multiple-precision numbers is to use a sequence of k-bit words with values $W_1, W_2, \ldots, W_r$ to represent the integer $W_r + 2^{k-1}W_{r-1} + 2^{2(k-1)}W_{r-2} + \cdots + 2^{(r-1)(k-1)}W_1$. Normally, the signs of the W's are all the same.

For floating-point multiple precision, we use a sequence of words with identical sign and exponents in a decreasing arithmetic progression. That is, if m bits are used for mantissas, and the exponent of the first is E, then the exponent of the second is $E - m$, the exponent of the third is $E - 2m$, and so on.

Example 1.29. Let us represent $(10,000)_{10}$ using triple-precision sign-and-magnitude fixed-point notation with 6-bit computer words. We find $(10,000)_{10} = (10011100010000)_2$. Since we need a sign bit (0 in this case) for each word, we break the latter string of bits into groups of five, starting from the right. Thus the third word has 0 for sign and 10000 for magnitude. The second word has 0 for sign and 11000 for magnitude and the first word has 0 for sign and 01001 for magnitude. Note that a leading 0 is attached, since we broke up a string of 14 bits. The representation of $(10,000)_{10}$ is thus 001001 011000 010000.

[†] The reader should be reminded that $e = 4$ and $m = 7$ was chosen for ease in working through examples. However, in practice, much larger values, say $e = 8$ and $m = 27$ are chosen, so that even relatively long series of calculations can be expected to produce around 20 significant places in binary, or equivalently, 6 to 7 places in decimal. It is only if numbers very close to each other are subtracted that many fewer significant places are obtained.

These three words are 9, 24 and 16, respectively. Since k = 6, the three together in triple precision represent $16 + 2^5 \times 24 + 2^{10} \times 9 = 16 + 768 + 9{,}216 = 10{,}000$. Note that the decimal point is assumed at the right end of the last word. ∎

Example 1.30. Let us use two 12-bit computer words to represent $(\frac{1}{3})_{10}$ as precisely as possible in floating-point. Assume, as before, that four bits are utilized for the exponent. Note that $(\frac{1}{3})_{10} = (.\overline{01})_2$. If we use the first scheme discussed in this section, the entire second word becomes part of the mantissa. We therefore have 19 mantissa bits. If we normalize, the exponent in the first word becomes -1, so the first word is 001111010101 and the second word is 010101010101.

By the second method, we use seven bits each for two mantissas. If we normalize the first word, the first exponent is -1 as before. Its mantissa is 1010101, also as before. The exponent of the second word is seven less than that of the first, that is, -8. Its mantissa is the seven bits in the binary fraction for $\frac{1}{3}$ following the mantissa of the first word, that is, 0101010. Thus, the second word is 000000101010. Note that the second word happens to be normalized because its exponent has the smallest possible value, -2^{e-1}. However, in general, the second word will not be normalized in this scheme. ∎

1.9 REPRESENTATION OF CHARACTER STRINGS

We have seen how the same computer word can be interpreted in several ways, either in fixed- or floating-point, and if in fixed-point, in several different formats. These interpretations are essentially numerical. A versatile computer also has the ability to deal directly with computer words that represent nonnumeric data, character strings in particular.

The notion of what constitutes a character we leave intentionally vague. However, the following are normally considered characters.

1. The letters. Upper and lower case letters are usually considered distinct characters.

2. Digits.

3. Arithmetic signs, e.g., $+$, $=$, ↑ (exponentiation).

4. Punctuation, e.g., parentheses, comma, period.

5. The blank (usually indicated ƀ).

Associated with each computer is a set of characters which may be internally represented in the computer. The internal representation is a string of bits, usually six to nine bits. The number of bits used to represent a character is called the *byte length* of the computer.[†] A string of bits of that length is called a *byte*. Usually, the

---

[†] Another common usage of the term "byte" is the smallest number of bits accessible as a unit in the computer memory. For many computers the "byte" in this sense is also the number of bits used to represent a character.

computer's word length is a multiple of the byte length, and a word (or several words) represents a string of characters. We may determine the string of characters by breaking the word or words into bytes and decoding the bytes.

Example 1.31. There are several encodings for characters which are in use or have been popular. They do not each encode the same set of characters, although certain characters are common to all. We list in Fig. 1.11 the encodings for the characters A, B, 0 and ♭ (blank) in three such codes using from six to eight bits.

	EBCDIC·	ASCII·	BCD·
A	11000001	1000001	010001
B	11000010	1000010	010010
0	11110000	0110000	000000
♭	01000000	0100000	110000

Fig. 1.11   Character codes. EBCDIC is used on IBM 360/370 series computers; BCD was used on IBM 7000 series computers; ASCII is used on most other presently manufactured computers, often with an eighth bit included with each byte.

Thus if the BCD code is used, we can encode the string AB0 in an 18-bit word: 010001010010000000.

1.10   REPRESENTING OTHER KINDS OF DATA

There is really no limit to the kinds of information which can be represented by strings of bits. The rule to bear in mind is that if we wish to encode m different items, we need $\log m$ bits.[†] Put another way, with k bits, we may encode 2^k items but no more.

Example 1.32.   Suppose a clothing store wishes to record in a computer its inventory of men's shirts, listing the collar and sleeve size of each. Suppose collar sizes range from $13\frac{1}{2}''$ to $17\frac{1}{2}''$, in steps of $\frac{1}{2}''$, and sleeve lengths range from $32''$ to $36''$, in steps of $1''$. There are five different sleeve sizes, and $\lceil \log_2 5 \rceil = 3$. Thus three bits are needed. For example, we might represent $32''$ by 000, $33''$ by 001, and so on; that is, we could represent sleeve size i by the binary equivalent of $i - 32$, with leading zeros if necessary to make three bits.

There are nine collar sizes, so four bits are needed. We might encode collar size j by the four-bit binary number $2j - 27$. For example, collar size 15 is represented by 0011.

It is interesting to note that there are $9 \times 5 = 45$ different kinds of shirts. Since $\lceil \log_2 45 \rceil = 6$, it appears that six bits are sufficient to represent a shirt, rather than the seven that are needed if we encode sleeve and collar separately. The disadvantage of using only six bits is that some calculation will be needed to evaluate either the

---

[†] $\lceil x \rceil$, the *ceiling* of x, is the smallest integer equal to or greater than x.

sleeve or collar size. Perhaps the best six-bit encoding is to encode sleeve size i with collar size j as $(i - 32) + 5 \times (2j - 27)$. ∎

Example 1.33. A frequent use of computer words is to represent decimal numbers. Since there are ten decimal digits, four bits per digit are needed. The usual code is the obvious one, $(0)_{10} = 0000$, $(1)_{10} = 0001, \ldots, (9)_{10} = 1001$. For example, 451 is represented by 010001010001. ∎

EXERCISES

1.1 Convert the following to decimal.

a) $(1100110)_2$

b) $(20112)_3$

c) $(AB3C)_{16}$

1.2 Perform the following conversions.

a) $(274)_{10}$ to binary

b) $(274)_{10}$ to ternary

c) $(1000)_9$ to base eleven

1.3 Convert the following to decimal.

a) $(10.011)_2$

b) $(4.203)_5$

* c) $(2.21)_3$

1.4 Perform the following conversions.

a) $(16.4)_{10}$ to base 5

b) $(27.115)_8$ to base 4

c) $(.205)_9$ to ternary

* **1.5** Find the decimal fraction having the same value as the repeating base 7 fraction $.2\overline{35}$.

** **1.6** Show that $\sqrt{2}$ is not a rational number.
Hint: Suppose $\sqrt{2} = a/b$ for integers a and b with no common factor greater than 1. Then $a^2 = 2b^2$, so a is divisible by 2. Can you proceed from there?

1.7 Find four significant places of

a) $(.73)_{10}$ in base 8

* b) $(.23)_5$ in base 8

* c) $(.3\overline{3})_{10}$ in base 7

1.8 Convert $(1011.00111)_2$ to octal.

1.9 Convert $(AF.7B0E)_{16}$ to binary.

*1.10 Give a simple algorithm to convert from base 4 to base 8. Do not begin "First convert to base 2, then. . . . " There is a more direct method.

1.11 Perform the following computations in octal.

a) $\begin{array}{r} 271 \\ +334 \end{array}$ b) $\begin{array}{r} 1001 \\ -\ 772 \end{array}$ c) $\begin{array}{r} 25 \\ \times 36 \end{array}$ d) $36\overline{)20167}$

1.12 Perform the following calculations in hexadecimal.

a)   CA7   b)   3BO   c)   654   d) 2E1⌐D7A3C
      +949   − 2EF   × 1D8

*__1.13__ Give algorithms similar to the one in Fig. 1.7 (p. 28) to perform in base r:

a) subtraction (assume the result will be nonnegative),

b) multiplication,

c) division (produce a quotient and remainder).

1.14 Represent the following numbers in sign-and-magnitude, ones'-complement and twos'-complement notation, using eight-bit computer words.

a) +127   b) −127   *c) −128   d) −37

1.15 Perform the following sums and differences in sign-and-magnitude, ones'-complement and twos'-complement notation, using eight-bit computer words.

a)   27   b)   27   c)   108   *d)   −47
     +(−33)   −(−33)   − 92   +(−92)

1.16 What is the relation between the one's- and two's-complement representation of the same negative number?

*__1.17__ Which of the following algebraic laws hold for fixed-point computer arithmetic?

a) The *commutative law of addition* $X + Y = Y + X$.
Hint: The answer depends on what you assume about how answer zero is to be represented.

b) The *commutative law of multiplication* $X \times Y = Y \times X$.

c) The *associative law of multiplication* $X \times (Y \times Z) = (X \times Y) \times Z$.

d) The *distributive laws of multiplication over addition* $X \times (Y + Z) = X \times Y + X \times Z$ and $(Y + Z) \times X = Y \times X + Z \times X$.

e) $X − (Y − Z) = (X − Y) + Z$.

1.18 Find floating-point numbers as close as possible to the following decimal numbers. Use four bits for the exponent and seven bits for the mantissa.

a) 7   b) 7.3   c) −.0014   *d) 150

1.19 Normalize the following floating-point numbers (four-bit exponent—seven-bit mantissa) and give their decimal values.

a) 010110011001

b) 100010001001

*__1.20__ What is the relationship between the representation of a number in excess-2^{k-1} code and as a k-bit twos'-complement number?

1.21 In Example 1.24 we represented 1.79 approximately by the floating-point number 010011110011, where $e = 4$ and $m = 7$. What number precisely is represented by this 12-bit word?

*__1.22__ Suppose 32-bit words have a seven-bit exponent E, in excess-64 code, and a 24-bit mantissa M, and that such a word represents number $\pm 16^E \times M$, depending upon the sign bit. Give a method of normalization for such numbers.
Hint: It is not possible always to make the leading mantissa bit 1.

1.23 Represent 16,383 in the format of Exercise 1.22.

*__1.24__ Suppose 36-bit words are used to represent numbers according to Fig. 1.12. The first bit represents the sign, as usual. The next four bits represent some number A in binary. A determines

Fig. 1.12 Arcane word format.

the number of bits used for the exponent. In particular, $4 + A$ bits are used, and the exponent E is represented in excess-2^{3+A} code. The remaining bits represent the mantissa, with the decimal point at the left end. The number represented is $\pm 2^E \times M$.[†]

  a) Find a representation for 2^{300}.

  b) What number is represented by $00101\,1000000011\,100000000000000000000$?

*1.25 Suppose all is as in Exercise 1.24, but the number represented is $\pm 3^E \times M$. Find a representation for 50.625.

**1.26 Suppose 36-bit words are formatted as in Exercise 1.24. Give normalization rules when the number represented is

  a) $\pm 2^E \times M$

  b) $\pm 3^E \times M$

*1.27 What are the advantages and disadvantages of representing numbers as in Exercise 1.24?

1.28 Let us use 15-bit words with $e = 5$ and $m = 9$ to represent floating-point numbers. Represent the following decimal numbers as closely as possible and perform the indicated operations. What is the percentage error in the results?

  a) $12.4 + 3.62$

  b) $12.4 - 11.6$

  c) $.0412 \times 25.19$ (use one word for the answer)

  d) $65.0/13.0$ (use one word for the dividend)

1.29 Let us use 9-bit computer words. Suppose three such words are used to represent an integer using the weighted sum method of Section 1.8. Show how to represent 3,141,592 in this format.

1.30 Use two 15-bit computer words to represent 7.4 as precisely as possible in double-precision floating-point with $e = 5$ and $m = 9$,

  a) treating the entire second word as an extension of the mantissa of the first,

  b) treating the two words as a sum.

**1.31 Give algorithms to perform the four arithmetic operations on multiple-precision numbers in the weighted-sum format of Section 1.8.

1.32 How many bits are required to represent

  a) a card from a poker (52 card) deck?

 * b) a card from a pinochle (48 card) deck?

 * c) a poker hand (five cards)?

** d) three cards from a pinochle deck?

  We may define the *residue of a modulo b* (or *a mod b*) to be the unique number c between 0 and $b - 1$ such that $a - c$ is divisible by b. When $a \geqslant 0$, a mod b is just the remainder when a is divided by b. For example, 7 mod 3 is 1, since $7 - 1 = 6$ is divisible by 3; and -13 mod 5 is 2, since $-13 - 2 = -15$ is divisible by 5.

---

† This scheme was, to the author's knowledge, first proposed by Robert Morris.

1.33 Find the following:

a) 27 mod 6

b) 35 mod 7

c) −16 mod 3

d) −85 mod 28

*1.34 Give an efficient algorithm to find a mod b when a is negative.

*1.35 Show that the twos'-complement representation of a is a mod 2^m, where m is the length of the computer word, and $-2^{m-1} \leqslant a < 2^{m-1}$.

*1.36 Show that the ones'-complement representation of a is a mod $2^m - 1$, where m is the length of the word, and $-2^{m-1} < a < 2^{m-1}$. (Zero has another representation—all 1's. Note that $(11 \ldots 1)_2$ mod $2^m - 1$ is zero!)

Programming Exercise

There are numerous simple algorithms throughout this chapter which could be implemented. To extend the skills learned in Chapter 1, we suggest the following problem.

1.37 It is surprisingly easy to generate a large number of places of e (the base of natural logarithms). First we note that

$$e = 2 + \sum_{i=2}^{\infty} \frac{1}{i!}.$$

That is, $e - 2 = \frac{1}{2} + \frac{1}{6} + \frac{1}{24} + \frac{1}{120} \cdots$.

We can represent any real number $0 \leqslant x < 1$ as a (possibly) infinite "variable radix" fraction $.a_1 a_2 \ldots$, if the digit a_i is permitted to be any of $0, 1, \ldots i$, and the number represented is:

$$\sum_{i=1}^{\infty} \frac{a_i}{(i + 1)!}.$$

For example, $\frac{3}{8}$ is represented by the truncated fraction $.021$, since $\frac{3}{8} = \frac{0}{2} + \frac{2}{6} + \frac{1}{24}$. The real number $e - 2$ is represented by the infinite fraction $.111 \ldots$, and thereby hangs a tale.

The algorithm of Fig. 1.5 (p. 26) can be used to convert a number x to decimal as long as we can compute the product $10x$ and find its integer part, independent of how x is actually represented. For example, we could represent x in the variable radix notation just described.

To multiply a truncated variable radix fraction $x = .a_1 a_2 \ldots a_m$ by 10 we execute the algorithm of Fig. 1.13.

We use i to indicate the "current" place and c to indicate the carry from the previous place. Initially $i = m$ and $c = 0$. Since a_j must be between 0 and j, we carry $j + 1$ from place j by subtracting $j + 1$ from that place and adding 1 to place $j - 1$. Note that this operation does not change the number represented. The product $10x$ is the final value of the integer c plus the variable radix fraction $.b_1 b_2 \ldots b_m$.

Example 1.33. To multiply $a_1 a_2 a_3 = .021$ by 10, we first set $c = 0$ and $i = 3$. Since $10 \times a_3 + c = 10$, $[10/(3 + 1)] = 2$ and $10 - 2 \times (3 + 1) = 2$, we set $b_3 = 2$ and $c = 2$. Then, $10 \times a_2 + 2 = 22$, $[22/(2 + 1)] = 7$ and $22 - 7 \times (2 + 1) = 1$. Thus, $b_2 = 1$ and $c = 7$. Finally, $10 \times a_1 + 7 = 7$, $[7/(1 + 1)] = 3$ and $7 - 3 \times (1 + 1) =$

```
begin
    c = 0;
    for i = m by −1 to 1 do
        begin
            d = 10 * a_i + c;
            c = [d/(i + 1)];
            b_i = d − c * (i + 1)
        end
end
```

Fig. 1.13   Algorithm to multiply variable radix fraction by 10.

1, so $b_1 = 1$ and $c = 3$. Thus, .021, which represents $\frac{3}{8}$, when multiplied by 10 gives the integer 3 plus the fraction .112, which represents $\frac{1}{2} + \frac{1}{6} + \frac{2}{24} = \frac{3}{4}$. That is $\frac{3}{8} \times 10 = 3\frac{3}{4}$. ∎

The suggested exercise is to produce e to 1000 decimal places by converting .11 ... 1, to m places, from the variable radix notation to decimal.[†] To properly choose m, we must know that the portion of the series

$$\sum_{i=1}^{\infty} \frac{1}{(i + 1)!}$$

thrown away by truncating at m places is negligible compared with 10^{-1000}. Since the value of each term in the series is very much smaller than the preceding term, we need only be sure that $1/(m + 2)!$ is small compared with 10^{-1000}. It is suggested that $m = 500$ be chosen.

FURTHER READING

Flores [1963] is a comprehensive book covering algorithms for performing fixed- and floating-point arithmetic. Knuth [1969] covers arithmetic from a more theoretical point of view, and a still more advanced viewpoint can be found in Aho, Hopcroft, and Ullman [1974].

Algorithms similar to laboratory exercise 1.37 computing e exist for various mathematical constants such as π and $\sqrt{2}$. A description of such algorithms can be found in Nievergelt, Farrar, and Reingold [1974].

[†] This technique was used by Kenneth Thompson and Robert Morris to compute e to 1,000,000 places. They used something over one month of PDP 11 time.

Chapter 2

A Simple Computer

In this chapter we shall discuss a computer which, although an oversimplification of modern computing systems, does exhibit many of the important concepts associated with computers and computing. In particular, we shall discuss the pieces into which a computer may be logically divided, and we shall describe a simple machine language. Then we shall introduce mnemonics for the machine instructions; such mnemonics form the basis of an "assembly language," a concept discussed in more detail in Chapter 4.

Incidentally, we shall break with tradition and not choose a name for the example computer we develop in this book. We use the term "our computer" whenever this particular example, rather than computers in general, is meant.

2.1 AN OVERVIEW OF A COMPUTER

We can, at a very macroscopic level, picture a computer as in Fig. 2.1. It consists of:

1. A *main* (or *core*) *memory*, which consists of a large number of easily accessible computer words. Present in the main memory are at least some of the instructions of the program which the computer is executing and at least some of the data upon which the program is to operate.

2. A *secondary memory*, typically having a much larger capacity than the main memory, although access to secondary memory is relatively slow. Typical secondary storage devices are magnetic tapes, disks, and drums.

3. A *control unit*, which determines the actions taken by the computer. The control unit reads instructions appearing in main memory and causes them to be executed.

4. An *arithmetic unit*, consisting of some *registers* (holding computer words) and electronic circuits to perform arithmetic and other operations on the words held in the registers or in main memory.

Communication with the outside world takes place through main memory. Typical devices for input are a card reader or a remote console. The characters punched on the cards or typed on the console are encoded into bit strings and placed directly in main memory. Output is produced, for example, by punching the contents of a portion of main memory on cards or by printing on a console or high-speed line printer.

It should be observed that communication with the outside world is typically character based. The representation in the computer of, for example, a printed line is a sequence of bytes representing the characters of the line. Thus, if we wish the computer to print a number, we must first convert the fixed- or floating-point representation of the number to a sequence of bytes representing the digits we desire to print.

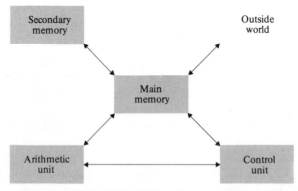

Fig. 2.1   Organization of a computer.

2.2   THE MAIN MEMORY

We may picture the main memory as shown in Fig. 2.2. The memory consists of M computer words, with numbers (*addresses*) $0, 1, \ldots, M - 1$.[†] Often, M is a power of 2, say $M = 2^k$ for some integer k. Typical values of k are 13 to 15 for a minicomputer and 16 to 18 for a large computer.[‡]

The only communication between the memory and the rest of the computer is through a *memory buffer* register. The memory buffer of a computer holds a single word, or perhaps some small number of consecutive words, depending on the computer. To obtain a word from memory it is necessary to copy it into the memory

---

[†] In many computers, memory words are divided into several bytes. For example, a 32-bit computer word could be regarded as consisting of four 8-bit bytes, as are IBM 360/370 machines. Each byte receives an address of its own, and words are given the address of their leftmost byte. Thus, in 360/370 series machines, the addresses of memory words are $0, 4, 8, 12, \ldots, 4M - 4$, if the memory consists of M words. The ith byte, $0 \leqslant i \leqslant 3$, of the jth word, $0 \leqslant j \leqslant M - 1$, is given address $4j + i$.

[‡] There is a simple way to convert powers of 2 to an approximately equivalent decimal number. Observe that 2^{10} is roughly $(1000)_{10}$ (1024 to be exact). Thus, 2^{20} is about a million, 2^{30} about a billion, and so on. For example $2^{12} = 2^{10} \times 2^2 \approx 1,000 \times 4 \approx 4000$. $2^{18} = 2^{20}/2^2 \approx 1,000,000/4 \approx 250,000$.

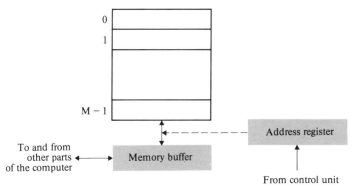

Fig. 2.2   Main memory.

buffer, from whence it may be shipped where needed. The memory buffer thus forms a bottleneck, forcing us to obtain just one or perhaps a few words from memory at a time. The hardware normally used to build a main memory makes this bottleneck necessary.

To read a word from memory, the address of the desired word is placed in the memory address register by the control unit. The circuitry of the memory will cause the contents of that word (and in some computers, several words following) to appear in the memory buffer.

To store a word into memory, the word is placed into the memory buffer register and the address into which it must be stored is placed in the address register.

The time taken to read a word into or from memory is on the order of a microsecond (10^{-6} second). Fast as this is, data can be shifted within those portions of the computer (control and arithmetic units) built of solid-state circuitry at least an order of magnitude faster, say 0.1 μs to 0.01 μs.[†] Thus, it is desirable that as much as possible of the data currently being processed be available in the fast registers of the arithmetic unit. Some computers come equipped with a sizable (several-thousand word) solid-state memory called a *cache*. Those portions of the main memory in heavy use may appear in the cache, and these portions may be accessed in order of magnitude faster than if they were in the main memory. Even "full-size" solid-state main memories are becoming economical and may be quite prevalent in the late 1970's.

Let us digress for a moment and comment on how digital data—0's and 1's—is stored in main memory and in solid-state registers. A core memory is composed of magnetic cores, one for each bit of each word. The donut-shaped cores are composed of small magnetic domains having a north and south pole which may be reversed by a current. A 0 is indicated by pole alignment in one direction around the circumference and a 1 by alignment in the other direction (as shown in Fig. 2.3).

The direction of magnetism may be sensed by passing current through wires that thread through the cores. In this way we may read the memory. The memory

---

[†] μs is the usual abbreviation for microsecond.

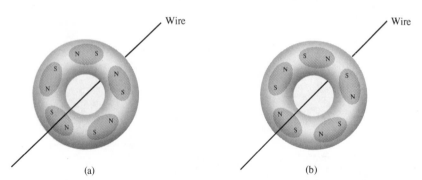

Fig. 2.3   Magnetic cores: a) Representing 0, b) Representing 1.

address register determines through which cores the current goes. Sufficient current in one direction or the other will alter the direction of magnetism, allowing us to write.

Registers such as the memory buffer or address register, as well as the entire control and arithmetic units, are composed of solid-state circuits. In these, 0's and 1's are represented by the presence or absence of voltage or electronic charge. In these circuits, computation can take place, in the sense that a voltage at one point can appear (with a time lag on the order of .01 μs to .001 μs) depending on the presence or absence of voltages at several other nearby points. Thus, data may be copied or manipulated logically, e.g., we can design a circuit that adds one row of voltage-represented bits to another such row, the answer appearing along a third row.

The actual physical mechanism behind solid-state or magnetic circuitry is beyond the scope of this book. We shall also omit a discussion of *logical design*, the methods whereby circuits are constructed to execute algorithms. The reader is asked to accept that circuitry can be designed to execute any algorithm which requires only a bounded amount of space for storage. For example, addition of k bit numbers in sign-and-magnitude notation requires $2k$ bits for its inputs, k bits for the answer, and k bits for carries. Thus, addition of k-bit words can be carried out by logical circuits.

2.3   THE CONTROL UNIT

A detailed picture of the control is shown in Fig. 2.4. The control unit repeatedly executes the *control cycle*, represented in Fig. 2.5. The location register holds a memory address, the address in which the control expects to find the next instruction to be executed.

To fetch an instruction, the contents of the location register are passed to the memory address register; the desired instruction appears in the memory buffer after a fixed delay. The location register is increased by one. The instruction is passed to the control, entering via the instruction register. The instruction is examined by circuitry called a *decoder*, which determines from the instruction exactly what the computer must do. The instruction is then executed; the control passes orders to the arithmetic unit for computation and/or to the memory to obtain or store data, whatever the instruction calls for.

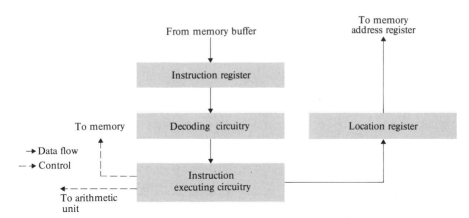

Fig. 2.4 The control.

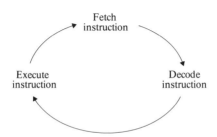

Fig. 2.5 The control cycle.

Normally, the location counter is increased by one, so the cycle may repeat, beginning with the fetch of another instruction. As an exception, some instructions call for "transfers." These instructions are executed by loading a particular address, specified by the instruction, into the location register. Instructions are then executed starting with that address, proceeding through higher addresses, until another transfer is reached. Note that a transfer instruction allows the computer to execute the same instructions repeatedly. In the absence of transfers, instructions in repeatedly higher addresses would be executed, once each.

Modern computers often allow some *instruction overlap*. If the instruction register can hold more than one word and the memory buffer is large enough, several instructions can be obtained at once from memory and one can be decoded while another is being executed. It is even possible to execute several instructions *in parallel*, that is, simultaneously. One must be careful not to execute in parallel two instructions one of which depends on the other. For example, if one instruction says "add A and B and call the result C," and another says "multiply C and D and call the result E," we cannot begin the second until we have completed the first. Nevertheless, typical programs present many opportunities for parallel execution that a sophisticated control unit can employ to advantage.

2.4 THE ARITHMETIC UNIT

The arithmetic unit consists of circuits to perform various operations, and also a small set of registers as shown in Fig. 2.6. The operations typically include arithmetic ones, e.g., addition in fixed- or floating-point format, as well as other operations which will be discussed when we introduce the instruction set of our computer. The operations take one or more arguments (*operands*); these arguments are computer words found either in one of the arithmetic registers or in a memory location. (Exceptions occur; for example an argument might be a byte or a sequence of consecutive words.) The result of the operation is placed in a register or a memory location, usually the former.

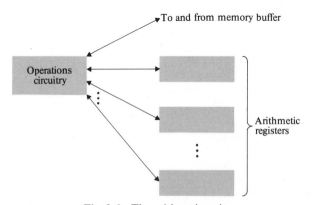

Fig. 2.6   The arithmetic unit.

Important special cases are operations which

1. copy the contents of one register into another register or into a memory location or

2. copy a memory location into a register.

These instructions, called *data-movement instructions*, are essential to any computer.

Often, some of the arithmetic registers may hold only certain kinds of arguments or only arguments for certain operations. For example, some registers might not be usable for the arguments of a floating-point arithmetic operation.

2.5 SECONDARY STORAGE

While the size of a main memory is large, a complete computer system requires the ability to store several orders of magnitude more data than the 2^{18} or so words of the largest main memories. A computer therefore needs secondary storage devices which have enormous capacity but whose data may be accessed or altered only slowly in comparison with the speed of main memory.[†]

The movement of data between secondary memory and the rest of the computer is only via the main memory. That is, data may be transfered from the main memory to the memory buffer to a secondary device, or the process may occur in reverse.

Since secondary devices (and the "outside world," as well) are typically much slower than main memory, large computers have one or more separate control units called *data channels*, whose job is to control the movement of data between the main memory and the secondary devices and the outside world. A typical situation follows. The control unit encounters an instruction to move some data, e.g., copy the contents of memory locations 100 to 200 onto a particular place in a disk storage unit. The control passes the instruction to a data channel, which moves the data as fast as it can. Meanwhile, the control unit proceeds to execute more instructions.

The control will not necessarily know when the data channel has finished its job. We shall briefly discuss communication between two essentially independent control units, such as the main control and a data channel in Section 2.16.

Three currently important secondary storage devices are magnetic tape, disk, and drum, and we shall discuss each of these in turn.

1. Magnetic Tape

We may write digital information on magnetic tape by lining up the magnetic domains in different directions to represent 0's and 1's. The tape passing under a tape head has its magnetic domains lined up in one of two directions. For example, N-S might represent 0 and S-N represent 1. To read the tape, the polarity of magnetism is sensed by the tape head.

Usually, a tape has several tracks. A common arrangement is for the number of tracks to be one more than the number of bits in a byte. One byte is written in a column, and the extra track gets a *parity bit*, chosen so the number of 1's in any column is an odd number.

Example 2.1. If eight-bit bytes are used, the 32-bit word

$$11000001\,11000010\,1\,100001\,1\,1\,1000100$$

would appear in four columns of nine-track tape as shown in Fig. 2.7. The parity bits are shown in the lowest track.

For example, the first eight bits 11000001 appear in the leftmost column of Fig. 2.7. Since there are already an odd number of 1's, the parity bit 0 is selected. If

---

[†] In fact, it should be observed that a computer has a hierarchy of memories, beginning with arithmetic registers which are fastest and most easily accessed, but few in number. The hierarchy may range through a cache (see Section 2.2) which has several orders of magnitude larger capacity than arithmetic registers, but whose words are not directly connected to the arithmetic performing circuitry, as are the arithmetic registers. Then comes the main memory, slower than a cache but of larger capacity. Finally, we have secondary memory, with the largest capacity but slowest access.

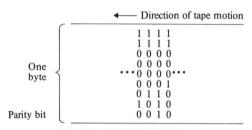

Fig. 2.7   Portion of a tape.

there had been an even number of 1's, parity bit 1 would be chosen, as in the third column. ∎

Data is packed much more closely along the tape than across it. The nine tracks across the tape occupy about an inch. However, along the tape 1600 columns per inch is typical.

A computer tape travels at a speed of about 100 inches/second. Despite this speed and density, the number of computer words that may be read in one second from tape is much less than what may be read from main memory. The following example illustrates the point.

Example 2.2.   Let us consider a computer with a 32-bit word length and 8-bit bytes. Its tapes travel 100 inches per second, and each track has 1000 bits per inch. Thus, in one second we can read $100 \times 1000 = 100,000$ bytes, or 25,000 words. If the same computer takes 1 μs to read a word from main memory, it can read 1,000,000 words, or 40 times as much from main memory as from tape in one second. Put another way, if a data channel is moving data between tape and main memory, only $\frac{1}{40}$th of the time is spent moving words in or out of memory. The other $\frac{39}{40}$th of the time, the main control unit has the main memory to use for its own computation.

However, let us consider the capacity of an entire tape, of 2400 feet. The tape stores 250 words per inch, so its entire length may hold $2400 \times 250 \times 12 = 7,200,000$ words. This is roughly the capacity of 27 2^{18} word core memories. ∎

In addition to the relative slowness of reading from tape, there is the much greater problem that in order to read a particular piece of data from the tape, we must move it to where the head is. This operation can take an enormous amount of time compared with the time to access a word from main memory, as the following example shows.

Example 2.3.   Let us consider the computer with the same parameters as in Example 2.2. It takes roughly 1050 inches to store the contents of a 2^{18} word memory. Thus, it could take over 10 seconds to go between two of these 2^{18} words. ∎

The conclusion is that one must be careful about how one uses tape for memory. There is considerably less freedom to access data in any desired sequence than with main memory. The desirable property of main memory that each word be accessible in the same amount of time is called *random access*. In comparison, the mode of access of tape is called *sequential*.

It is worth noting that in order to keep track of one's position on the tape, blank (unmagnetized) regions called *interrecord gaps* of about an inch may be placed on the tape. The data between two interrecord gaps is called a (*physical*) *record*. The tape may be brought to rest with the head at any one of these gaps.

2. Magnetic Disk

A disk unit consists of several circular plates with tops and bottoms made of mag- netizable material. The plates are stacked on a central axis, and the entire conglomera- tion rotates at perhaps 1000 or more revolutions per minute. Each plate has two heads attached to arms, one to read or write on the top surface, the other for the bottom. The heads can be positioned at any desired radius from the axis, to read or write on a track located at that radius.

Normally, there is one path upon which data travels between a disk unit and the main memory. Thus, at most, one track at a time can be read or written upon, although there are many heads. A disk unit is pictured in Fig. 2.8.

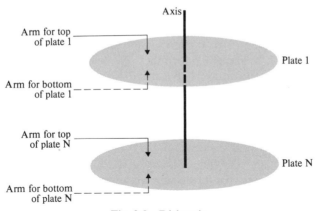

Fig. 2.8   Disk unit.

As mentioned, each surface contains up to several-hundred tracks arranged in concentric circles around the axis; as shown in Fig. 2.9. Each track typically stores on the order of 100,000 bits. Storage is done magnetically, as it is for tape. One sector, called the *switching gap*, is left unmagnetized, to mark the beginning of the tracks and to allow time for the head to move between adjacent tracks as the disk rotates. Often, one track is used to indicate, by its contents, positions around the disk. Thus it is possible to locate data at any desired angle (relative to the switching gap) around the disk.

The disk is used in a way that is part random access, part sequential. Any piece of data may be accessed in the time it takes to:

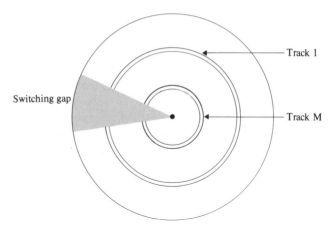

Fig. 2.9   A surface of a disk.

i) move the appropriate head to the appropriate track (called *seek* time), and

ii) wait until the desired portion of the track moves under the head (called *latency* time).

If the disk is rotating at 1000 rpm, the latency time is no more than $\frac{1}{20}$th of a second (compare with Example 2.3 for tape). The seek time can be several times as large as this, although if motion between adjacent tracks is desired, this can be accomplished in the time it takes the switching gap to pass under the head. Some of the implications of these figures on timing are considered in the next example.

Example 2.4. Suppose we have a disk unit rotating at 1000 rpm with 10 plates (20 surfaces), 50 tracks per surface, and 100,000 bits per track. The total capacity of the unit is $20 \times 50 \times 100,000 = 100,000,000$ bits. In terms of 32-bit words, this is 3,125,000 words, comparable to the capacity of the tape discussed in Example 2.2.

Let us compute the number of 32-bit words which may be read in one second. Assume the words are on consecutive tracks of one disk or tracks of one *cylinder* (tracks at a fixed radius on different surfaces). We may then disregard seek and latency times. In one second, the disk rotates $16\frac{2}{3}$ times, so we may read that number of tracks, a total of 833,333 bits or about 26,000 words. This number compares with the figure given for a typical tape in Example 2.2 and is considerably slower than that for main memory. ∎

3. Magnetic Drum

A drum is a revolving cylinder covered with magnetic material, as shown in Fig. 2.10. The surface is covered with tracks around the circumference, and a head is permanently positioned to read each track. Normally, only one head at a time can be used for reading or writing, as in a disk unit.

The speed of rotation and capacity of the tracks is similar to that of a disk. However, since heads never need to move, there is no seek time. On the negative

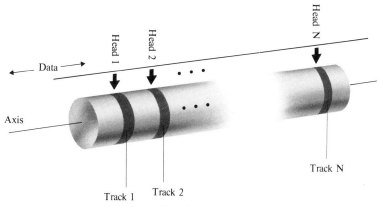

Fig. 2.10   Magnetic drum.

side, the capacity of a drum is less than that of a disk of equal volume. If we compare Figs. 2.8 and 2.10, we note that both the disk and drum occupy a cylindrical volume. The disk stores data throughout the volume, but the drum stores it only on the surface.

2.6   THE KINDS OF COMPUTER INSTRUCTIONS

The instructions of a computer can, with a few exceptions, be classified into the following types:

1. data motion,
2. operations,
3. control transfers,
4. input/output.

The usual format of an instruction is shown in Fig. 2.11. Often, each instruction takes up one word of memory. In many computers, variable length instructions are permitted. For example, instructions needing no memory address could be placed in half a word. (The address portion is often half the total length.) It might be convenient to have two addresses in some instructions, in which case we could use a word and a half. If instructions whose lengths involve a fraction of a word are permitted and instructions are packed as closely as possible; then some instructions will begin in the middle of a word. The control unit must be able to keep track of not only in which word the next instruction begins, but where in the word it begins. If each byte has its own address, then there is no problem.

At the left are some bits which we call the *instruction code*. These are the bits which the control unit examines in order to determine what action must be taken. At the right is a memory address, which indicates some data needed by the instruction, e.g., the location of an operand if the instruction is an arithmetic operation or the location of the next instruction if a transfer. The address portion is not actually

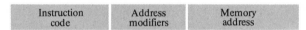

| Instruction code | Address modifiers | Memory address |

Fig. 2.11   Instruction format.

needed for all instructions. In the middle may be some bits which can be used to modify the address portion in ways we shall discuss later.

We shall now begin the specification of our computer. This computer will be used to explicate ideas for the remainder of the book. Our computer has a word length of 30, each of which may be regarded as composed of five bytes of six bits each, and 2^{12} words of main memory. It has seven arithmetic registers of 30 bits each; these will be referred to as registers 1 through 7. Its instructions are all one word in length. The first twelve bits of instructions form the instruction code. The next six are for address modifiers, and the right-hand twelve bits are for the memory address.

In the next sections we shall explore some of the ideas connected with the various types of instructions. We shall also learn the comparatively simple set of instructions used by our computer.

2.7   DATA-MOTION INSTRUCTIONS

A *data-motion* instruction causes the contents of one memory location or arithmetic register to be placed in another (the "target").[†] The data also stays where it was, so two copies of the data are made. The data formerly in the target location disappears.

Such an instruction must indicate which two registers or memory locations are involved and in which direction data is to move. Often, the sizes of a computer word and the main memory are such that it is not possible to fit two memory addresses and an instruction code in one computer word. For this reason, many computers do not have in their repertoire single instructions which move data directly from one memory location to another. One has to move the data from memory to an arithmetic register and thence to memory again by another instruction.

When we discuss the instructions of our computer it is convenient to represent the bits of the instruction in octal. The twelve bits of the instruction code can be easily represented by four octal digits, the address modifier by two octal digits, and the memory address by another four octal digits.

The instruction code itself will be divided in half. The first six bits (two octal digits) will indicate an action and the next six bits will indicate up to two arithmetic registers. Registers 1 through 7 may be represented by the octal digits 1 through 7, either in bits 7 to 9 or bits 10 to 12. We use octal 0 to indicate that no register is designated.

We shall use octal 01 (binary 000001) in bits 1 to 6 to indicate a data-motion instruction. Bits 7 to 9 indicate the place whose data is to be copied. Any of the digits 1

[†] We classify instructions which move data between main and secondary memory as input/output instructions. The distinction is made because the latter movements of data usually involve use of a data channel, while data-motion instructions, as the term is used here, do not.

through 7 there indicate that the data is copied from the register with that number. A 0 there indicates that the data is to be copied from a memory address, the one found in the address portion of the instruction.

Bits 10 to 12 indicate the target location. The same code applies. However, note that octal 0 in both bits 7 to 9 and 10 to 12 does not make sense. It says, in effect, copy some memory address into itself. We may treat this combination as an invalid instruction or as a "no-op," an instruction having no effect.

We shall now consider some examples of data-motion instructions in our computer. We shall sometimes use rectangles to exhibit instructions. These rectangles are partitioned into three portions representing the contents of the instruction-code, address-modifier, and memory-address portions of the instruction, all in octal. Since we have not yet discussed address modifiers, we shall, for the time being, leave the middle blank. The reader can assume it to be all 0's.

The instruction in Fig. 2.12(a) says that data is to be moved from register 5 to memory location 473.[†] The data also stays in register 5, of course. The former contents of location 473 are lost.

The instruction in Fig. 2.12(b) causes the contents of register 1 to be copied into register 2. The memory address is irrelevant in this case.

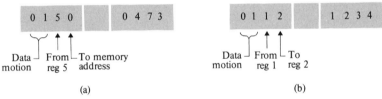

(a)   (b)

Fig. 2.12 Two instructions.

2.8 OPERATIONS

Let us now take up those instructions, called *operations*, which manipulate data. These instructions often specify three locations; two tell where the operands are, and one indicates someplace to put the result. As we commented regarding data-motion instructions, there often is not enough room in one computer word to hold two memory addresses, so the typical repertoire of instructions includes only those in which all, or all but one, of the locations involved are registers. In fact, it is common to restrict operation instructions to take one operand in a register, the other in memory (or perhaps another register), and for the result to appear in the register holding the first operand.

Our computer will have eight arithmetic and several other operations. These operations will be the four usual ones ($+$, $-$, $*$, $\div$) in fixed- or floating-point. Fixed-

---

† We shall always use octal numbers for the address of our computer so we omit the subscript 8.

point numbers are in sign-and-magnitude notation. Floating-point numbers have a
sign bit, a seven-bit exponent and a 22-bit mantissa.[†] We assume the results of arithmetic operations will be normalized in the way suggested in Chapter 1. The first
six bits of the instruction codes are:

Operation	Octal code
Fixed-point addition	02
Floating-point addition	03
Fixed-point subtraction	04
Floating-point subtraction	05
Fixed-point multiplication	06
Floating-point multiplication	07
Fixed-point division	10
Floating-point division	11

Bits 7 to 9 of the instruction code will always be a register number. This register
will hold the first operand as well as the result. Bits 10 to 12 will give the location of
the second operand. Zero there indicates that the location is the memory address
found in the right half of the instruction. A number from 1 through 7 indicates a
register as for data motion. For example

0	4	1	0		0	4	7	3

is an instruction to subtract the contents of memory location 473 from the contents
of register 1, leaving the result in register 1 and treating the contents of register 1
and memory location 473 as fixed-point numbers.

All multiplications will produce a single-word product, and all divisions take a
single-word dividend. An overflow occurs if a product has more than 29 bits. There
are no multiple-precision arithmetic operations.[‡]

We shall also have some *logical* operations, ones which treat computer words
as a string of bits—no more, no less. The "and" operation ($\wedge$) looks at corresponding
bits of each of its two operands and places a 1 in that position if both operands have
a 1 there. The "or" operation ($\vee$) places a 1 in a position if either operand has a
1 there. The "exclusive or" ($\oplus$) operation places 1 in a position if exactly one of its
operands has a 1 there.

[†] This selection of exponent and mantissa size is not really sufficient to provide the accuracy
needed in many applications. However, our computer is designed to provide an example of a
computer, not to be a perfect computing tool. In this situation, and several others as well, we
sacrifice "usefulness" to avoid unnecessary complications such as inconveniently long word length.
[‡] This is another "unreasonable" design decision made for the sake of simplicity. The decision
should not, however, hinder our basic understanding of computers and computing.

$$
\begin{array}{ll}
W_1 & 11110000 \\
W_2 & \underline{10101010} \\
W_1 \wedge W_2 & 10100000 \\
\end{array}
\qquad
\begin{array}{ll}
W_1 & 11110000 \\
W_2 & \underline{10101010} \\
W_1 \vee W_2 & 11111010 \\
\end{array}
\qquad
\begin{array}{ll}
W_1 & 11110000 \\
W_2 & \underline{10101010} \\
W_1 \oplus W_2 & 01011010 \\
\end{array}
$$

$$\text{(a)} \qquad\qquad\qquad \text{(b)} \qquad\qquad\qquad \text{(c)}$$

Fig. 2.13 Logical operations.

Let us consider an example on eight-bit computer words. If $W_1 = 11110000$ and $W_2 = 10101010$, then $W_1 \wedge W_2$ is computed as in Fig. 2.13(a). The "or" function is computed as in Fig. 2.13(b). $W_1 \oplus W_2$ is shown in Fig. 2.13(c)

We use 12, 13 and 14 in bits 1 to 6 to indicate the "and," "or" and "exclusive or" operations, respectively. Bits 7 to 12 of the instruction code have the same meaning as for the arithmetic operations. Thus,

1	3	4	0		0	4	7	3

tells the computer to apply the "or" function to the contents of register 4 and memory location 473, leaving the result in register 4.

We shall also have several single argument (*unary*) operations. These apply only with the lone operand in a register. The result appears in the same register; no memory address is involved. Bits 7 to 9 will hold the number of the register involved and bits 10 to 12 must be 0. The unary operations are:

Operation	Instruction code
not	15
complement	16
shift left	17
shift right	20

The "not" operation ($\neg$) is a logical one, which changes 0's to 1's and vice versa. Thus $\neg (11011010) = 00100101$.

The complementation operator changes the sign (first bit of the word) leaving the rest of the word unchanged.

The shift operators move all bits of the word left or right. The number of places that bits are moved will be found in the memory-address portion of the instruction. (Note that this use of the memory-address portion differs from the use of that portion by other instructions.) Bits shifted beyond the end of the word are lost, and 0's are brought in from the other end.

For example, let register 7 hold $(1234567654)_8$. The instruction

2	0	7	0		0	0	1	1

shifts that register $(11)_8$, i.e., $(9)_{10}$ places right, leaving 0001234567. (Recall that each octal digit represents three bits.) If we then execute the instruction

1	7	7	0		0	0	0	6

we are left with 0123456700. Note that bits shifted outside the computer word do not reappear.

In the next example, we see how the instructions defined so far can be put together to form a simple piece of a program.

Example 2.5. Let us write a sequence of instructions which might form part of a larger program. These instructions will compute $C = (A + B) * (A - B)$, assuming A, B, and C are floating-point numbers held in memory locations 100, 101, and 102, respectively. We suppose that the instructions are found in memory locations beginning at 34. Fig. 2.14 gives the program. ∎

	Instruction		
Location	Bits 1 to 12	Bits 19 to 30	Comments
34	0101	0100	Copy A (location 100) into register 1.
35	0112	0000	Make another copy of A in register 2. Note that the address of this instruction is not used.
36	0310	0101	Add B (location 101) to register 1 in floating point. Register 1 now holds $A + B$. (We assume no overflows occur.)
37	0520	0101	Subtract B from register 2, which now holds $A - B$.
40	0712	0000	Multiply registers 1 and 2. The result, $(A + B) * (A - B)$ appears in register 1.
41	0110	0102	Store the result (register 1) in the location reserved for C (102).

Fig. 2.14   Program to compute $C = (A + B) * (A - B)$

2.9   TRANSFER INSTRUCTIONS

Transfer instructions may override the normal sequencing of instructions by altering the location register. The effect of the *unconditional transfer* is to load a specified number (the address portion of the instruction) into the location register. Various types of *conditional transfers* test for the occurrence of certain conditions and load a specified number (the address portion, again) into the location register if the condition is met. If the condition is not met, the location register is not changed, and the instruction in the next higher location will be executed next, as usual. Typical conditions that might be tested are:

1. Is a certain arithmetic register holding all 0's?
2. Is the value in a certain arithmetic register positive?
3. Has there been an instruction which caused a division by zero since the last time this test was made? (This presumes that the computer has a special register to remember such an occurrence.)

Our computer will have an unconditional transfer, which is indicated by $(2100)_8$ in the first twelve bits and causes the address portion of the instruction to be placed in the location register. It will also have five conditional transfers.

The first, indicated by 22 in the first six bits and a register number in bits 7 to 9 causes the location register to receive the address portion if the sign (first bit) of the designated register is 0. (i.e., the value of the number in the register is nonnegative.) Thus

2	2	1	0		1	2	3	4

causes the instruction in location 1234 to be executed next if register 1 has a positive sign.

The second, indicated by 23 in bits 1 to 6, causes the transfer of control to occur if the sign bit of the register designated by bits 7 to 9 is 1, i.e., the number represented in that register is negative.

The third, indicated by 24 in bits 1 to 6, causes the transfer if the register designated by bits 7 to 9 holds all 0's. That is, instruction 24 is a test for a normalized zero (either fixed or floating point).

The fourth (code 25) causes the transfer if the register indicated by bits 7 to 9 is not all 0's.

The fifth (code 26) causes the location register to receive the memory address of the instruction if there has been an arithmetic "disaster" since the last time an instruction with code 25 was executed. By an arithmetic disaster, we mean any operation whose result does not fit in the place allocated for its result. Examples are:

1. a division by zero;
2. a fixed-point addition of two numbers whose sum is greater than or equal to 2^{29}, or less than or equal to -2^{29}.

It is assumed that a circuit somewhere in our computer "remembers" the occurrence of such a disaster and is reset to indicate "no disaster" each time instruction 26 is executed. ∎

With the addition of transfer instructions, we now have a repertoire sufficient to write pieces of programs containing loops.

Example 2.6. Consider the piece of machine-language program which might be produced by a compiler in response to the statement:

$$\textbf{for } I = 1 \textbf{ to } 10 \textbf{ do}$$
$$K = K + 2 * I$$

Instruction

Location	Bits 1 to 12	Bits 19 to 30	Comments
0	0101	0100	The first two instructions take the constant 1
1	0110	0103	and place it in location 103, reserved for I. Note that one instruction cannot move data between two memory locations, so the transfer occurred via register 1.
2	0101	0101	The next four instructions perform the body of
3	0610	0103	the loop, the statement $K = K + 2 * I$. We load
4	0210	0104	2 (location 101) into register 1, multiply it by
5	0110	0104	I (location 103), add K (location 104) and store the result in K.
6	0101	0103	To go around the loop again, we add 1 to I.
7	0210	0100	
10	0110	0103	
11	0102	0102	To test whether I has reached 10, we load 10
12	0421	0000	(location 102) into register 2 and subtract register 1, which still holds the new value of I, even though that value has been stored in memory location 103.
13	2220	0002	We now test whether register 2 is nonnegative. Since our computer normalizes, we know that zero always has a positive sign. The jump to location 2 will therefore take place if $10 - I \geqslant 0$, that is, $I \leqslant 10$. If I has reached 11, the computer executes the instructions in locations 14, 15, ... Note that the jump is to location 2, not 0, since we wish to repeat the body of the loop, not the initialization, which set $I = 1$.

Fig. 2.15   Program for Example 2.6.

Assume that the compiler uses locations 100–104 for storing the fixed-point constants 1, 2, and 10 and the fixed-point variables I and K, respectively. Since we are dealing with a piece of a program, we may suppose that K has already been set to some value. Also assume that the piece of the machine-language program corresponding to these statements begins in location 0.[†] Machine instructions that perform the calculation represented by the above statement are shown in Fig. 2.15.

Let us observe that we have been somewhat wasteful of instructions in the above program. Since I and K are used repeatedly, it would be wise to initialize the loop by bringing them to their own registers (say 3 and 4) and storing them in memory locations 103 and 104 only after the loop has ended (i.e., when I becomes 11). ∎

[†] It is not likely that a piece of program such as this would actually begin in location 0. However, the point at which we begin the instructions does not affect the essential ideas, and so we shall hereafter begin sample programs at location 0.

In our next example, we shall see how transfers of control are useful for making decisions as well as repeating loops. We shall also see the use of some of the logical operations and how a computer can compute its own instructions.

Example 2.7. Let us write a program that converts a floating-point number to an equivalent fixed-point integer. We recall, however, that not every floating-point number is an integer, so we must be satisfied with the integer part of the number. Moreover, some floating-point numbers are larger than the largest fixed-point number that can be represented. We shall not worry about what happens in this case.[†]

Recall that, in our computer, floating-point numbers are represented as follows.

1. Bit 1 holds the sign.
2. Bits 2 to 8 hold the exponent in excess-2^6 code.
3. Bits 9 to 30 hold the mantissa.

As usual, we can express the value of the floating-point number as $\pm 2^E \times M$, where E and M are the integer and fraction represented by the exponent and mantissa. It is useful to express the value in terms of e and m, the binary integers that actually appear in bits 2 to 8 and 9 to 30 respectively. Since E is represented in excess-2^6 code, the relation $E = e - 64$ holds. Since M was evaluated assuming the decimal point at the left end of the mantissa, while m assumes it at the right, the relation $M = m \times 2^{-22}$ holds. Thus, $\pm 2^E \times M = \pm 2^{e-86} \times m$.

Our strategy will be to isolate the sign bit, e and m, using logical operations. The algorithm is flowcharted in Fig. 2.16. The following constant words will be of use.

Location	Contents (octal)	
101	4000000000	(1 in bit 1)
102	3760000000	(1 in bits 2 to 8)
103	0017777777	(1 in bits 9 to 30)
104	0000000126	($(86)_{10}$ in fixed-point)
105	2010000000	(the instruction code to shift register 1 to the right)
106	1710000000	(the instruction code to shift register 1 to the left)

The floating-point number to be converted appears in location 100. We list in Fig. 2.17 the sequence of instructions to do the conversion. It is suggested that the reader "hand simulate" the program by listing the contents of each register at each step. Do the simulation for one value of e greater than 86 and one less. ∎

[†] It is a grave fault to write programs assuming that the data on which it will be used will be in the proper range (or meet any other desirable restrictions). Nevertheless to highlight the essential details of the floating-fixed conversion, we shall make that assumption. A wise programmer would include tests to insure that his assumptions were being met at critical stages of the program.

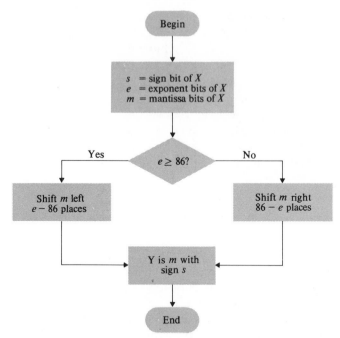

Fig. 2.16   Conversion of floating-point X to fixed-point Y.

Location	Instruction Bits 1 to 12	Bits 19 to 30	Comments
0	0101	0100	The floating-point number is copied into register 1.
1	0102	0101	101 holds a word with 1 in the first bit and 0's elsewhere. It is placed in register 2.
2	1221	0000	The "and" operation between register 2 and 1 has the effect of placing the sign bit of register 1 in register 2. Other bits of register 2 remain 0, as the "and" function requires.
3	0103	0102	102 holds a word with 1's in positions 2 to 8 (those representing the exponent) and 0's elsewhere. It is placed in register 3.
4	1231	0000	Register 3 now holds the exponent of the word in register 1.
5	1210	0103	103 holds a word with 1's in the mantissa positions, 9 to 30. At this point the word has been broken up—the sign in register 2, the exponent in 3, and the mantissa (the integer we have called m) in 1.

Fig. 2.17   Program to convert a floating-point number to a fixed-point number.

| | Instruction | | |
Location	Bits 1 to 12	Bits 19 to 30	Comments
6	2030	0026	The exponent is shifted to the rightmost 8 positions. Note $(26)_8 = (22)_{10}$. Register 3 now holds the integer we have called e.
7	0430	0104	Then, the number 86 (held in location 104) is subtracted from e.
10	2230	0017	A jump to location 17 occurs if $e - 86 \geqslant 0$.
11	0104	0105	If we reach this step, we have $e < 86$, and the mantissa must be shifted right. Location 105 holds a "dummy instruction," whose first 12 bits hold 2010, an instruction to shift register 1 right. The remaining bits are 0. We bring this word to register 4.
12	1630	0000	Register 3 is negated and now holds $86 - e$, which is greater than zero.
13	1343	0000	Registers 3 and 4 are "or"ed together. Since register 4 had 0's in bits 13 to 30, and register 3 had 0's in bits other than the last 7, the effect is to place the contents of register 3, (which is $86 - e$) in the address portion of the dummy instruction of register 4.
14	0140	0015	Register 4 is stored in location 15, which is the next instruction to be executed. The computer has thus computed its own instruction!
15	—	—	The initial contents of location 15 are unimportant. They will be filled before they are executed. At this point, we shift m to the right $86 - e$ places, which has the effect of multiplying it by 2^{e-86}.
16	2100	0023	Here, we jump to rejoin the branch in which $e - 86 \geqslant 0$.
17	0104	0106	We reach this step from instruction 10 only if $e - 86 \geqslant 0$. The instructions 17 to 22 are analogous to instructions 11 to 15. Location 106 holds a dummy left shift instruction.
20	1343	0000	
21	0140	0022	
22	—	—	
23	1312	0000	Here, we are rejoined by the branch in which a right shift was required. In either case, register 1 holds the integer's magnitude, that is, $2^{e-86} \times m$, and register 2 holds the sign. The two are "or"ed together.
24	0110	0100	Finally, we store the fixed-point number in location 100.

Figure 2.17 (*continued*)

2.10 INPUT/OUTPUT INSTRUCTIONS

As was previously mentioned, large computers have data channels to communicate between their main memory and either secondary storage or the outside world. Our timing examples 2.2 through 2.4 showed that, for a typical disk or tape, it took on the order of forty times as long to transfer a sequence of words between main memory and the disk or tape as it did to move the words between locations in main memory. Put another way, we could execute something on the order of forty instructions in the time it takes to move one word between main and secondary memory.

   Thus, if we cause our computer to wait each time data must be moved in this way, a small amount of input/output will be the dominant cost of executing a program. The need for data channels is clear. They operate while the control unit is doing other things. Relatively infrequently, compared with the rate at which the control unit moves instructions or data in or out of memory, a data channel will itself move a word in or out of main memory.

   If a computer has a data channel (or channels), there must be instructions in the repertoire of the control unit that cause orders to be given to the channel. Also, a conditional transfer to test if the data channel has finished its job is useful. Either this or another similar technique must be used for the control to know that data needed had finally been placed in main memory, or that the contents of certain locations of main memory have been copied into secondary storage and can safely be overwritten. Another method of communication between controls and data channels, called "interrupts," will be discussed in Section 2.16.

   Despite the obvious efficiency of a data channel, our computer will dispense with one. We shall assume the control unit performs all movement of data between main memory and secondary memory or input/output devices. It should be emphasized that this choice is made only to avoid being bogged down in additional details. It does not reflect current practice for any but small computers.

   Our instruction to input data from secondary storage or an input device has 27 in bits 1 to 6. The instruction to output data has 30 in these bits. Bits 7 to 12 of these instructions indicate the secondary storage unit or input/output device involved. We shall not specify what all of these devices are, but shall use the following codes for some of them.

Bits 7 to 12	Device[†]
00	the printer
01	the card reader
02	the card punch
03	the disk unit

   The address portion of the instruction holds an address where we can find more relevant information, in particular the first and last memory location to be copied, or into which incoming data is to be stored.

[†] We assume one device of each type. There is no reason a computer cannot have more than one unit of a type, especially tapes, disks, and drums; in this case, a distinct code would be needed for each one.

Example 2.8. The instruction:

3	0	0	0		0	3	0	2

together with the word:

1	0	0	0		1	1	7	7

in location 302 causes the contents of locations 1000 through 1177 to be printed. That is, bits 1 to 12 of word 302 indicate the first location and bits 19 to 30 indicate the last location in the block of words being printed.

The instruction:

2	7	0	1		0	3	0	4

with:

1	2	1	0		1	2	1	7

in location 304 causes a card to be read and its contents placed in locations 1200 through 1217. ∎

The input/output instructions form an example of "indirect addressing"; that is, the address portion of the instruction does not hold the location upon which the instruction is to be performed. Rather, it tells where we may find out upon what location (or locations, in this case) we are to perform the instruction. We shall discuss indirect addressing in more detail shortly.

We should also observe that if the input/output device is a disk or drum, we must provide some additional information, namely what track contains the data (if it is an input instruction) or is to receive the data (if it is an output instruction). We shall store this information in the location following the one mentioned in the address portion of the instruction. For example, the instruction:

2	7	0	3		0	3	0	6

with the following words in locations 306 and 307:

306:	1	0	1	0		1	0	3	7

307:	0	0	1	4		0	0	0	7

causes the contents of locations 1000 through 1037 to be written on track $(14)_8$ of surface $(7)_8$ (wherever that may be).

If tape units are to be manipulated, a set of instructions to manipulate the tape is necessary. For example, we need instructions which cause the tape head to be moved forward or backward to the next interrecord gap. ∎

2.11 MISCELLANEOUS INSTRUCTIONS

Many computers have instructions which do not even vaguely fit the classification we have made. For example, most computers have a "no-op," which does nothing. Or they may have an instruction which does both some operation and a (conditional) jump. We shall have only one additional instruction in the repertoire of our computer. We use 00 in bits 1 to 6 to indicate that the computer is to halt.

The 25 instructions of our computer are summarized in the appendix.

2.12 ADDRESS MODIFICATION—IMMEDIATE AND INDIRECT ADDRESSING

We shall now describe what the mysterious six bits between the instruction code and the memory address in our computer's instructions are used for. In general, we can get more versatility out of the address portion of an instruction by the use of an optional address modifier. The address modifier, if it is not zero, tells the computer that the address portion refers to something other than the memory location whose address appears in the address portion of the instruction. There are many possible meanings, and we shall only suggest some of the more common ones.

One possibility, called *immediate addressing*, is that the address portion is to be taken literally. Instead of interpreting the address portion as a memory location, it is to be treated as an operand itself. Since the address portion is shorter than a full computer word, zero's must be attached to the address portion in some way to make a full computer word.

We shall have two types of immediate addressing in our computer. The first, *left-immediate addressing*, adds eighteen 0's to the right end of the address portion and treats that computer word as the operand. The second, *right-immediate addressing*, is the same, but adds the 0's at the left end. These address modes will be denoted by 1 and 2, respectively, in bits 13 to 15. Bits 16 to 18 are presumably zero.

Example 2.9. Let us consider the program of Example 2.7 (p. 69). Instruction 11 was:

0	1	0	4	0	0	0	1	0	5

which loaded a word with 2010 in bits 1 to 12 into register 4. We can use left-immediate addressing to dispense with the need for location 105. The first 12 bits of location 105 are $(2010)_8$. The right-hand 18 bits of location 105 are all 0's. Thus we could replace the instruction in location 11 by:

0	1	0	4	1	0	2	0	1	0

This instruction appends eighteen 0's to the binary equivalent of $(2010)_8$ and loads that computer word into register 4. This effect is exactly the same as that of the previous instruction, which found this computer word in location 105.

The advantage of using immediate addressing is that we have saved the time necessary to fetch the contents of location 105 out of the memory, as well as having saved location 105 itself for another use.

We can use right-immediate addressing to replace instruction 7 of Example 2.7:

0	4	3	0	0	0	0	1	0	4

which subtracts $(86)_{10}$ from register 3 by

0	4	3	0	2	0	0	1	2	6

Note $(126)_8 = (86)_{10}$.

Another mode of address modification, called *indirect addressing*, interprets the address portion of the instruction not as the location of an operand, but as the location where we shall find the location of the operand.

We shall use 3 in bits 13 to 15 to indicate a mode called *left-indirect addressing* in which bits 1 to 12 of the address named by the instruction are treated as the address of the desired operand. A 4 in bits 13 to 15 will indicate *right-indirect addressing*, that is, bits 19 to 30 of the address named by the instruction form the address of the desired operand.

Example 2.10. Let the contents of some memory locations be:

100:

0	2	0	0	0	0	0	3	0	0

200:

7	7	7	7	7	7	7	7	7	7

300:

0	0	0	0	0	0	0	0	0	0

Then instruction:

0	1	0	1	4	0	0	1	0	0

would place all 0's in register 1, because right indirect addressing is called for. Bits 19 to 30 of location 100 contain 0300 and location 300 contains all 0's. The instruction:

0	1	0	1	3	0	0	1	0	0

would place all 1's in register 1. ∎

We do not permit a register to substitute for a memory location for indirect addressing. In the next section, we shall see that "indexing" serves as right indirect addressing through a register, among other things.

2.13   ADDRESS MODIFICATION BY INDEXING

Still another form of address modification is *indexing*. Here the address portion of an instruction is modified by adding the integer found in a register.[†] Often, several registers are set aside expressly for the purpose of holding numbers for addition to addresses. These registers are then called *index registers*.

In our computer all registers can be used for indexing. Octal numbers 1 through 7 in bits 16 to 18 will indicate indexing by registers 1 through 7, respectively.

Example 2.11.   The instruction:

0	2	1	0	0	2	0	0	4	0

causes the contents of memory location x to be added to register 1, where x is $(40)_8$ plus the contents of register 2. Thus, if register 1 held $(14)_8$, register 2 held $(17)_8$, and memory location $(57)_8$ held $(6)_8$, the result of executing the above instruction would be to leave $(22)_8$ in register 1. That is, to compute the desired memory address, we add $(40)_8$, the number found in the address portion of the instruction, to $(17)_8$, the number held in register 2. Then, we perform the addition as though the instruction were:

0	2	1	0	0	0	0	0	5	7

By holding a number just slightly less than 2^{12} in the register used for indexing, we can appear to subtract from the address of the instruction rather than add. For example, if register 2 held $(7761)_8 = 2^{12} - (17)_8$ in bits 19 to 30, the effect of:

0	2	1	0	0	2	0	0	4	0

would be to add the contents of location $(21)_8$ to register 2. That is, we add $(40)_8 + (7761)_8 = (10021)_8$. We throw away the leading 1, since the sum has 13 bits; that is, we add modulo 2^{12}. Note that the contents of bits 1 to 18 of register 2 have no effect whatsoever on the address computed by indexing.   ∎

We now give a sample program showing how indexing can help us to access arrays.

Example 2.12.   Consider the statement:

$$\textbf{for } I = 1 \textbf{ to } 100 \textbf{ do}$$
$$A(I) = 0.$$

[†] This sum may produce more than the number of bits needed for an address. We can ignore leading bits if necessary. For example, our computer would use only the 12 rightmost bits of the sum; that is, it would compute the address modulo 2^{12} (see the exercises of Chapter 1 for an explanation of modular arithmetic).

This statement sets to zero the elements of a one-dimensional array A of size 100. A program to do the same thing in our computer's machine language is given in Fig. 2.18. We assume that A is stored in locations 1000 to 1143, with $A(1)$ in location 1000, $A(2)$ in 1001, and so on. In general, $A(I)$ is stored in location $(777)_8 + I$. ∎

		Instruction		
Location	Bits 1 to 12	Bits 13 to 18	Bits 19 to 30	Comments
0	0101	20	0001	Using right immediate addressing we load the integer 1 into register 1. That register will hold the loop index I, so we have set I to 1. Note that no memory location is used for I.
1	0102	20	0000	Zero is brought to register 2, again using immediate addressing.
2	0120	01	0777	Here, we store zero (register 2) into some address. That address can be calculated by adding $(777)_8$ and the contents of register 1. Since register 1 holds I, that address is the one reserved for $A(I)$.
3	0210	20	0001	Add 1 to I.
4	0103	20	0144	We compute $100 - I$ and jump
5	0431	00	0000	back to the beginning of the loop
6	2230	00	0002	body if $100 - I \geqslant 0$, i.e., $I \leqslant 100$. If not, we have completed the **for** loop and can proceed.

Fig. 2.18   Program for Example 2.12.

We have assumed that address modifiers use either immediate or indirect addressing or indexing, but not both. Some computers have modes of address modification which involve more than one of the three address modifications we have discussed.

In our computer, if the indexing bits (16 to 18) are not zero and bits 13 to 15 call for immediate or indirect addressing, we perform the indexing operation first.

Example 2.13. The instruction:

0	2	1	0	3	2	0	4	0	0

adds to register 1 the word W determined in the following way. Let register 2 hold

m_1. Let m_2 be the contents of bits 1 to 12 of location $(400)_8 + m_1$. Then W is the contents of location m_2.

The meaning of:

0	2	1	0	1	2	0	4	0	0

is to add to register 1 a word consisting of 0's in bits 13 to 30 and the sum of $(400)_8$ and the contents of register 2 in bits 1 to 12. ∎

2.14 CHARACTER ADDRESSING

A considerable fraction of the processing done by computers is concerned with alphanumeric data, that is, strings of characters. For example, if a six-place integer is read from a punch card, what appears in memory is not the fixed-point equivalent of that integer, but rather six characters in the internal code of the computer. These six bytes must be converted to the appropriate fixed-point number.

To make matters easier, modern computers have methods enabling the programmer to bring individual bytes of the words in main memory to a register. Conversely, it is also possible to store into a "byte-sized" portion of a word without disturbing the rest of the word.[†]

Recall that in our computer words may be regarded as composed of five bytes, each of which are six bits long. The bytes are in bits 1 to 6, 7 to 12, ..., 25 to 30. We can give each byte of each word a number in the same way IBM 360/370 machines (see p. 52) and various other machines do. The first byte (bits 1 to 6) of word 0 is given byte number 0. Bits 7 to 12 of word 0 are given byte number 1, and so on. In general, the ith byte of word j receives byte number $5j + i - 1$. The pattern is shown in Fig. 2.19.

Bits

		1 − 6	7 − 12	13 − 18	19 − 24	25 − 30
Word	0	0	1	2	3	4
	1	5	6	7	8	9
	2	10	11	12	•••	
	⋮					

Fig. 2.19   Byte numbering pattern.

---

† These operations can, of course, be done with sequences of instructions of the type already described for our computer, in particular, using the "and" and "or" operations to separate pieces of words and put pieces together as we did in Example 2.7. However, it is desirable that one instruction be sufficient to perform these operations.

In our computer, a 5 in bits 13 to 15 indicates that the operand is a single byte, whose number is given by five times the address portion of the instruction plus the contents of the index register (if any) indicated in bits 16–18. If the instruction is any but one which stores the contents of a register in a memory location, we construct the 30-bit operand by placing 24 0's before the six bits of the designated byte.

An instruction to store a register into a memory location, modified by 5 in bits 13 to 15, indicates that the rightmost six bits of the register are to be stored in the designated byte. The four other bytes in the same word as the designated byte are unchanged. Thus byte operations take place exclusively in bits 25 to 30 of registers, and if we are doing calculations on bytes, we can pretend that these six bits are the entire register.

Example 2.14. Suppose register 7 holds $(12345)_8$. Then the instruction:

0	1	0	4	5	7	1	0	0	0

brings byte $5 \times (1000)_8 + (12345)_8 = (17345)_8$ to bits 25 to 30 of register 4. Byte $(17345)_8$ is bits 25 to 30 of word $(3055)_8$, since $5 \times (3055)_8 + 5 - 1 = (17345)_8$, and the fifth byte of any word is bits 25 to 30.

The instruction:

0	1	4	0	5	7	0	7	7	7

stores bits 25 to 30 of register 4 into byte number $5 \times (777)_8 + (12345)_8 = (17340)_8$. That is, we store into bits 25 to 30 of word $(3054)_8$, since $5 \times (3054)_8 + 5 - 1 = (17340)_8$. Bits 1 to 24 of word $(3054)_8$ are not changed. ∎

Our computer needs a six-bit character code. We shall not specify all the characters that may be encoded, but the following may be easily remembered.

1. The first ten octal codes, 00 through 11 are for the digits 0, 1, . . . , 9, in that order.

2. The next 26 codes, that is 12 through 43, are for the letters, $A, B, \ldots, Z$, in that order.

3. 44 designates the blank (b).

Example 2.15. Let us write a program to examine a string of 100 characters held in locations $(3000)_8$ through $(3023)_8$. All A's found are to be replaced by blanks. We use register 1 to indicate the "current" byte to be examined. Initially, we set register 1 to zero. With an address of $(3000)_8$ and 51 address modification, we can refer to the first byte of word $(3000)_8$. As we add to register 1, we step through the bytes of the string in order. A test whether register 1 has reached 100, i.e., passed the last byte of word $(3023)_8$, completes the loop. The program is shown in Fig. 2.20.

Location	Instruction Bits 1 to 12	Bits 13 to 18	Bits 19 to 30	Comments
0	0101	20	0000	Bring zero to register 1.
1	0102	20	0044	This instruction loads $(44)_8$, the code for b, into the rightmost bits of register 2. We shall use this byte to store a blank into whichever bytes now hold A.
2	0103	51	3000	This instruction begins a loop. It brings a byte in the string to bits 25 to 30 of register 3.
3	1430	20	0012	This instruction applies the "exclusive or" operation to the byte in register 3 and a word having $(12)_8$, the code for A, in bits 25 to 30. The effect of the "exclusive or" operation is to give all 0's if and only if its two arguments are identical, i.e., the byte in register 3 is A.
4	2530	00	0006	If the byte is not A, we skip the next instruction, which stores b in place of A.
5	0120	51	3000	This instruction stores b in the place where A came from.
6	0210	20	0001	Both paths join at this point.
7	0113	00	0000	We increase register 1 by one
10	0430	20	0144	and test if it has reached $(100)_{10}$.
11	2330	00	0002	If not, we jump to location 2 to repeat the loop.

Fig. 2.20   Program to replace A's by blanks.

2.15 ASSEMBLY LANGUAGE

Programming in machine language is extremely rare today. Most programming is, of course, done in a "high level" programming language. Only those programs which are run very frequently such as systems programs (e.g., compilers) are thought to justify resorting to machine language.† Actually, even for programs which appear to justify the use of machine code, we find that a "mnemonic" version of machine code is almost always used. Such a language is called an *assembly language*, and the program which translates assembly code into machine code is termed an *assembler*.

---

† Even here, there are advocates of specialized "systems programming" languages such as BLISS or BCPL mentioned in the bibliographic notes of Chapter 0.

We shall consider how to design an assembler in Chapter 4, but here we shall simply introduce the concept of an assembly language to make the reading and writing of machine code easier.

In its rawest form, an assembly language provides two types of mnemonics.

1. The instructions are given names.
2. Memory locations used for data or instructions are given names.

Translating instruction names into their equivalent binary numbers is a simple table lookup. Translating location names into their denoted memory addresses is a bit harder; we shall discuss how to do so in Chapter 4.

In our computer's assembly language, we use the mnemonics for instructions shown in Fig. 2.21. For each possible value in bits 1 to 6, we have a sequence of letters forming a word that helps us remember the meaning of the instruction. This sequence

	Machine code		Mnemonic
Bits 1 to 6	Bits 7 to 9	Bits 10 to 12	
00	—	—	HALT
01	a	b	COPYab if $a \neq 0$ and $b \neq 0$
			LOADb if $a = 0$ but $b \neq 0$
			STOREa if $a \neq 0$ but $b = 0$
02	a	b	ADDa(b)
03	a	b	ADDFLa(b)
04	a	b	SUBa(b)
05	a	b	SUBFLa(b)
06	a	b	MULTa(b)
07	a	b	MULTFLa(b)
10	a	b	DIVa(b)
11	a	b	DIVFLa(b)
12	a	b	ANDa(b)
13	a	b	ORa(b)
14	a	b	XORa(b)
15	a	—	NOTa
16	a	—	COMPa
17	a	—	SHIFTLa
20	a	—	SHIFTRa
21	—	—	JUMP
22	a	—	JPLUSa
23	a	—	JMINUSa
24	a	—	JZEROa
25	a	—	JNONZa
26	—	—	JDIS
27		c	READc
30		c	WRITEc

Fig. 2.21 Instruction mnemonics for our assembly language. (b) indicates that b is appended if and only if it is not zero. For instructions 27 and 30, bits 7 to 12 are treated as one entity, the input/output device to be used.

of letters is followed by up to two digits that denote registers for those instructions for which bits 7 to 9 and 10 to 12 denote registers.

Example 2.16. Suppose we wish to compute $E = (A + B) * (C + D)$. We could write the following instructions in our assembly language.

```
LOAD1       A
ADDFL1      B
LOAD2       C
ADDFL2      D
MULTFL12
STORE1      E
```

We see from Fig. 2.21 that LOAD indicates 01 (octal) in bits 1 to 6 and 0 in bits 7 to 9. The 1 following LOAD indicates register 1 is the target, so 1 (octal) appears in bits 10 to 12. If A represents the location 3000, then the machine language equivalent of LOAD1 A is 0101003000. If we suppose that A, B, C, D and E represent locations 3000 to 3004, respectively, then the machine language equivalent of the entire program is

```
0101003000
0310003001
0102003002
0320003003
0712000000
0110003004   ∎
```

Note that we did not bother to specify an address for the MULTFL12 instruction since it is irrelevant. This is an example of a *default condition* (the absence of an indication has a prespecified meaning). A missing address will be taken to be zero.

Another default condition we shall use is that for instructions mentioning only register 1 and mentioning it only once, we may delete the 1. Thus, LOAD1 can be written LOAD, but MULTFL12 cannot be written MULTFL2. Also, MULTFL11[†] cannot be written MULTFL.

It is also useful to introduce mnemonics for the address modifiers.

In our assembly language, we shall use Xa to indicate a in bits 16 to 18 ($a \neq 0$) and 0 in bits 13 to 15. The mnemonics for modifiers with 0 in bits 16 to 18 but not in bits 13 to 15 are:

Bits 13 to 15	Mnemonic	
1	IMML	(immediate left)
2	IMMED[‡]	(immediate right)
3	INDL	(indirect left)
4	IND	(indirect right)
5	CH	(character modification)

[†] Many computers do not allow both arguments of an operation to be in the same register anyway.

[‡] We shall find that right-immediate and right-indirect addressing are much more common than their left variants. Thus we use L to indicate "left" but do not append R to indicate "right." This is another example of a useful default condition.

To denote an address modifier which is zero neither in bits 13 to 15 nor in bits 16 to 18, we shall take the mnemonic for bits 13 to 15 and follow it by the mnemonic for bits 16 to 18.

We shall place the address modifier after the address, surrounded by parentheses.

Example 2.17. If name *A* were given location 100, the instruction:

> LOAD A(IND)

would be translated by the assembler to:

> 0101400100.

The instruction:

> LOAD2 A(CHX3)

would translate to:

> 0102530100.

In order to refer to an instruction by name or *label* (if it is the target of a jump instruction) we shall optionally prefix a name, which may be any FORTRAN identifier, followed by a colon, to an instruction.

Example 2.18. Suppose the labeled instruction:

> HERE: LOAD A

happened to be placed in location 200 by the assembler. Then the instruction:

> JUMP HERE

would be translated to:

> 2100000200 ▮

We can now summarize the format of our assembly language instructions. They consist of the following, in order from the left:

1. An optional label for the instruction. (The *label field.*) If there is a label, it is a FORTRAN identifier followed by a colon.

2. An instruction (the *instruction field*). This must be one of the mnemonics defined in Fig. 2.21. (We shall relax this condition in Chapter 4.)

3. An address, either a FORTRAN identifier, denoting an unspecified memory address, or the address actually intended (a literal address). In the latter case we use either (i) a decimal integer (ii) an octal integer preceded by OCTAL, or (iii) a quoted string of one or two characters. Literal addresses are generally used with immediate address modification or shift instructions. They are always filled out with leading zeros to make 12 bits if necessary.

4. An optional address modifier, one of the mnemonics defined. If a modifier is present, it must be surrounded by parentheses. Together (3) and (4) form the *address* field.

5. Following the address field, we may have a comment preceded by /* and followed by */.

Example 2.19. The program of Example 2.15 (Fig. 2.20) can be written in assembly code as follows. We assume ARRAY is the name of the first word of the block holding the string of 100 characters. That is, ARRAY denotes the word $(3000)_8$ used in Example 2.15.

```
           LOAD1    0(IMMED)
           LOAD2    ' '(IMMED)†
   LOOP:   LOAD3    ARRAY(CHX1)
           XOR3     'A'(IMMED)
           JNONZ3   SKIP
           STORE2   ARRAY(CHX1)
   SKIP:   ADD1     1(IMMED)
           COPY13
           SUB3     100(IMMED)
           JMINUS3  LOOP   ▮
```

2.16 SOME MACHINE FEATURES WE'VE OMITTED

A modern ("third generation") computer system embodies a number of features which we have not included in our computer. It is expected that the resulting simplicity in our computer will make it easier to grasp the programming system concepts actually discussed in this book. However, for perspective, let us list some of the key ideas that are found in current day large scale computers, but which have not been included in our computer.

1. *Multiprocessing.* We have already alluded to the fact that a real computer larger than a "mini" will have data channels, which are really extra control units dedicated to communication between the main memory, the secondary memory, and the input/output devices. In fact, a large computer may have more than one complete control unit and each of these may be working on programs simultaneously, or several may work on parts of a single program.

2. *Interrupts.* An interrupt is an automatic transfer of control to a fixed location in memory when a specific situation occurs. Interrupts are useful in a number of ways. For example, arithmetic "disasters" of various kinds can be made to cause interrupts, whereupon a portion of the operating system is called upon to fix the situation.‡ For example, the remedy for an overflow might be to put the largest possible floating-point number into the overflowed register, but a more likely solution is to expel the offending program from the computer with a diagnostic message indicating what happened. The use of interrupts, if our computer had them, would obviate the need for the JDIS instruction.

---

† Note that this address represents the code for ƀ, that is, $(44)_8$.

‡ The *operating system* is a program residing permanently in memory (secondary memory except for those portions currently in use) which handles a number of details necessary to make the system run smoothly. For example, it schedules the jobs needing computer service, bills for service, allocates space on secondary memory devices, feeds programs to compilers or assemblers when necessary, and handles abnormal situations such as arithmetic disasters.

A second use of interrupts is to catch infinite loops. When a program begins, a clock is set with its estimated time limit. When that time is up, an interrupt occurs and the program is expelled from the machine.

A third use of interrupts is in communication between independent processors. For example, if a data channel is reading data from a secondary device into a block of main memory, a program will not want to read data from that block until it is sure the input operation has been completed. One way for the data channel to communicate with the main control unit is for the data channel to interrupt the main control when the former has completed its input operation.

3. *Memory protection.* If several programs are in main memory at once it is essential that none be able to write into the portion of memory used by another. Even more important, no program should be allowed to write into the portion of memory used by the operating system; since it could then seize control of, and monopolize, the entire computer system.

One simple scheme utilizes pairs of bounding registers (which are distinct from the arithmetic registers). Each program is assigned a particular pair of registers, which hold two memory locations between which the program resides. A program may not read or write a memory location outside the limits imposed by the bounding registers. To prevent alteration of the contents of bounding registers except by the operating system, the computer might require that an instruction to load a bounding register have a particular secret sequence of bits (*key*) in part of the word forming the instruction. Of course, the key would be known to the writers of the operating system, and when the operating system received control after an interrupt, it could access the entire memory if it wished.

A convenient way to protect bounding registers and other parts of the computer is to switch the computer between two "modes," called *master* and *slave* modes. In master mode any instruction may be executed, but in slave mode certain instructions are forbidden. For example, forbidden instructions would be those that set bounding registers or do input/output. The instruction to change from slave to master mode can be executed only with a secret key. Thus master mode operations such as protection of memory and the handling of input/output devices are reserved to the operating system.

4. *Virtual memory.* Many computers allow the programmer to write instructions whose address portions are numbers (*virtual addresses*) higher than the size of main memory. Most of such a program will be in secondary memory at all times. Only those portions of the program that are in current use will appear in main memory, and at different times the same instruction may appear in different locations. Specialized circuitry translates from the virtual address of a word to the actual locations in main memory occupied by the word. If a needed word is not in main memory, it (and a block of, say, 1024 surrounding it) is brought into main memory. These replace another block of words, hopefully words not currently needed. The latter block of words is returned to secondary memory.

In Chapter 5 we shall discuss "base registers," one method of organizing a computer to support virtual memory.

EXERCISES

2.1 In round figures:

a) 2 to what power is a billion?

b) What is 2^{44} in decimal?

2.2 Suppose a tape unit travels at 100 inches per second, has 7 tracks (one parity), and stores 1000 bits per inch on each track.

a) How much tape is required to store 2^{18} 36-bit words?

b) How many bits per second can be read or written?

2.3 Suppose a disk unit is in the shape of a cylinder with radius r inches and height h inches. Suppose that there are two disk plates per inch of height and on each surface, only the outer half of the surface is covered with tracks (i.e., from radius $r/2$ to r). Where there are tracks, they are packed 10 to the inch. The density of bits around each track is such that on the innermost track (at radius $r/2$) there are 1000 bits per inch of circumference.[†] Find the number of bits stored on the disk as a function of r and h.

2.4 Suppose a drum has the same dimensions as the disk of Exercise 2.3. Let tracks be packed 10 to the inch along the cylinder, and suppose the bits are packed 1000 to the inch around each track. What is the number of bits stored on the drum as a function of r and h?

2.5 For what values of r and h will the disk and drum of Exercises 2.3 and 2.4 have the same capacity?

2.6 What are the capacities of the aforementioned disk and drum when $r = 10$ and $h = 20$?

* **2.7** A *no-op* is an instruction which when executed does not change the contents of any register or memory location, and which will after execution cause the next instruction in sequence to be executed. For which of 00, 01, . . . , 30 in bits 1 to 6 do there exist contents of bits 7 to 30 which will make the instruction a no-op? You may assume that the location in which the instruction appears is known.

2.8 Suppose that register 1 holds 0123456765 and register 2 holds 0000000777 (octal). The contents of some memory locations are:

Location	Contents (octal)
1000	2000003000
1001	0000000001
2000	4040404040
3000	7373737373

Describe the effect on register 1 of the following instructions.

a) 0210101000

b) 1210301000

c) 1310401000

d) 0210021001

e) 0210320001

f) 0101522632

[†] The other tracks have lesser densities, so the number of bits per degree of arc is a constant independent of the track.

2.9 Write machine- or assembly-language programs to perform the same function as the following statements. In part (b), assume A and B are arrays of length 100, and that A and B are the names of the first locations of the blocks of 100 consecutive words used to hold each array.

a) **for** I $= 1$ **to** 10 **do**

   $A = A + B$

b) **for** I $= 1$ **to** 100 **do**

   $A(I) = B(I) * A(I)/A(1)$

2.10 Rewrite the programs of

a) Example 2.6 (p. 67).

b) Example 2.7 (p. 69).

using address modification where appropriate. If you wish, use assembly language, giving names to the pieces of data referenced.

*__2.11__ Suppose that a memory access (either to read an instruction or to read or store data) requires 1 μs on our computer, and that 0.1 μs is required to decode and execute an instruction, exclusive of memory access. For example LOAD X requires 2.1 μs; the reading of the instruction requires 1 μs, decoding requires 0.1 μs, and obtaining the contents of location X requires 1 μs. Instruction ADD12 requires only 1.1 μs. How long do each of the following instructions take?

a) ADD X(IND)

b) ADD X(IMMED)

c) ADD X(CHX2)

*__2.12__ Using the timing rules of Exercise 2.11, compare the time for the programs of Examples 2.6 and 2.7 with revisions in Exercise 2.10.

*__2.13__ Write an assembly-language program which examines a string of 200 characters beginning in location TEXT and deletes blanks, shifting the following characters forward in the string so no gaps appear. Your program should produce a count of the number of characters of the remaining string, but bytes which no longer hold part of the string need not hold anything in particular. Try to make your program as efficient as possible. In particular, do not, each time a blank is found, immediately shift all following characters.

**__2.14__ Write a program which reads the first 10 characters of a punch card and stores them in two consecutive locations. Check that each of the ten characters is an octal digit (0 through 7) and that the first is three or less. If so, the program must compute a fixed-point number having the value of the string of 10 characters (treated as an octal number).

*__2.15__ Write a program to convert a positive fixed-point number to a string of decimal digits and print out the digits.

*__2.16__ Many real machines are equipped with indexing, but not indirect addressing. Show how we can simulate the effect of an instruction like LOAD A(IND) by a sequence of instructions using indexing but no indirect addressing.

**__2.17__ Show how the effect of character addressing as described for our computer can be simulated by a sequence of our computer's instructions without using character addressing.

FURTHER READING

Bell and Newell [1971] is a good source on varieties of computer organization. Donovan [1972] discusses the IBM series of computers, and Gear [1974] and Stone [1971] each discuss that and the organization of a specific minicomputer. For information on the electronic principles underlying computer hardware see Lo [1968], and for the subject of the design of computer circuits (switching circuits) see Booth [1971] or Kohavi [1970]. More information on the design of "third generation" computers and their operating systems can be had from Denning [1970] and Hansen [1973]. Coffman and Denning [1973] give a more theoretical treatment of the subject.

Chapter 3

Introduction to Data Structures

We have seen that a basic repertoire of instructions is sufficient to handle data in the form of numbers and character or bit strings. Using indexing, we can handle arrays, as well. However, in systems programs and in many applications there is a need to handle data of a more general nature, in which there are "objects" connected in a variety of ways. In this chapter we shall study such data and some of the most important forms of connection—lists, trees and "associative structures."

3.1 DATA STRUCTURES

There are many problems whose solution is simplified by organizing pieces of data in such a way that significant relationships between the pieces are made clear and can be easily utilized. Many such organizations can be visualized as a collection of objects which we shall call *records*. Each record consists of one or more *fields*, and each of these fields holds either some data or a *pointer* to another record. The pointers connect that record to other records and serve to represent the significant relationships between records.

Example 3.1. Fig. 3.1 shows a collection of records which could be used to represent a family group. Record 1 represents a couple. It has two data fields giving the names of the mother and father. There are also two pointer fields, pointing to the records representing the two children. Records 2 and 3 represent the children. They each have a data field representing the child's name and pointers to the parents and to each other. In this case, each record has a pointer to all the others. However, if the sibling relationship were not important, then those pointers need not appear in records 2 and 3.

  Note that in this example we are making the assumption that each couple has two children. If a couple could have more than two children we would need larger records for both couples and children, in the former case to hold more pointers to children, in the latter case for additional sibling pointers. We shall discuss in Example 3.2 methods of handling records of essentially the same type but of varying size. ∎

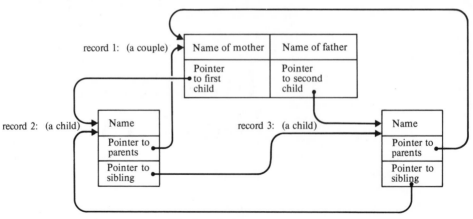

Fig. 3.1   A data structure.

It is quite likely that the reader, if he has programmed extensively, is familiar with the notions of fields, records, and pointers, perhaps in another guise. For example, in PL/I if we wished a collection of, say, 100 records for couples and 200 records for children as in Example 3.1, we might write:

```
DECLARE 1 COUPLE(100),
          2 MOTHER CHARACTER(20),
          2 FATHER CHARACTER(20),
          2 CHILD1 POINTER,
          2 CHILD2 POINTER;
DECLARE 1 CHILD(200),
          2 NAME CHARACTER(20),
          2 PARENTS POINTER,
          2 SIBLING POINTER;
```

MOTHER, FATHER, and NAME are fields of character type, while CHILD1, CHILD2, PARENTS, and SIBLING are pointer fields. Then, if child number 143 were the first child of couple 12, we might assign

$$\text{CHILD1(12)} = \text{ADDR(CHILD(143))} \qquad (3.1)$$

In FORTRAN we can do essentially the same thing by declaring arrays MOTHER, FATHER, CHILD1, and CHILD2 of length 100 and arrays NAME, PARENTS, and SIBLING of length 200. We would probably use integers to represent the names of parents and children, since long character strings cannot be easily manipulated in FORTRAN. However, integers are a very reasonable substitute for the pointer identifiers in PL/I. The FORTRAN assignment

$$\text{CHILD1(12)} = 143$$

is an effective substitute for the PL/I assignment, expression (3.1), above.

It is not hard to implement a record in a computer memory. One chooses enough consecutive memory locations that there is space to store all the data held by the record and all its pointers. We may treat the first (lowest) memory location of the record as its *address*. Hence, a pointer to any record is simply the address of that record stored in a designated place. The pointers possessed by the record in question are thus the addresses of other records and require m bits, if the computer has a memory[†] of size 2^m.

Unless the positions of pointers and data within a record are "known" by the program which examines them, each record needs data in a fixed location to decode the format of the record, that is, to tell where the pointers and data may be found. The fewer different formats being used for records, the less information about format need be carried in the record. Ultimately, however, the only thing which must be in a known place is data indicating the format.

Example 3.2. Let us consider a data structure which might be used in a tic-tac-toe playing program (although we do not want to suggest that it is essential to a good tic-tac-toe program). There are seventeen important objects in the game—the nine *boxes*, which we number as in Fig. 3.2, and the eight *lines*, that is, three rows, three columns and two diagonals. We shall have a record for each box and a record for each line.

Fig. 3.2   Tic-Tac-Toe.

The records for the lines each have three pointers, one to each of the records for the boxes on the line. In addition, we shall link all the records for the lines together, as we may wish to visit each in turn, for example, to see if there were any line in which our opponent had two marks. Thus, we order the records for the lines any way we wish, and have each record point to the next line on the list. A known memory location will hold the address of the first record on the list, and the last record will have no pointer to another line.

[†] If the region of memory in which the records are known to be placed is smaller than the entire main memory, we can do with fewer bits to represent pointers. Conversely, if records are located in secondary as well as main memory, additional bits may be required for each pointer.

The data in the line records will indicate the number of X's and the number of O's in the line. Since these numbers each range from 0 to 3, two bits would be sufficient. However, to make use of character addressing in our computer, let us store each number in one byte. The number of X's will appear in the leftmost byte of the first word of the record and the number of O's in the second byte of that word. The remaining three bytes of the first word will not be used. The second and third words of the record will hold the four pointers mentioned above, with the leftmost or rightmost 12 bits utilized for each pointer. The arrangement of the record for the lines is shown in Fig. 3.3. Since the format of a line record is known, no formatting information is needed.

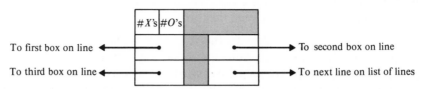

Fig. 3.3   Records for lines: a) box on 4 lines; b) box on three lines; c) box on 2 lines.

Note that we could compact the data into two words if we wished, and, should we choose to do so, there would be very little efficiency loss, if any.

The record for each box will hold data indicating its status (X, O, or unoccupied). It will have a pointer to each line on which it is present. These pointers are useful if, say, we place an X in a box. We may follow the pointers to increase the count of X's for all and only the lines containing the box. Since each box is on two, three or four lines, it is useful to have as data a count of the number of pointers in the record. This is all the formatting information we need for boxes. We shall store the status of the box in the first byte of the first word and the number of pointers in the second byte. The first pointer will be in the rightmost 12 bits of the first word, and the left and right 12 bits of subsequent words. Fig. 3.4 shows the three types of records for boxes. S stands for the status information. $S = 0$ means unoccupied; $S = 1$ means X; and $S = 2$ means O. All pointers are to records for lines.

Let us suppose that the lines are ordered as follows: 123, 456, 789, 147, 258, 369, 159, 357. Suppose that the addresses of the line records are $(1000)_8$, $(1010)_8 \ldots$,

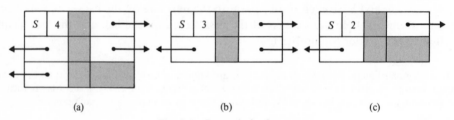

      (a)   (b)   (c)

Fig. 3.4   Records for boxes.

$(1070)_8$, respectively. Let the addresses of the records for boxes 1 to 9 (See Fig. 3.2) be $(2000)_8$, $(2010)_8, \ldots, (2100)_8$, respectively. Suppose the current board is shown in Fig. 3.5. Then the contents of the three words for line 147 (locations 1030 to 1032) would be:

$$
\begin{array}{ll}
1030: & 0101000000^\dagger \\
1031: & 2000002030 \\
1032: & 2060001040
\end{array}
$$

The record for box 7 occupies words 2060 and 2061. It has three pointers, to lines 147, 789, and 357. The contents of its words are:

$$
\begin{array}{ll}
2060: & 0203001030 \\
2061: & 1020001070
\end{array}
$$

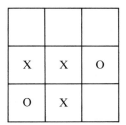

Fig. 3.5   Tic-Tac-Toe position.

3.2 LINKED LISTS

A common form of data structure is a *linked list* of records. The records are ordered in some way (such as the records for lines in Example 3.2) and each points to the next one in the order, as shown in Fig. 3.6(a). The last record has no pointer, of course, although for uniformity it will likely have a field for the pointer, filled with zeros.

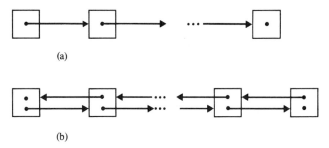

(a)

(b)

Fig. 3.6   Linked lists: a) singly linked; b) doubly linked.

---

† We place 0's in unused portions of records.

The records shown in Fig. 3.6(a) are *singly linked*; that is, pointers connect them in one direction only. In Fig. 3.6(b), we see a *doubly linked* list. If a list is doubly linked, one can scan the records in various ways by following pointers. In a singly linked list, one is restricted to scan in the direction of the pointers.

A vital part of a linked list is a method for indicating the ends. This problem is essentially one of indicating the absence of a pointer that we might reasonably expect to be present. Two possible strategies are:

1. Carry in each record data indicating which, if any, of its pointer fields are absent. This approach treats absence of pointers as a change in record format.

2. Use all 0's in the place where a pointer is expected, to indicate no pointer. If this method is used, we must be sure that no record has address 0. Actually, as we shall see in subsequent chapters, a computer system will most probably not allow the programmer to use location 0 for his data anyway.

We shall now consider an example of a program that scans a list to obtain some information.

Note that indirect addressing is quite handy when dealing with pointers. In this example, the pointers will be in registers, and we shall use indexing in lieu of indirect addressing through memory locations.

Example 3.3.   Suppose we have a singly linked list of records. Each record consists of two words, the first word holding data—a floating-point number—and the second holding in bits 19 to 30 a pointer to the next record. The end of the list is marked by a "pointer" of all 0's. It is desired to determine if some record holds a (normalized) floating-point 1.0 and jump to location YES if so. If not, we must jump to location NO. We suppose that initially, location HEAD holds a pointer to the first record, in bits 19 to 30. Should the list be empty, HEAD will hold 0's in bits 19 to 30 Register 7 will hold a pointer to the record "currently" being scanned as we move down the list. Briefly, the strategy used to scan the list can be expressed:

> **while** register 7 does not hold zero **do**
>   **if** record pointed to by register 7 holds 1.0 **then**
>   succeed (go to YES)
>   **else**
>   copy pointer to next record into register 7

The program in Fig. 3.7 will perform as desired. It is suggested that the reader hand simulate this program twice through its loop. Make any assumption you like about the locations of the first three records.

3.3 STACKS

An important feature of linked lists is the ability to add or delete records from one end (the *top*). We call such a list a *stack*. In order to add records, it is necessary that there be some source of new records, called an *available space list*. The available

Instructions		Comments
LOAD7	HEAD	Initialize register 7 to point to the first record on the list.
LOOP: AND7	OCTAL7777(IMMED)	We make all but the rightmost 12 bits of register 7 hold 0. (This is safer than assuming that there are 0's in bits 1 to 18.)
JZERO7	NO	If the new pointer is zero, we have reached the end of the list without finding 1.0 as data. We jump to location NO.
LOAD1	0(X7)	We bring the first word of the record pointed to by register 7 to register 1. Note that indexing with a zero address has the effect of right-indirect addressing through a register.
XOR1	OCTAL2014(IMML)	We apply the **exclusive or** operation to the data in the record and a word (constructed by left-immediate addressing) that is a normalized floating-point 1.0.
JZERO1	YES	If register 1 now holds 0, we have found the desired datum and jump to location YES.
LOAD7	1(X7)	We load register 7 with the second word of the current record. Note that the contents of register 7 do not change until after the desired address is determined. Register 7 now holds the pointer of the record just considered. Unless that record was last on the list, register 7 now points to the next record.
JUMP	LOOP	We examine the next record. A jump to the second instruction repeats the loop.

Fig. 3.7   Program to search a linked list.

space list will be a stack itself, and can supply records to any number of other stacks, provided that one size record suits all stacks. When records are deleted from the top of a stack, it is essential that the record be returned to available space, else we shall eventually run out of records. The chief application we shall make of true stacks—ones in which records are both added and deleted from the stack—are in Chapters 7 and 8. There we shall see how stacks are useful in the implementation of recursive procedures and in "parsing" computer programs—as an aid to the compiler.

Example 3.4. Let us suppose an available-space list of two-word records. The available-space list will be singly linked, with a pointer in bits 19 to 30 of its first word. A zero pointer will mark the end of the available space list. Suppose we have a stack of two-word records. Location TOP has a pointer in bits 19 to 30 to the first record of our stack, and location AVAIL points to the first record of available space, also in bits 19 to 30. The following program moves the first record of available space to the top of the other stack.

```
LOAD1    AVAIL(IND)
LOAD2    TOP
LOAD3    AVAIL
STORE2   AVAIL(IND)
STORE1   AVAIL
STORE3   TOP
```

The initial arrangement of pointers is shown in Fig. 3.8(a). The first three steps load the important pointers into three registers. The arrangement after the third instruction is in Fig. 3.8(b). The next steps store the pointers where they belong. The situation after each of the three remaining instructions is shown in Fig. 3.8(c) through (e). Note that the registers not shown in Fig. 3.8(c) through (e) continue to point as in Fig. 3.8(b). We omit them because they are not needed.

The net effect is that the top record of available space is transferred to the top of the other stack. The former top record of the stack becomes the second record; it has been *pushed down*. The second record of available space has reached the top. We say the available-space list has been *popped up*. ∎

It is important to observe a programming flaw that occurs in Example 3.4. The available space list is not infinite, so it could be exhausted. We detect this situation

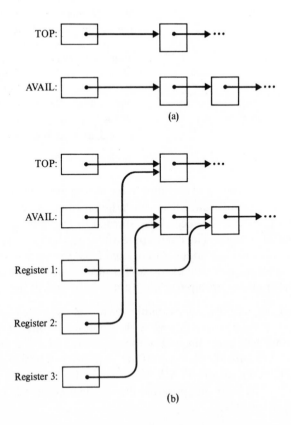

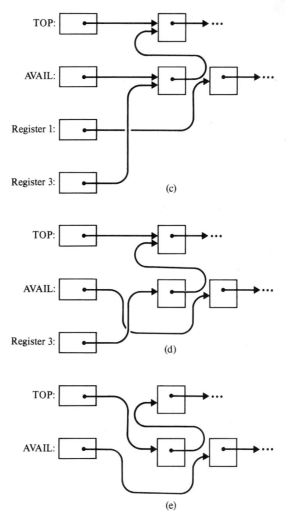

Fig. 3.8   Moving a record from available space.

by 0's in bits 19 to 30 of location AVAIL, since the bottom of the list was marked by a pointer of 0's in Example 3.4. A correct program would test for all 0's in location AVAIL before proceeding. The steps were omitted for simplicity.

To pop a stack, we may transfer its top record to available space by reversing the roles of locations TOP and AVAIL in Example 3.4.

3.4   THE TABULAR METHOD OF LIST STORAGE

In the previous sections we visualized a situation in which records were being moved around from one list to another. Chapters 8 and 9 provide several examples where one needs such a facility. However, in many applications, there is no real "motion" of records. Lists are either fixed in advance, or they may grow, but they never shrink. In this situation, a far simpler representation of lists suffices. It is possible to place the records of a list in consecutive locations in memory. The block of memory allocated to the list is termed a *table*. In fact, records of a related type which are not linked in a list, (e.g., the records for boxes in Example 3.2) are often placed in consecutive memory locations. The term "table" may be applied to such a collection of records, as well.

If all records on a list are of the same size, say c words, no pointers linking the list are needed if they are stored as a table, and in fact the list can be considered doubly linked. If we know the address of the "current" record, we can find the address of the next record by adding or subtracting c, depending on whether the list is stored up or down in memory, i.e., whether the first record is at the highest or lowest memory location. We can find the address of the previous record by subtracting or adding c, respectively.

We need some mechanism for detecting the end of a list. It is sufficient to record the address of the first word following the last record of the list or a related piece of data, e.g., the address of the last record. If the list will be used as if it were doubly linked, we need similar information to detect the beginning. Of course, it is presumed that the address of the first record is known, else the list could never be reached.

Example 3.5. Let us reconsider Example 3.3, using a table to hold the list. Recall that we had a list of records, each of which held a floating-point number. It was desired to determine if one of those numbers was 1.0, jumping to location YES if so and to NO if not.

Suppose there are 100 records. We may store the data of the 100 records in one word each. The table of the 100 words holding the list will begin in location HEAD with the top of the list at the low end of the block. The program in Fig. 3.9 may then serve in place of the one in Example 3.3. ∎

	Instructions		Comments
	LOAD7	0(IMMED)	Initialize register 7 to point to the beginning of the table. When we reference the table we shall use address HEAD with indexing by register 7. Thus setting register 7 to 0 makes it point to the first record in the table.
LOOP:	LOAD1	HEAD(X7)	Begin a loop by testing whether the current record holds 1.0.
	XOR1	OCTAL2014(IMML)	
	JZERO1	YES	
	ADD7	1(IMMED)	Add 1 to register 7. Test if that register is still less than 100. If so, return to the beginning of the loop. If not, jump to NO.
	COPY76		
	SUB6	100(IMMED)	
	JMINUS6	LOOP	
	JUMP	NO	

Fig. 3.9 Searching a tabularly stored list.

Even if the size of records on a list is not constant, one can store them in a table. Each record requires data in a fixed position telling how many words the record has. To move down the list, we add or subtract that number to or from the current record's address, depending on whether the list runs up or down memory.

Example 3.6. Suppose that the records of a particular list are from 1 to 63 words long, and the first byte of the first word holds the size of the record. Let location CURRENT hold in bits 19 to 30 a pointer to the "current" record. The program in Fig. 3.10 makes location CURRENT point to the next record on the list, assuming that record to be stored in the next available higher numbered locations. We omit a test to see if the current record is the last, in which case the program should not be executed, of course.

Instructions		Comments
LOAD1	CURRENT(IND)	Move the first word of the current record to register 1.
SHIFTR1	24	Shift the first byte of the first word of the record to the rightmost six bits of register 1, simultaneously setting all other bits of register 1 to zero.
ADD1	CURRENT	Add the size of the "old" current record to the value of
STORE1	CURRENT	CURRENT to obtain the address of the new current record.

Fig. 3.10 Program to find the next record in a tabularly stored list of variable-sized records.

Even a stack may be stored in tabular form. For available space, we allocate a suitably large block of memory. A pointer indicates the current top record, as shown in Fig. 3.11. When adding a record to the list, we add the size of the "old" top record to the pointer which indicates the top of the stack.[†] We must then check that space is available by comparing the address calculated for the next record, plus the size of that record, with the end of available space. If available, the fields of the next record may then be filled as desired.

Example 3.7. Suppose a stack is stored in the 1000 words beginning at location STACK, with the bottom of the stack at the low end. Let location TOP be a pointer (bits 19 to 30) to the current top record. Suppose all records are four words long. The program in Fig. 3.12 tests whether there is room to add a record and if so, jumps to location PROCEED, presumably to fill the fields of the record. If not, we jump to location HELP.

[†] It should be noted that in Fig. 3.11, the top of the stack is at the bottom of the page and vice versa. There is a sensible explanation for why this awkwardness occurs. To begin, we normally picture main memory with word 0 at the top of the page and the highest numbered word at the page bottom. This convention makes sense, since we want to picture a program written on the page as placed in memory in the same order as the program's instructions appear on the page. Second, it is appealing to take an increase in the pointer as corresponding to a push operation, since the stack size then increases. We are thus forced to show the top of stack near the bottom of the page.

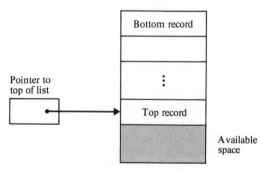

Fig. 3.11   Stack in tabular form.

Instructions		Comments
LOAD1	TOP	Add 4 to the address of the current top record.
ADD1	4(IMMED)	
COPY12		Test if there is not room to push a record onto the
SUB2	STACK+997(IMMED)	stack.
JPLUS2	HELP	
STORE1	TOP	Otherwise, store the address of the new top record in
JUMP	PROCEED	TOP and proceed to fill the record.

Fig. 3.12   Test for available space. The expression STACK + 997, used as an address, represents 997 plus the location named STACK, that is, the smallest number which is too large to be the address of a four-word record fitting into the block reserved for the stack. (For a discussion of the use of expressions in assembly-language addresses, see Section 4.5.)

We may pop a record from the list by the reverse procedure of moving the pointer one record toward the bottom. We must check that we do not try to pop a record when the stack is already empty. It is worth noting that if the stack grows and shrinks, there may be data from records left in the current available space region. This data is not part of the stack. If the stack is scanned beginning at the current top record and moving down to the bottom record, such data will not be scanned.

3.5   TREES

A *tree* is a particular kind of data structure built on a collection of entities called *nodes* (or *vertices*) linked together by edges, which are drawn as arrows from one node to another. The tree data structure has a variety of applications, a few of which we shall encounter in Section 3.7 and in Chapters 8 and 9.

In a tree, *paths* (sequences of nodes with edges from one node to the next) fan out from a special node called the *root* like the branches of a tree,[†] never meeting once they have diverged. Figure 3.13 is an example of a tree with nodes labeled *A* through *J*. The root is *A*.

The nodes of a tree are usually represented in the computer by records. It is also

---

[†] Perversely, computer scientists draw their trees with the root in the air.

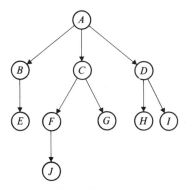

Fig. 3.13   A tree.

possible that edges will be directly represented by pointers. However, other schemes exist for representing trees by pointers that do not exactly reflect the edges, but from which the edges can be determined. We shall discuss some of these representations shortly.

In a sense, a tree represented by nodes and edges is a mathematical abstraction, while the representation of a tree by records and pointers is a computer implementation of the concept. The situation is analogous to the mathematical abstraction of an integer which, as we saw in Chapter 1, has various computer implementations, such as sign-and-magnitude or twos'-complement notation.

Some terminology is necessary before we proceed. If there is an edge from node X to node Y, we say that X is the *parent* of Y, and Y is a *child*[†] of X. A node with no children is called a *leaf*. A sequence of nodes $N_1, N_2, \ldots, N_n$ such that N_1 is the parent of N_2, which is the parent of N_3, and so on, is called a *path*. We say the path is *from* N_1 *to* N_n. If there is a path from X to Y, we say X is an *ancestor* of Y and Y is a *descendant* of X.

Example 3.8.   In Fig. 3.13, C is the parent of F and also of G. D is a child of A. The sequence A, C, F, J is a path from A to J; C, F is a path from C to F; A is an ancestor of J. F is a descendant of C as well as a child.   ∎

We can define a tree precisely by the following rules.

1. There is one node called the *root* which has no parent.

2. There is a path from the root to every other node in the tree.

3. Every node except the root has exactly one parent.

The children of any given node may be ordered. We shall assume that this order corresponds to the way in which the tree is drawn, with the child drawn leftmost being first. For example, in Fig. 3.13, the children of A are ordered B, C, D.

---

† Tree terminology is a curious mixture of male-descent terms and botanical terms. Being a friend of nature, but no male chauvinist, I have retained the botany but replaced the masculine gender terms with their corresponding unisex terms.

As we have mentioned, there are numerous computer implementations of a tree. The straightforward one is to have a record for each node with an indication of the number of children of the node contained in the record and pointers to each child also contained therein.

Example 3.9. Let us suppose that the data for each node of the tree in Fig. 3.13 can be held in 24 bits. We shall use the first byte of the first word of each record to hold the number of children and the remaining 24 bits to hold the data. Subsequent words of the record will hold pointers to the children. The pointer to the first (leftmost) child will be in bits 1 to 12 of the second word. The pointer to the second child in bits 19 to 30 of that word, the pointer to the third child in bits 1 to 12 of the third word, and so on. Fig. 3.14 shows the tree of Fig. 3.13 represented in this fashion. ▮

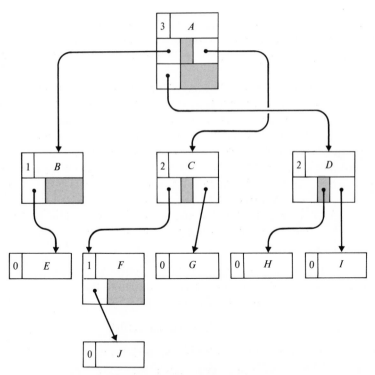

Fig. 3.14   Tree representation.

Another representation of trees limits the number of pointers in any record to two, no matter how many children a node has. Of course, the pointers no longer reflect the edges of the tree, but the structure of the tree will still be understandable.

We define the *right sibling* of a node X to be the node having the same parent as X and immediately to the right of X in the ordering of the children of X's parent. For example, in Fig. 3.13, C is the right sibling of B; D has no right sibling.

The implementation we have in mind gives each node a pointer to its leftmost child and to its right sibling.

Example 3.10. Let us consider the tree of Fig. 3.13 again. We can use records of two words, the first of which holds data. In bits 1 to 12 of the second will be a pointer to the leftmost child, and in bits 19 to 30 a pointer to the right sibling. The absence of a child or right sibling may be indicated by 0's in place of a pointer. The data structure for this tree representation is shown in Fig. 3.15.

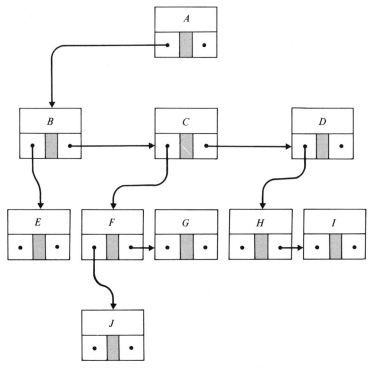

Fig. 3.15   Data structure representing tree.

It should be noticed that the pointers in Fig. 3.15 do not correspond to the edges in Fig. 3.13. However, for every path in Fig. 3.13, there is a sequence of pointers in Fig. 3.15 connecting the records. Depending on the way in which the tree will be scanned or operated upon by the program, this arrangement may well be satisfactory. ▋

3.6 ASSOCIATIVE MEMORIES AND ASSOCIATIVE STRUCTURES

One of the important data handling jobs which computers do is to associate information with a large number of objects. For example, we could suppose that the ASPCA maintains a file of lost dogs, giving certain pieces of information about each, e.g., favorite bone size and number of spots. From time to time, they wish to feed their computer the name of some dog, find out whether he is on their list, and if so, get all the information in the file on that dog.

One way to implement such a file would be to create a linked list with one record for each dog. The data portion of the record will hold the name of the dog and the information about him. Given a name, we may scan down the list, comparing the given name with the name found in each record. When a match is found, the remaining data in the record is the desired information and may be printed out.

If the given name is on the list, on the average half the list will be scanned before it is found. If the name is not on the list, the entire list must be scanned before this fact is discovered. For long lists the cost of accessing the list for data can be prohibitive, and it might be asked if there is a better way to implement this kind of data structure.

First of all, what precisely is it that we wish to implement? Ideally (as a mathematical abstraction) it is a collection of records, each consisting of a *key* (the name of the dog in the above discussion) and data associated with each key (bone size and number of spots). The arrangement of records is shown in Fig. 3.16.

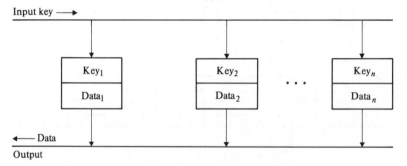

Fig. 3.16   Idealized associative memory.

We imagine that there is an input to the array of records on which keys (e.g., names of dogs) appear. This key is compared with the keys in each record "simultaneously," and the record whose key matches sends its data to the output. The other records send no data. Additionally, we wish to be able to add and delete keys and their records at will. Such a scheme is called an *associative memory*. The important feature of an ideal associative memory is that all records are scanned simultaneously. The time needed to find a key does not depend on the number of records in the memory.

It is likely that eventually one will be able to buy hardware that acts as an associative memory with a substantial number of records. For the present, we are forced to use the main memory of the computer to act like (*simulate*) an associative memory. We call a data structure that simulates an associative memory an *associative structure*. There is no known way to use the main memory to simulate an associative memory in amount of time that does not increase as the number of records increases. However, this increase can be made quite slow on the average.

One possible method, the linked list, has already been discussed. We saw that the average time to find the data associated with a key was half the length of the list. Certainly, the lookup time for a linked list grows with the number of records, in fact, it is proportional to the number of records. The time to add a new key does not increase as the list gets longer (just push a new record onto the list).

3.7   BINARY SEARCH TREES

A better method of simulating an associative memory puts a tree structure on the records. The average time to find a given key varies as the logarithm of the number of records. Most kinds of keys can be ordered in some way. For example, if the keys are integers, an appropriate order is smallest first. If the keys are character strings, as they usually are, they may be ordered alphabetically. We arrange the records in a *binary tree*, which has the following properties.

i) No node has more than two children.

ii) Each child is either a left or right child. No node has more than one of each, but it may have a right child without having a left one or vice-versa. We draw left children extending diagonally left and downward; right children are drawn similarly to the right.

Our tree must have the following property. Suppose a given record X holds key α. Let β be the key held by any record which can be reached from X by a path starting with the left child of X. Then β comes before α in the ordering. Let γ be the key held by a record reached by a path starting with the right child of X. Then γ comes after α in the ordering. We call such a tree a *binary search tree*.

Example 3.11.   Let keys be strings of letters, and let the ordering on keys be alphabetical. Then Fig. 3.17 shows a binary search tree. (We show no data associated with the keys.)   ∎

The algorithm in Fig. 3.18 finds a desired key α in a binary-search tree. P is a pointer to a node in the tree. Initially, P points to the root. As the algorithm proceeds, we compare α with the key β at whatever node N is currently pointed to by P. If $\alpha = \beta$, we are done. Otherwise, α is compared with β. If α precedes β, we make P point to the left child of N. If N has no left child, then P will be given the value 0, which is used here to represent the absence of a pointer. We may detect $P = 0$ and determine that α is not in the tree. The case where α follows β is handled similarly, with P passing to N's right child. We assume ROOT is the address of the root of the tree and KEY(P) is the key at the node pointed to by P. Also, LEFTCHILD(P) and RIGHTCHILD(P) are the addresses of the left and right children of the node pointed to by P or 0 if no such children exist.

Example 3.12.   Suppose we have the search tree of Fig. 3.17, and we wish to find DONNER. We first compare DONNER with DASHER, the root, and find that DASHER precedes DONNER. We make P point to PRANCER and compare that

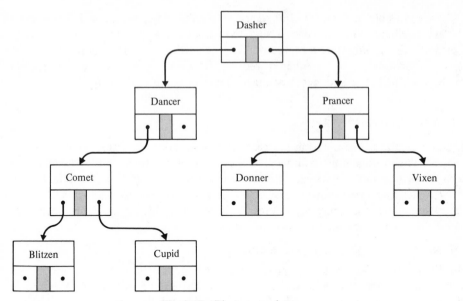

Fig. 3.17   Binary search tree.

```
        begin
(1)         P = ROOT;
(2) LOOP:   while true do
(3)             if P .EQ. 0 then
                    begin
(4)                     PRINT, 'KEY NOT PRESENT';
(5)                     break LOOP
                    end
                else
(6)                 if  α .EQ. KEY(P) then
                        begin
(7)                         PRINT, 'KEY FOUND AT', P;
(8)                         break LOOP
                        end
                    else
(9)                     if  α .LT. KEY(P) then
(10)                        P = LEFTCHILD(P)
                        else
(11)                        P = RIGHTCHILD(P)
        end
```

Fig. 3.18   Algorithm to find key α on a binary-search tree. The **while true do** loop in step 2 will continue indefinitely until either α is found or we pass to a nonexistent left or right child.

with DONNER. Since DONNER precedes PRANCER, we go to PRANCER'S left child and find the desired record at the next step. ∎

In many applications, we wish to add records to the search tree from time to time. To do so, follow the algorithm of Fig. 3.18 until we discover a missing child at line (3). Make the new record be the child found missing.

Example 3.13. Suppose we wished to add RUDOLPH to the tree of Fig. 3.17. We compare RUDOLPH with DASHER and find the former follows the latter. We then move to the right child of DASHER, which is PRANCER. Comparing RUDOLPH with PRANCER again sends us right, to VIXEN. When we compare RUDOLPH to VIXEN, we are sent to the left child of VIXEN. But there is no such node, and therefore, RUDOLPH is inserted into the tree as the left child of VIXEN. ∎

Although it is impossible to guarantee so without periodically rearranging the tree, we may expect that a <u>random</u> binary search tree will be roughly "balanced," that is, the number of descendants reached from the left child of a node will approximate the number of descendants reached from the right child. If these numbers are exactly equal in all cases, then all paths from the root to a leaf are of the same length, say k.[†] It is then possible to reach any node by visiting no more than k nodes. Figure 3.19 shows a completely balanced binary tree with $k = 4$.

We may ask how many nodes does a completely balanced binary tree have if its paths between roots and leaves are of length k? There is one root, two children of the root, four children of the children of the root, . . . , and 2^{k-1} children of the . . . children of the $(k - 1$ times) root. The total number of nodes n is thus given by

$$n = 1 + 2 + 4 + \cdots + 2^{k-1} = 2^k - 1. \tag{3.2}$$

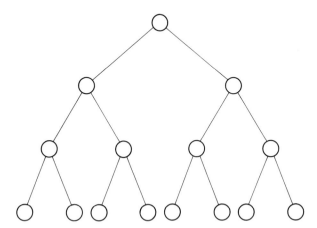

Fig. 3.19 Completely balanced tree with four nodes on each path.

[†] By the *length* of a path, we mean the number of nodes on the path.

If we solve (3.2) for k in terms of n, we get $2^k = n + 1$ or

$$k = \log_2 (n + 1). \tag{3.3}$$

While (3.3) holds for a completely balanced tree, it does not hold for a "random" binary-search tree. Analysis has shown that k, the average length of the path followed to find a particular node out of n in a "random" tree, is roughly given by

$$k = 1.4 \log_2 n. \tag{3.4}$$

Thus the average time to find a key in a binary-search tree does not remain constant as the number of keys increases, but the time grows more slowly than for a linked list. There, the relation comparable to (3.3) was $k = n/2$. If $n \geqslant 9$, we find 1.4 $\log_2 n < n/2$, and for large n, 1.4 $\log_2 n$ is considerably smaller than $n/2$. We consider that a binary search tree is generally superior to a linked list as an associative structure.

3.8   SCATTER STORES

Another type of associative structure, known as *hashing* or *scatter storage*, is comparable or superior to the binary-search-tree method.[†] Such a system is depicted in Fig. 3.20.

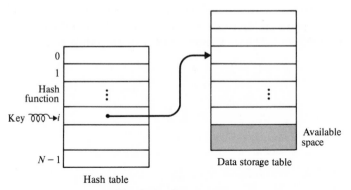

Fig. 3.20   Scatter store.

A scatter store consists of N consecutive computer words, which we shall refer to as the "*hash table*."[‡] Some or all of the words in the hash table hold pointers to records of the *data-storage table*. Each record of the data-storage table holds both a key and the data associated with that key. (Often two tables are used: one for keys,

---

[†] One feature of a binary-search tree makes it preferable to a hash table in certain circumstances. It is comparatively easy to find the smallest element in the tree. Exercise 3.19 shows an example of where this feature is important.

[‡] Often "hash table" is used synonymously with "scatter store," but we reserve the former term for one part of the scatter store.

the other for data. In that case, an entry in the hash table has two pointers, one to each.) The data-storage table can be thought of as a stack which only grows and which is stored in tabular form. Thus, a block of memory is allocated for the data-storage table and its available space. A pointer indicates the first word of available space.

A key can in general be regarded as a string of bits. For example, if the key is a character string, we may take the corresponding bit string to be the coded characters, perhaps filled out with the code for ƀ to make a string of fixed length. To find the record for a given key, we apply a *hashing function* to its string of bits. This function takes the bits of the key, and operates on them to produce an integer between 0 and $N - 1$, where N is the size of the hash table. The hashing function must be complicated, in the sense that the relationship between the key and the result is not easy to predict. (That is to say, the hashing function "hashes up" the key.) On the other hand, the hashing function must be one which can be quickly calculated by the computer.

Example 3.14. A common example of a hashing function is the following. It works only if N, the size of the hash table, is a power of 2.

1. Break the string of bytes forming the key into strings of k bytes each, filling the last string out with blanks if necessary. For example, if $k = 2$, then *ABCDE* would be broken into *AB*, *CD*, and *Eƀ*.

2. Add all the strings together, treating the character codes for the strings as though they were integers. For example, if the code for our computer (See Example 2.14) were used, the three strings *AB*, *CD* and *Eƀ* would be treated as the binary integers:

AB	001010001011
CD	001100001101
Eƀ	001110100100

The sum of these three numbers is 100100111100.

3. Remove enough leading bits from the sum so that the remaining bits are equal in length to one of the summands. In our example, each summand is 12 bits (2 bytes × 6 bits/byte). Therefore, no deletion is necessary here.

4. Square the result. In our example, the 24 bit result would be

010101010100011000010000.

5. Select m particular bits from the middle of the word, where $N = 2^m$. The positions of these bits is fixed, independent of the result. In our example, if $N = 1024 = 2^{10}$, a logical choice would be bits 8 to 17, the exact center of the word. These bits are 1010001100. Thus, the hashing function applied to key *ABCDE* is $(652)_{10}$, and we would expect to find in the 653rd word of the hash table a pointer to the data associated with *ABCDE*. (Recall that the words of the hash table are indexed, beginning with zero not one, so the word number 652 is the 653rd word of the hash table.)   ∎

In the next example we shall use a particularly simple hashing function and see how keys begin to fill up the hash table and data-storage table.

Example 3.15.   The simple hashing function we use is the following.

1. Assign the number 1 to *A*, 2 to *B*, and so on.
2. Given a key which is a string of letters, sum the numbers for each letter.
3. Divide by 10 and let the remainder be the result.

This hashing function maps keys to the integers 0 through 9, so we shall take $N = 10$ for the size of our hash table.

We shall allow our hash table to occupy locations $(100)_8$ to $(111)_8$. Initially, these each hold zero, to indicate that no pointers to the data-storage table have been set up.

The data-storage table will be in locations 112 to 177, and bits 19 to 30 of location 200 will be a pointer to the first available location in the data-storage table. Initially, the whole data-storage table is available, so location 200 points to 112.

Keys will be arbitrary strings of letters, and we shall assume that two words are required for the data associated with any key.

Let us suppose that the first key to be entered into the scatter storage system is *ABCDEFGHI*. The hashing function is applied to *ABCDEFGHI* by summing $1 + 2 + \cdots + 9 = 45$ and dividing by 10 to leave a remainder of 5. Thus, word 5 of the hash table (location 105) will become a pointer to the record of the data-storage table for *ABCDEFGHI*. This record begins in the location pointed to by 200, i.e., location 112. First, we must store *ABCDEFGHI* itself. (Why we must do this will become apparent later.) We place the character code for *ABCDEFGHI* in as many consecutive words of the record as needed. Since our computer has five bytes per word, *ABCDE* will go in location 112 and *FGHIƀ* in location 113. Note that since keys may be arbitrarily long, at least one blank is needed as an *endmarker* to signal the end of the key. Thus, a word of five characters actually requires two words, the second all blank.

We then use the next two words, 114 and 115 to store the data associated with *ABCDEFGHI*. Then, since 116 is now the first available location, we make 200 point there. The scatter store now looks as in Fig. 3.21.

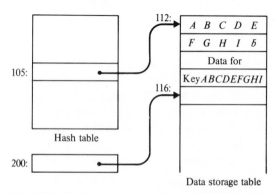

Fig. 3.21   Scatter store after placing ABCDEFGHI.

Let the next key be XY. The result of hashing XY is 9, so a pointer to the record for XY, is placed in location 111 (word 9 of the hash table). That record begins in location 116, and consists of three words, since $XY\textit{ƃƃƃ}$ fits in one word. The present configuration of the scatter store is shown in Fig. 3.22.

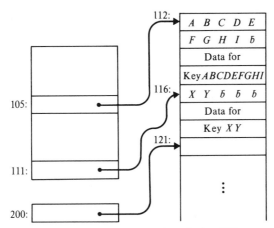

Fig. 3.22   Scatter store after placing XY.

Now suppose we desire to read the data for key XY. We again apply the hashing function to XY, yielding result 9, i.e., location 111. Location 111 points to 116, so we scan the characters stored in 116 and following locations, until we reach the first blank. These characters are XY, so we are satisfied that we have reached the record for this key. Since $XY\textit{ƃƃƃ}$ fills location 116, we know that the data for XY will be in the next two locations, 117 and 120. ∎

However, all is not so simple as the algorithm depicted in Example 3.15. As we enter more keys into the scatter store, we may very well find two or more that yield the same value when the hashing function is applied. Such a situation is called a *collision*. We have a collision when we find a pointer already in a hash table location which we intended to fill. There are many methods of handling collisions; we shall discuss two of them here.

1. Provide a method for finding alternate locations in the hash table when the location indicated by the hashing function is already occupied.

2. Add extra space in the records of the data storage table for a pointer. Then the records for all keys whose value after hashing is the same can be linked in a list.

The simplest strategy of type (1), *linear hashing*, is summarized as follows. If a collision occurs because the ith word of the hash table is already filled, search words $i + 1, i + 2, \ldots$, in order, until an empty word is found. In that word, place a pointer to the data-storage record for the new key. However, note that $N - 1$ is the highest numbered word of the hash table. If, in our search, we reach word $N - 1$, we must go to the beginning of the table and search $0, 1, 2, \ldots$. That is, from any position j we next look at position $j + 1$ modulo N.

To find a key α, we hash α. Suppose the hashing function applied to α yields i. We search the data storage records pointed to by word, $i, i + 1, i + 2, \ldots$ of the hash table until we find a record holding α or find a hash-table location with no pointer. In the latter case, we may conclude that α has not been entered into the table.

Fig. 3.23 is a flowchart of a linear-hashing scheme for inserting key α into a hash table of size N, using hashing function h. A check is made to avoid a loop if all entries are filled.

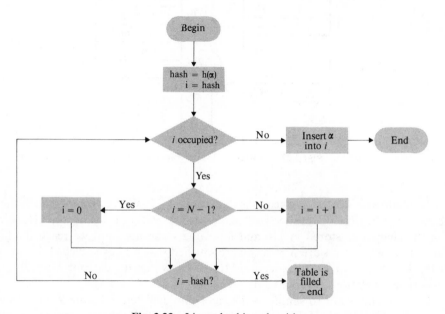

Fig. 3.23   Linear hashing algorithm.

Example 3.16. Let us use linear hashing to resolve conflicts in the scatter store described in Example 3.19. Suppose we wish to enter key Y in the scatter store depicted in Fig. 3.22. The hashing function applied to Y gives value 5. Since location 105 is filled, we next look at 106, find it empty and place the pointer for key Y there. The new configuration of the scatter store is shown in Fig. 3.24.

Suppose we now wish to find the data for the key BC (which is not in the scatter store, as we can see). The result of hashing BC is again 5, so we look in location 105. That location points to 112, so we examine the key in the record with address 112. We find that this key is not BC, so we have reached the wrong record.

Since we are using linear hashing, BC could have been placed in 106 instead. We see, however, that 106 points to 121, which begins the record for Y. It is not possible that BC was placed in 107, because that word is empty. It is also impossible that a pointer to a record for BC exists anywhere else in the hash table. (Think about

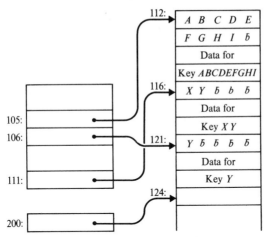

Fig. 3.24   Scatter store after placing Y.

this. If there were such a pointer, how did it get there?) We thus conclude that *BC* is not in the scatter store.   ∎

The second method we shall consider for resolving conflicts links those records in the data-storage table whose keys have the same value when the hashing function is applied. At the expense of space for a pointer in each data-storage record, we may save ourselves the trouble of searching through records whose key has the wrong hashing function value. This method of handling conflicts is called *chaining*.

Example 3.17.   Suppose that the scatter store used is essentially that of Example 3.14, but we use the last word of each data-storage record to hold a pointer to the next record having the same hashing value, if there is one. Then the configuration of the store after entering keys *ABCDEFGHI* and *XY* (corresponding to Fig. 3.22) is shown in Fig. 3.25. Note that neither of the words for pointers are in use yet.

Suppose we again wish to enter key *Y*. We hash *Y* and obtain value 5. As in Example 3.16, we enter *Y* and its data in a record beginning with the first available word of the data-storage table (location 123 in Fig. 3.25). However, instead of placing a pointer to 123 in 106, as we did in Example 3.16, we place a pointer to 123 in the last word of the record for *ABCDEFGHI*. Word 106 remains empty. The resulting configuration is shown in Fig. 3.26. We have shown the record for *Y* appended to the end of the list of keys with hash value 5, rather than the beginning, since we will have to search to the end of that list anyway to check that a record for *Y* was not already there.

If we wish to find the record for *BC*, we again go to location 105, and thence to the record for *ABCDEFGHI*. We then travel via the pointer in word 116 to the record for *Y*. Since *Y* ≠ *BC* and the record for *Y* has an empty pointer, we conclude that *BC* is not present, as before. To see what the pointers in the data-storage table have bought, compare looking for key *F* (hashing value 6) in Figs. 3.24 and 3.26. In the former case, we would go to the record for *Y* before discovering *F* not to be present. In Fig. 3.26, we know this immediately, since there is no pointer in location 106.   ∎

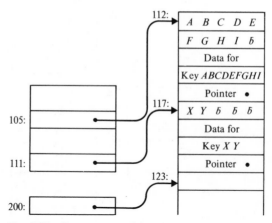

Fig. 3.25   Scatter store with pointers in data storage.

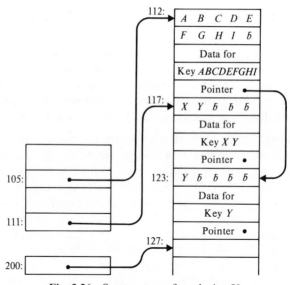

Fig. 3.26   Scatter store after placing X.

EXERCISES

3.1 Let us suppose that a tic-tac-toe board is represented as in Example 3.2 (p. 91). Suppose location LINES holds a pointer to the first line record in bits 19 to 30. (The lines and box records have addresses which are unknown and can only be found by following pointers; we may not assume the lines are in 1000,1010, . . . , as in Example 3.2.)

   a) Write a program to check whether any line has two X's and an empty box, and

   b) if so, place O in the empty box and update the information in the lines containing that box.

3.2 Suppose we have a doubly linked list with records of two words each; the second word holds pointers backward (bits 1 to 12) and forward (bits 19 to 30) as in Fig. 3.27. Write a program that removes from the list the record pointed to by bits 19 to 30 of a word named REMOVE. Do not forget to check if the removed record was first or last (indicated by a zero pointer forward or backward, respectively).

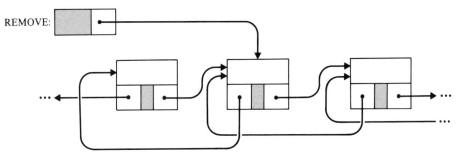

Fig. 3.27 Doubly linked list.

3.3 Write a program to insert the record pointed to by the word named ADJOIN (in bits 19 to 30) in front of the record pointed to by the word BEFORE in the list of Exercise 3.2. Can the operations of these two exercises be done conveniently if the list is stored as a table?

* **3.4** Suppose we are given the singly linked list of Example 3.3 (p. 94), but with the first word of each record holding an integer between 0 and $2^{12} - 1$ in bits 19 to 30, and the sign (first) bit of the first word indicating by a 1 that the record has no record following it on the list. Write a program to test whether some record holds the integer 49.

3.5 Suppose we have a doubly linked list of records as in Exercise 3.2, with a singly linked available-space list. Let location AVAIL hold in bits 19 to 30 a pointer to the first record of available space. Assume that the absence of a pointer is indicated by 0. Write two programs to move records from the list to available space and vice-versa, checking that you do not attempt to move a nonexistent record to the other list (i.e. "pop" an empty list).

** **3.6** Show how two stacks may be stored as tables and use the same available space. Can you do the same with three stacks?

3.7 In Fig. 3.28, identify

a) The parent of E,

b) The children of E,

c) The right sibling of J,

d) The right sibling of E,

e) The leaves,

f) The root,

g) The longest path in the tree.

3.8 Show the links between records if the tree of Fig. 3.28 is implemented

a) as in Example 3.9 (p. 102),

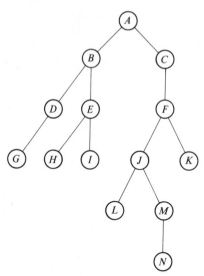

Fig. 3.28   Tree.

b) as in Example 3.10 (p. 103),

c) as in Example 3.10 but with the addition of a pointer to the parent in each record.

* **3.9** Place the letters $A, B, \ldots, N$ at the nodes of Fig. 3.28 so that the tree becomes a binary-search tree. For each node with one child, indicate whether it is a left child or a right child.

*__3.10__ Suppose a binary-search tree is implemented in the style of Example 3.10 (p. 103). Write a program to find the rightmost (highest in the ordering of keys) key in the tree.

*__3.11__ Repeat Exercise 3.10 with the tree implemented as in Example 3.9 (p. 102).

3.12 Let keys be strings of letters and let the order on keys be alphabetic. Fig. 3.17 (p. 106) shows the structure of the binary search tree grown as in Section 3.7 when presented with the list of keys DASHER, DANCER, PRANCER, VIXEN, COMET, CUPID, DONNER, BLITZEN.

a) Show the search tree grown by the same method when presented with these keys in reverse order.

b) Insert RUDOLPH into your answer to (a).

3.13 Using the hashing function of Example 3.15 (p. 110), with the linear strategy to resolve collisions, insert DASHER, DANCER, PRANCER, VIXEN, COMET, CUPID, DONNER, BLITZEN, RUDOLPH into the (empty) scatter store of that example. Assume one word of data is needed for each entry. Then, attempt to find SANTA in the scatter store. How many locations of the hash table are examined (*probed*) before it can be determined that SANTA is not present?

*__3.14__ A *queue* is a list which has records added at one end (the *bottom*) and removed from the other end (the *top*). If we are sure the list will not grow beyond a fixed length N (or are willing to call it an error if it does), then we can implement the queue by a ring of records, with two pointers, one indicating the first available record for additions and the other indicating the top record, at which deletions can be made. The arrangement is shown in Fig. 3.29. Write

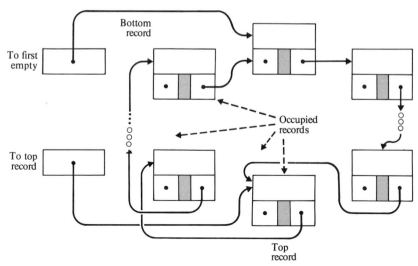

Fig. 3.29   Implementation of a queue.

programs which will insert or delete entries from the queue by advancing one of the two pointers clockwise. Be sure to check that there is room to add an entry to the queue before moving the pointer to the first empty record.

*3.15 Show how to implement a queue as a table with implicit pointers. *Hint:* make one of the "implicit pointers" be from one end of the table to the other.

**3.16 Design an algorithm (you needn't write the program) which deletes an entry from a binary-search tree. Note that the structure of the tree must be preserved. If the node to be deleted is not a leaf, we cannot simply disconnect it from the tree. A leaf must be found to take its place and preserve the properties of the binary-search tree.

3.17 Often a list must be *sorted* by key, that is, records must appear least key first. If the keys are integers, they are in numerical order; if the keys are character strings, they are in alphabetic order. One simple algorithm to sort a list of N records, presumably stored in a table, is given in Fig. 3.30. The algorithm is called *insertion sort*, since it inserts the record which was originally the ith into its proper place among the first $i - 1$ records, for $i = 2, 3, \ldots, N$ in turn. We assume KEY(i) is the value of the key in the ith record, and that $<$ is the ordering on keys.

```
for i = 2 to N do
    begin
        j = i;
        while j .GT. 1 and KEY(j) < KEY(j − 1) do
            begin
                exchange the jth and j − 1st records;
                j = j − 1
            end
    end
```

Fig. 3.30   Insertion sort.

a) Determine the sequence of exchanges made if the initial keys are 3, 1, 4, 1, 5, 9, 2. Note that < on keys just means the ordinary "less than" (FORTRAN .LT.) in this case.

* b) What is the largest number of exchanges that can be made on N records?
Hint: Consider what happens if the keys initially are largest first.

*3.18 Another way to sort N records is:

1. form a binary-search tree from the records, and then

2. repeatedly select and delete the least record from the tree.

How fast does this sorting algorithm work if the average path length from the root to a leaf in the tree is about $\log_2 N$ (as it will be if the initial order of the keys is "random")? Is this time faster than for insertion sort?

*3.19 One task of an operating system is to keep track of jobs submitted for execution by the computer and to select an equitable order for their execution. One "equitable" method is to select for execution the job with the shortest estimated execution time whenever the computer becomes available. Show how to keep jobs in a binary-search tree, ordered by estimated execution time, inserting new jobs as they are submitted and selecting the shortest job when the computer is available. Could you conveniently keep jobs in a hash table instead?

Programming Exercises

3.20 Implement a growing binary-search tree with integer keys. For various numbers of keys, say $N = 10, 30, 100, 300, 1000$, generate a large number of random sequences of keys. Obtain an average path length by averaging over all nodes of all the trees with a fixed number N of nodes. How close does your average come to $1.4 \log_2 N$? Be sure to take a large enough sample that statistical fluctuations can be neglected. How large does this sample have to be?

3.21 Design a scatter store with a hash table of eleven locations. Let the keys be sequences of four letters. To determine the hashing function h:

1. Sum the "values" of the letters where A has value 1, B has value 2, and so on.

2. Divide by 11 and take the remainder.

To resolve collisions when h applied to the key gives location j, we use one of two rules:

a) Linear hashing.

b) "Pseudo-random" hashing. In this, when j is filled we try, in turn, the location $j + 3$ (modulo 11), $j + 6$ (modulo 11), $j + 12$ (modulo 11), ..., and in general try $j + 3 \times 2^{i-1}$ (modulo 11), at the ith try to resolve the collision.[†]

Generate a large number of sequences of 11 keys and insert them into the scatter store using first (a) and then (b). Plot the expected number of collisions as a function of the number of already-filled entries, both for linear and for pseudo-random hashing. You should find that

---

[†] Note that we can compute 3×2^i (modulo 11) as $[3 \times 2^{i-1}$ (modulo 11)$] \times 2$ (modulo 11). That is, it is not necessary to compute large powers of 2, since $3 \times 2^{i-1}$ (modulo 11) will always be between 0 and 10. Also, it happens that this method works, because 2 is *primitive* with respect to 11, meaning that its powers modulo 11 give all the numbers between 1 and $11 - 1 = 10$. However, the reader should not assume that 2 is primitive with respect to an arbitrary number, or he may find himself failing to look at all the locations in the hash table.

pseudo-random hashing is superior when the table is mostly filled (except for the last item inserted, when both are the same), and no worse than linear when the table is mostly empty.

3.22 Compare the hashing function h of Example 3.15 (p. 110) with the hashing function g defined by:

1. computing the sum of the values of the letters, as in Example 3.15 or Exercise 3.21,
2. squaring the result, and
3. taking the second decimal digit from the right end as the hash-table location.

   Use $N = 10$ for the size of the hash table and generate a large number of sequences of 10 keys, each key four letters long. Use the linear strategy to resolve collisions in both cases. You should find that h is superior to g regardless of whether the table is mostly full or mostly empty. Why?

FURTHER READING

   Knuth [1968a] was a pioneering text developing the data structure point of view. The reader is referred there for more information about trees, lists, stacks, and queues. The use of binary-search trees, hash tables, and other associative structures is covered in Knuth [1973] and Aho, Hopcroft, and Ullman [1974], as is the topic of sorting.

   Morris [1968] is another good source on scatter storage. Additional material on the subject matter of this chapter can be found in Berztiss [1971] and Stone [1972, 1973].

Chapter 4

Assembly Languages and Assemblers

In Chapter 2 we introduced a rudimentary assembly language, in which each instruction was a mnemonic version of a machine instruction. In this chapter we shall discuss two issues: the first is how to write an assembler—a program that converts assembly code to machine code; the second is a collection of extensions to the assembly language of Chapter 2 that make it far more convenient to use. Chief among these extensions is a "macro" facility that can be used both as a shorthand and as a way of "simulating" a variety of computer designs.

4.1 THE ASSEMBLY PROCESS

An *assembler* is a program whose input is a string of characters forming an assembly-language program and whose output is a string of computer words forming a machine-language program "equivalent" to the assembly-language program. This machine-language program can then be run on the computer as can any other program in the machine language of that computer. The arrangement is shown in Fig. 4.1.

The assembler may place the program it generates in available memory locations and transfer control to it (a *load and go* assembler), or the output of the assembler may be presented to another program called a loader. The loader places the machine-language program in memory for phase II. We shall discuss the role of the loader in the next chapter.

There are two essential jobs which the assembler must perform. First, it must replace instruction and address-modifier mnemonics by their binary equivalents. Second, it must determine locations for the *symbolic addresses* (variables used as an address field) and replace all references to a given symbolic address by the binary number of the chosen location.

To help select the locations to be used for the symbolic addresses, the assembly language makes available to the programmer certain "pseudo-operations." These tell where, relative to the executable instructions, the words represented by symbolic addresses are to appear. (Usually, data is placed immediately following the last executable instruction.) We are thus led to the general topic of pseudo-operations.

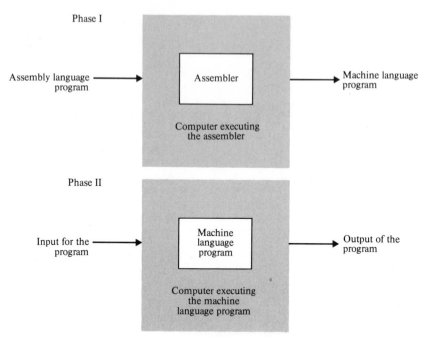

Fig. 4.1   The assembly and execution of a program written in assembly language.

4.2   PSEUDO-OPERATIONS

To create a convenient assembly language, we must build in certain additional features. These are generally called *pseudo-operations*, because they are not converted to
machine-language instructions, but rather tell the assembler something about its job.

The first type of pseudo-operation that we need is a data-defining pseudo-
operation. Such a pseudo-operation allows us to designate that certain symbolic
addresses represent program variables, and that memory locations are to be left
vacant for them. Often, it is possible to indicate an initial value for the variable as well.

We shall have in our assembly language the following types of data defining
pseudo-operations. It should be noted that the address field of a pseudo-operation
will not in general have the format of the executable instructions defined in Chapter 2.
Rather, various lists of quantities with various meanings can be used.

1. A pseudo-operation of the form:

$$\alpha: \text{DATA } \beta$$

tells the assembler that the memory location named $\alpha^\dagger$ is to hold data, and that its

---

$\dagger$ The presence of a name on this and all other pseudo-operations is optional. In this case, it's
rather useful, though, and will be present as a rule.

initial value is to be β. If β is an integer, we shall place the fixed-point equivalent of that integer in the location. If β is a FORTRAN floating-point constant (e.g., 6.8 or $1.02E - 3$), we shall place the floating-point equivalent in the location. If β is a string of up to five characters, surrounded by quotation marks,[†] we shall place the character code of our computer for these characters in the location, filled out with the blank code $(44)_8$ to the left, if necessary. Finally, if β is OCTAL followed by up to ten digits 0 to 7, we shall treat these digits as an octal integer and convert it to a 30-bit binary integer, filling it out with 0's at the left end if needed.

2. A pseudo-operation of the form:

$$\alpha: \text{BLOCK } i$$

reserves i (written in decimal) consecutive words for a block. The first of these words has the symbolic address α. The remaining words of the block have no symbolic address, but we shall see that they are quite easy to access. All words of the block will hold 0's initially.

3. It is often useful to define one location, say α, to be a pointer to another, say β. We need a data-defining instruction that tells the assembler to place the actual location of β in either bits 1 to 12 or bits 19 to 30 of α. We shall have a pseudo-operation of the form:

$$\alpha: \text{POINTER } \beta$$

The location named α will hold the location corresponding to β in bits 19 to 30. For example, if the above instruction appeared somewhere in an assembly-language program, then LOAD α(IND) has the same effect as LOAD β.

We shall have another pseudo-operation

$$\alpha: \text{POINTERS } \beta, \gamma$$

which places the address of β in bits 1 to 12 of the location named α and places the address of γ in bits 19 to 30 of that word.

Example 4.1. As a sample program, let us read the first 60 columns of a card into a block of 12 words named A, and then delete blanks, moving all nonblank characters as far left as possible. We use register 6 to count the number of bytes scanned so far and register 7 to count the number of nonblank characters encountered. Since the READ instruction requires another word with two pointers, one to the first and one to the last word of block A, we shall define block A by two consecutive instructions, A: BLOCK 11 and B: DATA 0. This arrangement allows us to give a name to the last word of the block as well as to the first. (The need for this awkward arrangement will be obviated when we discuss expressions as addresses.) The program in Fig. 4.2 does the job. ∎

[†] There is a little problem of what to do if one of the characters is a quotation mark. Let us assume that quotes are not permissible characters in this context, although this is really no solution to the problem.

Instruction		Comments
READ1	PTR	We read a card into block *A*. PTR holds *A* in bits 1 to 12 and *B* in bits 19 to 30. Note the POINTERS pseudo-operation defining PTR at the end of the program.
LOAD6	0(IMMED)	Initialize registers 6 and 7 to zero.
LOAD7	0(IMMED)	
LOOP: LOAD1	A(CHX6)	Here we begin a loop and bring the next character to be considered to register 1.
COPY12		We compare the character with our computer's code for blank.
XOR2	' '(IMMED)	
JZERO2	SKIP	If the character is ƀ, we skip the next two instructions.
STORE1	A(CHX7)	In this step, we store the character in the first avail-
ADD7	1(IMMED)	able space and increment register 7 by 1.
SKIP: ADD6	1(IMMED)	Here, we are rejoined by the flow of control when
MOVE65		the character is blank. We increment register 6 and
SUB5	60(IMMED)	compare it with 60. If it is less than 60, we repeat the
JMINUS5	LOOP	loop.
.		
.		
.		The remainder of the program appears here.
A: BLOCK	11	Finally, we have the data-defining pseudo-opera-
B: DATA	0	tions.† *A* and *B* together define 12 words, initially
PTR: POINTERS	A,B	all zero, whose first word is named *A* and whose last is *B*. PTR is a word with the address of *A* in bits 1 to 12 and the address of *B* in bits 19 to 30.

Fig. 4.2   Program to delete blanks.

We shall mention one pseudo-operation not concerned with data. This is the END pseudo-operation. It has no name or address fields. The END pseudo-operation simply informs the assembler that it has reached the last line of the assembly program.

4.3 A SIMPLE ASSEMBLER

Let us now consider how an assembler does its job. We have introduced only a few of the concepts present in a typical assembly language; but, using these, the ideas behind the working of a simple assembler can be illustrated. Initially, the assembly-language program is found in a region of main or secondary memory.

† The data need not be last, but if placed in the middle of a program, we must jump over data to avoid "executing" it.

The assembler usually works in two phases or *passes*. Each pass consists of reading the assembly program, instruction by instruction. After they have been read and processed, the instructions are stored, preferably in the same region in which they were placed initially.

The first pass cleans up the program, by deleting superfluous blanks and comments. But its most important job is to assign a number to each executable instruction and data-defining pseudo-operation. This number is the location which will be reserved for the machine-code version of the assembly-language instruction.

In most assembly languages the assignment of locations to instructions is quite easy, since almost all instructions use an easily determined number of words. In our language, one word per instruction is the rule. However, certain data-defining instructions and other pseudo-operations represent more than one location. For example, the instruction BLOCK i represents i locations. If BLOCK i is assigned location j, then the next instruction is assigned location $i + j$. Also, some pseudo-operations such as END generate no instruction at all.

While assigning numbers to instructions on the first pass, we match these numbers to the names of the instructions. To do so, the assembler must have an associative structure, typically a scatter store, in which the keys are names (symbolic addresses) given to instructions, and the data is the location that the name represents and perhaps some other information. This associative structure is called the *symbol table*, and it usually has the capacity to store several thousand names.

We also have use for another associative structure. This one has keys which are mnemonic instruction codes and contains data such as:

1. the bits of the instruction code represented by the mnemonic, and
2. information as to how many machine instructions are generated by the assembly instruction (usually 0 or 1). In cases such as the BLOCK instruction, it indicates how to determine the number of instructions (look at the integer following).

It would seem that this associative structure has fixed size—the number of different mnemonics and pseudo-operations. However, in a "macro" assembly language (to be discussed subsequently) this table needs sizable additional capacity. Note that the information in the instruction-code table (or a portion of it, in the case of a macro assembler) is built into the assembler, while the information of the symbol table is entered as the assembler operates.

It is worthwhile discussing how the assembler goes about locating name, instruction, and address fields in a line of an assembly-language program. Many assemblers use a *fixed format*; e.g., the name begins in position 1, the instruction code begins in position 8, and the address and modifiers begin in position 15. In these instances, it is easy to determine whether a name is present and to isolate its characters. Similarly, one can easily isolate the instruction code and the other pieces of the instruction.

In the case of our assembly language, which is comparatively *free format*, things are not so simple. The following algorithm suffices, however. Scan the instruction until a nonblank character is reached. This character begins either the name field, if there is one, or the instruction field. We scan through consecutive letters and digits.

If we come to a colon before seeing a blank, we have isolated a name. If we reach a blank before seeing a colon, we have the instruction field. If we have found the name, the next nonblank character begins the instruction field. The end of the instruction field is indicated by a blank. Anything following that is the address field.

When we begin the second pass of the assembler, all instruction names will have been assigned location numbers, which may be found in the symbol table. In the second pass, the instructions are again scanned one by one. From each, we construct the corresponding machine-language instructions (normally one instruction). The instruction field is replaced by the sequence of bits for which it stands. Likewise, address modifiers are replaced by the bits they represent.[†] Symbolic addresses found in the address field are replaced by the location they represent; this information is found in the symbol table.

Pseudo-operations may generate none, one, or more than one instruction. The initial values for computer words generated from data-defining instructions are computed from these instructions in the obvious way. For example, in our assembly language, the instruction DATA 100 gives rise to a word $(0000000144)_8$. BLOCK 10 gives rise to ten words of zeros. Fig. 4.3(a) flowcharts the first pass of the assembler, and Fig. 4.3(b) flowcharts the second. Error checks, such as for ill-formatted lines or for two lines with the same name, are omitted. For the time being, the letter A indicating one box in Fig. 4.3(b) can be ignored.

Example 4.2.   Let us consider the simple assembly program:

```
        LOAD1    A
        ADD1     B
        STORE1   C
        HALT
    A:  DATA     1
    B:  DATA     2
    C:  DATA     0
        END
```

The first instruction LOAD1 A is given location 0. We find that it has no name, and that its instruction field is one which gives rise to one machine instruction. Thus the location counter (COUNT in Fig. 4.3a) is increased by 1, and we consider the second instruction, ADD1 B. The next two instructions are treated similarly: no entries are made in the symbol table, since there are no names for the instructions; and COUNT is incremented by one for each instruction.

The fifth instruction, A: DATA 1, is assigned location 4. We see that it has a name A, so A is placed in the symbol table with information that the location reserved for A is 4. Similarly, B and C are placed in the symbol table and given locations 5

[†] These two jobs could be done in the first pass as well. If so, the assembler is often called *one pass*, even though a second pass to substitute memory locations for symbolic addresses is still needed. We can dispense with the second pass altogether if we make a list, for each name α appearing in an address field, of the instructions in which α appears. When the instruction with name α is found on pass 1, we immediately substitute the location of that instruction for all uses of α.

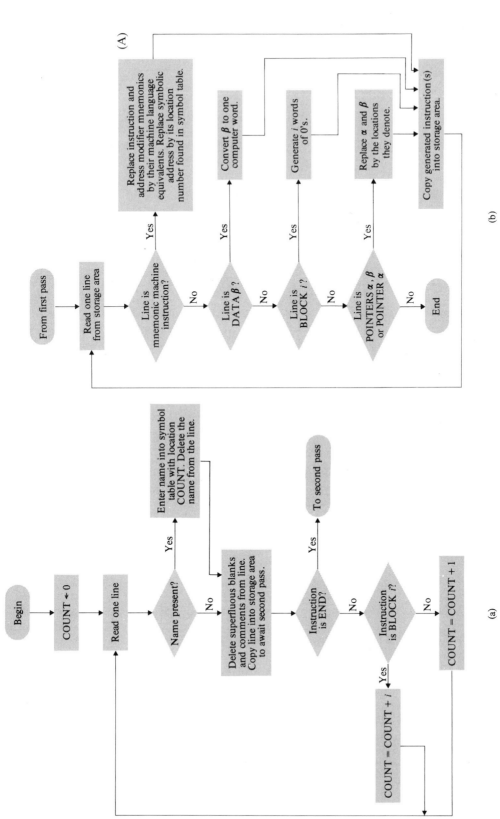

Fig. 4.3 Flowchart of a simple assembler: a) Pass one; b) Pass two.

Pass one (a):

Begin → COUNT ← 0 → Read one line → Name present?

- Yes → Enter name into symbol table with location COUNT. Delete the name from the line.
- No → Delete superfluous blanks and comments from line. Copy line into storage area to await second pass.

→ Instruction is END?

- Yes → To second pass
- No → Instruction is BLOCK i?
  - Yes → COUNT = COUNT + i
  - No → COUNT = COUNT + 1

Pass two (b):

From first pass → Read one line from storage area → Line is mnemonic machine instruction?

- Yes → Replace instruction and address modifier mnemonics by their machine language equivalents. Replace symbolic address by its location number found in symbol table.
- No → Line is DATA β?
  - Yes → Convert β to one computer word.
  - No → Line is BLOCK i?
    - Yes → Generate i words of 0's.
    - No → Line is POINTERS α, β or POINTER α?
      - Yes → Replace α and β by the locations they denote.
      - No → End

(A) → Copy generated instruction(s) into storage area.

and 6, respectively. The last instruction is the pseudo-operation END. It is given no location, but indicates the end of the first pass.

In the second pass, we again examine the first instruction. The mnemonic LOAD1 is replaced by $(0101)_8$ in bits 1 to 12. We further scan the first instruction and find the symbolic address A. Consulting the symbol table, we find that A stands for location 4. Thus we replace A by $(0004)_8$ in bits 19 to 30. There is no modifier, so bits 13 to 18 of the generated computer word are 0.

The second and third instructions are translated similarly to:

$$0210000005$$
$$0110000006$$

The fourth instruction has no address field and is translated to all 0's.

When we reach the fifth instruction, we see that DATA, the instruction field, is not a mnemonic machine instruction. The assembler must translate this instruction in a special way. Namely, the string of nonblank characters following DATA must be interpreted as a FORTRAN constant, octal constant, or character string and replaced by the appropriate 30-bit computer word. In this case, the constant is the integer 1, so the assembler must create the fixed-point constant 1 as the translation of A: DATA 1.

Similarly, the next two instructions yield fixed-point constants 2 and 0. The END instruction again generates no instructions but signals the end of the pass.

The entire machine-language program is:

Location	Contents
00	0101000004
01	0210000005
02	0110000006
03	0000000000
04	0000000001
05	0000000002
06	0000000000

4.4 LITERALS

Several additional features are necessary for a useful assembler. Here, we shall discuss "literals," and in the following sections, expressions in address fields, the "myself" symbol, and macros.

As we have seen, the immediate form of address modification is quite handy when we wish to refer to known constants that fit in the address portion of an instruction. Many assembly languages have a feature that looks similar, but allows full word constants to be referred to "literally."

In our assembly language, let an address $=\alpha$ where α is a FORTRAN constant, an octal number of up to 10 places preceded by OCTAL, or a quoted character string of up to 5 characters refer to a location in memory which will be created by the assembler and initialized with α. That is:

$$\text{LOAD} \quad = \alpha$$

means the same as:

$$\text{LOAD} \quad \text{X}$$
$$\vdots$$
$$\text{X:} \quad \text{DATA} \quad \alpha$$

The only difference is that there is no need to write the DATA instruction or even to mention its name. These details are handled by the assembler.

Let us consider the modifications needed to make the simple assembler we discussed handle literals. After the first pass, we know how many computer words are needed for the program, exclusive of literals. The locations immediately after the last one used for the program will be used to hold the values of the literals.

We shall need another associative structure, called the *literal table*, which associates with certain 30-bit computer words (those designated by literals) the location where they will be found. During the second pass, if the literal $=\alpha$ is encountered, α is converted to the 30-bit word represented by α (e.g., if α is an integer, it is converted to the 30-bit fixed-point equivalent). We then check to see if this word is already in the literal table. If so, we replace $=\alpha$ by the associated location. If not, we enter it into the literal table and assign it the next available location. The counter indicating the next available location is increased by 1. We may then replace $=\alpha$ by the next available location.

At the end of the second pass, the computer word for each literal is placed in its proper location at the end of the program.

Example 4.3.   Consider the assembly program:

$$
\begin{array}{lll}
& \text{LOAD}^\dagger & =1 \\
& \text{ADD} & =2 \\
& \text{MULT} & =2 \\
& \text{STORE} & \text{A} \\
& \text{HALT} & \\
\text{A:} & \text{DATA} & 0 \\
& \text{END} &
\end{array}
$$

In the first pass, we find that A represents location 5, and that 6 is the first available location following the program. In the second pass, LOAD $=1$ is found to contain a literal which is $(0000000001)_8$. Since this word is not in the literal table, we place it there, assigning it location 6, and translate LOAD $=1$ to 0101000006.

The second instruction, ADD $=2$, also has a literal $(0000000002)_8$. That word is not yet in the literal table, so we give it location 7 and translate ADD $=2$ to 0210000007.

$\dagger$ Recall that 1 may be omitted from instructions, so LOAD means the same as LOAD1.

For the third instruction, we again find a literal representing computer word $(0000000002)_8$. This word is in the literal table and represents location 7. We thus translate MULT $=2$ to 0610000007. The last two instructions are translated in the obvious way. The resulting machine language program is:

Location	Contents
00	0101000006
01	0210000007
02	0610000007
03	0110000005
04	0000000000
05	0000000000
06	0000000001
07	0000000002 ∎

We should comment that an extension of the literal concept will allow us to avoid specifying instructions of the form:

$$\alpha: \text{DATA } 0$$

The assembler could create such an instruction for α if it is used as a symbolic address but not otherwise given a location.

4.5 EXPRESSIONS FOR ADDRESSES

It is often convenient to allow an address to be an arithmetic expression, rather than a single name. Most assemblers will allow some of these expressions and will evaluate them during the second pass. There is one condition which must be met by such expressions, due to the fact that assemblers normally generate "relocatable" machine code, which will be discussed in the next section.

The maximal permissible class of expressions (most assemblers permit only a subset of these) consists of operands chosen from the symbolic addresses of the program and integers. The operators are typically $+, -,^\dagger *$ and $/$. Division is integral; i.e., the remainder, if any, is thrown away. The special condition is that should all symbolic addresses, say α, be replaced by $\alpha + \Delta$, where Δ is a fixed constant (the same constant for all symbolic names) then the resulting expression must either be algebraically equivalent to the original or be equivalent to the original plus Δ. In the former case, say the expression is *constant-like* or *nonrelocatable*; in the latter case it is *name-like*, or *relocatable*.

Example 4.4. $2 * A - B$ is an acceptable name-like expression. If we substitute $A + \Delta$ for A and $B + \Delta$ for B we obtain $2 * (A + \Delta) - (B + \Delta)$ which simplifies to $2 * A - B + \Delta$.

---

† Minus may be binary or unary.

$A - B$ is an acceptable constant-like expression, since $(A + \Delta) - (B + \Delta) = A - B$.

$A * B$ is not acceptable, since $(A + \Delta) * (B + \Delta)$ is equivalent neither to $A * B$ nor to $A * B + \Delta$. ∎

In the great majority of cases, the expression will be of the form $\alpha \pm c$, where α is a symbolic address and c a constant. The condition is clearly satisfied in this case. Since $(\alpha + \Delta) \pm c = (\alpha \pm c) + \Delta$, we see that $\alpha \pm c$ is a relocatable expression.

Example 4.5. Let us reconsider Example 4.1. There, we had a block A of 12 words and a word PTR which held pointers to both the first and last words of the block. In Example 4.1 we expressed this arrangement by:

```
  A:   BLOCK      11
  B:   DATA       0
PTR:   POINTERS   A,B
```

We could more simply write:

```
  A:   BLOCK      12
PTR:   POINTERS   A,A+11
```

The name B has been replaced by the expression $A + 11$. ∎

Negative constants or any other expression which yields a negative value when locations are substituted for symbolic addresses are an interesting kind of expression. We might ask how such an address is to be interpreted. Our approach is to treat $-c$ as if it were $M - c$, where M is the size of main memory. In general, all addresses should be computed modulo the size of main memory.

In Fig. 4.4, we see a replacement for the box marked (A) in Fig. 4.3(b) (p. 127). It indicates the handling of expressions and literals in the address field. Note that COUNT remains set after pass one, and that a constant or symbolic address is a special case of an expression.

4.6 THE MYSELF SYMBOL

It is sometimes useful to have a way for an instruction to refer to itself or to a neighboring instruction, usually for the purpose of jumping to the designated instruction. Of course, we could give a name to any instruction we choose, but a shorthand is useful for this common situation. We shall therefore use * as an operand[†] to mean the location of the instruction in which it appears.

[†] Note that we can distinguish uses of * as an operand from its uses as the multiplication symbol. In the former case it must have an adjacent operator, in the latter case not. In Chapter 8 we shall take up "parsing" and see how expressions such as **3 − 2** can be deciphered. (The first and last *'s are "myself"; the inner two are "times.")

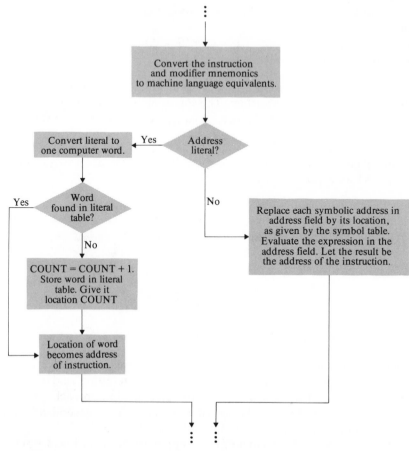

Fig. 4.4   Pass two processing of addresses with literals and expressions.

Example 4.6.   We recall Example 4.1, which had the following sequence of instructions:

```
LOOP:   LOAD1     A(CHX6)
        COPY12
        XOR2      ' '(IMMED)
        JZERO2    SKIP
        STORE2    A(CHX7)
        ADD7      1(IMMED)
SKIP:   ADD6      1(IMMED)
        MOVE65
        SUB5      60(IMMED)
        JMINUS5   LOOP
```

Since the only references to SKIP and LOOP are those shown, we could eliminate these names and replace the addresses SKIP and LOOP by * plus or minus the distance from the conditional transfer instruction to the target location.

Thus, JZERO2 SKIP could become JZERO2 *+3. Similarly JMINUS5 LOOP could be replaced by JMINUS5 *−9. We could then delete the names from the first and seventh instructions. ∎

It should be observed that the "myself" symbol is treated like any symbolic address. Thus, *+3 and *−9 are name-like expressions. In the second pass of the assembler, we may substitute for * by giving it the number of the instruction in which it appears. If we adopt this strategy, we must count each instruction in pass two as we do in pass one. An alternate strategy is to substitute for * in pass one, requiring that addresses be examined in detail to distinguish the operator * from the myself symbol.

The reader should be warned that an assembler will treat *+c as referring to c memory locations after the location of the instruction in which it appears—not c assembly language statements after the current one.

Example 4.7. Suppose we wish to insert a block of ten words in the middle of a program. We should not write:

```
         JUMP    *+2
A:       BLOCK   10
         LOAD    XYZ
```

This will land us at the second word of block A. Rather, we should write:

```
         JUMP    *+11
A:       BLOCK   10
         LOAD    XYZ  ∎
```

In practice, most assembly languages restrict their expressions so that their evaluation is trivial. A typical rule would insist that operators and operands alternate, with no parentheses and with all operators associating from the left; i.e., $A + B * C - D$ means $((A + B) * C) - D$.

4.7 MACROS

Many assembly languages are *extensible*, meaning that they have within them the ability to define additional instruction mnemonics, called *macros*, which can then be considered part of the language and used repeatedly. These new definitions apply only within the program in which they appear. In fact, they normally apply only in the portion of the program following the definition. The assembler will replace these macro instructions by their definitions, consisting of the predefined mnemonics for machine instructions and/or previously defined macro instructions.

To define a macro instruction, we write a *macro definition*, which specifies:

1. the name of the new instruction,
2. a list of dummy arguments, (*formal parameters*), and

3. a "meaning" of the new instruction (the macro body), which is a sequence of assembly instructions, with fields chosen from among the formal parameters and the usually available items appropriate to the various fields.

In our assembly language, we shall have two pseudo-operations MACRO and ENDM. If we see the pseudo-operation

$$\text{MACRO } \alpha(\beta_1, \beta_2, \ldots, \beta_n)$$

then all instructions following up to the next ENDM will be the definition of the new macro instruction. Here, α is the name of the macro and $\beta_1, \beta_2, \ldots, \beta_n$ are its formal parameters.

Example 4.8. Our computer does not have a "transfer if not equal" instruction. However, we can simulate the effect of such an instruction and also provide a convenient shorthand by the following macro definition:

```
MACRO   JNEQ(A,B,GOTO)
LOAD    A
SUB     B
JNONZ   GOTO
ENDM
```

The JNEQ macro body computes $A - B$ for fixed-point numbers A and B, then jumps to GOTO only if $A \neq B$. Thus it appears that the instruction named GOTO will be jumped to whenever $A \neq B$, and that the next instruction will be reached if $A = B$. ∎

It should be emphasized that the macro definition is a model, not executable code. Thus the program may not even have data locations A and B or an instruction named GOTO. In fact, if such names do exist in the program, they are not related to the formal parameters such as A, B and GOTO mentioned in the macro definition.

If a program contains a macro definition, we may use the macro to generate some executable code by a *macro use*. The macro use specifies:

1. the name of the macro to be used, and
2. the symbols (called *actual parameters*) to be substituted for the formal parameters in the macro body.

When the assembler encounters the use, it replaces the formal parameters in the macro body by the corresponding actual parameters, in the order of appearance. The assembler then replaces the macro use by the instructions resulting from this substitution and proceeds to assemble those instructions in the normal way.

In our assembly language, we shall use the macro named α by writing α in the instruction field and a list of actual parameters separated by commas in the address field.

Example 4.9. Suppose an assembly-language program has the macro definition JNEQ of Example 4.8. Further on in the program we can use macro JNEQ. Let us suppose it is desired at some point to determine whether all three of X, Y, and Z are equal, and to jump to instruction YES if so and to NO otherwise. The relevant portions of the program are:

```
MACRO   JNEQ(A,B,GOTO)
LOAD    A
SUB     B
JNONZ   GOTO
ENDM
  .
  .
  .
JNEQ    X,Y,NO
JNEQ    X,Z,NO
JUMP    YES
```

Upon encountering the pseudo-operation MACRO JNEQ(A, B, GOTO) in pass one, no machine instructions are generated by the assembler for this instruction, for any of the instructions of the macro body, or for ENDM. However, an entry for JNEQ is made in the instruction code table indicating JNEQ is a macro and listing its formal parameters, A, B, and GOTO, and its body:

```
LOAD    A
SUB     B
JNONZ   GOTO
```

Then when the assembler reaches the macro use JNEQ X, Y, NO, it goes to the macro body (which it has stored), substitutes X for A, Y for B, and NO for GOTO. The assembler then replaces JNEQ X, Y, NO by the three instructions:

```
LOAD    X
SUB     Y
JNONZ   NO
```

The second macro use is treated similarly, with X replacing A, Z replacing B and NO replacing GOTO in the macro body. The three instructions

```
JNEQ    X,Y,NO
JNEQ    X,Z,NO
JUMP    YES
```

are thus treated by the assembler as if they were:

```
LOAD    X
SUB     Y
JNONZ   NO
LOAD    X
SUB     Z
JNONZ   NO
JUMP    YES
```

Those familiar with subroutines or procedures in a programming language will likely notice a similarity between the concepts of macro and subroutine. It is therefore necessary that we emphasize the difference. The definition of a macro causes no machine code to be generated by the assembler; while the definition of a subroutine does cause the compiler to generate code to execute the subroutine.

The use of a macro causes the assembler to generate the code of the macro body with actual parameters substituted for formal parameters. For the call of a subroutine the compiler simply generates a jump to the code for the subroutine. The actual parameters for the call of the subroutine are passed in one of several ways which we shall discuss in subsequent chapters.

4.8   A MACRO ASSEMBLER

Let us consider the modifications necessary to permit the simple assembler previously discussed to handle macros. The changes all occur in the first pass. In that pass, each instruction code must be checked to see if it is the pseudo-operation MACRO or if it is a name previously defined to be a macro.

If we encounter an instruction MACRO $\alpha(\beta_1, \beta_2, \ldots, \beta_n)$, we must enter α into the table of instruction codes (or a separate table for macro instruction codes). Associated with α will be

1. the fact that it is a macro,[†]

2. the list of formal parameters used in the macro definition, and

3. the body of the definition. For convenient storage, inessential blanks (all blanks except those marking the end of instruction codes in our assembler) may be deleted. It is also convenient to mark each occurrence of a formal parameter, so that when the macro is used, the substitution of actual formal parameters may easily be carried out. For example, the ith formal parameter could be replaced by the character code for # followed by i in binary, with, say, 6 bits allocated for i.

The macro definition, up to and including the ENDM instruction, is then deleted from the program. It will not be needed on the second pass.

Now let us see how to handle the situation in which an instruction code is found to be a macro (a macro use). This macro must have been previously defined, so information about it will appear in the table of instruction codes. Let the formal parameters in the macro definition be $\beta_1, \beta_2, \ldots, \beta_n$ and the actual parameters in the use of the macro be $\gamma_1, \gamma_2, \ldots, \gamma_n$. The body of the macro definition is scanned and a new copy made. Each time an argument, say β_i, is encountered in the original definition, γ_i is substituted in the copy.

Note that the order of the arguments in the macro definition is part of the information about the macro stored in the instruction code table. Thus the pairing of β_i and γ_i for each i can be carried out simply.

[†] Which means that instruction mnemonics must have a bit indicating the opposite if all are to be kept in one instruction code table.

The new copy of the macro body now becomes part of the program being processed by the assembler; it is placed in front of all the instructions remaining to be processed on the first pass. If the macro use had a label, that label is attached to the first instruction of the copy of the macro body. Thus the list of instructions operates as a stack. We remove each instruction as it is processed. (Unless the instruction is part of a macro definition, it is placed at the end of a list of instructions waiting for the second pass.) When a macro use is expanded, the copy of the body is pushed on top of the list of instructions waiting for the first pass.

Note that when expanding a macro use, the count of locations used is not increased. It is the instructions in the copy formed that will increase the location counter as they are processed in turn.

Example 4.10. In our assembler we could store information about macros in the following format.

1. The first words hold the name of the macro followed by the character $, which will act as an endmarker.

2. This is followed by the macro body with inessential blanks deleted, $'s separating instructions, and formal parameters replaced by one of the character strings #1, #2, ..., #9. That is, the ith formal parameter is represented by #i for $1 \leq i \leq 9$. We are thus restricted to nine formal parameters, although it is easy to see how a change in format could obviate the need for this restriction. Note that since formal parameters are used only as place markers for actual parameters, we can use any distinct symbols we like for actual parameters when we store the macro body.

3. Two $'s mark the end of the body.

For example, the macro definition

```
MACRO    MULTIPLY(X,Y,Z)
LOAD1    X
MULT1    Y
STORE1   Z
ENDM
```

would be stored as the following sequence of words:

```
M U L T I
P L Y $ ƀ
L O A D 1
ƀ # 1 $ M
U L T 1 ƀ
# 2 $ S T
O R E 1 ƀ
# 3 $ $ ƀ
```

When the macro is used, say, MULTIPLY A, B, CD, we find the record of the instruction table with the information about MULTIPLY. The body is scanned, and every # and its following digit *i* is replaced by the *i*th actual parameter. Then, instructions in the body are separated, an easy task since $'s mark the separation.

In this example, we substitute *A* for #1, *B* for #2, and *CD* for #3 in the body, yielding the three instructions

```
LOAD1    A
MULT1    B
STORE1   CD
```

in place of

```
MULTIPLY A, B, CD.  ▮
```

Example 4.11 illustrates the following points about macros.

1. Macros may be used not only as shorthand, but to make the programmer think he is programming a machine with a variety of features not actually possessed by the machine.

2. Macros may use other macros as part of their definition.

3. Pieces of instructions other than addresses may be formal parameters of a macro.

Example 4.11. We mentioned that ideally the binary operations of machines should have three addresses: two for the operands, and one for the result. However, few machines have large enough words that three memory addresses can be specified. Let us write a set of macros to make it appear that our computer has three address instructions. To begin, we define a macro DO to use as a shorthand. DO takes three addresses and an instruction mnemonic as actual parameters. The definition of DO is:

```
MACRO   DO(OP,A,B,C)
LOAD    A
OP      B
STORE   C
ENDM
```

Now, we can define macros such as:

```
MACRO   3ADD(X,Y,Z)
DO      ADD,X,Y,Z
ENDM
```

for a three-address fixed-point addition, or:

```
MACRO   3SUBFL(A,B,C)
DO      SUBFL,A,B,C
ENDM
```

for a three-address floating-point subtraction. Note that three of the actual and formal parameters of DO are the same in the latter case. This is of no consequence; what is important is that each macro use will ultimately be replaced by instructions whose addresses correspond to actual locations.

Suppose we have a program which begins with the above three macros and then has the instruction 3ADD DING, DONG, BELL. The three macros will be processed in pass one and their bodies stored in the instruction table. When the use of 3ADD is reached, the location counter is still at zero. Then the use 3ADD DING, DONG, BELL is replaced by DO ADD, DING, DONG, BELL at the top of the list of instructions remaining to be processed. The location counter remains at zero. Then the DO instruction, which is also a macro, is processed and is replaced by:

```
LOAD    DING
ADD     DONG
STORE   BELL
```

The location counter is still zero, but now, the new top instruction LOAD DING is processed. It is not a macro and so is given location 0. Then the next two instructions are similarly processed and given locations 1 and 2. ∎

4.9 CONDITIONAL ASSEMBLY

To realize the maximum potential of the macro facility, the assembler needs the ability to compute instructions by means more versatile than the simple substitution of actual parameters for formal ones in a macro use. A variety of useful pseudo-operations that tell the assembler to perform some computation are known. We shall discuss only two of them here. The first pseudo-operation

$$\text{IF } \alpha$$

tells the assembler to include the next instruction in a macro expansion only if the value of expression α is zero.

Example 4.12. Let us reconsider the macro JNEQ (A, B, GOTO) first introduced in Example 4.8 (p. 134). There we assumed that A and B were fixed-point numbers. However, we might wish to handle the case in which they were floating-point numbers (or characters or pointers for that matter). To distinguish between fixed- and floating-point computation in a single macro we might add a fourth parameter TYPE to JNEQ. Presumably, the fourth actual parameter in a use of JNEQ will be 0 (indicating fixed-point) or 1 (indicating floating-point). The macro body might be written:

```
MACRO   JNEQ(A,B,GOTO,TYPE)
LOAD    A
IF      TYPE
SUB     B
IF      TYPE-1
SUBFL   B
JNONZ   GOTO
ENDM
```

The use JNEQ X, Y, NO, 1 is replaced by:

```
LOAD    X
IF      1
SUB     Y
IF      1-1
SUBFL   Y
JNONZ   NO
```

When processing the above instructions, we find that IF 1 has an expression whose value is not 0, so we remove both IF 1 and the following instruction, SUB Y, from the list of instructions. However, IF 1 − 1 evaluates to 0, so the following instruction, SUBFL Y, is not removed, leaving:

```
LOAD    X
SUBFL   Y
JNONZ   NO
```

A second useful type of computation in macros is the concatenation of strings to form apparently indivisible components of instructions, such as operation codes or address fields. We shall use ‖ in macro bodies to indicate concatenation (juxtaposition) of strings with no intervening blanks. In our assembly language, which attaches register numbers to operation mnemonics without separation, this feature enables us to pass a register number to a macro as a parameter.

Example 4.13. Suppose we were content to allow JNEQ to handle only fixed-point arguments, but did not wish it necessarily to destroy the contents of register 1 with each use. We can introduce a parameter REG to indicate which register JNEQ should use, as follows:

```
MACRO        JNEQ(A,B,GOTO,REG)
LOAD‖REG     A
SUB‖REG      B
JNONZ‖REG    GOTO
ENDM
```

Then the use JNEQ X, Y, NO, 3 would be expanded as follows:

```
LOAD3    X
SUB3     Y
JNONZ3   NO
```

EXERCISES

4.1 Write pieces of assembly language programs corresponding to the following statements. Use data defining pseudo-operations to indicate storage for all data used by the programs.

a) **for** I = 1 **to** 100 **do**
   for J = 1 **to** 10 **do**
       A(I, J) = I + J

b) **begin**
$$A = 1.5;$$
    repeat
        begin
$$B = (A + 2./A)/2.;$$
$$C = (B - A)**2;$$
$$A = B$$
        end
    until
$$C\ .LE.\ 1.E-5$$
end

4.2 Write an assembly-language program that determines (jumps to YES) if a string of 80 characters (stored in 16 consecutive words of memory) begins with a name field as defined for our assembly language, that is, a (possibly empty) string of blanks, then a string of letters and digits, and a colon. Recall that $(44)_8$ is our code for ƀ and let $(55)_8$ be the code for colon(:).

4.3 Simulate the assembler on the following program. Show the contents of the symbol table at the end of pass one and show the final machine-language program.

```
                LOAD7    =99
      LOOP2:    LOAD3    0(IMMED)
      LOOP1:    LOAD1    A(X3)
                SUBFL1   A+1(X3)
                JPLUS1   *+5
                LOAD1    A(X3)
                LOAD2    A+1(X3)
                STORE1   A+1(X3)
                STORE2   A(X3)
                MOVE31
                SUB1     =99
                JPLUS1   *+3
                ADD3     1(IMMED)
                JUMP     LOOP1
                SUB7     =1
                JPLUS7   LOOP2
                HALT
         A:     BLOCK    100
                END
```

* **4.4** Which of the following programs compute $C = A + B$?

```
a)      LOAD    A       b)      LOAD    A
        JUMP    *+2             ADD     B
  D:    BLOCK   100             STORE   2*B-A
        ADD     B               HALT
        STORE   C       A:      DATA    47
        HALT            B:      DATA    31
  A:    DATA    47      C:      DATA    0
  B:    DATA    31              END
  C:    DATA    0
        END
```

4.5 Which of the following expressions are

a) constant like

b) relocatable (name-like)?

  i) $(A-B)*C$

  ii) $5*A-3*(B+1)$

  iii) $(A+1)*2-B-C$

  iv) $(A+B)*2-3*C$

4.6 Some assemblers permit *doubly relocatable expressions*, which, when $A + \Delta$ is substituted for each variable A, leaves the expression plus 2Δ. Which, if any, of the expressions of Exercise 4.5 are doubly relocatable?

* **4.7** We wish to write a macro WORK (A, B, I) which sets $A = A + B$ if $I \neq 0$ and sets $A = A - B$ if $I = 0$. Why is the following macro unsuitable?

```
            MACRO    WORK(A,B,I)
            LOAD1    I
            LOAD2    A
            JZERO1   SUBTR
            ADD2     B
            JUMP     STO
   SUBTR:   SUB2     B
   STO:     STORE2   A
            ENDM
```

Hint. What happens if the macro is used twice?

4.8 Write a macro WORK as in Exercise 4.7 which does "work."

a) using the IF pseudo-operation of Section 4.10,

b) without using IF.

** **4.9** Suppose we attempt to represent double-precision fixed-point numbers in our computer by two consecutive words with the same sign. The magnitude of the number is bits 2 to 30 of the first word followed by bits 2 to 30 of the second, as described in Section 1.8. Write a macro DBLADD (A, B, C) which adds the double-precision number located in words A and $A + 1$ to that located in B and $B + 1$, storing the result in C and $C + 1$. *Hint.* The disaster check (JDIS) can be used to detect carries from the second word (low-order bits) to the first.

*4.10 Write a macro JNEQ (A, B, GOTO, TYPE, REG) which jumps to GOTO if $A \neq B$, uses register REG for computation and assumes A and B are of type TYPE, where TYPE $= 0$ means fixed-point, TYPE $= 1$ means floating-point, and TYPE $= 2$ means pointer in bits 19 to 30 (do not assume bits 1–18 are zero in this case).

**4.11 Write a macro 3ADD (A, B, C, W, X, Y, Z) which sets $C = A + B$ for floating-point A, B, and C, where $W = 0$ means A is a memory location and $W = 1$ means A is a register number. X and Y are similarly related to B and C. Z gives a register number in which computation may be performed. For example,

$$3ADD \quad 1,Q,2,1,0,1,3$$

should be expanded to:

```
            COPY13
            ADDFL3   Q
            COPY32
```

Programming Exercise

Of course, the natural project for this section is to write an assembler. The project has a wide range of difficulty, depending on the number of "features" implemented. At the lowest level of difficulty, the following project is suggested.

4.12 Write a simple assembler as described in Section 4.3, with the following modifications:

1. All symbolic addresses are single letters. Thus, the symbol table can be implemented as an array of length 26, and we can avoid hashing.

2. A statement label, if it occurs, must be in column 1. No colon is necessary.

3. The operation code must begin in column 3. Note that in our assembly language, each operation code is a sequence of letters, which determine bits 1 to 6, followed by a sequence (possibly none) of numbers which determine bits 7 to 12. One can therefore determine bits 1 to 6 and bits 7 to 12 independently.

4. The address field must begin in column 12.

FURTHER READING

The fundamental paper on the macro assembler is McIlroy [1960]. Barron [1969] is a source for further information about assemblers. Some of the theory pertaining to macro assembly can be found in Wegner [1968].

Chapter 5

Loaders and Link Editors

In real computer systems, almost every program executed has the ability to be put in memory with different beginning addresses (*origins*). The program which places other programs into memory is called a *loader*. Often associated with the loader is a *link editor*, which has the ability to take several programs (typically a main program and its subroutines) and establish communication of data between them.

In this chapter, we shall introduce the ideas of a loader and link editor. We shall also discuss subroutines and give one method of transferring data between a subroutine and the program calling it.

5.1 RELOCATION OF INSTRUCTIONS

We have had our assembler generate computer words that appear to be placed into consecutive memory locations starting with zero. However, the lowest memory locations are usually taken up with words having special significance and are not available to store a program. Moreover, in a large computer system, several programs may appear in main memory at once. Clearly not all these programs can begin at the first location available. We are faced with the problem that the output of the assembler must be able to run when placed in memory starting at any location—a location which the assembler cannot predict in advance.

What actually happens in most computer systems is that a program called a loader sits in memory and places the program to be executed in empty memory locations. The loader may be a separate program or part of a "load and go" assembler or compiler. The loader *relocates* a program by adding a constant c to every string of bits that represents an address. When the loader has placed the program in memory (possibly along with some subroutines), control passes to the first location used for the program. The constant c is chosen so that location c and sufficient locations above c are available to hold the words of the program.

The loader for our computer might be presented with information such as:

Location	Contents
43	1710000012

It is easy to see that c must be added to 43 to tell where the word 1710000012 goes. However, the loader may have to modify the above word if some portion of it refers to a memory location.

The word 1710000012 could have several valid interpretations, among them:

1. a floating-point number, namely .0312501;
2. a string of five characters, F800A in the code for our computer;
3. a fixed-point number;
4. an instruction to shift register 1 left $(10)_{10}$ places; or
5. a pair of pointers in bits 1 to 12 and 19 to 30.

In the first four cases, no modification of the word is necessary, although if the instruction represented in case (4) were any but a shift, it would be necessary to add c to bits 19 to 30. In case (5), we must add c to bits 1 to 12 and 19 to 30, independently.[†]

Since we cannot expect the loader to guess the interpretation of an arbitrary computer word, the assembler must tell it what piece or pieces of each computer word represent locations. The code for this information is somewhat arbitrary, but in general, an assembler (or programmer writing in machine code) must give the following pieces of information about each computer word in the machine-language program:

1. the *offset* (*absolute address*), i.e., the location in which the word should be placed if the program started at location zero;
2. which, if any, bits are part of an address; and
3. the contents of the computer word.

A machine-language program with this information is termed *relocatable*. We see now that Fig. 4.1 describing the role of the assembler is really an oversimplification. A truer picture is found in Fig. 5.1. In fact, the process of link editing, which we shall later discuss, is also present in what we have shown in Fig. 5.1 as "Phase II."

Our assembler generates words in three different classes, as far as relocation is concerned:

1. no bits need be relocated (e.g., shift instructions or DATA pseudo-operation);

[†] If there is a carry from bit 19, the program being loaded will not fit into available memory, and the loader should indicate this fault. In fact, since the loader itself must take up space while doing its job, it is not normally possible to utilize all the highest-numbered memory locations for the program being loaded. Thus, in our computer, certain addresses less than $2^{12} - 1$ must cause a fault.

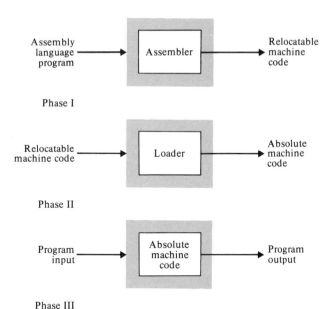

Phase I

Phase II

Phase III

Fig. 5.1   Role of the assembler and loader.

2. bits 19 to 30 must be relocated (e.g., most instructions or the POINTER pseudo-operation);
3. bits 1 to 12 and bits 19 to 30 must be relocated independently (the POINTERS pseudo-operation).

Thus, if our assembler is to produce relocatable programs, it must produce triples of the form: offset-relocation code-contents. The offset is the value of the location counter at the time the word is generated by the assembler. The relocation code is 1, 2, or 3, with code i indicating case (i) above. The contents are the 30 bits which are to be placed in the location by the loader, subject to modification according to the relocation code.

Example 5.1.   The program in Fig. 5.2 reads the first five characters of 100 cards. It sets up a linked list of 100 records of two words each. The first word of each record will hold the five characters and the second will hold a pointer to the next record in bits 19 to 30 (zeros indicate the end of the list). We use B, a block of 200 words, to hold the list. Register 1 will point to the next available record and will also be used to count the 100 cards to be read. BUFFER will hold the five characters when they are read in.

We shall make the reasonable convention that whenever the address field of an instruction is a name-like expression (including a symbolic address as the usual case) the assembler will assume the address portion to be relocatable. If the address field is constant-like (including a constant, of course), we shall assume it is not relocatable.

Instruction number (decimal)		Instruction	
1		LOAD1	0(IMMED)
2		READ1	READPTR
3		LOAD2	BUFFER
4		STORE2	B(X1)
5		ADD1	2(IMMED)
6		STORE1	B-1(X1)
7		COPY13	
8		SUB3	200(IMMED)
9		JMINUS3	*-7
10		HALT	
11	BUFFER:	DATA	0
12	READPTR:	POINTERS	BUFFER,BUFFER
13	B:	BLOCK	200
		END	

Fig. 5.2   Sample program.

A literal should be treated as name-like and relocated, since a location will be generated to hold the value of the literal. This location must be relocated along with the rest of the program.

With this convention in mind, we see that instructions numbered 1, 5, 7, 8, 10, 11, and 13 yield words that are not relocated (relocation code 1). Instruction 12 requires both the leftmost and rightmost 12 bits to be relocated (code 3), and the remaining instructions have their rightmost 12 bits relocated (code 2). The assembler thus produces the triples shown in Fig. 5.3.

Offset	Relocation code	Contents
0	1	0101200000
1	2	2701000013
2	2	0102000012
3	2	0120010014
4	1	0210200002
5	2	0110010013
6	1	0113000000
7	1	0430200310
10	2	2330000001
11	1	0000000000
12	1	0000000000
13	3	0012000012
14	1	0000000000
⋮	⋮	⋮
323	1	0000000000

Fig. 5.3   Relocatable code produced from program of Fig. 5.2.

Suppose the loader wishes to load the program with origin $(500)_8$. Then Fig. 5.4 summarizes the actions taken by the loader. We see that $(500)_8$ is added to the right-most 12 bits of instructions with relocation codes 2 and 3, and that $(500)_8$ is also added to the leftmost 12 bits of instruction 13 with relocation code 3. ∎

Into location	Place the word
500	0101200000
501	2701000513
502	0102000512
503	0120010514
504	0210200002
505	0110010513
506	0113000000
507	0430200310
510	2330000501
511	0000000000
512	0000000000
513	0512000512
514	0000000000
⋮	⋮
1023	0000000000

Fig. 5.4   Placement of program of Fig. 5.2.

It should also be observed that if a programmer wishes to program in machine language and use the loader, he must restrict himself to the relocation codes accepted by the loader. For example the programmer could, if he wished, treat bits 10 to 21 of the words of our computer as an address; however, there would be no appropriate relocation code if he did this.

5.2   LOADING IN A MACHINE WITH BASE REGISTERS

For various reasons, many machines are designed to include an additional address modification similar to indexing for almost every instruction. The register utilized for this extra, mandatory indexing is called a *base register*. For example, on the IBM 360/370 series machines, 16 bits are used for the address portion of instructions, but the first four of these specify one of 16 possible base registers.

Using base registers, almost all addresses need no relocation. The strategy for using base registers is to attempt to keep the base-register contents fixed; however, as long as the base register is fixed, the number of different locations which can be referred to via this base register is limited. In the case of the 360/370 arrangement, only 12 bits of the address portion may be used for a total of 4096 different bytes[†] or 1024 words.

[†] Recall these machines address each byte of eight bits individually.

If the program references more than this number of words, two strategies may be used.

1. Change the value in the base register as needed.
2. Use several different base registers and keep each fixed.

The advantage of the base register concept as far as the loading of programs is concerned is that almost no address needs relocation. The only relocation which the loader must then perform is on the instructions which load base registers. By adding c to the constant loaded into a base register, we can increment every address using that base register by c. In fact, if the base registers remain fixed throughout the program, the loader itself could set the base register.

Let us suppose, for the purposes of this section only, that our computer uses base registers. We shall use bits 19 to 21 to indicate which of registers 1 to 7 is being used as a base register for the address. The remaining 9 bits will be treated as the address, subject to modification by adding the contents of the base register *before* any address modification indicated in bits 13 to 18.

Example 5.2. The instruction

0 1 0 1	42	7	0 3 3

loads register 1 with the contents of the location ℓ computed as follows.

1. Add $(33)_8$ to the contents of register 7 (the base register) to obtain location ℓ_1.
2. Add location ℓ_1 to the contents of register 2 (the index register) to obtain location ℓ_2.
3. Since indirect-right addressing is next called for, we consult bits 19 to 30 of location ℓ_2. Let bits 19 to 21 of ℓ_2 have octal digit b (the base register for this address) and bits 22 to 30 have ℓ_3. Then ℓ is ℓ_3 plus the contents of register b. ∎

A little reflection will serve to determine that for each form of address modification allowed in our computer, we might or might not want to make a base register part of the address. Intuitively, if an assembly instruction has a relocatable address, then when converting the instruction to the machine code of our computer with base registers, we shall want a base register in the address. If the address of the assembly instruction is not relocatable, then we do not want to use a base register. Fortunately the following convention will serve in most cases, and we adopt it for the interpretation of addresses in our computer with base registers. We take bits 19 to 21 to indicate a base register unless immediate address modification is called for (bits 13 to 15 hold 1 or 2).

Example 5.3. Let us convert the program of Example 5.1 to machine code for our computer with base registers. The entire program is less than 512 words long, and all words could be accessed with one base register kept fixed. However, to demonstrate the versatility of base register use, let us divide the program into two *segments*:

the first consisting of the executable instructions; the second of the data, each having its own base register. Then a loader can place the instructions and data in separate portions of the memory, and the instructions will be able to access the data independent of its distance, provided base registers 5 and 6 are set properly.

We use base register 5 for the segment containing instructions and base register 6 for the data segment. The machine code generated from the program of Fig. 5.2 is shown in Fig. 5.5.

Instruction segment, base register 5

Offset	Contents
0	0101200000
1	2701006001
2	0102006000
3	0120016002
4	0210200002
5	0110016001
6	0113000000
7	0430200310
10	2330005001
11	0000000000

Data segment, base register 6

Offset	Contents
0	0000000000
1	6000006000
2	0000000000
⋮	
311	0000000000

Fig. 5.5   Machine code for our computer with base registers generated from Fig. 5.2.

For example, the instruction STORE1 B-1(X1) gets address 6001. The 6 stands for base register 6. The 001 is selected for bits 22 to 30, since the address B-1 is the second word (offset 1) of the data. Instruction JMINUS3 $*-7$ gets address 5001, since $*-7$ is an address in the instruction segment, requiring base register 5, and the particular word of that segment denoted by $*-7$ happens to be the second (offset 1, again).

Suppose we wish to load the first segment into locations beginning at 1000 and the second segment into locations beginning at 2000. The loader could place 1000 in register 5 and 2000 in register 6. It would then place the word of segment 1 with offset i in location $1000 + i$ and the word of segment 2 having offset i in location $2000 + i$. ∎

Observe from Example 5.3 that when we loaded a program for our computer with base registers, we did not have to worry about which instructions were relocatable, because none were. The loader had only to copy the instructions from secondary memory to main memory and initialize the base registers for the two segments. This circumstance is quite convenient, since it minimizes the loader's job.

All is not as simple as we made it appear in Example 5.3, however. A program may require that base registers change their values. For example, we may wish to use only one register as a base register so that the remainder are available for computation. Then, if the program were longer than the number of words that could be accessed with a set base register (512 words for this version of our computer), we would be forced to change the value held in the base register from time to time. The instructions that placed a new value in a base register would have to be relocated by the loader. To facilitate changing base register values while a program is running, two things are necessary.

1. The assembly language must have a pseudo-operation with which the programmer can indicate to the assembler the base register that will be used, and its value (relative to the beginning of the program) at various points in the program.

2. The loader must receive a list of the relocatable statements of the program from the assembler.†

5.3 EXTERNAL REFERENCES

Most assemblers give the programmer the option of defining the location represented by certain symbolic addresses when the assembled program is loaded, rather than when the program is assembled. One use of such a feature is to allow several subroutines to access the same data, much the way COMMON data is used in FORTRAN.

Another important use of this idea is with subroutines. That is, a main program is compiled (if in a high-level programming language) or assembled separately from its subroutines. It may also call upon some library subroutines that are available in relocatable machine-language form. Each subroutine knows that it is a subroutine, and it knows by what name it will be called. The main program and each subroutine calling another uses the name of that subroutine.

Suppose that the main program calls a subroutine named XYZ. What must physically happen is that the main program stores in a designated place (usually a specific register) that place to which XYZ must return control when it finishes. It is important to record the place to return (the *return address*), since there may be several places which call subroutine XYZ. Then, the main program transfers to the

---

† Note that there will be comparatively few instructions requiring relocation, so a list of those requiring relocation will probably be far more efficient than providing a relocation/nonrelocation bit for each instruction. Contrast this situation with the problem of providing relocation information for our computer (without base registers). There, about half the instructions required relocation and half did not, so providing a relocation code with each instruction was as efficient a scheme as exists.

The reader should perceive a general rule about encoding information. If there are two (or more) alternatives, and one occurs almost invariably, then make a list of the exceptions. If several different alternatives occur frequently, use a sequence of bits to represent the information.

entry of XYZ. Normally, the entry of a subroutine is its first instruction, although it could be otherwise. In fact, a subroutine may have more than one entry.

Example 5.4. Suppose the entry of a subroutine is an instruction named ENTRY. Suppose also that the main program and the subroutine have "agreed" that when the subroutine is called, register 7 will hold the location to which the subroutine must jump to give control back to the calling program. Then the following instructions serve to call the subroutine:

```
LOAD7   *+2(IMMED)
JUMP    ENTRY
```

When the jump to ENTRY occurs, bits 19 to 30 of register 7 will hold the location following the JUMP instruction.

The subroutine must be careful not to disturb register 7. If it wishes to return to the return address, it executes the instruction JUMP 0(X7). This instruction transfers control to the location found in bits 19 to 30 of register 7. That is, the next instruction which the computer will execute is the one following the instruction of the main program which transferred to the subroutine.

It should be emphasized that there may be several apparently identical pairs of instructions:

```
LOAD7   *+2(IMMED)
JUMP    ENTRY
```

within the program. However, since * always represents the location of the instruction in which it appears, each such sequence will be assembled into different machine instructions. Thus, by the instruction JUMP 0(X7) the subroutine will return to whichever one of these places caused the jump to the subroutine. ▌

Suppose we are assembling a program which makes reference to an entry, say ENTRY, of a subroutine. Since ENTRY is not a location of the program being assembled, it is not possible for the assembler to replace ENTRY by a location. The subroutine containing ENTRY may not be assembled until tomorrow, or may not be assembled at all, if it is written in, say, FORTRAN. Therefore the assembly language must have some provision to tell the assembler that a given symbolic address is *external*; that is, it refers to a location of some other program which will be loaded with the program being assembled.

The assembler in turn needs a method of telling the loader that part of the contents of a word represents an external name and must be replaced by the location of that name. The routine which matches external names of one program with their locations in other programs is called a *link editor*.

In many systems, the link editor joins a main program and its subroutines together into one relocatable program with no external references. This program is called a *load module*. The load module may then be passed to the loader and placed in memory as in Sections 5.1 or 5.2.

Let us now consider how an assembly program can indicate an external name and how the assembler might pass the information to the loader and link editor.

We can use a pseudo-operation such as

$$\text{EXTERNAL } \alpha$$

to indicate that α is an external name, either a piece of data or a subroutine entry. In the case that α is a datum, it can be referenced like any other address, for example, LOAD α. However, the assembler has no way of knowing how to generate a triple of offset-relocation code-contents for LOAD α. The presence of α in an EXTERNAL pseudo-operation alerts the assembler to the fact that α is external, so only bits 1 to 18 of the word for LOAD α can be determined by the assembler. Our assembler will use relocation code 4 to indicate that bits 19 to 30 of the word must be determined by the link editor. We shall see how in Section 5.5. In the next section, however, we consider in more detail how subroutine calls are handled in assembly language.

5.4 SUBROUTINE LINKAGES

Our assembly language will have a pseudo-operation:

$$\text{CALL } \alpha(\beta_1, \ldots, \beta_n).$$

The meaning of this instruction is intended to be the same as that of a FORTRAN subroutine call. The subroutine (and its entry, as well)[†] is named α and its arguments are $\beta_1, \ldots, \beta_n$—which we restrict here to be either symbolic addresses or constants.

The assembler treats the CALL pseudo-operation almost as though it were a macro standing for the following code, known as a *calling sequence*.[‡]

```
EXTERNAL    α
LOAD        *+2(IMMED)
JUMP        α
POINTER     β'₁
POINTER     β'₂
              .
              .
              .
POINTER     β'ₙ
```

Here, β'_i stands for β_i if β_i is a symbolic address. If β_i is a constant, however, then β'_i is $= \beta_i$, a literal.[§]

[†] In what follows, we shall not distinguish between a subroutine and its entry. More precisely, we assume each subroutine has one entry and that the name of the subroutine is the name of the entry.

[‡] In fact, had we defined macros with variable numbers of operands, as are available in most assembly languages, it would be preferable for the user to define his own macros generating calling sequences as he wished.

[§] A better arrangement is to make β'_i the address of a DATA β_i instruction. This way, should the subroutine change the value of its ith argument, it will not change the value of the literal β_i, which may be used many times by the calling program and should not be changed.

Example 5.5. CALL *XYZ*(A, 1, B) is treated as though it were:

```
        EXTERNAL  XYZ
        LOAD7     *+2(IMMED)
        JUMP      XYZ
        POINTER   A
        POINTER   =1
        POINTER   B
```

As before, the assembler can translate each of these instructions into triples of offset-relocation code-contents, with the exception of the instruction JUMP *XYZ*. The latter is treated like any other external name. ∎

In the next example we shall see that once the link editor has replaced the external reference (*XYZ* above) by the actual entry of the subroutine, the CALL pseudo-operation and its resulting calling sequence are sufficient for the called subroutine to obtain its arguments. In truth, there are many methods of making arguments available to a subroutine; we shall discuss the principal ones in Chapter 6.[†] Here we shall consider only the scheme we have already introduced, *call by reference* (also known as *call by location* or *address*). A distinguishing feature of this method is that the subroutine, by using the register set to hold the return address (register 7 above), can find pointers to the values of its arguments.[‡]

Let us now consider an example of how a subroutine can be written to obtain and use the values of its arguments when call by reference is used.

Example 5.6. Let us suppose that XYZ is a subroutine which makes its third argument equal to the sum of its first two arguments. If XYZ is called by reference, the calling sequence generated from CALL XYZ(A, 1, B) is the one given in Example 5.5. Fig. 5.6 shows the pointers in the calling sequence. The order of *A*, *B* and =1 in the main memory may differ from that shown, and assembly instructions are used to represent their machine language equivalent.

To bring the value of *A*, for example, to a register, XYZ must use a combination of indexing by register 7 followed by indirect addressing. In particular, the instruction LOAD1 0(INDX7) will first find the location pointed to by register 7 and then follow the pointer found there to the location of *A*. The value of *A* will thus be brought to register 1. One possible program for XYZ is:

```
        ENTRY   XYZ
XYZ:    LOAD1   0(INDX7)
        ADD1    1(INDX7)
        STORE1  2(INDX7)
        JUMP    3(X7)
        END
```

[†] The choice of a method is not arbitrary, as subtle differences in the results produced by subroutines occur when different linkage conventions are used.

[‡] As an example of an alternative, we would instead have used *call by value*, where the values of the arguments *A*, 1 and *B* would have been placed in the calling sequence instead of pointers to those values as we do for call by reference.

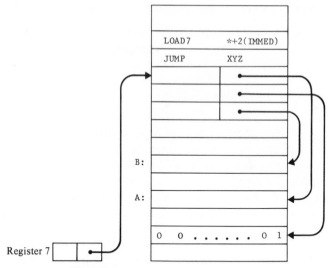

Fig. 5.6   Pointers for call by reference.

We are using ENTRY as a pseudo-operation to tell the assembler that XYZ is a name which will be referred to as an external name by another program. The above six instructions can be assembled in isolation, without the assembler knowing about any program which calls XYZ.

Observe that the jump to 3(X7) returns control to the point immediately after the locations used to pass parameters to XYZ.   ∎

It should be noted that a good discipline to follow is to ensure that a subroutine leaves the arithmetic registers with the same contents they held when the subroutine was called. The subroutine would have its own storage locations to hold the initial contents of whatever registers it uses. These registers would then be restored just before the subroutine returned control to the calling program.

Example 5.7.   The subroutine XYZ of Example 5.6 keeps all registers but number 1 intact. We could write XYZ as in Fig. 5.7 to store the contents of register 1 into a location REG1 available for that purpose. Register 1 is then reloaded from REG1 just before the return.   ∎

```
             ENTRY   XYZ
      XYZ:   STORE1  REG1
             LOAD1   0(INDX7)
             ADD1    1(INDX7)
             STORE1  2(INDX7)
             LOAD1   REG1
             JUMP    3(X7)
      REG1:  DATA    0
             END
```

Fig. 5.7   Subroutine XYZ with Register 1 preserved.

5.5 IMPLEMENTATION OF A LINK EDITOR

Let us now resolve the question of how the assembler loader and link editor are to handle subroutine calls and other external references. As we have seen, the assembler can generate calling sequences from CALL statements almost as if CALL were a macro. However, there are several differences between the treatment of a CALL instruction, in our examples, and the treatment of a macro.

1. The format of the CALL pseudo-operation differs slightly from the format for the use of a macro. That is, CALL XYZ(A, B, C) would probably be written CALL XYZ, A, B, C if CALL were a macro. This difference should not present great difficulty to the person writing the assembler. In the first pass, one observes the CALL pseudo-operation and breaks what follows into its constituent parts in an obvious manner, e.g., XYZ(A, B, C) into XYZ, A, B, and C.

2. The CALL statement takes a variable number of arguments, while we have defined only macros with a fixed number of arguments. This difference again presents little difficulty, since the assembler treats each argument of the subroutine similarly. For example, in the calling sequence one instruction POINTER β_i' is generated for each argument β_i, independent of the total number of arguments.

3. The most important difference, however, is that in the CALL statement, it is not possible to directly assemble the instruction JUMP α, where α is the name of the subroutine. The best the assembler can do is to leave the string of characters α in place and assemble the rest of the program.[†] The link editor then substitutes an appropriate address for α when it knows the location into which it places the entry α.

We can draw an analogy between the way an assembler determines the location for each symbolic address and the way a link editor determines the location for external names. As the assembler scans its input, it sees uses of symbolic addresses (address fields) and locations for symbolic addresses (name fields). Not every use is preceded by its location. Therefore the assembler must make two passes, one to gather all the locations for the symbolic addresses and the second to substitute locations for the symbolic addresses.

Similarly, the link editor encounters uses of certain symbolic addresses (external names) and locations for these names (the entries of subroutines or pseudo-operations defining data referenced externally). Depending on the order in which

---

Actually, what is done in many cases is that the assembler gives distinct numbers, 1, 2, ..., to each external name referenced. The number then replaces the character string. The fact that the number i refers to the ith external name, rather than location i, is indicated by a special relocation code, say 4 for our computer. A table associating external names and their numbers is included with the assembler's output. The advantage of such a scheme is that it allows each instruction output from the assembler to have the same length, while the presence of character strings of arbitrary length prevents this uniformity.

An alternative is for the assembler to generate a special word, tacked on to the beginning or end of the program, for each external name. To jump to external address α, we execute JUMP β(IND), where β is the address of the special word for external name α. Since the assembler knows the location of β, no special relocation code is necessary. The link editor will place the address of α in β before loading. This scheme is known as the *transfer vector* approach.

the main program and its subroutines are presented to the link editor, the use of a name may precede its location.

We may thus think of two passes for the link editor. As programs are scanned, the link editor makes a table of all the places where external names are used and a table of the location for each name referenced to externally. When all such locations are known, the link editor can, in a second pass, substitute a location for each external name in each program.

A common use of the link editor is in the construction of a *load module* from a main program and its subroutines. The load module is constructed by scanning the main program and subroutines, resolving the uses of external names as we have described above, as though the programs would be loaded consecutively starting at location zero (see Fig. 5.8). The addresses of jump instructions to subroutines and

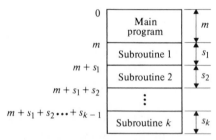

Fig. 5.8   A load module.

other references to external data are made relocatable (relocation code 1). A load module is thus a relocatable machine-language program with no external references. It consists of a main program and all of its subroutines, whether programmer written or library routines. The entire process of transforming an assembly-language program into executable machine code is summarized in Fig. 5.9.

EXERCISES

5.1 Give the triples (offset-relocation code-contents) which the assembler would produce as output given the assembly language programs of

a) Example 4.3 (p. 129).

b) The answers to Exercise 4.1 (p. 140).

c) The program of Exercise 4.3 (p. 141).

5.2 Load the programs of Exercise 5.1, beginning at location 300.

5.3 Rewrite the programs of Exercise 5.1 to be run on our computer with base registers, as defined in Section 5.2. Assume each program, including its data, uses base register 7.

5.4 Give the calling sequence to be generated from CALL SUB(A, 4, B, C), assuming call by reference as in Section 5.3.

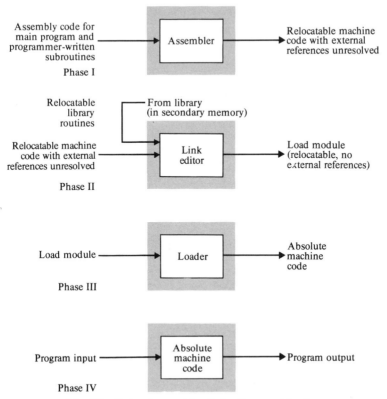

Fig. 5.9 Role of assembler, link editor, and loader.

5.5 Write subroutine SUB(W, X, Y, Z) which sets Y to $W + X$ and Z to $W - X$, if the call is by reference. Preserve the values of any registers used by your subroutine.

* **5.6** Write a subroutine MM(A, B, C, N) which multiplies two $N \times N$ matrices A and B, placing the result in C. MM is to be called by reference, with pointers to the first locations of blocks holding A, B, and C as the first three parameters. Assume that the element of A in row I and column J is in word $N * (I - 1) + J$ of the block for A and similarly for B and C.

* **5.7** Some computers do not have indirect addressing. Show how without using indirect addressing one could write subroutines called by reference

a) using indexing on our computer without base registers

b) on our computer with base registers. *Hint:* Use a base register to indicate the place from whence the call came.

Programming Exercise

5.8 The natural exercise for this chapter is to write a simple link editor and loader. Your program will receive input from cards rather than from an assembler, and the cards will be in the following format; almost every card represents one triple of offset-relocation code-contents.

1. Columns 1 to 3 will be a generalized relocation code, as follows
   000 –address of contents (columns 36 to 47) is external
   001 ⎫
   010 ⎬ –same as relocation codes 1 to 3 from Section 5.1.
   011 ⎭
   100 –card indicates beginning of subroutine (The first "subroutine" is the main program.)
   101 –card indicates end of subroutine

2. If columns 1 to 3 hold 000 through 011, then columns 5 to 16 are the offset of the instruction and columns 18 to 47 are the contents. In the case of relocation code 000, columns 36 to 47 are an "external name." We take all external names to be integers between 0 and $2^{12} - 1$, for convenience.

3. If columns 1 to 3 hold 100, then columns 5 to 16 are the name of the subroutine. These names are integers between 0 and $2^{12} - 1$, as those integers are the only permissible external names.

4. If columns 1 to 3 hold 101, then the rest of the card is blank.

   Your loader and link editor must resolve external references and load routines into memory, beginning at location $(100)_8$; i.e., the words of memory occupied and the contents of each must be listed. References to external names which are not among the subroutine names loaded should be detected and a warning printed. Another warning should be printed if an address exceeds $2^{12} - 1$ after relocation.

FURTHER READING

The reader can consult Barron [1969] or Presser and White [1972] for more information on loaders and link editors.

Chapter 6

Basic Programming Language Concepts

The remainder of this book is devoted to various topics in the field of programming languages. This chapter and the next are devoted to the terminology associated with programming languages. In Chapters 8 and 9 we discuss aspects of compiling, the algorithms whereby programs written in a high-level programming language are translated to assembly or machine code. Finally, Chapter 10 discusses how to prove programs correct. Knowledge of this field, if properly understood, can be an aid both in writing programs correctly and in debugging them. The first section of this chapter provides a more detailed overview to Chapters 6 and 7.

6.1 AN OVERVIEW OF PROGRAMMING LANGUAGES

There are at least four separate issues to which we must address ourselves to develop an understanding of programming languages.

1. How do we determine the legal programs in a given programming language? The specification of legal programs is called the *syntax* of a language. In Chapter 8 we shall discuss "context-free grammars," a useful tool for specifying the syntax of programming languages and an aid in building compilers as well.

2. What is the meaning of a given program?

3. What machine code should the compiler generate in response to a given program?

4. How should we design a compiler to translate programs from the programming language in which they are written to the proper machine code as defined by question (3)? Chapter 9 discusses compiler design.

It should not go unobserved that questions (2) and (3) are related. In fact, an answer to (3) is in a sense an answer to (2), since if we know what the computer should do to "simulate" a program, we must know what that program "means." Often the term *semantics* of programming languages is applied to the issues raised by Questions (2) and (3). Chapter 9 will mention "syntax-directed translation schemes," a tool that aids in specifying the answers to (2), or more often (3), in much the way that the context-free grammars of Chapter 8 will help answer question (1).

In this book we shall sometimes wish to make a distinction between questions (2) and (3). For question (2) we shall refer to the *abstract meaning* of programming language features, and for question (3) we shall use the term *implementation*. As an example of the distinction between the abstract meaning and the implementation of a programming-language feature, consider the following.

Example 6.1. Let us consider the assignment statement $A = B + C$. The identifiers A, B, and C have as an abstract meaning that they denote quantities (probably real numbers or integers, though we could not be certain without seeing possible declarations in the program containing this assignment). Let us say that A, B, and C denote integers. In their abstract meaning, the integers can be of any size; they do not have to fit into a computer word.

For an implementation of $A = B + C$ we might take:

```
LOAD    B
ADD     C
STORE   A
```

or an equivalent sequence of computer instructions. On the implementation level we might concern ourselves with the fact that A, B and C are represented in fixed-point by single computer words of some specified length. Thus they are subject to the vagaries discussed in Section 1.5, such as possible violations of the associative law that do not afflict integers on the abstract level.

For a second example, the abstract meaning of an associative structure is effectively described by Fig. 3.12 (p. 100). To describe one implementation of an associative structure we might specify a scatter store, describe the amount of memory to be allocated for the hash and data storage tables, and provide programs to compute the hash function, handle collisions, and enter and retrieve data from the data storage table (as in Section 3.8). ∎

There is a second, orthogonal way in which we shall partition programming-language concepts. We can view programming languages as built from a hierarchy of objects, beginning with identifiers at the lowest level. Identifiers are the primary constituents of expressions, which are, in turn, formed into statements. In their turn, statements are formed into subprograms. By a *subprogram* we mean a piece of a program having the capability of defining its own identifiers. Examples of subprograms are **begin** . . . **end** blocks and procedures in ALGOL or PL/I, or subroutines in FORTRAN. Clearly a program is a special case of a subprogram.

In the area of identifiers, we shall first discuss (Section 6.2) the basic identifier types, from the point of view of both their abstract meaning and their implementation. In Section 6.3 we discuss the implementation of arrays. Next, we consider the distinction between dynamic and static storage allocation for identifiers (Section 6.4) and discuss an implementation of dynamic storage allocation in Section 6.5. Chapter 7 is also concerned to a large extent with one type of dynamic storage allocation called stack allocation.

The next portion of this chapter is devoted to expressions. Some useful terminology concerned with the syntax of expressions—operators in particular—is discussed in Section 6.6. Section 6.7 introduces the two kinds of meaning associated with expressions, often called ℓ- and r-values. An ℓ-value is the abstract meaning or implementation of an expression on the left of an assignment symbol; usually this value is a location in memory. An r-value is similarly the value of an expression appearing on the right side of an assignment, e.g., a numerical value.

The abstract meaning and implementation of statements is covered briefly in Section 6.8.

Finally, in Sections 6.9 through 6.12 as well as in Chapter 7, we cover issues at the subprogram level of the hierarchy. Section 6.9 covers binding of identifiers. If one subprogram, such as a subroutine, makes mention of an identifier X, to which of the possibly many X's defined as identifiers by various subprograms does this mention of X refer? The answer depends not only on the program in question, but on the identifier binding rules of the programming language in which it is written. Sections 6.10 through 6.12 discuss parameter passing between a routine and one of its subroutines. We have already discussed the implementation of one form of parameter passing, call-by-reference, in Section 5.3. Some other methods of passing parameters will now be covered, from the point of view of both their abstract meaning and their implementation. Finally, Chapter 7 will be devoted in its entirety to the important subject of recursion and its implementation in machine language.

The scope of Chapters 6 through 9, expressed in terms of the two dimensional partition of programming-language concepts discussed above, is illustrated in Fig. 6.1.

	Syntax	Abstract meaning	Implementation	Compilation
Identifiers		Identifier types — Section 6.2 Arrays — Section 6.3 Dynamic/static storage — Section 6.4 Dynamic storage allocation — Section 6.5		Compilers Chapter 9
Expressions	Types of operators Section 6.6	ℓ-values and r-values — Section 6.7		
Statements		Types of statements — Section 6.8		
Subprograms		Binding of identifiers — Section 6.9 Parameter passing — Sections 6.10–6.12 Recursion — Chapter 7		
General	Context-free grammars — Chapter 8	Syntax directed translation — Sections 9.9–9.11		

Fig. 6.1 Division of programming-language concepts.

6.2 IDENTIFIERS AND THEIR IMPLEMENTATION

Identifiers are used in programming languages to represent elementary pieces of data which the program will manipulate.[†] It should be borne in mind that each identifier in a program ultimately represents a single computer word, a fraction of one word, or a consecutive block of computer words (with the possible exception of certain identifiers representing data structures). It is to be expected that each identifier will represent data of a type that is easily handled by the computer.

For example, most computers can do integer (fixed-point) arithmetic, so most programming languages allow certain identifiers to denote integers. When the program is compiled, we can expect that the computer words represented by integer identifiers will be operated upon by fixed-point arithmetic operations.

Let us enumerate some of the types of identifiers permitted in various programming languages. Not all these "types" represent mutually exclusive properties (or *attributes* as they are usually called). For example, an identifier can be both integer and double precision.

1. *Integers* (*Fixed-Point Numbers*). Recall Example 6.1 (p. 162) which discusses the distinction between the abstract meaning of an integer and its implementation as a fixed-point number.

2. *Real* (*Floating-Point*) *Numbers.* Identifiers whose abstract meaning is that of a real number are implemented by single computer words and by floating-point arithmetic.

3. *Complex Numbers.* An identifier whose abstract meaning is that of a complex number can be implemented by two consecutive computer words, the first of which represents the real part and the second the imaginary part. Usually, the real and imaginary parts are represented by floating-point numbers. These numbers can be added, subtracted, or multiplied in the normal way for complex numbers. Usually, more than one machine instruction is involved when an arithmetic operation is applied to complex numbers.

4. *Multiple Precision Numbers.* Numbers, either integer or real, in k-tuple precision can be stored in k consecutive computer words. They can be manipulated in the usual arithmetic ways. Many machines have single instructions for double-precision arithmetic operations. If these are not available, or if more than double precision is involved, a sequence of machine instructions or a subroutine can be used for an arithmetic operation on multiple precision numbers.

5. *Pointers.* A variable which acts as a pointer is stored in one word, or perhaps part of a word. A programming language permitting pointer variables will have operators to manipulate them. Such manipulation would include instructions to make a particular pointer variable, say A, point to a particular identifier, say B. In

---

[†] Identifiers also denote objects other than data, particularly labels and subroutines. The meaning of a label should be obvious, and we shall discuss aspects of subroutine implementation later in this chapter and in the next.

the machine language equivalent, the address of B would be placed in the location reserved for A. Immediate addressing is particularly useful here.

Example 6.2. We can make A point to B by the instructions:

```
LOAD   B(IMMED)
STORE  A
```

The location named A will then hold a pointer to B in bits 19 to 30.

Another essential pointer manipulation is to use the pointer to refer to the object it points to. We might encounter a statement that said "Let C have the value of the thing pointed to by A." In our machine language, we can use the indirect mode of address:

```
LOAD   A(IND)
STORE  C
```

6. *Bit Strings.* These are usually of fixed length, but they may require more than one word, and their length may not be an even multiple of the word length of the computer. The usual operations on bit strings are logical "and," "or," "exclusive or," and "not." If the length of a bit string identifier is declared, the compiler knows the number of words used for the bit string and whether any bits of the last word are not part of the string.

Example 6.3. Let us consider several bit strings of length 50, each stored in two consecutive words of our computer. The last 10 bits of the second words are not used and may hold anything. Suppose we wish to compute $C = A \wedge B$, where A, B, and C are each bit strings of length 50, and A, B, and C are the symbolic addresses of the first words used for each string. The following is code to do the assignment:

```
LOAD   A
AND    B
STORE  C
LOAD   A+1
AND    B+1
STORE  C+1
```

Suppose we now wished to test if C was all 0's, and jump to ZEROS if so. We must first make sure that the last 10 bits of location $C + 1$ are zero. (They might not be if, for example, we had at some time done the assignment $C = \neg C$ in the obvious way.) The following code makes the test:

```
LOAD   C
JNONZ  *+4
LOAD   C+1
AND    =OCTAL7777776000
JZERO  ZEROS
```

7. *Boolean Variables.* These are in effect a special case of a bit string, the case in which the string is of length 1. Since the length is known and the "string" always fits

in one word, there is little trouble representing a Boolean variable in the computer. Often, a whole word is made available for a single Boolean variable but, if space is important, then many can be placed in one computer word.

The two values a Boolean variable may take are often referred to as **true** and **false**, rather than 1 and 0. When translated to machine language, however, 1 replaces **true** and 0 replaces **false**. In some languages, any nonzero value is taken as **true**.

8. *Character Strings.* If a string of characters is of fixed length, its implementation is much the same as that of a bit string. A fixed-length block of consecutive words is allocated for the string. Some languages, such as SNOBOL, permit character strings of arbitrary length, and here implementation of character strings is more difficult. The machine-language program produced by the compiler must have an available space list of some kind. We shall discuss one method of providing this space in Section 6.5.

Implementation of varying length character strings is simplified if the programmer is required to declare a maximum possible length for the string, as in PL/I. Then, an available space list is not necessary. The compiler can simply allocate sufficient space to hold a string of the maximum possible length. The current length of the string can be indicated by selecting the first k bits of the first word, for some k fixed in advance, to hold the current length of the string. An alternative method is to use some byte which has no meaning as a character (called an *endmarker*) to follow the character string.

Example 6.4. Suppose we have a character string named X of maximum length 7 whose current value is *ABCDE*. Using the first mentioned scheme we could allocate two words for X, with the first byte of the first word holding the current length. The current value of X would then be:

$$0512131415$$
$$16????????$$

The question marks indicate octal digits whose value is irrelevant.

Using the second scheme, we might suppose that $(77)_8$ does not represent a character in our computer's character code. Then the value of X would be:

$$1213141516$$
$$77????????$$ ▌

An important operation on character strings, called *concatenation*, should be mentioned. The concatenation of string α with string β is α followed by β. For example, if the value of α is DEFG and that of β is ABC, then the value of $\alpha\|\beta$[†] is DEFGABC. Exercises 6.3 to 6.5 contain a discussion of how the concatenation operation can be carried out.

[†] We use the symbol $\|$ for concatenation, as in Chapter 4.

6.3 ARRAYS

The most common data structure available in programming languages is the array. Abstractly, an array is a collection of elements of some fixed data type. We visualize the elements as arranged in a k-dimensional grid for some fixed k. Along each dimension, grid points between some limits are filled with elements; no elements exist outside those limits.

Syntactically, the usual representation of a k-dimensional array is to provide an identifier name, say A, for the entire array. $A(I_1, I_2, \ldots, I_k)$ denotes the element at the grid point whose coordinate along the jth grid axis is equal to the value of I_j, for each j, $1 \leqslant j \leqslant k$.

The implementation of an array is normally by a block of consecutive words, with the various elements stored according to a formula such as the ones we shall develop below. To begin, let us consider arrays as defined in FORTRAN, where the occupied grid points along each coordinate run from 1 to some fixed upper limit defined in advance by a DIMENSION statement.

Under these assumptions, a one-dimensional array A whose elements require one word each is usually stored so that A names the first location of the block, and $A(I)$ is stored in the Ith location of the block. Thus, in our computer we may bring $A(I)$ to register 1 by a sequence such as:

```
LOAD2   I
LOAD1   A-1(X2)
```

Note that the address of the second instruction is $A - 1$ rather than A. For example, if the current value of I is 1, we wish to bring the contents of A itself to register 1. With LOAD A(X2) we would instead bring location $A + 1$, which holds $A(2)$, to register 1.

A two dimensional array A of m rows by n columns can be stored row by row (in *row major* form) in a block of mn words. It could also be stored column by column (*column major* form) in an analogous manner. We use A for the name of the first word of the block. Then using row major form, we store $A(I, J)$ in the $n(I - 1) + J$th word of the block. $A(I, J)$ may be accessed by computing $nI + J$ in, say, register 2, and then using address $A - n - 1(X2)$. For example, if $n = 20$, the code to bring $A(I, J)$ to register 1 is:

```
LOAD2   I
MULT2   20(IMMED)
ADD2    J
LOAD1   A-21(X2)
```

Row major form can be generalized to k dimensions as follows. Suppose A is a k-dimensional array of size $n_1 \times n_2 \times \cdots \times n_k$. We store $A(I_1, I_2, \ldots, I_k)$ in the $n_2 n_3 \ldots n_k(I_1 - 1) + n_3 n_4 \ldots n_k(I_2 - 1) + \cdots + n_{k-1} n_k(I_{k-2}) + n_k(I_{k-1} - 1) + I_k$th word of the array. The code in Fig. 6.2 brings $A(I_1, I_2, \ldots, I_k)$ to register 1, where $m = n_2 n_3 \ldots n_k + n_3 n_4 \ldots n_k + \cdots + n_{k-1} n_k + n_k + 1$.

```
LOAD2   I₁
MULT2   n₂(IMMED)
ADD2    I₂
MULT2   n₃(IMMED)
          .
          .
          .
ADD2    I_{k-1}
MULT2   n_k(IMMED)
ADD2    I_k
LOAD1   A-m(X2)
```

Fig. 6.2 Code to access an array.

Many languages, such as ALGOL and PL/I, do not fix the limits of an array in advance. Rather, these limits are permitted to change as the program runs, and a dynamic storage allocation scheme such as that discussed in Section 6.5 is needed to provide a block of appropriate size. In this situation, the limits of the various co-ordinates and possibly the number of dimensions itself become part of the value of the array. Usually a set number of words (called a *dope vector*) at the beginning of the block holding the array are used to hold these values. We shall give two examples of dope vectors and leave some interesting and more complicated situations as exercises.

Example 6.5. Consider the first representation for character strings discussed in Example 6.4, where the length of the string preceded the string itself. We can regard a character string as a one-dimensional "array" whose elements are of character data type. The length of the string, placed in the first byte of the first word, can be thought of as a rudimentary "dope vector," since it tells us about the size of the "array" and is in a fixed place, obtainable without knowing the current size. ∎

Example 6.6. Suppose we have a three-dimensional array A whose lower limits are always 1 along each coordinate, and whose upper limits are currently n_1, n_2, and n_3. If we examine Fig. 6.2, we see we can store the array in row major form, with the accessing function depending on n_2 and n_3, but not on n_1.[†] Thus if the array were known to be three dimensional, and the lower limits of each coordinate were known to be 1, the values of n_2 and n_3, stored in the first two words of the block, would be sufficient for a dope vector in this simple case.

Since a variable-size array is not likely to begin at a fixed location in memory, let us assume that storage for it is allocated dynamically and that APTR points to the first word of the block, as suggested in Fig. 6.3. Then $A(I_1, I_2, I_3)$ is stored in word $n_2 n_3(I_1 - 1) + n_3(I_2 - 1) + I_3 + 2$ of the array. The term 2 at the end represents the length of the dope vector. Code to load the value of $A(I_1, I_2, I_3)$ into

---

[†] We would, however, need n_1 if we wished to check that the location actually reached by the code of Fig. 6.2 lay inside the current block used for storage of array elements.

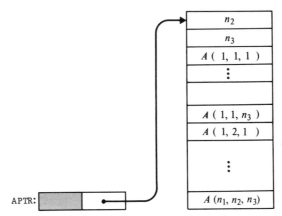

Fig. 6.3   Representation of variable-sized array.

register 1 is shown in Fig. 6.4. It is possible to save two steps from the code of Fig. 6.4 if we move each array element to the next higher word and use a third word of the dope vector to hold the quantity $n_2 n_3 + n_3 - 2$. We could then delete the two SUB3 1(IMMED) instructions and replace ADD3 1(IMMED) by a subtraction of $n_2 n_3 + n_3 - 2$. ∎

```
LOAD2   APTR
LOAD3   I₁
SUB3    1(IMMED)
MULT3   0(X2)         /* n₂(I₁ − 1) */
ADD3    I₂
SUB3    1(IMMED)
MULT3   1(X2)         /* n₂n₃(I₁ − 1) + n₃(I₂ − 1) */
ADD3    I₃
ADD3    1(IMMED)
ADD32
LOAD1   0(X3)
```

Fig. 6.4   Code to obtain $A(I_1, I_2, I_3)$.

More difficult problems regarding access to variably sized arrays are discussed in the exercises.

6.4   STATIC AND DYNAMIC STORAGE ALLOCATION

In the previous section on arrays, we saw that code to access an array can be made more efficient if space for the array can be determined *statically* (once and for all) by the compiler, rather than if space is allocated *dynamically*, i.e., the space alloted changes in size and position while the program is running. (Compare the code of Fig. 6.2 with that of Fig. 6.4.) One of the chief virtues of FORTRAN (but also the source of some of its awkwardness) is that all storage is allocated statically. The principal points in the language design that ensure the feasibility of static allocation are:

1. All arrays are of fixed length declared in the program.
2. Subroutines cannot be recursive.

Thus by (1), each routine has associated with it a fixed number of words needed to store its arrays and simple identifiers, much as an assembly language program does. By (2), at most one copy of any subroutine is ever active, so the space required for a main program and its subroutines is just the sum of the space required for each individually.[†]

At the opposite extreme are languages like SNOBOL, APL and LISP, where all identifiers are allocated storage dynamically. Although these languages are convenient to use, they are considerably slower than FORTRAN[‡] for many jobs. For an example of why these languages tend to run slower than FORTRAN, consider SNOBOL. Here the compiler cannot even determine the complete set of identifiers, since the names of new ones may be computed while the program is running. The only way to obtain the current value of an identifier α is to probe an associative structure (usually implemented by a hash table) with key α and find as associated data a pointer to a place in memory where the value of α may be found. The place for the value of α is allocated dynamically by a scheme such as that of the next section.

ALGOL also allocates storage for its identifiers dynamically. However, here the allocation is far less chaotic than in SNOBOL, and accessing of identifier values is more efficient in ALGOL than in SNOBOL. ALGOL's method of dynamic storage allocation, called *stack allocation* is discussed in Section 7.1.

PL/I in a sense combines the best features of static and dynamic storage,[§] since identifiers will be allocated storage statically as in FORTRAN, if that is feasible. The programmer can also declare identifiers to be allocated storage dynamically. In PL/I, an AUTOMATIC declaration causes the identifier to be allocated storage on a stack when its subprogram is entered, as in ALGOL. A CONTROLLED identifier is given storage or has that storage taken away on execution of ALLOCATE and FREE, respectively.

6.5 DYNAMIC STORAGE ALLOCATION

In Section 3.3 we introduced the available space list, a method whereby records of fixed size could be provided as needed and to which these records could be returned

---

[†] In case this remark appears too obvious, Chapter 7 will cover the inplementation of recursion. Thus we shall see that when a routine is recursive, many sets of its identifiers can be present in memory at once, with an identifier having different values in different sets.

[‡] Dynamic storage allocation accounts for only part of this inefficiency. Other factors costing time in SNOBOL, APL, and LISP are the way identifiers are bound to their declarations (see Section 6.9) and the potential need for repeated "garbage collection" (see Section 6.5).

[§] Another problem, however, arises here, making it hard for a PL/I program to compare with a FORTRAN program for efficiency. PL/I is so complicated that a PL/I compiler has a hard time putting out code that is as well optimized as that of a FORTRAN compiler (see Section 9.8).

for reuse. To get a general view of the problem of providing storage space for various uses, imagine a large block of memory (often called a *heap*) partitioned into variable-sized used and unused records. Each used record holds the value of some identifier (or whatever we wish to store). The unused records are linked together by pointers in their first word. Also found in the first word of each record is a count of the number of words in the record, information needed when we require a place in which to store new data.

Example 6.7. In Fig. 6.5 we see a block of $(1000)_{10}$ words used for dynamic storage allocation. The words are numbered 0 through 999; these numbers should be regarded as offsets from the first word of the block rather than as absolute memory locations. There are three identifiers A, B, and C currently having their values (e.g., long character strings or arrays) stored in the block of available space. A, B, and C each have a fixed location outside of available space in which is held a pointer to the block of available space used to hold its value. In Fig. 6.5, A uses the 100 words from 200 to 299, B uses 450 to 699, and C uses 800 to 849.

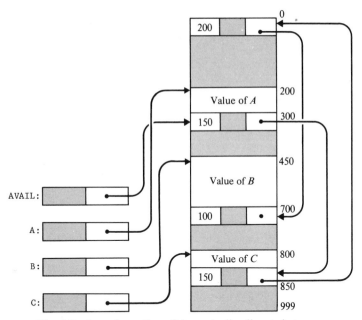

Fig. 6.5   A configuration of dynamically allocated storage.

There are four blocks of unused space. These are linked together in no particular order, starting from an outside word called AVAIL. Bits 19 to 30 of the first word in each unused block contains a pointer to the next unused block, and bits 1 to 12 contain a count of the number of words in the block. For example, the first block on the list is words 300 to 449. Word 300 contains the length of the block, 150, and a pointer to the next block of available space, which in this case begins at 850.   ∎

If a new block of space is needed we must select from among the available blocks and divide that block in two parts. One part, of the desired size, is used as needed, and the remainder of the block stays on the available space list. If the available block is exactly the size needed, then it is removed entirely from the available space list.

There are various strategies which may be used to select the block from which space is to be taken for the new use. An elaboration of these methods and a comparison of their merits is beyond the scope of this book. We shall discuss only the simplest possible approach in the next example.

Example 6.8. Suppose that identifier C in Example 6.6 is given a new value, one which requires 175 words. We can scan down the list of available blocks. When we examine bits 1 to 12 of words 300 and 850, we find that 300 to 449 and 850 to 999 are too small, but that 0 to 199 is of sufficient size. We allocate words 25 to 199 for the new value of C,[†] and words 0 to 24 remain on the available space list. Bits 1 to 12 of word 0 are made to hold 25 instead of 200.

Then we may return words 800 to 849, which held the old value of C, to available space.[‡] The simplest strategy is to push the block onto the top of available space. We give word 800 a pointer to word 300 and make AVAIL point to 800. Bits 1 to 12 of 800 are given the value 50.[§] The configuration of the dynamically allocated storage after these changes is shown in Fig. 6.6. ∎

Figure 6.6 points up one serious problem which must be handled in a dynamic-storage allocation scheme. We note that of the 1000 words in Fig. 6.6, 475 are unused. Yet we could not satisfy a request for a block of 475 words because of *storage fragmentation*, the tendency of the available words to be divided among small nonadjacent blocks, as blocks are used and returned in "random" order. In fact, in the case shown in Fig. 6.6 we could not immediately satisfy a request for a 300-word block, even though the 300 words 700 to 999 are all available.

If a block is requested, but a search of the available space list determines that no sufficiently large block exists, we must perform a *garbage collection* to attempt to create such a block. Various garbage collection strategies exist. Perhaps the simplest is to attempt to find adjacent unused blocks such as 700 to 799, 800 to 849 and 850 to 999 in Fig. 6.6 and to combine them into a single block. To do this we sort the list of

---

[†] Note that this is a better choice than using words 0 to 174 for the new value of C. If we did the latter we would have to move the pointer in word 0 to word 175 and make the pointer in 850 point to 175 instead of 0.

[‡] We assume here that used blocks hold a count of the number of pointers to them (a *use count*), and that the count is updated as pointers change, otherwise we could not tell that the block 800 to 849 was no longer used. It should be noted that while we show here only one pointer to each used block, there are natural circumstances under which more than one pointer to a block would be present. For example, suppose A and B are character strings and we execute the assignment $A = B$. The most efficient way to proceed is to make A's pointer point to the same block as B's pointer. Then the value of B would have at least two pointers pointing to it, and its use count would be incremented by one. The use count for the old value of A would be decremented by one and that block would be returned to available space if the use count reached zero.

[§] Let us assume that values of identifier include a dope vector with sufficient information to determine the length of the block returned to available space. If not, we could require that used blocks as well as unused ones have their length in their first word.

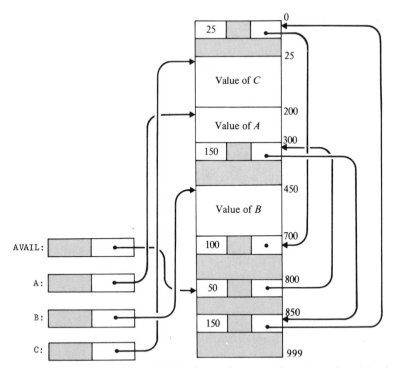

Fig. 6.6   Configuration of dynamically allocated storage after change in value of C.

first words of available blocks, so two blocks that are adjacent in memory will appear adjacent on the list.

We can test whether blocks beginning at ℓ_1 and ℓ_2 are consecutive. If the length of the block beginning at ℓ_1 is b, then that block is immediately followed by the block beginning at ℓ_2 if and only if $\ell_2 = \ell_1 + b$.

Example 6.9.   The sorted list of available blocks for Fig. 6.6 is:

First word	Length
0	25
300	150
700	100
800	50
850	150

We find that the block beginning at 800 immediately follows that at 700, since $800 = 700 + 100$. But the block beginning at 700 is separated from the block starting at 300 by used space, since $700 \neq 300 + 150$. ∎

Should the above method fail to find a block of sufficient size, we have only one recourse. We must move the used blocks around in memory. To even contemplate doing so we must introduce a new set of pointers into configurations such as those illustrated in Figs. 6.5 and 6.6. In particular, from each used block we must be able to get to all words that point to that block in order to adjust the pointers when the block is moved. We are thus required to have in each used block a pointer to the beginning of a list of all locations that point to that block. This list must be initialized when a new block β comes into use and must be altered every time we make another pointer point to β or change a pointer so it no longer points to β.

6.6 EXPRESSIONS AND OPERATORS

Every programming language has a facility to build expressions by combining operators and identifiers. At this, the second level of our hierarchy there is some useful syntactic terminology to learn. We can classify operators by the number of arguments they take and the positional relationships between the arguments and the symbol or symbols denoting the operator.

An operator taking k arguments is called *k-ary*. The common special cases are $k = 1$, which is called *unary*, $k = 2$, which is *binary*, and $k = 3$, which is *ternary*. Sometimes we shall find an operator such as MIN or MAX which can take any number of arguments, e.g., $\text{MIN}(X_1, X_2, \ldots, X_n)$. We call such an operator *variadic*.

A unary operator can have its operator symbol precede its argument, in which case it is called *prefix*. If the symbol follows the argument, the operator is called *postfix*. A *general form* unary operator has symbols both preceding and following the argument.

Example 6.10.   Minus $(-)$ can be a unary prefix operator. If A is an identifier, then $-A$ is an expression. If our operator set includes binary $+$, then $A + B$ is an expression, and therefore so is $-(A + B)$. Note that parentheses around the argument of $-$ is needed in $-(A + B)$ [to distinguish it from $-A + B$] but not in $A + B$ alone.

Any function taking one argument can be considered a unary prefix operator. For example, a function such as $\text{SIN}(A)$ can be regarded as having operator SIN and expression (A) as operand. Note that parentheses around the operand are essential when the operator is a function name, although they could be omitted when the operator was $-$, and the operand was a single identifier.   ∎

A binary operation in which the operator symbol appears between its arguments is called *infix*. A general form of binary operator has three symbols which we may denote θ_1, θ_2, and θ_3. These surround the two operand expressions $\mathscr{E}_1$ and $\mathscr{E}_2$ to form an expression $\theta_1 \mathscr{E}_1 \theta_2 \mathscr{E}_2 \theta_3$. Possibly one or more of the θ's are not actually there. (If only θ_2 is present we have an infix operator.) If θ_1 distinguishes the operator from all other permissible operators, we may call it *prefix*, and if θ_3 distinguishes the operator, we may call it *postfix*.

Example 6.11.   The usual arithmetic operators are all binary infix. Thus, we may build expressions such as $A + B$, $A - B$, and $(A + B) * (A - B)$. Subscripting for one dimensional arrays can be regarded as an example of a general form binary operator.

That is, $A(I)$ can be considered a binary operator, where θ_1 is missing, θ_2 is (, and θ_3 is) . ∎

The general form of a k-ary operator is $\theta_1 \mathscr{E}_1 \theta_2 \mathscr{E}_2 \ldots \theta_k \mathscr{E}_k \theta_{k+1}$, where the $\mathscr{E}$'s are to denote the operands. Some of the θ's may not be present. As for unary and binary operators, we may call a k-ary operator prefix if θ_1 uniquely determines the operator and postfix if θ_{k+1} does so.

Example 6.12. The ALGOL operator **if** $\mathscr{E}_1$ **then** $\mathscr{E}_2$ **else** $\mathscr{E}_3$ can be regarded as a ternary operator if $\mathscr{E}_1$ is a Boolean-valued expression. The intended value is the value of $\mathscr{E}_2$ if $\mathscr{E}_1$ is **true** and the value of $\mathscr{E}_3$ if $\mathscr{E}_1$ is **false**. Here, $\theta_1 = $ **if**, $\theta_2 = $ **then**, $\theta_3 = $ **else** and θ_4 is missing. The operator can be regarded as prefix unless some other operator has **if** preceding the first operand. ∎

When we build an expression by applying an operator to smaller expressions, we should theoretically place parentheses around each of the operands to avoid possible confusion. For example, if we saw $A + B * C$, we could not be sure whether $(A + B) * C$ or $A + (B * C)$ was meant. However, certain conventions are in common use to imply that parentheses have been deleted, e.g., $A + B * C$ usually is taken to mean $A + (B * C)$.

Operators are generally ranked according to their *precedence*. This precedence may vary from language to language. If an operator φ_1 is of "higher" precedence than φ_2, then we look for φ_1's operands and group (parenthesize) them before we look for φ_2's. Among operators of equal precedence, we generally group the left-most occurrence first,[†] with the exception of exponentiation, which is usually grouped from the right.

Example 6.13. In FORTRAN, the order of precedence of operators from highest to lowest is:

1. subscripting operator (parentheses around array subscripts)
2. functions, e.g., SIN or user-defined functions[‡]
3. ** (exponentiation)
4. unary $-$[§]
5. * and /
6. + and binary $-$

[†] An exception would occur if a language had a *right associative* infix operator, which is one that must be grouped from the right. In most languages, infix operators are regarded as *left associative*, and are grouped from the left. It is worth noting that APL violates this "rule"; all operators have equal precedence and are right associative.

[‡] Actually, since functions surround their arguments with parentheses, the order of precedence is not too important for functions. The same applies to the subscripting operator.

[§] We can identify a unary minus by the fact that it is either the first character in an expression or has a left parenthesis or operator symbol immediately to its left.

Thus, if we are given $A + B * C$, we first look for the operator with highest precedence, $*$. We know $*$ is a binary infix operator so we look for expressions to its left and right, and find B and C, respectively, we thus group $A + B * C$ as $A + (B * C)$. The next operator in order of precedence is $+$, and we find A to its left and $(B * C)$ to its right. Thus, the entire expression may be grouped around the $+$ as $(A + (B * C))$.

Suppose we are given

$$\texttt{MAX(A+MAX(B,C)-D,E)}$$

to parenthesize. The operator with highest precedence is MAX, so we first work on the leftmost occurrence of MAX. Our first job is to scan right from MAX(until we encounter a legal expression followed by a comma. That is, the comma between B and C does not qualify, since $A + $ MAX(B is not a legal expression. Then, the comma after D is considered, and we find it to be the one we are looking for, since $A + $ MAX($B, C) - D$ is an expression. Then, we repeatedly look further right for expressions followed by commas or right parentheses. When we find the latter, we have grouped the arguments of MAX. In this case, we immediately find E) and complete the grouping of the arguments of MAX.

Next, we group the second MAX, and find its arguments to be B and C. We then turn to the operators $+$ and $-$ at the lowest level of precedence. The leftmost occurrence, the plus sign, has arguments A and (MAX(B, C)). Then, the other occurrence, the minus sign, is given arguments $(A + ($MAX$(B, C)))$ and D. The complete parenthesization is:

$$\texttt{(MAX(((A+(MAX(B,C)))-D),E))} \qquad \blacksquare$$

6.7 SEMANTICS OF EXPRESSIONS

The abstract meaning and implementation of the usual operators found in programming languages should present no surprises. Some of this material was discussed in Section 6.2 when we covered identifiers and mentioned some of the natural operations on them. The reader will find it a worthwhile exercise to write code to implement various operators when no single machine instruction suffices (e.g., for multiplication of complex numbers or concatenation of character strings). Some of these problems are mentioned in the exercises section of this chapter.

There is another issue regarding the semantics of expressions which is not fully covered by considering the semantics of identifiers and operators separately. There are two different values which may be associated with any given expression, depending on whether the expression appears on the left or right side of an assignment.[†]

The usual meaning of an expression is that of the value produced by applying

---

[†] Note that when we speak of two values for an expression we are not referring to the dichotomy between abstract meaning and implementation. Each of the values of an expression has both an abstract meaning of its own and an implementation of its own.

the operators to the operands as one would expect. This value we call the *r-value*, because it is the value normally intended when the expression appears to the right of the assignment symbol.

There are certain expressions that have another value, called the *ℓ-value* because it is the value normally intended when the expression is on the left of an assignment symbol. Not every expression has an *ℓ*-value, just as not every expression can appear on the left of an assignment. Intuitively, the abstract meaning of an *ℓ*-value is a memory location. For example, the *ℓ*-value of the trivial expression $A^†$ is the location reserved for A. The *ℓ*-value of $A(I)$ is the location in the array A reserved for its *i*th element, where *i* is the current "value" of I (that is, its *r*-value). Let us now consider some examples of how *ℓ*- and *r*-values of expressions are implemented.

Example 6.14. Consider the assignment statement $A = B$. The two expressions A and B do not "mean" the same thing, even though syntactically they are the same, that is, they are each expressions consisting of single identifiers. For B, we expect the compiler to generate code which brings its *r*-value to a register, e.g., LOAD B. For A we want only its *ℓ*-value, that is, the symbolic address A. These two pieces can be put together with a STORE instruction to form code to execute the assignment statement:

```
            LOAD    B
            STORE   A
```

Let us take a more complex case, the assignment $A(I, J) = B(K, L) + C$, where A and B are 10×10 arrays and C is a real number. Again we require code to bring the *r*-value of the expression on the right to a register, code such as:

```
        LOAD2   K
        MULT2   10(IMMED)
        ADD2    L
        LOAD1   B-11(X2)
        ADDFL1  C
```

What we need for $A(I, J)$ is code which will enable us to compute the address of $A(I, J)$. A possible sequence is

```
        LOAD2   I
        MULT2   10(IMMED)
        ADD2    J
        -       A-11(X2)
```

together with a notation that address $A-11(X2)$ refers to the location of $A(I, J)$ after executing the above three instructions. The two sequences can then be put

---
† A single identifier is a special case of an expression, of course, in fact it is really the most common kind of expression used.

together with a STORE to form code for the assignment statement:

```
LOAD2    K
MULT2    19(IMMED)
ADD2     L
LOAD1    B-11(X2)
ADDFL1   C
LOAD2    I
MULT2    10(IMMED)
ADD2     J
STORE1   A-11(X2)
```

For a somewhat more subtle example, suppose P is a pointer and I is an integer. The PL/I assignment P = ADDR(I) makes P point to I. In terms of ℓ- and r-values, what happens is this. ADDR is a unary operator such that the r-value of the expression ADDR($\mathscr{E}$) is the ℓ-value of the expression $\mathscr{E}$. Fortunately, I is an expression which has an ℓ-value; that ℓ-value is the location reserved for I. Like any assignment, we generate code to bring the r-value of the expression on the right to a register. That is, we must bring the ℓ-value of I to a register with an instruction such as LOAD I(IMMED). This instruction is followed by an instruction STORE P, placing the computed value into the location which is the ℓ-value of expression P. Thus, since P is a pointer, its own r-value is something else's ℓ-value.   ∎

It is worth noting that various languages treat the assignment operator as any other binary operator. Using the concept of ℓ- and r-values, we can see the logic in this arrangement. The implementation of the assignment "expression" $\mathscr{E}_1 = \mathscr{E}_2$ is to place the r-value of $\mathscr{E}_2$ in the ℓ-value of $\mathscr{E}_1$ (assuming $\mathscr{E}_1$ has an ℓ-value). The r-value of the expression $\mathscr{E}_1 = \mathscr{E}_2$ is the same as the r-value of $\mathscr{E}_2$, and $\mathscr{E}_1 = \mathscr{E}_2$ does not have an ℓ-value. Thus, we may write statements (which are really expressions) having more than one assignment operator.

Example 6.15.   If = associates from the right, we may write $A = B = C$ to mean the same as

```
B = C
A = C
```

That is, $B = C$ is "evaluated" first, by placing the value of C in the location of B. The r-value of $B = C$ is the value of C, so $A = B = C$ is then evaluated by placing the value of C in the location of A.

On the assumption that = has lowest precedence, the statement

```
B = C * (A = A + 1)
```

has the effect of the statements

```
A = A + 1
B = C * A
```
                                                                                    ∎

6.8 SEMANTICS OF STATEMENTS

There are few surprises when we discuss the abstract meaning of statements, but let us now cover the salient parts. We can group statements, with a few exceptions, into the following four categories.

1. *Assignment Statements.* The typical syntax and semantics of this statement were covered in Example 6.14.

2. *Control Statements.* Unconditional transfers, such as the FORTRAN GOTO are implemented by the unconditional jump instruction of the computer. Conditional transfers, such as IF in FORTRAN, are implemented by the evaluation of an expression, followed by one or more conditional jump instructions of the computer, each conditioned on the value just computed. Nested control statements, such as WHILE or IF . . . THEN . . . ELSE from PL/I or DO from FORTRAN are implemented by a combination of conditional and unconditional jumps.

3. *Declarations.* These statements are not implemented by executable computer code. Rather they tell the compiler something about identifiers, and their "implementation" is the storage of data by the compiler in its own symbol table (akin to the symbol table of an assembler). The data stored by the compiler concerns the identifiers mentioned in the declaration statement and reflects the information about these identifiers contained in the declaration. Examples are the REAL, INTEGER, and DIMENSION statements of FORTRAN.

4. *Input/output Statements.* These play the role indicated by their name. Their usual implementation is by a call to a library subroutine that handles conversion between character strings and numerical data, as well as controlling input/output devices.

6.9 BINDING OF IDENTIFIERS

The remainder of this chapter and all of the next are concerned principally with phenomena at the level of subprograms, although this section has aspects involved with the semantics of identifiers as well. Recall that in this book we use the term *subprogram* to refer to a part of a program that has private (or *local*) identifiers, whether or not it can be "called" as can a subroutine. The principal examples of subprograms are **begin** . . . **end** blocks in various languages such as PL/I and ALGOL and the usual callable subprograms known as subroutines, procedures, or functions.

In the typical language, a subprogram can contain uses of certain identifiers which are not local to the subprogram in the sense of being declared in that subprogram and having storage for that identifier somehow connected with the subprogram. Suppose XYZ is such an identifier mentioned in subprogram S. Presumably the use of XYZ in S refers to an identifier local to some subprogram other than S. The determination of the local identifier to which XYZ refers to is called *binding* this use of identifier XYZ to its declaration. We can divide programming languages into two classes, those for which binding can be done by the compiler (*static* binding) and those for which binding must be done while the program is running (*dynamic binding*).[†]

FORTRAN uses what is probably the simplest static binding scheme. To begin, FORTRAN has no blocks, so the only subprograms are the main program and its subroutines and functions. With the exception of data in COMMON and the formal parameters of a subroutine or function, all identifiers mentioned in a subprogram must be local to that subprogram. The FORTRAN compiler will allocate storage for each identifier at the end of the subprogram. Thus the FORTRAN compiler can surely bind these identifiers.

Moreover, since the storage for identifiers local to a subprogram appears at the end of the subprogram when the compiler translates FORTRAN into, say, assembly code, the compiler can generate direct references to storage for the identifiers. For example, $A = B + C$ in a FORTRAN program could be translated into:

```
          LOAD    B
          ADD     C
          STORE   A
            .
            .
            .
A:        DATA    0
B:        DATA    0
C:        DATA    0
```

The above may not seem remarkable until we realize that in other situations we might have to do considerably more work to get at the locations of A, B, and C. For example, if the assignment $A = B + C$ appeared in a language using dynamic storage as in Section 6.5, we would have to go indirectly through a pointer to get at these identifiers. In fact, even in ALGOL, another language using static binding, we must go through pointers to get at A, B, and C. The direct reference saves time on some machines when compared with indirect addressing or indexing, so we now see another design decision which makes FORTRAN capable of producing efficient machine code. As with the decision to allocate storage statically in FORTRAN, we pay a price in versatility of the language.

We have yet to cover the use of formal parameters and COMMON identifiers within a FORTRAN subprogram. In FORTRAN, parameters are passed by reference as described in Section 5.3. The FORTRAN compiler generates calls and accesses actual parameters in essentially the manner described in that section. Identifiers in COMMON are declared in a COMMON statement, which also determines their offset relative to the beginning of a block of COMMON data. Thus the FORTRAN compiler has no problem determining to what storage location COMMON identifiers refer. In the machine code, direct references to these identifiers can be made

---

[†] It should not be missed that the same static/dynamic dichotomy was used to describe allocation of storage. In general, "static" means "doable by the compiler," while "dynamic" means "must be done while the program is running."

after processing by the link editor, which treats blocks of common data as it does a subroutine.

ALGOL is another language using static binding, but here the rule used to resolve identifier uses is more complicated than in FORTRAN. In an ALGOL program both blocks (sequences of statements surrounded by **begin** and **end**) and procedure definitions can occur, but any two such subprograms must either have no overlap or be nested, one wholly inside the other. Thus for each subprogram S we may define an *environment* consisting of a sequence of subprograms $S_1, S_2, \ldots, S_n$ such that S_1 is S, S_2 is that subprogram most closely surrounding S_1, S_3 stands in the same relation to S_2, and so on (note that the case $n = 1$, when S is the outermost subprogram, is possible). A subprogram may use identifiers declared by any of the subprograms in its environment.

If subprogram S, as above, uses an identifier XYZ, and more than one of S_1, $S_2, \ldots, S_n$ declare an identifier with that name, then XYZ in S refers to the XYZ of the first subprogram in the list $S_1, S_2, \ldots, S_n$ declaring an identifier with the name XYZ. Thus, the ALGOL compiler can perform the binding of identifiers, using the rule: "An identifier α mentioned at some point in the program is bound to the declaration of α in that subprogram which declares α and most closely surrounds the point." We shall call this the "*most closely nested*" rule.

Example 6.16. Let us consider the ALGOL program suggested by Fig. 6.7. In that figure all subprograms are indicated as blocks, but they could just as well be procedure definitions. Consider the assignment statement AB := CD + EF in Block 1. Since AB is declared in Block 1, that block is the most closely nested subprogram declaring AB and surrounding the assignment statement. It is to this declaration that AB refers, and the value computed by the assignment will be stored in the location allocated for the AB belonging to Block 1.

However, CD is not declared in Block 1. The environment of Block 1 consists of blocks 1, 2, and 3 in that order. The first subprogram on the list having a declaration

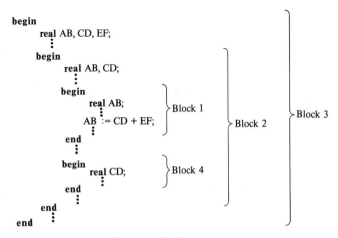

Fig. 6.7   Block structure.

of CD is Block 2, so it is to that CD that the CD in the assignment statement refers. The declarations of CD in Blocks 3 and 4 are not the ones referred to, in the former case because Block 2 precedes Block 3 on the environment list for Block 1, and in the latter case because Block 4 is not even in the environment of Block 1. Finally, the use of EF in Block 1 refers to the declaration of EF in Block 3, since the blocks on the environment list preceding Block 3 do not declare EF, while Block 3 does.

It is worth noting that each subprogram in an ALGOL program has storage created for the identifiers it declares, so the identifiers declared with name CD in Blocks 2, 3, and 4 occupy four distinct locations. This is also the case for other names declared in two or more subprograms. Section 7.1 describes storage allocation for ALGOL, and the mechanism whereby distinct storage locations are created for different declarations of the same name will be deferred until then. ∎

There are certain languages such as SNOBOL, APL, and LISP in which identifiers cannot be bound by the compiler. For each of these languages, dynamic binding, that is, binding while the program is running must be used; and for each of these languages, the same binding rule is used. A use of identifier α refers to the declaration of α in that subprogram which was most recently initiated[†] (prior to this use of α) and which has a declaration of α. We call this rule "*most recently initiated.*"

Example 6.17.   Suppose we are using this form of dynamic binding, and subroutine *A* calls subroutine *B* which calls subroutine *C*. Suppose also that *C* uses identifier XYZ. If *C* also declares XYZ, then it is to this declaration that the use refers. If *C* does not declare XYZ but *B* does, then the use is bound to the declaration in *B*. Only if neither *B* nor *C* declare XYZ can the use of XYZ refer to a declaration within *A*. ∎

In Section 7.4 we shall discuss ways to implement this commonest form of dynamic binding. Let us close with an example to fix firmly in mind the fact that static binding as used in ALGOL is different from this type of dynamic binding.

Example 6.18.   Consider the skeleton of an ALGOL program exhibited in Fig. 6.8. The program consists of an outer Block 1 with the definition of procedure PRO and an inner Block 2 nested within. According to the ALGOL static binding rule, the environment of PRO consists of itself and Block 1. Thus, the uses of AB in the assignment AB := AB + 1 in PRO clearly refer to the declaration of AB in Block 1.

However, suppose now that the program of Fig. 6.8 were written in some language resembling ALGOL syntactically, but in which dynamic binding using the "most recently initiated" rule was required. Then when the program began, Block 1 would commence execution. The definition of PRO is not executed, just as macro definitions are not executed in an assembly program. Finally, control would reach Block 2, which would call PRO. Now when the assignment AB := AB + 1 is executed, the most recently initiated subprogram is PRO, which does not have a declaration of

---

[†] In the case a subprogram is a block we can consider the block "initiated" if control is within the subprogram surrounding that block, and control reaches the **begin** of the block. A subroutine initiates when it is called.

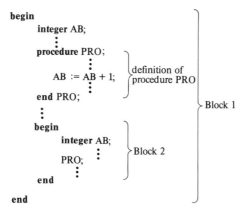

Fig. 6.8   Skeleton ALGOL program.

AB. The next most recently initiated subprogram is Block 2, not Block 1, so it is to
the declaration of AB in Block 2 that this assignment refers. ▌

6.10 PARAMETER PASSING

We saw in Section 5.3 one discipline, call-by-reference, for passing parameters to a
subroutine. This method is standard in many languages such as FORTRAN and
PL/I. One extension of the technique described in Section 5.3 should be mentioned.
It is usual in programming languages to allow expressions as actual parameters.[†]
Certain simple expressions such as $A(I, J)$ have ℓ-values, and we may compute and
pass to the subroutine a pointer to the location denoted by that expression. Other
expressions, such as $X + Y$, have no ℓ-value. For these we evaluate the expression
and put the value in a location reserved for the purpose. In the calling sequence we
have a pointer to that location.

Example 6.19.   Let us consider a subroutine EXCHANGE(X, Y) which might be
written as in Fig. 6.9.

```
begin
      INTEGER TEMP;
      TEMP = X;
      X = Y;
      Y = TEMP;
      RETURN
end
```

Fig. 6.9   The subroutine EXCHANGE (X, Y)

---

† The terms *actual* and *formal* parameters were introduced in Section 4.8 in connection with
macros. Their meaning here is essentially the same. Actual parameters are the arguments used
in a subroutine call. Formal parameters are the ones used in the subroutine definition.

If the calling sequence for EXCHANGE is as indicated in Section 5.3, the assembly code for that routine might be as in Fig. 6.10.

```
EXCHANGE:    LOAD    0(INDX7)
             STORE   TEMP
             LOAD    1(INDX7)
             STORE   0(INDX7)
             LOAD    TEMP
             STORE   1(INDX7)
             JUMP    2(X7)
    TEMP:    DATA    0
             END
```

Fig. 6.10   Assembly code for EXCHANGE assuming call-by-reference.

The implementation of CALL EXCHANGE (A + B, C) would be:

```
LOAD7     A
ADD7      B
STORE7    ARG1
LOAD7     *+2(IMMED)
JUMP      EXCHANGE
POINTER   ARG1
POINTER   C
```

with ARG1 defined by a DATA statement at the end of the program. Note that EXCHANGE puts the value of $A + B$ into C and the value of C into ARG1. The values of A and B are not affected. This example illustrates the important point that it makes little sense to use an expression without an ℓ-value as an argument if the subroutine assigns a value to that argument. In this case, EXCHANGE has not in any sense "exchanged" $A + B$ with C.

Consider now the implementation of CALL EXCHANGE(J, N(J)). Since $N(J)$ has an ℓ-value, we can compute its location. Assuming N is a FORTRAN array, the following is one possible calling sequence:

```
LOAD7     N-1(IMMED)    /* PLACE POINTER    */
ADD7      J             /* TO N(J) IN       */
STORE7    *+4           /* CALLING SEQUENCE */
LOAD7     *+2(IMMED)
JUMP      EXCHANGE
POINTER   J
POINTER   0             /* POINTER TO N(J)  */
```

The reader should simulate EXCHANGE by hand to see that, if J has value j_0 before the call, it does in fact set J to $N(j_0)$ and $N(j_0)$ to j_0. ∎

We also briefly mentioned in Section 5.3 the possibility of call-by-value linkage. There the value, rather than a pointer to the value, is passed to the subroutine. In a strict call-by-value linkage, the subroutine produces results which can only be placed in the calling sequence and subsequently used by the calling program. In a language with pointer identifiers, however, we can use a subroutine called by value to affect the values of data in the calling program by passing to the subroutine ℓ-values, i.e., pointers to the data to be modified.

Example 6.20. An implementation of A = SIN(X), if call-by-value were used would be:

```
        LOAD7    X              / * PLACE VALUE OF X      */
        STORE7   *+3            / * IN CALLING SEQUENCE   */
        LOAD7    *+2(IMMED)
        JUMP     SIN
        DATA     0              / * VALUE OF X            */
        DATA     0              / * PLACE FOR RESULT      */
        LOAD7    *-1
        STORE7   A              / * ASSIGN RESULT TO A    */
```

A more general form of call-by-value is called *copy-restore* linkage. Before calling a subroutine we evaluate its actual parameters and their locations if they have one, placing all this information in the calling sequence, as we did for call-by-reference. After the subroutine returns, we take the current values out of the calling sequence and place them in their locations, which were computed before the call and not changed by the subroutine.

Example 6.21. Let us again consider the routine EXCHANGE of Fig. 6.9. An appropriate calling sequence for CALL EXCHANGE(J, N(J)), assuming copy-restore linkage is shown in Fig. 6.11. The implementation of EXCHANGE is some-

```
        LOAD7    J
        STORE7   *+10      /*  VALUE OF J          */
        LOAD7    J(IMMED)
        STORE7   *+9       /*  LOCATION OF J       */
        LOAD7    N-1(IMMED)
        ADD7     J
        STORE7   *+8       /*  LOCATION OF N(J)    */
        LOAD7    0(X7)
        STORE7   *+5       /*  VALUE OF N(J)       */
        LOAD7    *+2(IMMED)
        JUMP     EXCHANGE
        DATA     0         /*  VALUE OF J          */
        DATA     0         /*  LOCATION OF J       */
        DATA     0         /*  VALUE OF N(J)       */
        DATA     0         /*  LOCATION OF N(J)    */
        LOAD7    *-4
        STORE7   *-4(IND)  /*  RESTORE J           */
        LOAD7    *-4
        STORE7   *-4(IND)  /*  RESTORE N(J)        */
```

Fig. 6.11   Calling sequence for EXCHANGE (J, N(J)) assuming copy-restore linkage.

what different, if the call is by copy-restore, from the implementation of Fig. 6.10, which assumed call-by-reference. We see in Fig. 6.12 an implementation of EX-CHANGE(X, Y) which will work if called with copy-restore linkage. The reader should check that the program of Fig. 6.12 called by the code of Fig. 6.11 does in fact work as intended. ∎

```
EXCHANGE:   LOAD    0(X7)
            STORE   TEMP
            LOAD    2(X7)
            STORE   0(X7)
            LOAD    TEMP
            STORE   2(X7)
            JUMP    4(X7)
    TEMP:   DATA    0
            END
```

Fig. 6.12   Assembly code for EXCHANGE assuming copy-restore linkage.

A final strategy for passing arguments is to arrange that no actual parameter is evaluated until it is needed, and each is evaluated afresh every time it is needed. This strategy is known as *call-by-name* and is the chief method of parameter passing used in ALGOL (although the programmer has the option of declaring any parameter to be passed by value). While the above definition may be somewhat vague, there is fortunately a precise statement of the abstract meaning of call-by-name, known as the ALGOL *copy rule*. The copy rule states that the subroutine so called must be implemented to behave as if its actual parameters were literally substituted for its formal parameters,[†] that is as if the call were a macro use. If an actual parameter is an expression, it must be surrounded by parentheses before substitution; the parentheses may be later removed if precedence of operators permits.

Example 6.22. Suppose we use call-by-name linkage for the subroutine EX-CHANGE of Fig. 6.9. If we execute CALL EXCHANGE(J, N(J)), we must arrange

---

[†] There is a "catch," however. If the subroutine uses a local variable that has the same name as one in the actual parameters of the call, we must first substitute a new name for that local variable, one which does not appear in the actual parameters. For example, if we called EXCHANGE (TEMP, A), where EXCHANGE is as in Fig. 6.9, we would have to first substitute another name, say DUMMY, for local variable TEMP, treating EXCHANGE as if it were written:

```
            begin
                INTEGER DUMMY;
                DUMMY = X;
                X = Y;
                Y = DUMMY;
                RETURN
            end
```

then substituting TEMP for X and A for Y in the above code.

that the call be implemented as if we instead executed Fig. 6.9 with J in place of X and $N(J)$ in place of Y. That is, we must execute:

```
begin
    INTEGER TEMP:
    TEMP = J;
    J = N(J);
    N(J) = TEMP;
    RETURN
end
```

It is interesting to observe that EXCHANGE does not work as expected if called by name. In particular, if J has value j_0 before the call, the above code will set J to $N(j_0)$ but then set $N(N(j_0))$ to j_0, rather than setting $N(j_0)$ to j_0 as it would do if called by reference or by copy-restore. There is apparently no way to implement a true "exchange" subroutine if it is to be called by name! ∎

The implementation of call-by-name is unfortunately not as easy as the specification of its abstract meaning. An implementation of call-by-name forms the subject matter of the next section.

6.11   THUNKS

If all arguments to subroutines are simple variables or constants, call-by-name can easily be implemented using pointers as we did in Section 5.3, and call-by-name becomes essentially call-by-reference. However, in a more general setting, arguments may be arbitrary expressions, possibly even expressions involving function calls themselves. In these cases a versatile means of argument representation must be used. One method which has found favor is to pass to the subroutine the locations of programs (actually subroutines with no parameters) which will compute the ℓ-values (if they exist) and r-values of each of the actual parameters. These programs are often called *thunks*.[†] The subroutine calls the appropriate thunk to obtain the ℓ- or r-value for one of its parameters whenever it needs that value. Note that no parameter need be passed to a thunk.

Example 6.22. Let us again consider the call EXCHANGE$(J, N(J))$, assuming call-by-name. We must write thunks to evaluate the ℓ- and r-values of J and $N(J)$. While it might be more efficient (as far as space is concerned) to evaluate the r-value of an argument by calling the ℓ-value evaluator and then obtaining the value found in that location, we shall not do so. Rather we shall write four separate routines. We assume that each thunk is called with register 6 holding the location to which it is to

---

[†] The reader clearly deserves an explanation for the term. Unfortunately we do not yet have the concepts needed to fully justify it. Suffice it to say that "thunk" is the sound a pointer makes when it is moved rapidly down a stack. In Chapter 7, where we discuss the stack implementation of storage allocation in ALGOL, we shall see how the execution of a thunk can cause a pointer to move down the stack.

return, and that it will put its answer (an ℓ- or r-value) in register 5. The routine to compute the ℓ-value of J is:

```
THUNK1L:   LOAD5   J(IMMED)
           JUMP    0(X6)
```

For the r-value of J we use:

```
THUNK1R:   LOAD5   J
           JUMP    0(X6)
```

For the ℓ-value of $N(J)$:

```
THUNK2L:   LOAD5   N-1(IMMED)
           ADD5    J
           JUMP    0(X6)
```

Finally, the r-value of $N(J)$ is obtained by:

```
THUNK2R:   LOAD5   N-1(IMMED)
           ADD5    J
           LOAD5   0(X5)
           JUMP    0(X6)
```

If we use register 7 to call EXCHANGE, the calling sequence could be:

```
LOAD7      *+2(IMMED)
JUMP       EXCHANGE
POINTER    THUNK1L
POINTER    THUNK1R
POINTER    THUNK2L
POINTER    THUNK2R
```

The program for EXCHANGE could be as shown in Fig. 6.13.

The reader should simulate the above program to see that it does what is expected of it. That is, if J has initial value j_0, it sets J to $N(j_0)$ and $N(N(j_0))$ to j_0. ∎

6.12   COMPARISON OF LINKAGE CONVENTIONS

It should be apparent from the examples of the previous two sections that the three linkage conventions defined there do not necessarily give the same answer when a particular subroutine is called with particular arguments. In this section we shall discuss some of the causes for different results when different linkage conventions are used. We do not wish to endorse one convention over another; each has its advantages and disadvantages. We simply desire that the reader acquaint himself with some of the situations in which he will have to think carefully about which convention to use (or which he is forced to use if he is writing in a particular programming language).

One source of discrepancy concerns *side effects*, the ability of a subroutine to change data not given to it as a parameter. For example, FORTRAN subroutines can manipulate variables in COMMON, and ALGOL or PL/I procedures can alter variables which are defined in a block surrounding the procedure.

It is possible that a subroutine has a side effect which changes a datum which is also one of its parameters. If called by value or copy-restore, the datum is evaluated

	Statement		Comments
EXCHANGE:	LOAD6 JUMP	*+2(IMMED) 1(INDX7)	Call the thunk to evaluate the r-value of the first argument, by jumping to its first location, that is, to the location found in the word after that pointed to by register 7. In the case that the calling sequence was as in the example, we would here call THUNK1R and evaluate J.
	STORE5	TEMP	When the thunk returns, the value of the first argument will be in register 5. Store it in TEMP to complete execution of the statement TEMP = X.
	LOAD6 JUMP COPY54	*+2(IMMED) 0(INDX7)	Next begin execution of statement X = Y. Call the thunk to evaluate the ℓ-value of the first argument, then copy it into register 4 for safe-keeping.
	LOAD6 JUMP STORE5	*+2(IMMED) 3(INDX7) 0(X4)	Obtain the r-value of the second argument and store its value in the location preserved in register 4, that is, the ℓ-value of the first argument.
	LOAD6 JUMP LOAD1 STORE1	*+2(IMMED) 2(INDX7) TEMP 0(X5)	Execute Y = TEMP by computing the ℓ-value of the second argument and storing the value held in TEMP in the location computed. Note that in the case discussed in this example, the call would be to THUNK2L, which would use the new value of J computed when we executed the assignment X = Y.
	JUMP	4(X7)	Return.
TEMP:	DATA END	0	

Fig. 6.13 Assembly program for EXCHANGE assuming call-by-name.

once and for all, so the side effect does not change the value of the parameter. However, if called by name or reference, the subroutine may reevaluate the datum, possibly changing values each time it is used.

Example 6.24. Let us consider the following FORTRAN subroutine:

```
SUBROUTINE SUB(I,J)
COMMON  K
K = I + 1
J = K * I
RETURN
END
```

which we may assume is called by copy-restore, a possible treatment for FORTRAN subroutine parameters which are variables or constants.

Suppose COMMON variable K of SUB is also known by the name K to a routine which calls SUB(K, L). Let K have the value 5 at this point (the value of L happens to be irrelevant). Then $K = I + 1$ sets K to $5 + 1 = 6$. The statement $J = K * I$ gets the value 6 for K from COMMON and the value 5 for I, since the value 5 for the first parameter was passed to SUB initially. The fact that the first actual parameter was K and that the value of K has changed is of no consequence under copy-restore linkage.

However, suppose SUB were instead called by name or reference. $K = I + 1$ would again set K to 6. When we execute $J = K * I$, we obtain the current value of K, namely 6, as before. But if SUB is called by name or reference, it will obtain the current value of I. That is, it must find the current value of its first actual parameter K (since I is its first formal parameter), finding 6 there. It thus computes $J = 36$ and returns. ∎

A second source of discrepancy between calls by name and by value occurs when a function or subroutine is *not defined* (that is, it halts or enters an infinite loop) for some of its arguments. A call by value must evaluate its arguments before calling the subroutine, even if some of these arguments involve function calls. If one of these arguments is not defined, the call by value never takes place. However, in a call by name, it is possible that this evaluation need not be done, so the subroutine might produce an answer if called by name.

Example 6.25.   Let us consider a subroutine EVAL(A, B, C) which is to set C equal to A if $B \neq 0$ and set C equal to 0 if $B = 0$. That is:

> **if**   B .NE. 0· **then**
>   C = A
> **else**
>   C = 0.

The intention is that EVAL will be called with expressions as its first and second parameters, and checking for the second parameter equal to zero protects against a division by zero when we evaluate the first argument. A typical call might be:

$$\text{CALL EVAL(X/Y + X/(Y-1), Y*(Y-1), Z)}$$

where

$$\frac{X}{Y} + \frac{X}{Y - 1}$$

involves a division by zero if and only if $Y = 0$ or $Y - 1 = 0$, that is, $Y * (Y - 1) = 0$.[†]

If we use call-by-name for EVAL, the above call would behave like the code:

> **if**   Y * (Y − 1) .NE. 0· **then**
>   Z = X/Y + X/(Y − 1)
> **else**
>   Z = 0.

[†] Let us ignore the fact that in floating-point arithmetic, we could have $Y * (Y - 1) = 0$ without $Y = 0$ or $Y - 1 = 0$.

formed by substituting actual parameters for formal. It is easy to check that the above code never causes a division by zero and sets Z to 0 if Y is 0 or 1.

However, if the call is by reference or copy-restore, the arguments are evaluated before the call; and if Y is 0 or 1, a division by zero will occur. On most computer systems, a division by zero can cause the program to be immediately terminated, surely a different result than when EVAL is called by name. Although on our simple computer, division by zero does not terminate the program, it does set a bit indicating "disaster" when EVAL is called by reference or copy-restore. That bit is not set if the call is by name. ∎

EXERCISES

6.1 Write macros to perform addition, subtraction, multiplication and division of complex numbers. Assume each argument is in a block of two words with real part in the first and imaginary part in the second. The parameters of the macros are the symbolic addresses for the first words of the blocks.

6.2 Let A, B, and C be bit strings of length 100.

a) Describe one way of allocating (static) storage for these identifiers.

* b) Write a program which tests if $(A \wedge \neg B) \vee C$ is all 1's.

6.3 Suppose we have two character strings A and B of length at most 14 and 9, respectively. Let these strings consist of letters only, and let the blank serve as an endmarker. Write a program in our assembly language to compute $A \parallel B$ and store it in a block beginning at C. Recall that in our computer, the character codes for the letters are $(12)_8$ through $(43)_8$ and $(44)_8$ is the code for blank.

6.4 Repeat Exercise 6.3 on the assumption that there is no end-marker, but the first byte of each string is an integer indicating the length of the string.

** **6.5** Another representation of character strings is a linked list of k-word records, with any unused space in the last record filled out with a special marker (say $). For example, if $k = 2$, the alphabet could be represented as in Fig. 6.14.

a) What are the advantages and disadvantages of such a representation, compared with the representation of character strings in blocks of consecutive words?

b) What factors influence the proper selection of k, the record size?

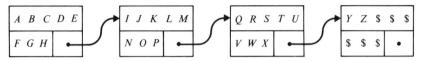

Fig. 6.14   Linked list character string representation.

6.6 Suppose a one dimensional array A is to be given dynamically allocated storage, and that the legal values of subscripts for A range from 1 up to some number which is the contents of word N. Also, suppose that A is stored in a block whose first word is pointed to by bits 19 to 30 of a word named PTR. Give assembly code to bring $A(I)$ to register 1 if $1 \leq I \leq N$ and branch to OUTOFBOUNDS otherwise.

6.7 Suppose A is a k dimensional array whose ith subscript may range from x_i through y_i, inclusive.

a) Give some rule for locating $A(I_1, I_2, \ldots, I_k)$ if A is the symbolic address for the first word of the block.

b) Show how to load $A(I_1, I_2, \ldots, I_k)$ into register 1.

6.8 Repeat Exercise 6.7 for the specific case that A is 3-dimensional, its first subscript ranges from -10 to $+10$, its second from 1 to 5, and its third from 0 to 4.

** **6.9** Suppose that x_i and y_i of Exercise 6.7 are not constants but may vary with time.

a) What is the minimum amount of information (functions of the x_i's and y_i's) which must be kept in a dope vector to enable us to access any element $A(I_1, I_2, \ldots, I_k)$ of the array?

b) Suggest a format for the array A based on your answer to (a).

c) Assuming $k = 3$, write an assembly language program to bring $A(I_1, I_2, I_3)$ to register 1, assuming the format from (b).

6.10 Two possible strategies for dynamic storage allocation are:

1. *First Fit.* Allocate the block as close to the low end of the available region as possible.

2. *Best Fit.* Allocate the block at the low end of the smallest empty block into which it fits.

For example, suppose available space consists of 1000 words, and we allocate blocks of 200, 50, 100 and 150 words, then return the first and third of these. Under either the first-fit or the best-fit strategy, the available space would appear as in Fig. 6.15. If we then allocate a block of 75 words, under first-fit we would place it in words 0–74. Under best-fit it goes into words 250–324, since the empty block of 250–349 is the smallest empty block of 75 or more words.

Your problem is to give two sequences of requests for space and returns to available space, one such that the first-fit strategy enables all requests to be met without garbage collection, but the best-fit strategy does not; second, such that the opposite occurs.

6.11 Assume we have three operators #, ¢ and $, where:

i) # is binary infix, left associative, and of highest precedence,

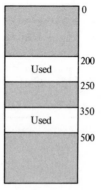

Fig. 6.15   Configuration of available space.

ii) ¢ is unary postfix and of next highest precedence,

iii) $ is binary infix, right associative, and of lowest precedence.

Fully parenthesize the following strings:

   a) A $ B # C ¢ $ D

   b) A # B ¢ $ C # D ¢

6.12 Which of the following FORTRAN expressions have *l*-values?

   a) A(I)

   b) A + B

   c) SIN(X)

6.13 In Fig. 6.16 we see the skeleton of an ALGOL program with blocks and a procedure declaration. Assuming:

   a) static binding of identifiers using the "most closely nested" rule, and

   b) dynamic binding using the "most recently initiated" rule, to which of declarations (1)–(4) do A, X, and Y refer in the assignment A := X + Y when PRO(X) is called?

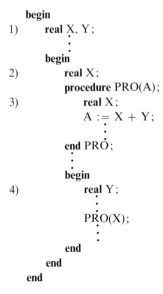

Fig. 6.16 Skeleton program.

6.14 If the only subprograms are blocks, rather than procedures, is there a difference between static binding using the "most closely nested" rule and dynamic binding by the "most recently initiated" rule? Why?

6.15 Give the calling sequences for:

CALL ASSIGN(A + B,C(I))

assuming:

   a) call-by-reference

   b) copy-restore linkage

in the style suggested in Section 6.10. *Hint:* Note that the first argument has no ℓ-value, so presumably ASSIGN does not assign to it. Thus, no restoration of its value is possible or necessary in part (b).

6.16 Write assembly code for ASSIGN of Exercise 6.15 assuming ASSIGN sets its second argument equal to its first and linkage is

   a) by reference

   b) by copy-restore.

*6.17 Write thunks for the arguments $A + B$ and $C(I)$ of the subroutine ASSIGN, assuming that calls are by name and that ASSIGN is as described in Exercise 6.15. Use the style of Section 6.11.

**6.18 In Example 6.25 we considered a subroutine EVAL which (if called by name) checked whether its second argument was zero before evaluating its first argument. There we observed that the particular expression $X/Y + X/(Y - 1)$ caused division by zero if and only if $Y * (Y - 1) = 0$. Is it true in general that for every expression $\mathscr{E}$ using operators $+$, $-$, $*$, and $/$ we may find another expression $\mathscr{E}'$ to use as the second argument of EVAL when $\mathscr{E}$ is its first argument; that is, evaluation of $\mathscr{E}$ causes division by zero if and only if $\mathscr{E}' = 0$? Neglect truncation problems caused by the fact that computer arithmetic rather than arithmetic on abstract reals is used.

*6.19 Let us consider the following FORTRAN function:

```
          FUNCTION FUN(X,Y)
    10    IF(X .EQ. Y) GOTO 10
          FUN = X + Y
          RETURN
          END
```

and the following subroutine:

```
          SUBROUTINE SUB(A,B,C)
          IF (A .LE. 0.) GOTO 20
          C = B
    20    RETURN
          END
```

What happens in response to the call:

$$\text{CALL SUB}(-1.,\text{FUN}(2.,2.),\text{D})$$

if the linkage is:

   a) by reference

   b) by name†

   c) by copy-restore

*6.20 It has been suggested that the problems which occur when the EXCHANGE subroutine of Fig. 6.9 (p. 183) is called by name could be eliminated by the routine:

---

† Note that this alternative is never implemented in FORTRAN.

```
begin
    INTEGER TEMP1, TEMP2;
    TEMP1 = X;
    TEMP2 = Y;
    Y = TEMP1;
    X = TEMP2;
    RETURN
end
```

Does the above routine work "correctly?"

FURTHER READING

Sammet [1969] is a compendium of a large number of programming languages. Peterson [1974] and Pratt [1975] introduce a selection of the more common ones. For more extensive treatments of programming-language concepts than is found here, refer to Pratt [1975], Elson [1973], or Harrison [1973]. Wegner [1968] and Galler and Perlis [1970] give more theoretical treatments of programming-language ideas. Dynamic storage allocation is covered extensively in Knuth [1969]. Rosen [1967] contains many of the original papers in programming languages and other topics covered in this book. The concept of "thunks" is introduced in Ingerman [1961].

Chapter 7

Recursion and Stack Allocation of Storage

The ability of a subroutine to call itself recursively is an important convenience in many programming languages. In this chapter we shall study the use of a stack for allocating storage and see how it helps implement recursive subroutines. Other aspects of stack allocation, including the implementation of both dynamic and static binding will also be discussed.

7.1 STACK ALLOCATION OF STORAGE

The use of a stack for providing storage space for data is an idea found in the implementation of a wide variety of languages. The general idea is as follows. Suppose a programming language has the (usual) property that if subprogram S_1 is initiated, and subprogram S_2 initiates after S_1 begins but before S_1 ends, then S_2 will end before S_1 does. Suppose further that there is a block of memory which will be used to hold all the data used by the entire program. The block will be treated as a stack of unequally sized records. Each time a subprogram S is initiated, a record, called an *activation record*, for the data belonging to S is pushed onto the stack. When S terminates, the activation record for S is popped off the stack. Our assumption that any subprogram initiated after S begins but before S ends will itself end before S does assures us that the activation record for S will be at the top of the stack when S ends. We are also assured that during the time S's activation record is on the stack, we shall not terminate any subprogram T whose activation record is below S's on the stack, since T must have initiated before S.

Example 7.1. Suppose we have the skeleton ALGOL program shown in Fig. 7.1. When the outer block, Block 1, initiates, we allocate a record of two words, one for A and one for B. The stack then appears as in Fig. 7.2(a). After Blocks 2 and 3 initiate, the stack is then as shown in Fig. 7.2(b). Finally when Block 3 terminates and Block 4 initiates, the stack is as shown in Fig. 7.2(c). ∎

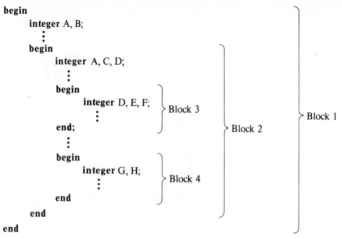

Fig. 7.1 Skeleton ALGOL program.

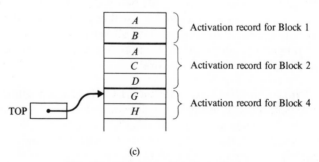

(a)

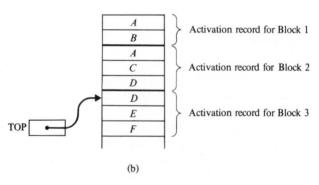

(b)

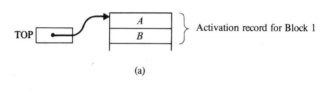

(c)

Fig. 7.2 Sequence of stack contents.

One advantage of stack allocation, as can be seen in Example 7.1, is that sub-programs can share the same memory in certain situations, as did Blocks 3 and 4 in that example. We recall from Section 6.9 that the "environment" of a subprogram consists of all subprograms in which it is physically nested, if static binding is used, as it is in ALGOL. It is exactly the environment of a subprogram S whose activation records should appear on the stack when S is in execution. For example, the environment of Block 4 in Fig. 7.1 is Blocks 4, 2, and 1. These appear on the stack, in exactly that order from the top, when Block 4 is in execution (see Fig. 7.2c). Note that Block 3 is not part of the environment of Block 4 and need not appear on the stack while Block 4 is running. Thus it is possible for Block 4 to use the same space Block 3 did, and stack allocation forces this sharing to occur.

In the simple situation depicted by Example 7.1, it is possible for any datum to be accessed via the pointer to the top of stack.

Example 7.2. Suppose we have the stack of Fig. 7.2(c), and the pointer denoted TOP is loaded into register 7. Imagine that in Block 4 we have the assignment A := B + G. Since static binding with the "most closely nested" rule is used in ALGOL, the compiler can determine by examining the program of Fig. 7.1 that A is from Block 2, B from Block 1, and G from Block 4. Then, because of the particular order chosen for the data within each activation record, G is in the word pointed to by TOP, A is three words below and B is four words below the word pointed to by TOP. Note that the compiler, knowing in this simple case how many words each activation record has, can determine these distances from the top.[†] A := B + G could then be translated as:

$$\begin{array}{ll} \text{LOAD} & -4\,(\text{X7}) \\ \text{ADD} & 0\,(\text{X7}) \\ \text{STORE} & -3\,(\text{X7}) \end{array} \qquad\qquad |$$

It should not be imagined that accessing activation records is as simple as depicted in Examples 7.1 and 7.2. In general, we must deal with a situation in which the size of an activation record is not known (for example, an array of varying length could be stored in an activation record) and in which many activation records for the same subprogram are simultaneously present on the stack. The latter situation occurs when one or more subprograms are recursive subroutines; we shall discuss this in the next section. A method of dealing with the situation where the distances between activation records are not known by the compiler is discussed in Section 7.3. The method is known as a "display" and consists of keeping an array of pointers to certain activation records that are currently on the stack.

7.2 RECURSION

Many common programming languages such as ALGOL, PL/I, and SNOBOL (but not FORTRAN) permit *recursion*, that is, a subroutine which may call itself. A

[†] In fact, it can determine the distance from the bottom of the stack, but to do so for accessing data would be at variance with the more general accessing strategies we shall discuss in the next sections.

recursive call can be *direct* (routine *A* calls *A*) or *indirect* (for example, *A* calls *B*, which calls *C*, which calls *A*). Whether direct or indirect, recursion can be related to stack allocation as follows: If a subroutine *A* is recursive, it will be necessary at some time to have two or more activation records for *A* on the stack simultaneously.

There are many kinds of programs which can be written more succinctly if recursion is used than if it is avoided. One large class of such programs concerns data structures such as trees. The reason trees lend themselves to recursion is that the notion of a tree is inherently recursive, that is, it can be defined in terms of itself. Specifically, a tree is either:

1. a single node, or

2. a node *N* (the root) with a collection of trees attached. The attached trees are the ones whose roots are the children of *N*.

Example 7.3. Let us return to the program of Fig. 3.18 (p. 106) which searched for a key α in a binary search tree. There we used an *iterative* (nonrecursive) program. We can write a recursive subroutine SEARCH(P) which looks for α at node *P*, and not finding α there, calls itself recursively on the left or right child of *P*, as appropriate. Such a subroutine SEARCH is written in Fig. 7.3. The program to find α on a binary search tree with root ROOT simply consists of:

CALL SEARCH(ROOT)

```
begin
    if P .EQ. 0 then
        PRINT, 'KEY NOT PRESENT';
    else
        if α .EQ. KEY(P) then
        PRINT, 'KEY FOUND AT', P
        else
        if α .LT. KEY(P) then
            CALL SEARCH(LEFTCHILD(P))
        else
            CALL SEARCH(RIGHTCHILD(P));
        RETURN
end
```

Fig. 7.3   SEARCH(P).

Of course, recursion is not necessarily efficient when implemented on a computer, so the program of Fig. 7.3 may actually require more time than that of Fig. 3.18. Nevertheless, implementation of recursion in machine language or in a nonrecursive language like FORTRAN is quite feasible, as we shall see in this section. Moreover, recursion often makes it easier for a person to write, debug, and understand a program, so it has merit even in those situations where a modest price in efficiency must be paid.

To keep our examples simple, we shall draw upon recursive arithmetic formulas for subsequent examples of recursive programs. It should be borne in mind that the recursive computation of arithmetic functions is almost never a sensible thing to do; an iterative program is generally as easy to read and write and far more efficient where arithmetic functions are concerned. Nevertheless, we shall draw upon an arithmetic function, the calculation of factorials, to begin our discussion of how to implement recursion.

Example 7.4. Perhaps the simplest example of a recursion is the computation of factorials recursively. We can use a recursive subroutine (actually a function as in FORTRAN) FACT(N), whose value is to be $N!$ if given $N \geqslant 1$ as argument. FACT(N) can be expressed as shown in Fig. 7.4. The program of Fig. 7.4 is based on the fact that $1! = 1$ and $n! = n*(n-1)!$ for $n > 1$.

> **if**   N .LE. 1 **then**
>   FACT = 1
> **else**
>   FACT = N * FACT(N − 1)

Fig. 7.4   Recursive computation of factorials.

Should some routine XYZ call FACT(3), an activation record for FACT would be set up, as in Fig. 7.5(a). FACT(3) calls FACT(2), and an activation record for FACT(2) is set up on top of that for FACT(3). Similarly, FACT(2) calls FACT(1), and another activation record is set up on top of the stack as indicated in Fig. 7.5(b). Although there is but one program for routine FACT, the three activation records in Fig. 7.5(b) represent three separate "calls" of FACT with different actual parameters. All three calls of FACT are "active" at once. For example, immediately after the activation record for FACT(1) is set up, FACT(3) is in the midst of computing 3 * FACT(2); FACT(2) is computing 2 * FACT(1); and FACT(1) is just beginning its computation.

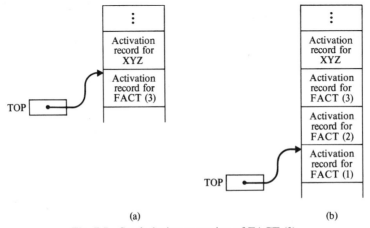

(a)   (b)

Fig. 7.5   Stack during execution of FACT (3).

The three calls of FACT will terminate in the order opposite to that in which they initiated (as all subroutine calls must). That is, FACT(1) will compute FACT = 1 with no further calls, the activation record for FACT(1) will be popped off the stack and we return to FACT(2) with FACT(1) equal to 1. We then compute FACT = 2 ∗ FACT(1) = 2, pop the record for FACT(2) off the stack and return to FACT(3) with FACT(2) = 2. FACT(3) then computes FACT = 3 ∗ FACT(2) = 6 and returns this value to XYZ, after the record for FACT(3) is popped off the stack. ∎

It should be observed that activation records for a recursive subroutine need not appear contiguously on the stack as they did in Example 7.4. For example, if A calls B which calls C which calls A, the stack would appear as in Fig. 7.6.

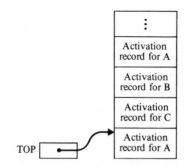

Fig. 7.6   Stack after indirect recursive call of A.

We shall now delve more deeply into the mechanics of recursive subroutine implementation with an extended example, in which, however, matters are still simpler than those which can be expected to occur in a recursive language such as ALGOL. In particular, the recursive subroutine we shall consider makes use only of its own local variables and the actual parameters with which it is called. The former can be accessed by going a fixed distance into the stack as we did in Example 7.2. The latter can be reached via pointers found in the calling sequences (the call will be by reference). There is thus no need for a "display." (This notion was mentioned at the end of Section 7.1 and will be described in detail in Section 7.3.)

Example 7.5.   The *combinations of M things out of N*, written $\binom{N}{M}$, is equal to

$$\frac{N!}{M!(N-M)!}.$$

A (highly inefficient) recursive formula for $\binom{N}{M}$ is given by:

$$\left.\begin{array}{l} \dbinom{N}{0} = \dbinom{N}{N} = 1 \\[2ex] \dbinom{N}{M} = \dbinom{N-1}{M} + \dbinom{N-1}{M-1} \text{ if } 0 < M < N \end{array}\right\} \qquad (7.1)$$

We can write a recursive subroutine COMB(N, M, P) based on Expression (7.1) to set P equal to $\binom{N}{M}$ as in Fig. 7.7.[†]

```
begin
      INTEGER P1, P2;
      if M .LE. 0 .OR. M .GE. N then
            P = 1
      else
            begin
                  CALL COMB(N − 1, M, P1);
                  CALL COMB(N − 1, M − 1, P2);
                  P = P1 + P2
            end
end
```

Fig. 7.7   Recursive procedure COMB (N, M, P).

Let us design an assembly-language subroutine, called by reference, that will implement the recursive subroutine COMB. To begin, let us determine what its activation record should look like.[‡] Surely P1 and P2, being local variables of the subroutine, will have words allocated for them in the activation record.

We do not provide locations for N, M, or P, since these are actual parameters. Their values will be accessed through pointers in the calling sequence as we have discussed, regarding call-by-reference, in Sections 5.3 and 6.10. However, since there are but two calls of COMB in Fig. 7.7, we can expect that the assembly code for COMB will have only two places where calling sequences are set up. On the other hand, if N and M are large there will be many more than two calls to COMB active at one time. For example, if we call COMB with $N = 10$ and $M = 3$, we immediately call COMB with $N = 9$ and $M = 3$, then with $N = 8$ and $M = 3$. We conclude that no matter what plan we adopt, the two calling sequences of COMB cannot hold all the pointers for all the calls to COMB that may be active at once. We therefore shall adopt the strategy of copying the calling sequence pointers onto the stack, and we shall make place in the activation record for them.

A similar observation applies to the return address. In Sections 5.3 and 6.10 we were dealing with nonrecursive subroutines, and we could leave register 7 intact. In the present case, register 7 cannot hold the return address for more than one call of COMB, so we shall have to store it in the activation record as well.

Finally, by the rules of call-by-reference, we shall have to compute the actual parameters $N - 1$ and $M - 1$, which are expressions. These values must be stored

---

[†] We could make COMB be a function taking only N and M as parameters, but to do so would introduce extra details which we choose to avoid.

[‡] It should be noted that the entire program of Fig. 7.7 should be regarded as a single subprogram. The **begin** ... **end** construct following the **else** in Fig. 7.7 is there to group the three statements following **else**, the way DO ... END does in PL/I. It should not be regarded as forming a block with local variables as in ALGOL.

in the activation record and pointers to them passed to COMB(N − 1, M, P1) and COMB(N − 1, M − 1, P2). In the first of these, no location for *M* is needed. COMB(N, M, P) was passed a pointer to *M*, and the same pointer can be passed to COMB(N − 1, M, P1). The format we shall choose for the activation record for COMB is shown in Fig. 7.8.

| Value of *P*1 |
| Value of *P*2 |
| Pointer to actual parameter *N* |
| Pointer to actual parameter *M* |
| Pointer to actual parameter *P* |
| Contents of register 7 |
| Value of *N* − 1 |
| Value of *M* − 1 |

Fig. 7.8   Activation record for COMB.

The format we shall use for the calling sequence is the same as that in Section 5.3. Register 7 holds the location from which the call came, with pointers to *N*, *M*, and *P* in that location and in the next two locations.

We shall use register 6 to point to the activation record on top of the stack. COMB expects register 6 to be set when it is called. In turn, just before COMB calls itself recursively, it will increment register 6 by 8 words, thus creating a new activation record on top of the stack for the new call of COMB. Similarly, when the call to COMB returns, the calling copy of COMB will subtract 8 from register 6, thereby popping the activation record of the called copy off the stack. Thus when a call of COMB returns, the copy of COMB which called it will make register 6 point to its own activation record.

A flowchart for COMB(N, M, P) is shown in Fig. 7.9, and assembly code for the subroutine is in Fig. 7.10. The code of Fig. 7.10 is far from efficient but is designed to implement each of the steps indicated by Fig. 7.9 in as direct a manner as possible.

Let us now simulate COMB(3, 2, X). To be specific, let us suppose that the routine which calls (COMB(3, 2, X) has constants 3 and 2 and variable *X* located in 400, 410, and 420, respectively, and sets register 7 to 300. Suppose also that the activation record for COMB(3, 2, X) begins at location 1000, so register 6 is set to 1000 when COMB begins. Finally, assume instruction 29 of COMB (the contents of register 7 for the first call) has location 500, and instruction 46 (the contents of register 7 for the second call) has location 521. Then after instructions 1 to 8, the stack would appear as in Fig. 7.11.

At instruction 13 we jump to 17. There, we compute *N* − 1 = 2 and place 2 in location 1006 on the stack. We compute pointers 1006, 410, and 1000 to place in instructions 29, 30, and 31, respectively. Then, we push a new activation record onto

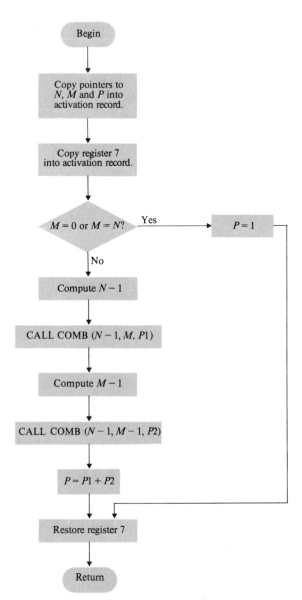

Fig. 7.9   Flowchart of COMB (N, M, P).

the stack and jump to COMB at instruction 28, effectively calling COMB with the
first and second arguments equal to 2 and with the third argument being the space
reserved for P1 in the activation record for COMB(3, 2, X). Register 7 holds address
500. After executing instructions 1 to 8 again, we are presented with the stack contents
shown in Fig. 7.12.

```
1.                  ENTRY     COMB
2. COMB:            LOAD1     0(X7)
3.                  STORE1    2(X6)        /* COPY POINTER TO N INTO ACTIVATION RECORD          */
4.                  LOAD1     1(X7)
5.                  STORE1    3(X6)        /* LIKEWISE M                                         */
6.                  LOAD1     2(X7)
7.                  STORE1    4(X6)        /* AND LIKEWISE P                                     */
8.                  STORE7    5(X6)        /* STORE REGISTER 7 INTO ACTIVATION RECORD           */
9.                  LOAD1     3(INDX6)
10.                 JZERO1    NOCALLS      /* TEST IF M = 0                                      */
11.                 LOAD1     2(INDX6)
12.                 SUB1      3(INDX6)
13.                 JNONZ1    CALLS        /* TEST IF M = N                                      */
14. NOCALLS:        LOAD1     1(IMMED)     /* HERE, M = 0 or M = N                               */
15.                 STORE1    4(INDX6)     /* SET P = 1                                          */
16.                 JUMP      RETURN       /* AND PREPARE TO RETURN AT LINE 53                   */
17. CALLS:          LOAD1     2(INDX6)     /* HERE 0 < M < N                                     */
18.                 SUB1      1(IMMED)
19.                 STORE1    6(X6)        /* COMPUTE N − 1 AND PLACE IN ACTIVATION RECORD */
20.                 COPY61
21.                 ADD1      6(IMMED)
22.                 STORE1    *+7          /* PLACE POINTER TO N − 1 IN CALLING SEQUENCE         */
23.                 LOAD1     3(X6)
24.                 STORE1    *+6          /* PLACE POINTER TO M IN CALLING SEQUENCE             */
25.                 STORE6    *+6          /* PLACE POINTER TO P1 IN CALLING SEQUENCE            */
26.                 ADD6      8(IMMED)     /* PUSH NEW RECORD ONTO STACK                         */
27.                 LOAD7     *+2(IMMED)
28.                 JUMP      COMB         /* CALL COMB(N − 1, M, P1)                            */
29.                 DATA      0            /* POINTER TO N − 1                                   */
30.                 DATA      0            /* POINTER TO M                                       */
31.                 DATA      0            /* POINTER TO P1                                      */
32.                 SUB6      8(IMMED)     /* POP RECORD FROM STACK                              */
33.                 LOAD1     3(INDX6)
34.                 SUB1      1(IMMED)
35.                 STORE1    7(X6)        /* COMPUTE M − 1 AND PLACE IN ACTIVATION RECORD */
36.                 COPY61
37.                 ADD1      6(IMMED)
38.                 STORE1    *+8          /* PLACE POINTER TO N − 1 IN CALLING SEQUENCE         */
39.                 ADD1      1(IMMED)
40.                 STORE1    *+7          /* PLACE POINTER TO M − 1 IN CALLING SEQUENCE         */
41.                 SUB1      6(IMMED)
42.                 STORE1    *+6          /* PLACE POINTER TO P2 IN CALLING SEQUENCE            */
43.                 ADD6      8(IMMED)     /* PUSH NEW RECORD ONTO STACK                         */
44.                 LOAD7     *+2(IMMED)
45.                 JUMP      COMB         /* CALL COMB(N − 1, M − 1, P2)                        */
46.                 DATA      0            /* POINTER TO N − 1                                   */
47.                 DATA      0            /* POINTER TO M − 1                                   */
48.                 DATA      0            /* POINTER TO P2                                      */
49.                 SUB6      8(IMMED)     /* POP RECORD FROM STACK                              */
50.                 LOAD1     0(X6)
51.                 ADD1      1(X6)
52.                 STORE1    4(INDX6)     /* P = P1 + P2                                        */
53. RETURN:         LOAD7     5(X6)        /* RESTORE RETURN ADDRESS                             */
54.                 JUMP      3(X7)        /* RETURN                                             */
```

Fig. 7.10   Assembly code for COMB.

We now discover $M = N$ at instruction 13, and at instruction 15 we set P1 from COMB(3, 2, X), to 1. This particular P1 is found at location 1000, not 1010, as we discover by following the pointer in 1014. We then jump to instruction 53, and return to instruction 32. The situation at this time is essentially identical to Fig. 7.11 but location 1000 now holds 1.

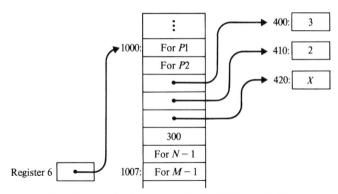

Fig. 7.11   After instruction 8 of COMB (3, 2, X).

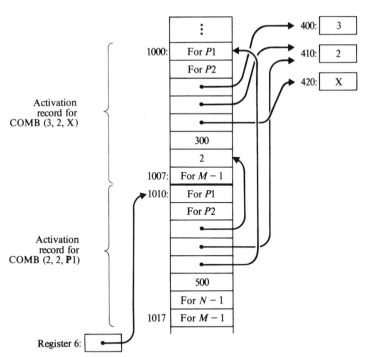

Fig. 7.12   After instruction 8 of COMB (2, 2, P1).

Now we proceed from instruction 32 with COMB(3, 2, X). $M - 1$ is found to be 1, and this value is placed in location 1007. The pointers 46 to 48 for the second calling sequence are computed to be 1006, 1007, and 1001, respectively. We jump back to COMB at instruction 45, effectively calling COMB(2, 1, P2). Register 7 holds address 521. After instructions 1 to 8 the stack is as shown in Fig. 7.13.

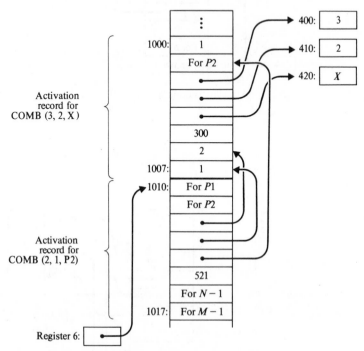

Fig. 7.13   After instruction 8 of COMB (2, 1, P2).

The tests of instructions 9 to 13 take us to 17, where we compute $N - 1 = 1$ and store this value in 1016. The pointers for instructions 29 to 31 are computed to be 1016, 1007, and 1010, respectively. We thus call COMB(1, 1, P1) at instruction 28. After instructions 1 to 8 of this call the stack contents are as shown in Fig. 7.14.

From the point shown in Fig. 7.1 we discover $M = N$ at instruction 13, set P1 at location 1010 to 1, and return to instruction 32. The stack at this time is essentially that shown in Fig. 7.13, but with location 1010 set to 1. We proceed with COMB(2, 1, P2), setting up a call to COMB(1, 0, P2) at instruction 45. This call sets P2 in location 1011 to 1 and returns to COMB(2, 1, P2) at instruction 49. The stack at that time is still similar to Fig. 7.13, but now both locations 1010 and 1011 hold 1. Instructions 50 to 52 add these two locations together, storing the result in 1001. We then return to COMB(3, 2, X) at instruction 49.

The situation now is akin to Fig. 7.11 (p. 207), but location 1000 has been set to 1 and location 1001 to 2. Instructions 50 to 52 add these and store the result in

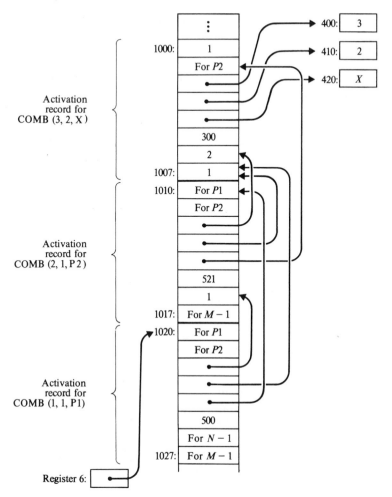

Fig. 7.14   After instruction 8 of COMB (1, 1, P1).

X, location 420. The return goes to that subprogram at location 303. We have set X to 3, which is $\binom{3}{2}$.   ∎

7.3   DISPLAYS

Throughout this section, let us discuss a programming language such as ALGOL which uses stack allocation and static binding using the "most closely nested" rule. In Section 7.1 we discussed a simple situation (Example 7.2) where, given a pointer to the top record on the stack, we could find any datum belonging to any of the subprograms in the environment of the currently executing subprogram. We could do this because we knew the number of words in each activation record. However, in a real programming language such as ALGOL there are several reasons why we might not know the position of a given activation record when the program was being compiled.

Example 7.6.   Fig. 7.15 shows the activation record for a block A which has arrays X and Y whose length can vary, depending on the values of some variables when A is entered. We could allocate storage for variable-length arrays in a heap, as discussed in Section 6.5. However, if we are already using a stack for storage allocation, it is convenient to rely on this method exclusively. Thus, supposing A had an integer variable Z as well as the variable-length arrays, we could format the activation record for A as in Fig. 7.15.

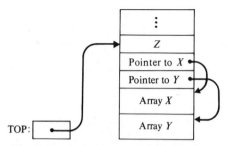

Fig. 7.15   Activation record for Block A.

We see that from TOP we can find Z directly and find the beginnings of X and Y (where dope-vectors are presumably kept) via pointers in the second and third words of the record. However, we don't know the length of the record; and, should we wish to push another activation record on the stack, we would need a pointer to the first available stack location, either in the activation record for A or in a fixed location outside the stack. Worse, should we then wish to pop an activation record above A on the stack, we would not know how to reset TOP to the beginning of the record for A.   ∎

Recursion is another source of problems when trying to access activation records inside the stack. The following example shows the type of problems that can arise.

Example 7.7.   Suppose subprogram A calls recursive subroutine B which calls itself many times. The situation on the stack is as shown in Fig. 7.16. Since the compiler cannot tell in advance how many activation records for B will appear on the stack, it cannot access data belonging to A via the top of stack pointer.

We can also dispense with the possibility that we could reach A's data via the bottom of the stack. Suppose A itself were a recursive procedure that called itself several times before calling B. The stack would appear as in Fig. 7.17. If B references a variable X local to A, it refers to the copy of X in that activation record for A

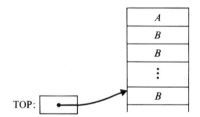

Fig. 7.16   Stack after recursive calls of B.

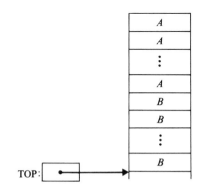

Fig. 7.17   Stack showing recursive calls of A and B.

closest to the top of stack.[†] That activation record is at a distance from the top of stack that depends on the number of calls of B and at a distance from the bottom that depends on the number of calls of A. Neither of these quantities can be known in advance. ∎

Having seen the problems that arise in accessing activation records, we must find a solution. Let us recall that in a programming language using static binding under the "most closely nested" rule, we can associate with each subprogram S_1 an environment $S_1, S_2, \ldots, S_n$ consisting of all those subprograms to whose local variables statements of S_1 could refer. When executing S_1, at least one activation record for each of these subprograms will appear on the stack. There may be more than one activation record for those S_i's that are recursive, but the top activation record for S_1 is above the top activation record for S_2, which is above the top activation record for S_3, and so on.

[†] This statement is in a sense an extension of the "most closely nested" rule for binding identifiers. In another sense, however, it represents a new kind of binding. In nonrecursive programs it is sufficient to bind identifier uses to declarations. In recursive programs, however, we must bind identifiers not only to declarations, but to a particular memory location out of possibly many on the stack that "represent" a particular declaration.

As we mentioned in Example 7.7, any reference to a local identifier of S_i by S_1 refers to the copy of that identifier in the top activation record for S_i. It is therefore only the top copies of the activation records for the S_i's whose data can be referenced and whose location must be known. We may therefore keep a stack of pointers to the top activation record for each subprogram in the environment. This stack is termed a *display*, and the entire arrangement is represented schematically in Fig. 7.18.

It is desirable that the display be kept in registers, but even if we cannot afford registers for the purpose we can conveniently access any datum through a display kept in memory.

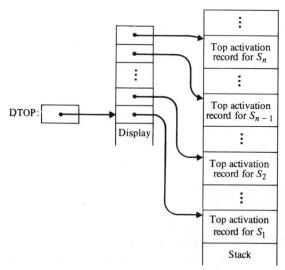

Fig. 7.18   Use of a display.

Example 7.8.   Suppose we have the display depicted in Fig. 7.16, and S_1 contains the assignment A = B, where A is a local variable of S_3. Suppose A is kept four words above the beginning of the activation record for S_3 and B is kept six words above the beginning of the activation record for S_5. Note that all the information contained in the above sentences can be determined by the compiler using the "most closely nested" rule. That is, the compiler can determine by looking at the program that A belongs to the third subprogram in the environment of S_1. The decision to put A four words from the beginning of S_3 is an arbitrary choice that can be made by the compiler. Similar statements hold for B. The compiler knows, therefore that B can be obtained by going to the fifth word on the display, following the pointer found there and going six words below the target of that pointer. Thus A = B could be carried out by code such as that of Fig. 7.19. Note that for efficiency one would certainly keep DTOP in a register, even if the whole display could not be kept in registers. ∎

```
LOAD2    DTOP
LOAD3    -4(X2)    /*   GET POINTER TO S₅    */
LOAD1    6(X3)     /*   GET B                */
LOAD3    -2(X2)    /*   GET POINTER TO S₃    */
STORE1   4(X3)     /*   STORE B INTO A       */
```

Fig. 7.19   Code for $A = B$.

We have seen that accessing the needed data using a display is not hard. To convince ourselves that a display is a feasible method for locating data we must now consider how the display is to be modified when a new subprogram initiates and when an old one terminates. There are two cases to consider, depending on whether the subprogram is a block or a subroutine. Since the block case is considerably simpler, we shall consider it first.

Suppose we are executing subprogram S_1 with environment $S_1, S_2, \ldots, S_n$ as in the previous example, and that S_1 contains within it a block S_0. When we reach the beginning of S_0 we push the activation record for S_0 onto the stack, as usual. We also push a new word onto the display and make it point to the activation record for S_0. The resulting configuration is as shown in Fig. 7.20. When S_0 terminates, we simply pop the display, effectively restoring the situation of Fig. 7.18.

If instead of entering a new block, S_1 calls a procedure P, the situation is more complex. In the case of block S_0 described above, we knew the environment of S_0 was $S_0, S_1, S_2, \ldots, S_n$. However, in a language like ALGOL, the environment of P

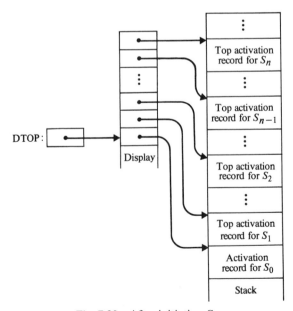

Fig. 7.20   After initiating S_0.

may not include all of $S_1, S_2, \ldots, S_n$. According to the ALGOL rules for procedure definition and use, P will be defined immediately within subprogram S_i, for some i between 1 and n. The environment of P will be P, $S_i, S_{i+1}, \ldots, S_n$.

We may not remove the activation records for $S_1, S_2, \ldots, S_{i-1}$, since when P terminates and S_1 resumes these records will again be needed. However, we may simulate their removal by popping the top $i - 1$ display pointers and storing them in the activation record for P. We then push a pointer to the activation record for P onto the display. By so doing we ensure that no matter where P was called from, and no matter how many pointers were on the display when P was called, when we execute P the display is sure to consist only of pointers to activation records for $P, S_i, S_{i+1}, \ldots, S_n$. An example will serve to clarify these ideas.

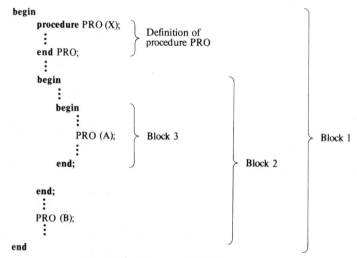

Fig. 7.21   Skeleton ALGOL program.

Example 7.9.   Consider the skeleton ALGOL program of Fig. 7.21. The environment of procedure PRO consists of itself and Block 1. PRO is called at two points, once inside Block 3 and once inside Block 1. Immediately before the call PRO(A) in Block 3, the stack and display are as shown in Fig. 7.22(a). When we call PRO(A), the first two members of the environment of Block 3 are no longer part of the "current" environment. We therefore pop two words off the display and store them in the activation record for PRO. This portion of the display is treated as a variable-length array, and we show the first word of the activation record for PRO pointing to the place where the display pointers are stored. These pointers are preceded by a "dope vector" consisting of a count of the number of pointers.

After popping two words off the display, we push a pointer to the activation record for PRO onto the display. The resulting configuration is shown in Fig. 7.22(b).

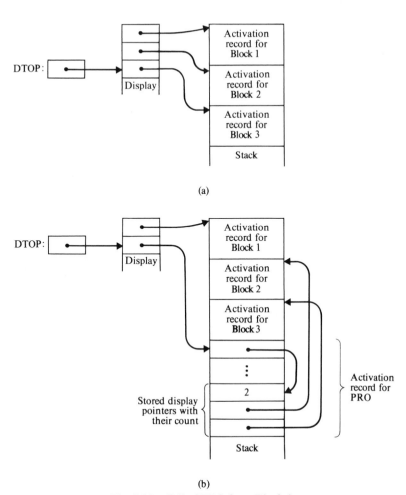

(a)

(b)

Fig. 7.22 Call of PRO from Block 3.

Now let us consider the call PRO(B) in Block 1. At the time of that call, the stack consists only of the activation record for Block 1 as in Fig. 7.23(a). To effect the call, no pointers need be popped off the display. We store an empty array of pointers in the activation record for PRO, as shown in Fig. 7.23(b).

It should be noted that the compiler can examine each procedure call and determine how many pointers, if any, to pop off the display and store in the activation record for PRO. For example, the call PRO(A) in Block 3 is at a point with an environment of length 3. The definition of PRO is at a place with an environment (excluding PRO itself) of length 1. Since $3 - 1 = 2$, we must effect the call PRO(A) by popping two pointers off the display. Similarly, the call PRO(B) occurs where the environment has length 1. We must pop $1 - 1 = 0$ pointers off the display. ∎

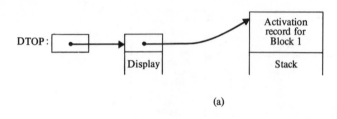

(a)

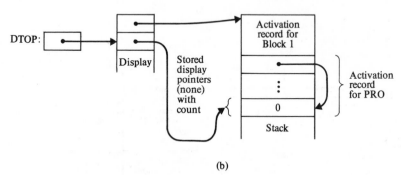

(b)

Fig. 7.23   Call of PRO from Block 1.

A comparison of Figs. 7.22(b) and 7.23(b) shows clear similarities. In each case the display consists only of pointers to activation records for Block 1 and PRO. The other activation records on the stack in Fig. 7.22(b) are not accessible. Thus whether the situation is as in Fig. 7.22(b) or 7.23(b), the code for PRO accesses its data in exactly the same way. Data belonging to Block 1 is found via the lower display pointer and variables local to PRO are found via the top display pointer.

The algorithm for completing a procedure call is simple. The display pointer to its activation record is popped and any display pointers stored in its activation record are pushed back onto the display. For example, when PRO of Example 7.9 terminates, Fig. 7.22(b) gives rise to Fig. 7.22(a) and Fig. 7.23(b) gives rise to Fig. 7.23(a).

7.4 STACK ALLOCATION WITH DYNAMIC BINDING

So far we have seen how a stack can be used to implement static binding under the "most closely nested" rule. It should also be apparent that a stack could be used for storage if binding of identifiers were under the dynamic "most recently initiated" rule. Under the rule that a subprogram has its activation record pushed onto the stack when it begins and popped when it terminates, we would at all times have a list of the active subprograms on the stack. The more recently the subprogram initiated, the higher on the stack it would be. The list of subprograms on the stack is thus analogous to the environment defined in Section 6.9 for subprograms having identifiers bound statically. To find the instance of X to which a use of identifier X refers, travel down the stack until the first activation record with a local variable X is found.

There would be no use for a display, since the compiler could not in general resolve references anyway. One strategy for resolving references is to make each activation record be an associative structure such as a scatter store[†] whose keys are the local identifiers. To find the value of an identifier X we look for X in each activation record, starting at the top, until a value for X is found. In this method, pushing new activation records onto the stack is not hard—we need only initialize the associative structure to "empty." Popping an activation record is easier still. We need only move the stack pointer. However, accessing values of identifiers is hard, since we may have to travel far down the stack before we find the identifier we are looking for.

An alternate strategy is to eschew a stack of activation records. Instead, make a private stack for each identifier mentioned by the program. When a subprogram initiates, push down the stack for each local identifier belonging to the subprogram. When the subprogram terminates, pop up the same stacks. While this method makes initiation and termination of subprograms relatively hard, it makes access of identifiers easy, since the value we want will always be on top of the stack for that identifier.

It is worth noting the situation in SNOBOL, which uses dynamic binding under the "most recently initiated" rule. Although SNOBOL permits dynamic creation of identifier names, the local variables of a subroutine (the only kind of subprogram in SNOBOL, since there are no blocks) must be declared in advance. This declaration makes it possible for us to use the second method described above. That is, we always have the information we need to push and pop the correct private stacks when a subroutine begins or ends.

EXERCISES

7.1 Suppose we have the skeleton of an ALGOL program as shown in Fig. 7.24.

a. Show the display and stack immediately before and after the call PRO(B) in Block 3.

b. Do the same for the call PRO(C) in Block 4.

* c. Suppose that after the call of PRO(C), PRO recursively calls PRO(A) in Block 2. Show the display and stack immediately before and after this call.

7.2 Suppose we have the ALGOL program represented in Fig. 7.1 (p. 198) and that the activation records for the blocks are formatted as in Fig. 7.2.

a. Show the contents of the display when Block 3 is in execution as in Fig. 7.2(b).

b. Assume that register 6 points to the top of the display. Write assembly code to execute $A := C + D$, making all data accesses via the display.

7.3 Write a recursive assembly-language program to compute $N!$ as described in Example 7.4 (p. 201). Specify your linkage conventions and activation record format.

[†] If a scatter store is chosen, data storage for all activation records can be in one table.

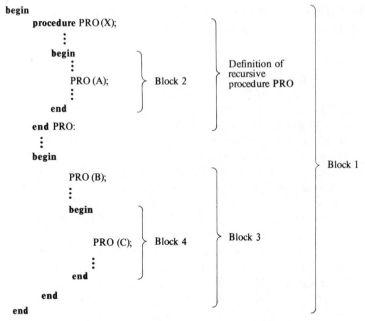

Fig. 7.24   Skeleton ALGOL program.

7.4 The nth triangular number[†] is $T_n = n(n + 1)/2$. The nth perfect square is $S_n = n^2$. The following identities are easy to show:

$$\left.\begin{array}{ll} S_n = T_n + T_{n-1} & \text{for } n \geqslant 2 \\ T_n = (S_{n-1} + 3n - 1)/2 & \text{for } n \geqslant 2 \end{array}\right\} \tag{7.2}$$

We may, based on Expression (7.2) write mutually recursive subroutines $T(N, M)$ and $S(N, M)$ which set M to the Nth triangular number and perfect square, respectively. These are shown in Fig. 7.25.

a. Implement the programs of Fig. 7.25 in assembly code, selecting formats for the activation records and a method of parameter passing.

b. Is a display necessary? Why?

c. Show the sequence of push and pop actions when T(4) is called.

7.5 The recursive procedure COMB of Example 7.5 was written in assembly code in Fig. 7.10 (p. 206). It exhibits certain inefficiencies because it was made to mimic the flowchart of Fig. 7.9 closely. Rewrite the program to save as many instructions as you can without tampering with the essential recursive nature of the program or with the fact that parameters are passed by reference using the calling sequence described in Section 5.3.

* **7.6** If we call COMB(10, 4, X), where COMB is from Example 7.5, what is the largest number of activation records to appear on the stack simultaneously?

[†] Triangular numbers are those numbers of marbles which can be arranged into an equilateral triangle. For example, 10 is a triangular number, as every bowler knows.

```
begin
    INTEGER M1, M2;
    if N .LE. 1 then
        M = 1
    else
        begin
            CALL T(N, M1);
            CALL T(N − 1, M2);
            M = M1 + M2
        end
end
```

(a)

```
if N .LE. 1 then
    M = 1
else
    begin
        CALL S(N − 1, M);
        M = (M + 3 ∗ N − 1)/2
    end
```

(b)

7.25 Mutually recursive programs: a) S(N, M); b) T(N, M).

Programming Exercise

7.7 The reader should obtain additional experience by implementing recursions in a nonrecursive language, such as the assembly language for his local machine or in FORTRAN. Some suggested problems are:

  a. searching a binary-search tree, as in Fig. 7.3 (p. 200).

  b. the square and triangular number programs of Fig. 7.25.

  c. deletion of an entry from a binary-search tree (see Exercise 3.6 on p. 115).

    If FORTRAN is chosen, the discussion of implementation of records in that language (Section 3.1) should be reviewed.

FURTHER READING

More detailed discussions of the stack implementation of languages such as ALGOL can be found in Randell and Russell [1964], Wegner [1968], Gries [1971] and Pratt [1975]. The idea of the display as we have presented it here is from Dijkstra [1960].

Chapter 8

Context-Free Grammars

We now introduce the notation called context-free grammars, which has obvious use in defining the syntax of a programming language. Moreover, by means of a so-called "parse tree," a context-free grammar gives a structure to programs that is useful when compiling the language. In this chapter we discuss context-free grammars and the construction of parse trees. In the next chapter we shall see how the parser forms an integral part of a compiler. To start, we consider the general notion of a recursive definition, of which a context-free grammar is a special case.

8.1 RECURSIVE DEFINITIONS

Many features of programming languages are defined "recursively." By a *recursive* (or *inductive*) *definition* we mean one in which the object is defined partially in terms of itself.

Example 8.1. We can define the class of "my enemies" as follows:

1. Anyone who harms[†] me is my enemy.
2. Anyone who is a friend to one of my enemies is also my enemy.

Thus, if A harms me, he is my enemy by rule (1). If B is A's friend, he is then my enemy by rule (2). Then, if C is B's friend, C is my enemy by a further application of rule (2).

To be precise, we should add another rule:

3. No one is my enemy unless his being so follows by a finite number of applications of rules (1) and (2).

Otherwise, we could not be sure that two of my friends, each of which was a friend of the other, were not my enemies. ∎

[†] Let us assume that the notions of "harms" and "friend" are understood by all.

The three statements of Example 8.1 are typical of recursive definitions. We see a method—statement (1)—of establishing certain things to be in the defined class initially. Then, we see some laws for constructing new members of the class from old ones—rule (2) is the lone example here. Finally, there is usually a statement, either implicit or explicit, that the class consists only of those items whose membership in the class follows from the other rules. Above, rule (3) is such a statement.

In a more complex form of recursive definition, several classes are defined at once. Often, only one of these classes is "important." We use the other classes to help define the important class.

Example 8.2.   Let us consider arithmetic expressions with operators + and * the only ones allowed. We can define the notions factor, term, and expression simultaneously. Intuitively, a *factor* is either a single identifier or an expression with parentheses around it. A *term* is a product of factors, and an *expression* is a sum of terms. We may use the following rules.

1. Any identifier is a factor. (This is how we get started.)
2. a) Every factor is a term.
   b) If $\mathcal{F}$ is a factor and $\mathcal{T}$ is a term, then $\mathcal{T} * \mathcal{F}$ is a term.
   c) Every term is an expression.
   d) If $\mathcal{T}$ is a term and $\mathcal{E}$ is an expression, then $\mathcal{E} + \mathcal{T}$ is an expression.
   e) If $\mathcal{E}$ is an expression, then $(\mathcal{E})$ is a factor.
3. Nothing else is a factor, term, or expression.

Thus, we can discover that $(A + B) * (C + D) * E$ is a term, and hence an expression by rule (2c). By rule (1), $A, B, C, D,$ and E are factors, and by rule (2a), $A, B, C,$ and D are each terms.[†] By rule (2c), A is an expression. By (2d) $A + B$ is an expression, and hence, $(A + B)$ is a factor by (2e). Similarly, we find that $(C + D)$ is a factor. By rule (2a), $(A + B)$ is a term. Thus, by (2b), $(A + B) * (C + D)$ and $(A + B) * (C + D) * E$ are terms. ∎

We should note that the recursive definition in Example 8.2 more or less fits the intuitive definitions of factor, term, and expression. Rules (2a) and (2b) together say "Any product of factors is a term," and rules (2c) and (2d) say "Any sum of terms is an expression." However, the recursive definition gives the feeling that one cannot use it to give a one paragraph description of a notion like "all terms." All we can do is find, by trial and error, whether a particular string of characters is or is not an expression, term, or factor.

Thus, it may be surprising to find that recursive definition is a useful and common description of programming languages and their constituent parts. There are three reasons why recursive definition is useful for this task.

1. One can find, in virtually all cases, an efficient algorithm for recognizing the programs of a particular programming language; most important, one can obtain this algorithm directly from a recursive definition of the programming language.

[†] Identifier E is a term as well, of course, but we do not need this fact.

2. Recursive definitions of programming languages tend to be considerably more concise than are other forms of description.

3. Recursive definitions do more than allow us to tell if a string of characters is a program. They help us to place a structure on the program which is quite useful in translating the program to machine language. This structure is similar in spirit to, but finer than, the hierarchical structure discussed in Chapter 0.

When we define languages recursively, the definition rules take on a special form. Since programs are character strings, it is not surprising that all objects claimed *a priori* to be in a defined class are themselves strings of characters. Moreover, the recursive rules say that members of some defined class can be formed by concatenating (writing next to each other) fixed characters and arbitrary members of certain defined classes, in some fixed order.

Example 8.3. Example 8.2 exhibits this type of definition. For instance, rule (2b) said that a term could be formed by concatenating any string in the class "term" with the character + and then with a string in the class "factor." Moreover, the only objects defined *a priori* to be in a class are identifiers, which are factors by rule (1). In any programming language, the permissible identifiers are strings of characters. ∎

Example 8.4. We can define statements and programs of a simple gotoless language as in Chapter 0 by the following rules.

1. A FORTRAN assignment, input/output statement, or declaration statement is a statement.

2. If $\mathscr{E}$ is a FORTRAN logical expression and $\mathscr{S}_1$ and $\mathscr{S}_2$ are statements, then **if** $\mathscr{E}$ **then** $\mathscr{S}_1$ **else** $\mathscr{S}_2$ is a statement.

3. If $\mathscr{E}$ is a FORTRAN logical expression $\mathscr{S}$ is a statement, then **while** $\mathscr{E}$ **do** $\mathscr{S}$ is a statement.

4. If $\mathscr{S}_1, \mathscr{S}_2, \ldots, \mathscr{S}_n$ are statements, then **begin** $\mathscr{S}_1 ; \mathscr{S}_2 ; \ldots ; \mathscr{S}_n$ **end** is a statement.

5. A statement is a program.

Here, we assume that the notions of "expression," "assignment statement," "input/output statement," and "declaration statement" are given. In practice there would be recursive rules defining these notions in terms of more primitive notions such as arithmetic signs and "identifier" (which itself can be defined as the concatenation of letters and digits). ∎

8.2 DEFINITION OF CONTEXT-FREE GRAMMAR

A context-free grammar is a shorthand for the recursive definition of a set of character strings. It is often referred to as a "BNF (Backus-Naur form or Backus normal form) description" of the language. The following are the necessary elements of a *context-free grammar* (or just *grammar*):

1. a set of *variables* (or *syntactic categories* or *nonterminals*), each of which represents a class of defined objects. Usually we shall give the variables names which have

triangular brackets around them, for example, ⟨program⟩ or ⟨expression⟩. One variable is *distinguished*, and represents the class of strings in which we are actually interested. The other variables are defined only to aid in the definition of the class of strings and to help put structure on those strings.

2. a set of *terminal* symbols, which could be characters or could be symbols representing some previously defined set of strings.[†]

3. a finite set of *productions* (or *rules*) of the form $A \rightarrow X_1 \ldots X_n$,[‡] where A is a variable and $X_1, \ldots, X_n$ are either terminal or variable symbols. The production $A \rightarrow X_1 \ldots X_n$ is intended to mean that one way to construct a member of the class A is to take:

$$\begin{Bmatrix} \text{the symbol } X_1, \text{ if } X_1 \text{ is a terminal, or} \\ \text{a member of class } X_1, \text{ if } X_1 \text{ is a variable} \end{Bmatrix},$$

and following it by

$$\begin{Bmatrix} \text{the symbol } X_2, \text{ if } X_2 \text{ is a terminal, or} \\ \text{a member of the class } X_2, \text{ if } X_2 \text{ is a variable} \end{Bmatrix},$$

followed by the symbol $X_3, \ldots$ and so on.[§]

The set of productions with A on the left of the arrow is called the set of *alternates* for A. Often, if $A \rightarrow \alpha_1, A \rightarrow \alpha_2, \ldots, A \rightarrow \alpha_n$ is the set of alternates for A, we write $A \rightarrow \alpha_1 \mid \alpha_2 \mid \ldots \mid \alpha_n$.

Example 8.5. Let us reconsider our expression-term-factor definition. Obviously, there are three variables, ⟨expression⟩, ⟨term⟩ and ⟨factor⟩. The first of these is distinguished. The terminal symbols are the characters (,), + and ∗, and the symbol **id**, representing the class of identifiers. The latter class must be considered defined *a priori*.

We may write the productions as:

i) ⟨expression⟩ → ⟨expression⟩ + ⟨term⟩ | ⟨term⟩

ii) ⟨term⟩ → ⟨term⟩ ∗ ⟨factor⟩ | ⟨factor⟩

iii) ⟨factor⟩ → **id** | (⟨expression⟩)

We obtain (i) from rules (2a) and (2b); (ii) is from (2c) and (2d); (iii) is from rules (1) and (2e) of the original definition.

[†] For example, the sets "expression," assignment statement," "input/output statement," and "declaration statement" must be considered defined *a priori* in the definition of "gotoless" programs of Example 8.4. In reality, we are not sure of their definition at all, but the control structure of gotoless programs does not depend on their definition. It is convenient to think of them as terminal symbols here.

[‡] Many times the symbol ::= is used in place of →.

[§] Here, we assume $n \geqslant 1$. Most definitions of a context-free grammar permit $n = 0$. That is, the *empty string*, whose length is 0 may be a member of certain recursively defined classes. While the notion of the empty string is often a convenience, we shall exclude it in our treatment of grammars for the sake of simplicity.

Rule (i) may be read: "An expression is either an expression followed by '+' followed by a term, or a term alone." Rule (ii) reads: "A term is either a term followed by '*' followed by a factor or a factor alone." The last rule reads: "A factor is either an identifier or '(' followed by an expression followed by ')'." ∎

Example 8.6. A grammar for gotoless programs is:

$$\langle \text{statement} \rangle \rightarrow \textbf{if exp then } \langle \text{statement} \rangle \textbf{ else } \langle \text{statement} \rangle \mid$$
$$\textbf{while exp do } \langle \text{statement} \rangle \mid$$
$$\textbf{begin } \langle \text{statement list} \rangle \textbf{ end} \mid$$
$$\textbf{as} \mid$$
$$\textbf{ios} \mid$$
$$\textbf{ds}$$
$$\langle \text{statement list} \rangle \rightarrow \langle \text{statement list} \rangle ; \langle \text{statement} \rangle \mid \langle \text{statement} \rangle$$

The terminals are the symbols **if, then, else, while, do, begin, end, exp, as, ios,** and **ds.** The last four stand for "expression," "assignment statement," "input/output statement," and "declaration statement." In a more complete definition of gotoless programs, these four "terminals" would be variables and be given productions of their own.

The variables are ⟨statement list⟩ and ⟨statement⟩. The rules for ⟨statement list⟩ say that a ⟨statement list⟩ is either a ⟨statement⟩ or a ⟨statement list⟩ followed by a semicolon followed by a statement, or put another way, a statement list is a list of statements separated by semicolons.

The rules for ⟨statement⟩ mirror the original definition, except for the rule:

$$\langle \text{statement} \rangle \rightarrow \textbf{begin } \langle \text{statement list} \rangle \textbf{ end}.$$

This rule replaces "If $\mathscr{S}_1, \ldots, \mathscr{S}_n$ are statements, then **begin** $\mathscr{S}_1; \ldots; \mathscr{S}_n$ **end** is a statement." Note that the statement in quotations means the same as the infinite set of productions:

$$\langle \text{statement} \rangle \rightarrow \textbf{begin } \langle \text{statement} \rangle \textbf{ end}$$
$$\langle \text{statement} \rangle \rightarrow \textbf{begin } \langle \text{statement} \rangle ; \langle \text{statement} \rangle \textbf{ end}$$
$$\langle \text{statement} \rangle \rightarrow \textbf{begin } \langle \text{statement} \rangle ; \langle \text{statement} \rangle ; \langle \text{statement} \rangle \textbf{ end}$$

and so on.

We cannot tolerate an infinite set of productions, and so introduced the variable ⟨statement list⟩ to help out. In so doing, we have replaced an infinite (but highly patterned) set of productions by three that "mean" the same thing. ∎

8.3 DERIVATIONS

We can describe those strings in the distinguished class of a grammar by means of "derivations." We may read the rule $A \rightarrow X_1 \ldots X_n$ as "An X_1 followed by an X_2 followed by ... is an A." We can also read the rule as "one way to form an A is to concatenate an X_1 with an X_2 with an etc." Extending this idea, suppose X_1 is a variable, and that one of its rules is $X_1 \rightarrow Y_1 \ldots Y_r$. We may put the rules $A \rightarrow X_1 \ldots X_n$

and $X_1 \rightarrow Y_1 \ldots Y_r$ together and say "One way to form an A is to follow a Y_1 by a Y_2 by a ... Y_r, then by an X_2 by an X_3 by an ... X_n."

By extending the idea of replacing variables by the right side of one of their rules we can generate all formulas for the composition of members of the desired class. The sequence of replacements made is called a *derivation* of the string of symbols constructed. Given a grammar, we can define its *sentential forms* recursively as follows.

1. The string consisting of the distinguished variable alone is a sentential form.

2. If $W_1 \ldots W_n$ is a sentential form, W_i is a variable, and one of W_i's rules is $W_i \rightarrow Z_1 \ldots Z_r$, then one new sentential form which we can construct is $W_1 \ldots W_{i-1}Z_1 \ldots Z_r W_{i+1} \ldots W_n$. We indicate that a step in a derivation can be made by writing $W_1 \ldots W_n \Rightarrow W_1 \ldots W_{i-1}Z_1 \ldots Z_r W_i \ldots W_n$.

3. Nothing else is a sentential form.

The sentential forms enable us to determine all the strings in the defined class. We say a sentential form is a *sentence* if it consists solely of terminal symbols. The sentences generated by a grammar are thus exactly the strings in the class denoted by the distinguished variable.

Example 8.7. When ⟨signed integer⟩ is the distinguished variable; ⟨sign⟩, ⟨digit⟩ and ⟨integer⟩ are the other variables; and 0, 1, +, and − are the terminals we can define binary integers with sign by the following productions:

$$⟨\text{signed integer}⟩ \rightarrow ⟨\text{sign}⟩⟨\text{integer}⟩$$
$$⟨\text{sign}⟩ \rightarrow + \mid -$$
$$⟨\text{integer}⟩ \rightarrow ⟨\text{digit}⟩⟨\text{integer}⟩ \mid ⟨\text{digit}⟩$$
$$⟨\text{digit}⟩ \rightarrow 0 \mid 1$$

Let us generate some sentential forms. We begin with the only string known *a priori* to be a sentential form, that is ⟨signed integer⟩. This sentential form has only one variable, and there is only one rule for the variable, so the one sentential form which we may immediately construct is ⟨sign⟩⟨integer⟩. We write ⟨signed integer⟩ $\Rightarrow$ ⟨sign⟩⟨integer⟩ to indicate that the latter sentential form has been constructed from the former by the replacement of one variable.

Now, with sentential form ⟨sign⟩⟨integer⟩ we have a choice of replacements. We may replace either ⟨sign⟩ or ⟨integer⟩, and we have two choices of production in either case—four choices in all. The four sentential forms we may derive from ⟨sign⟩⟨integer⟩ are:

$$+⟨\text{integer}⟩$$
$$-⟨\text{integer}⟩$$
$$⟨\text{sign}⟩⟨\text{digit}⟩⟨\text{integer}⟩$$
$$⟨\text{sign}⟩⟨\text{digit}⟩$$

One possible sequence of replacements we may make, starting from the third of these is:

$$⟨\text{sign}⟩⟨\text{digit}⟩⟨\text{integer}⟩ \Rightarrow ⟨\text{sign}⟩\ 1\ ⟨\text{integer}⟩$$
$$\Rightarrow ⟨\text{sign}⟩\ 1\ ⟨\text{digit}⟩ \Rightarrow +1\ ⟨\text{digit}⟩ \Rightarrow +10.$$

That is, we first replace ⟨digit⟩ by 1, then ⟨integer⟩ by ⟨digit⟩, next ⟨sign⟩ by +, and, finally, ⟨digit⟩ by 0. Since + 10 is a sentential form and consists of terminals only, it is a sentence, and we conclude that + 10 is in the class ⟨signed integer⟩. The sequence of steps in the derivation of + 10 which we have constructed[†] is summarized below.

$$\begin{aligned}
\langle\text{signed integer}\rangle &\Rightarrow \langle\text{sign}\rangle\langle\text{integer}\rangle \\
&\Rightarrow \langle\text{sign}\rangle\langle\text{digit}\rangle\langle\text{integer}\rangle \\
&\Rightarrow \langle\text{sign}\rangle\, 1\, \langle\text{integer}\rangle \\
&\Rightarrow \langle\text{sign}\rangle\, 1\, \langle\text{digit}\rangle \\
&\Rightarrow +1\, \langle\text{digit}\rangle \\
&\Rightarrow +10
\end{aligned}$$

We could have discovered that + 10 is a signed integer without the aid of derivations. For example, the rules that are used in the derivation could also be used in reverse order to make the following sequence of inferences.

i) 0 is a ⟨digit⟩.

ii) + is a ⟨sign⟩.

iii) Since 0 is a ⟨digit⟩ it is an ⟨integer⟩.

iv) 1 is a ⟨digit⟩.

v) Since 1 is a ⟨digit⟩ and 0 is an ⟨integer⟩, 10 is an ⟨integer⟩.

vi) Since + is a ⟨sign⟩ and 10 is an ⟨integer⟩, + 10 is a ⟨signed integer⟩.

We should observe that + 10 is not the only sentence generated by this grammar. By varying the choice of replacements made at the steps of a derivation we can derive from ⟨signed integer⟩ an infinity of different sentential forms and an infinity of different sentences. ∎

Suppose we have a sequence of sentential forms $\alpha_1, \ldots, \alpha_n$, such that each is derived from the previous one by the replacement of one variable according to some production. That is, $\alpha_1 \Rightarrow \alpha_2 \Rightarrow \cdots \Rightarrow \alpha_n$. Then we say the sequence $\alpha_1, \alpha_2, \ldots, \alpha_n$ is a *derivation of α_n from α_1*. Thus, a string of terminals is a sentence if and only if there is a derivation of it from the distinguished variable.

8.4   PARSE TREES

It is possible to represent derivations by trees, and these trees put an interesting and useful structure on the derived sentence.

First let us talk about trees in general. Our definition of a tree (from Section 3.5) places an order on the children of each node. We have called this order "to the left" and have exhibited the order of children in that way. We can extend the "to-the-left" notion to determine which of any two leaves is to the left of the other. Given two

---

[†] It should be noted that there are other derivations of + 10 found by changing the order in which the variables are replaced.

leaves n_1 and n_2, as in Fig. 8.1, trace the paths from n_1 and n_2 to the root. At some point, say node n_3, the paths will join. Now, let n_4 and n_5 be the children of n_3 along the paths from n_1 and n_2, respectively.

We say n_1 is to the left of n_2 if n_4 is to the left of n_5, and n_2 is to the left of n_1, otherwise. In this manner, all the leaves of a tree can be ordered.

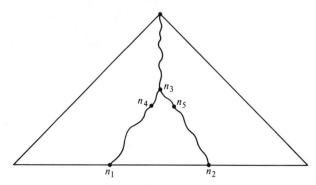

Fig. 8.1   Paths in a tree.

Example 8.8.   Consider the tree of Fig. 8.2. We find that n_7 is to the left of n_8. The paths from these nodes to the root meet at the root itself. Since n_7 reaches the root from n_2, n_8 reaches the root from n_3, and n_2 is to the left of n_3, it follows that n_7 is to the left of n_8. Similarly, the paths from n_8 and n_{11} to the root meet at n_3. Since n_8 is to the left of n_9, it follows that n_8 is to the left of n_{11}.

The complete ordering of the leaves is $n_4, n_6, n_7, n_8, n_{11}, n_{10}$.   ∎

Often, a tree has symbols (called *labels*) at its nodes. If so, then we may form a string, called the *yield* of the tree, consisting of the labels of the leaves, in order from the left.

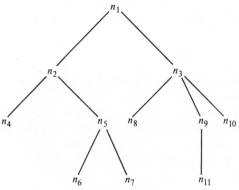

Fig. 8.2   Example tree.

Let us now define parse trees for a context-free grammar. Our definition of a parse tree will encompass one of the two common methods of constructing the parse tree for a given sentence. This method, called *top down*, takes a derivation of the sentence and builds the parse tree fro... it starting at the root (top) and working down to the leaves. In the next section we shall discuss *bottom up* construction of parse trees, and this method also assumes we already know a derivation for the sentence. As the reader may guess, bottom up construction works from the leaves until the root is constructed.

As we apparently need to know a derivation for a sentence before we may construct its parse tree, we should consider how easy it is to find a derivation and/or a parse tree for a given sentence. The obvious method of "try all possible derivations" until we find one for the sentence at hand is grossly inefficient. There is a nonobvious method that requires, at worst, time proportional to the cube of the length of a sentence to find a derivation for that sentence in a given grammar. While we shall not discuss this method, in Section 8.6 we shall consider a highly efficient method that works for some grammars, including at least one for most any programming language you choose.

We may associate a tree with each sentential form. The tree is labeled with a variable or terminal symbol at each node. We define the *parse* (or *derivation*) *tree* for a given sentential form recursively as follows. First note that the parse tree for sentential form α has yield α, so we can identify each symbol of α with a particular leaf of the tree in a left to right manner. That is, the ith symbol of α is identified with the ith leaf from the left. Then follow the rules below:

1. The sentential form consisting of the distinguished variable alone is associated with the tree of one node; the node is labeled by the distinguished variable.

2. Suppose $X_1 \ldots X_n$ is a sentential form and T is its associated tree. Let X_i be a variable and $X_i \to Y_1 \ldots Y_r$ a production. Then $X_1 \ldots X_{i-1} Y_1 \ldots Y_r X_{i+1} \ldots X_n$ is a sentential form, and its tree is constructed from T by:

i) finding the leaf of T identified with X_i,
ii) creating r children for that node, and
iii) labeling them $Y_1, \ldots, Y_r$, from the left.

Example 8.9. Let us consider the grammar of Example 8.7 and the derivation:

$$\begin{aligned}
\langle \text{signed integer} \rangle &\Rightarrow \langle \text{sign} \rangle \langle \text{integer} \rangle \\
&\Rightarrow \langle \text{sign} \rangle \langle \text{digit} \rangle \langle \text{integer} \rangle \\
&\Rightarrow \langle \text{sign} \rangle\, 1 \,\langle \text{integer} \rangle \\
&\Rightarrow \langle \text{sign} \rangle\, 1 \,\langle \text{digit} \rangle \\
&\Rightarrow +1 \,\langle \text{digit} \rangle \\
&\Rightarrow +10
\end{aligned}$$

The tree for the sentential form ⟨signed integer⟩ is a single node with that label. To obtain the tree for the next sentential form, ⟨sign⟩ ⟨integer⟩, we create two children and label them ⟨sign⟩ and ⟨integer⟩, respectively. The resulting tree is shown in Fig. 8.3(a).

Next, the node labeled ⟨integer⟩ is "expanded" according to the production ⟨integer⟩ → ⟨digit⟩⟨integer⟩, just as that production is used to create the sentential form ⟨sign⟩⟨digit⟩⟨integer⟩ from ⟨sign⟩⟨integer⟩. The next tree, shown in Fig. 8.3(b) has two children for the node labeled ⟨integer⟩ in Fig. 8.3(a).

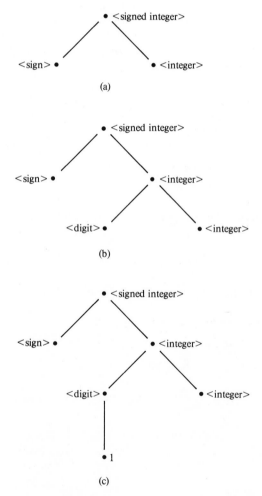

Fig. 8.3   Parse trees: a) For ⟨sign⟩ ⟨integer⟩; b) For ⟨sign⟩ ⟨digit⟩ ⟨integer⟩; c) For ⟨sign⟩ 1 ⟨integer⟩.

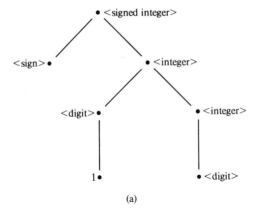

(a)

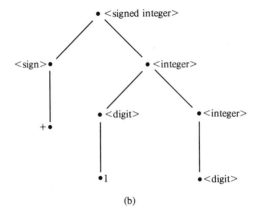

(b)

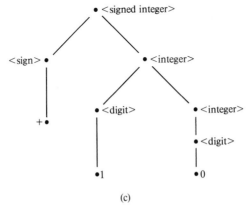

(c)

Fig. 8.4 Further construction of the parse tree: a) For ⟨sign⟩ 1 ⟨digit⟩; b) For +1 ⟨digit⟩;
c) For +10.

In the next sentential form, $\langle$digit$\rangle$ is replaced by 1, according to the production $\langle$digit$\rangle \rightarrow 1$. Thus, the tree for sentential form $\langle$sign$\rangle$ 1 $\langle$integer$\rangle$ is found by adding one child labeled 1, to the node labeled $\langle$digit$\rangle$ in Fig. 8.3(b). The result is shown in Fig. 8.3(c).

The trees corresponding to the last three sentential forms of the derivation are shown in Fig. 8.4(a), (b), and (c), respectively. ∎

We should observe that the last tree has a yield of $+10$. In addition to demonstrating that $+10$ is a sentence, the tree also provides a structure for $+10$. For example, the tree indicates that $+10$ is formed from a $\langle$sign$\rangle$ and an $\langle$integer$\rangle$, these being the children of the root. (Admittedly, the structure is rather trivial in this case.)

In general, many derivations have the same derivation tree. For example, the derivation:

$$\langle \text{signed integer} \rangle \Rightarrow \langle \text{sign} \rangle \langle \text{integer} \rangle$$
$$\Rightarrow \langle \text{sign} \rangle \langle \text{digit} \rangle \langle \text{integer} \rangle$$
$$\Rightarrow \langle \text{sign} \rangle \langle \text{digit} \rangle \langle \text{digit} \rangle$$
$$\Rightarrow \langle \text{sign} \rangle \langle \text{digit} \rangle \, 0$$
$$\Rightarrow \langle \text{sign} \rangle \, 10$$
$$\Rightarrow +10$$

produces the derivation tree of Fig. 8.4(c) as well.

8.5 BOTTOM-UP CONSTRUCTION OF PARSE TREES

We may also build a parse tree from a derivation starting from the sentence derived, which corresponds to the leaves, and working up the tree toward the root. Corresponding to each sentential form $X_1 \ldots X_n$ will be a collection of trees (called, not surprisingly, a *forest*) whose roots, in a designated order, read $X_1 \ldots X_n$ from the left.

Initially, there will be one tree for each symbol of the sentence. These trees will each have one node, labeled by the symbol it represents. The order of the trees is the obvious one—the same as the order of the symbols of the sentence. We consider the sentential forms of the derivation in their reverse order. Finally, we shall have constructed the "forest" for the sentential form consisting of the distinguished symbol alone. This forest has only one tree, whose root is labeled by the distinguished symbol. We shall see that it is a parse tree for the derived sentence.

To explain how a parse tree can be built bottom up, we have only to explain how, given the forest for some sentential form $X_1 \ldots X_n$, we may find the forest for the previous sentential form in the derivation, that is, the sentential form $X_1 \ldots X_i Z X_j \ldots X_n$ such that $X_1 \ldots X_i Z X_j \ldots X_n \Rightarrow X_1 \ldots X_n.^\dagger$ Apparently, the production applied at this step was $Z \rightarrow X_{i+1} \ldots X_{j-1}$. When going from $X_1 \ldots X_n$ back to $X_1 \ldots X_i Z X_j \ldots X_n$, we shall often say that $X_{i+1} \ldots X_{j-1}$ was *reduced* to Z.

$\dagger$ Note that there may be more than one string of symbols from which we could produce $X_1 \ldots X_n$ by applying one production. However, we are talking about one particular derivation, and in this derivation there will be a unique sentential form immediately preceding the sentential form $X_1 \ldots X_n$ in question.

Suppose we have the forest for $X_1 \ldots X_n$. Find the roots of the trees which correspond to $X_{i+1} \ldots X_{j-1}$, that is, the $i + 1$st through $j - 1$st roots from the left. Create a new node labeled Z and make its children be the roots of the aforementioned trees. The new node will be the root of the tree corresponding to Z in the sentential form $X_1 \ldots X_i Z X_j \ldots X_n$.

Example 8.10. Let us consider the grammar of Example 8.7 again and the derivation:

$$\begin{aligned}
\langle \text{signed integer} \rangle &\Rightarrow \langle \text{sign} \rangle \langle \text{integer} \rangle \\
&\Rightarrow \langle \text{sign} \rangle \langle \text{digit} \rangle \langle \text{integer} \rangle \\
&\Rightarrow \langle \text{sign} \rangle \, 1 \, \langle \text{integer} \rangle \\
&\Rightarrow \langle \text{sign} \rangle \, 1 \, \langle \text{digit} \rangle \\
&\Rightarrow +1 \, \langle \text{digit} \rangle \\
&\Rightarrow +10
\end{aligned}$$

To construct the parse tree for $+10$ we begin with its forest, shown in Fig. 8.5(a). The previous sentential form, $+1\langle \text{digit} \rangle$ is obtained by reducing 0 to $\langle \text{digit} \rangle$. We therefore create a node labeled $\langle \text{digit} \rangle$ and give it one child, the node labeled 0 in Fig. 8.5(a). The resulting forest is shown in Fig. 8.5(b).

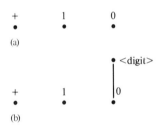

Fig. 8.5   Forests: a) For $+10$; b) For $+1 \langle \text{digit} \rangle$.

Proceeding backwards through the derivation, we see that we must first reduce $+$ to $\langle \text{sign} \rangle$ then $\langle \text{digit} \rangle$ to $\langle \text{integer} \rangle$ and then 1 to $\langle \text{digit} \rangle$. The forest which results from these three reductions is shown in Fig. 8.6.

Next, $\langle \text{digit} \rangle \langle \text{integer} \rangle$ must be reduced to $\langle \text{integer} \rangle$. We create a node labeled integer and give it two children, the roots labeled $\langle \text{digit} \rangle$ and $\langle \text{integer} \rangle$ in Fig. 8.6. The resulting forest is shown in Fig. 8.7.

Fig. 8.6   Forest for $\langle \text{sign} \rangle \, \langle \text{digit} \rangle \, \langle \text{integer} \rangle$.

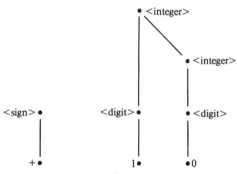

Fig. 8.7 Forest for ⟨sign⟩ ⟨integer⟩.

In the last step of the reduction process (first step of the derivation) we must reduce ⟨sign⟩⟨integer⟩ to ⟨signed integer⟩. We create a node labeled ⟨signed integer⟩ and give it two children the two roots in Fig. 8.7. The resulting forest is a single tree, shown in Fig. 8.8. This tree is identical to the parse tree constructed by the top-down definition in Fig. 8.4(c). ∎

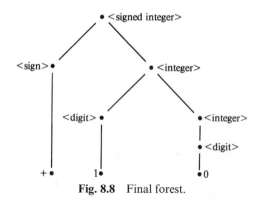

Fig. 8.8 Final forest.

While we shall not attempt a proof here, we should point out that in every case the parse trees constructed from a given derivation by the top-down and bottom-up techniques will be the same.

8.6 A PARSING ALGORITHM

Until now, we have assumed that we are given a derivation of a particular sentence in a particular grammar. However, a compiler is given only the sentence and must construct a derivation or, equivalently, a parse tree for the sentence. There are myriad ways of doing this. Some are more efficient than others, and in general, the more efficient ones do not work for an arbitrary grammar. Fortunately, we can find algorithms which are quite efficient and which work on many common grammars. We shall discuss one of them here, with the curious name of a *weak precedence parser.*[†]

To begin our description of this method, we must talk about rightmost derivations. We recall that many sentential forms have more than one variable, and we can replace any one of these to make a new sentential form. If starting with the distinguished variable, we always replace the rightmost variable by one of its productions, then we have a *rightmost derivation*, and every sentential form so generated is called a *right sentential form*. Every sentence has a rightmost derivation. In essence, this is because the order of replacement of variables does not affect the end result; only the choice of productions is important.

Example 8.11. Let us consider the following grammar for assignment statements involving identifiers with no subscripts and expressions over operators + and ∗. The terminals are =, + , ∗ and parentheses, as well as the symbol **id**, standing for any identifier. The productions are:

$$\langle\text{asgn stat}\rangle \rightarrow \mathbf{id} = \langle\text{exp}\rangle$$
$$\langle\text{exp}\rangle \rightarrow \langle\text{exp}\rangle + \langle\text{term}\rangle \,|\, \langle\text{term}\rangle$$
$$\langle\text{term}\rangle \rightarrow \langle\text{term}\rangle * \langle\text{factor}\rangle \,|\, \langle\text{factor}\rangle$$
$$\langle\text{factor}\rangle \rightarrow \mathbf{id} \,|\, (\langle\text{exp}\rangle)$$

with ⟨asgn stat⟩ being the distinguished variable.

Here is a rightmost derivation in this grammar: *top-down*

$$\langle\text{asgn stat}\rangle \quad \text{Root}$$
$$\mathbf{id} = \langle\text{exp}\rangle$$
$$\mathbf{id} = \langle\text{exp}\rangle + \langle\text{term}\rangle$$
$$\mathbf{id} = \langle\text{exp}\rangle + \langle\text{term}\rangle * \langle\text{factor}\rangle$$
$$\mathbf{id} = \langle\text{exp}\rangle + \langle\text{term}\rangle * \mathbf{id}$$
$$\mathbf{id} = \langle\text{exp}\rangle + \langle\text{factor}\rangle * \mathbf{id}$$
$$\mathbf{id} = \langle\text{exp}\rangle + \mathbf{id} * \mathbf{id}$$
$$\mathbf{id} = \langle\text{term}\rangle + \mathbf{id} * \mathbf{id}$$
$$\mathbf{id} = \langle\text{factor}\rangle + \mathbf{id} * \mathbf{id}$$
$$\mathbf{id} = \mathbf{id} + \mathbf{id} * \mathbf{id} \qquad\qquad \blacksquare$$

The weak-precedence parser will build a parse tree for a sentence bottom up. While doing so, it will in effect trace through the steps of a rightmost derivation for

---

[†] This particular type of parser has been used in only a few compilers (see the bibliographic notes). However, it is relatively simple to understand and works on some natural looking grammars, so it is probably a good choice for an introduction to parsing. It is related to the more common "simple precedence" parser. However, we have chosen to discuss weak rather than simple precedence parsing because the former works on a variety of useful grammars on which the latter does not.

The earliest forms of parsing, such as "recursive descent" or "operator precedence" are not really based on a context free grammar, but are ad hoc techniques which can work well if the user is experienced. There are numerous pitfalls, however, in these methods. Operator precedence works well on expressions but is not sufficiently general. Recursive descent can surprise the user by being much slower than he expected, or by failing to parse a string he thought should be parsable.

the sentence, but in reverse order, starting with the sentence and ending with only the distinguished symbol. It is logical that the derivation should be discovered in reverse order, since that is the order in which the sentential forms are needed when building a parse tree bottom up. As mentioned previously, the weak precedence parsing strategy will not work on every grammar, but will work on many. Those grammars on which it works are called *weak-precedence grammars.*

We have not yet told the secret of how to look at a right sentential form (of a weak-precedence grammar) and tell which symbols should be reduced to construct the previous right sentential form. This we shall explain now. The parser will consist of two lists. The first list is a stack (referred to as *the stack*) whose top we show on the right. Initially, the stack holds only one symbol, called the *endmarker* (which we shall denote by $). The endmarker is not a terminal or variable.

The second list is the input, and initially it holds the sentence whose tree we are about to construct, followed by the endmarker symbol. The top of the input will be shown at the left and it will be a stack which only gives up symbols. Each record of the stack and input holds $ or one grammar symbol (terminal or variable) and a pointer to the node of the parse tree corresponding to that symbol.[†] The symbols on the input are all terminals, except for the endmarker.

We shall picture a parser as in Fig. 8.9. If the parser is part of a compiler, the stack records will have other information besides grammar symbols. The grammar symbols read left to right, $X_1 \ldots X_n Y_1 \ldots Y_m$ in Fig. 8.9, are always a right sentential form if the initial input was a sentence.

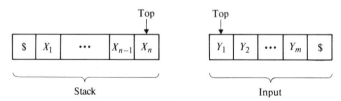

Fig. 8.9   The weak-precedence parser.

The two basic actions of the parser are *shift* and *reduce*. A shift action takes the top symbol off the input list, creates a node for it, and pushes it onto the top of the stack. That is, the record for the symbol is moved left across the gap in Fig. 8.9.

In a reduce action, we examine the symbols at the top of the stack and find the longest production right side that appears with its rightmost symbol at the top of the stack. (The *right side* of a production is the string of symbols to the right of the arrow, i.e., $X_1 \ldots X_n$ in the production $Y \rightarrow X_1 \ldots X_n$.) If there is no right side, we have an error, and the original input was not a sentence.

[†] Actually, we shall see that we never need to know the nodes for the symbols on the input list. A typical parser will create leaves for these symbols only when they reach the top of the input list (as symbols are removed from that list).

The symbols of the right side found are popped from the top of the stack and the left side of the same production[†] is pushed onto the stack. Thus, we have effected a reduction. If we are constructing a parse tree, we may create a node for the symbol pushed onto the stack.

Example 8.12. Suppose we have the grammar of Example 8.11, and the stack and input are as shown in Fig. 8.10. Pointers to the nodes of the tree under construction are shown for the records of the stack. Symbols on the input list correspond to leaves which are not shown.

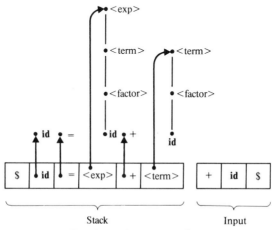

Fig. 8.10   Parser snapshot.

Suppose that the parser decides to reduce. (We shall understand why with this stack and input the parser will make that decision, once we see how such decisions are made.)

On top of the stack we see ⟨term⟩, which is the right side of a production. However, this is not the longest right side. That honor belongs to ⟨exp⟩ + ⟨term⟩, and this is the right side which we must use.

Thus, we reduce ⟨exp⟩ + ⟨term⟩ to ⟨exp⟩ and create a new node for the new symbol ⟨exp⟩. The revised stack and tree are shown in Fig. 8.11. Note that the top three records on the stack were removed and replaced by a new record for ⟨exp⟩. That record points to the new node, which is the parent of the nodes pointed to by the three records popped from the stack. ∎

Now we shall see how the weak precedence parser decides whether to shift or reduce. From a weak precedence grammar we construct a table (called the *shift-reduce table*) having a row for every symbol—terminals, variables and the end-marker. The table has a column for every terminal and the endmarker. Its entries

---

[†] One of the conditions for a grammar to be a weak precedence grammar is that no two productions have the same right side. Thus, this left side is unique.

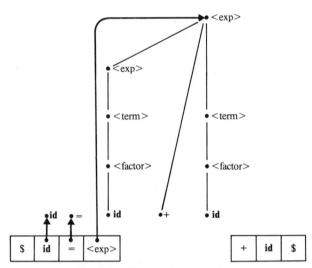

Fig. 8.11   Parser after reduction.

are shift (S), reduce (R), or blank. A blank indicates that the input to the parser
was not a sentence if that table entry is consulted by the parser.

The steps of the weak precedence parsing algorithm are as follows:

1. Initially we have a stack consisting of one record, holding the endmarker ($).
The sentence to be parsed is the input list followed by $.

2. Here we begin a loop. Repeatedly we consult the shift-reduce table to determine
an action, perform that action, and repeat the loop. If the stack has only $ and the
distinguished symbol, and the input has only $, then halt. The parse tree has been
constructed. Otherwise, let X be the contents of the top stack record and Y the top
(leftmost) input symbol. Examine the entry of the shift-reduce table in row X and
column Y. If it is blank, the original input was not a sentence, so we halt.[†] If the
entry is S, do step (3); if it is R, do step (4).

3. In this case, we shift. The first input symbol, Y, is popped from the input and
a record is pushed onto the stack. This record has the contents Y and a pointer to a
newly created node of the parse tree. The new node has label Y. Go to step (2).

4. Here, we must attempt a reduction. Examine the symbols at the top of the
stack for the longest right side of a production. (If there is none at all, the input was
not a sentence, so halt or call an error recovery routine.) Let this longest right side
be $X_1 \ldots X_n$. (X_n is X, of course, since X is the topmost symbol.) Let $A \rightarrow X_1 \ldots X_n$

[†] In practice, a compiler using the weak-precedence parsing algorithm would call an "error
recovery routine" which would print a diagnostic and attempt to make some simple change to
the stack and/or input so that parsing would proceed. In this way, a compiler can detect many
errors in a program rather than just the first error.

be the unique production with this right side.[†] Create a new node of the parse tree labeled A. Its children, from the left, are the nodes pointed to by the records for $X_1, \ldots, X_n$ on the top of the stack, in that order. Pop the records for $X_1, \ldots, X_n$, then push onto the stack a record with contents A and a pointer to the new node. Go to step (2). Fig. 8.12 flowcharts the parsing algorithm.

Example 8.13. In Fig. 8.13 is the shift-reduce table for the grammar of Example 8.11. In the next section we shall show how to construct such a table from a weak precedence grammar.

Let us parse the sentence **id** $=$ **id** $+$ **id** $*$ **id**. We shall show the "snapshots" of the parser, called *configurations* at successive steps of the parsing process. The initial configuration is shown in Fig. 8.14(a).

The top stack symbol is $\$$ and the top input symbol is **id**. We therefore look at row $\$$ and column **id** in Fig. 8.13. We find S there, so we shift **id** onto the stack and create a node for it. The next configuration is shown in Fig. 8.14(b).

Now, we find **id** on top of the stack and $=$ on top of the input. The entry in row **id** and column $=$ is again S, so we shift $=$ to the stack and create a node for it. This will create a configuration with $=$ on top of the stack and **id** on top of the input. The $(=, \textbf{id})$ entry is also S, so a third shift is called for. The resulting configuration is shown in Fig. 8.15.

Now, the $(\textbf{id}, +)$ entry of Fig. 8.13 is consulted, and we find R there. We must reduce, and **id** is the longest (and only) right side on top of the stack. Thus, we reduce by production $\langle\text{factor}\rangle \to \textbf{id}$; we pop the record for **id** off the top of the stack and push down a record for $\langle\text{factor}\rangle$ in its place. We create a node labeled $\langle\text{factor}\rangle$; its lone child is the node which was pointed to by the record just popped. The resulting configuration is shown in Fig. 8.16.

When we examine the $(\langle\text{factor}\rangle, +)$ entry, we find another reduction called for. This time, $\langle\text{factor}\rangle$ is the longest right side on top of the stack, and it is reduced to $\langle\text{term}\rangle$. Then a third reduction is called for; $\langle\text{term}\rangle$ is the right side and it is reduced to $\langle\text{exp}\rangle$. The result of these two reductions is shown in Fig. 8.17.

The $(\langle\text{exp}\rangle, +)$ entry calls for a shift, as does the $(+, \textbf{id})$ entry. After making these shifts, **id** is on top of the stack and $*$ is the first input symbol. Thus a reduction of **id** to $\langle\text{factor}\rangle$ and then to $\langle\text{term}\rangle$ is called for. The resulting configuration is shown in Fig. 8.18.

Now the $(\langle\text{term}\rangle, *)$ entry calls for another shift, as does the $(*, \textbf{id})$ entry. Thus, $*$ and **id** are shifted onto the stack, and the $(\textbf{id}, \$)$ entry calls for a reduction of **id** to $\langle\text{factor}\rangle$. Fig. 8.19 gives the configuration at this point.

Now, the $(\langle\text{factor}\rangle, \$)$ entry calls for a reduction. The longest right side on top of the stack is $\langle\text{term}\rangle * \langle\text{factor}\rangle$, so the next configuration is the one in Fig. 8.20.

Two more reductions succeed in producing $\$\langle\text{asgn stat}\rangle$ on the stack and $\$$ on the input. The last two configurations are shown in Fig. 8.21. Note that in Fig. 8.21(b), the identifiers surrounding $*$ have been grouped together at a lower level of

---

[†] We are, of course, assuming the grammar is a weak-precedence grammar, so the production is unique given $X_1 \ldots X_n$.

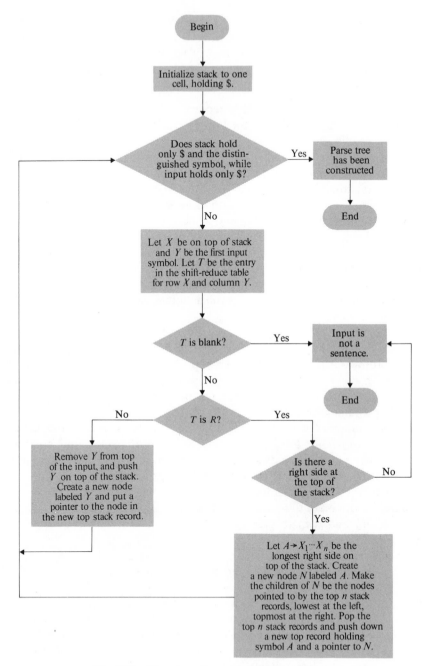

Fig. 8.12 Flowchart for weak-precedence parser.

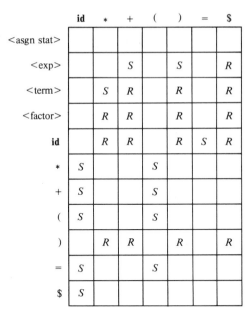

	id	*	+	(	)	=	$
\<asgn stat\>							
\<exp\>			S		S		R
\<term\>		S	R		R		R
\<factor\>		R	R		R		R
id		R	R		R	S	R
*	S			S			
+	S			S			
(	S			S			
)		R	R		R		R
=	S			S			
$	S						

Fig. 8.13   Shift-reduce table.

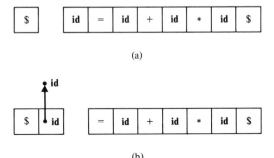

(a)

(b)

Fig. 8.14   First two parser configurations: a) Initial configuration; b) Second configuration.

Fig. 8.15   Fourth configuration.

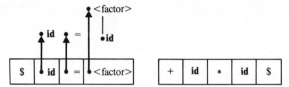

Fig. 8.16 Fifth configuration.

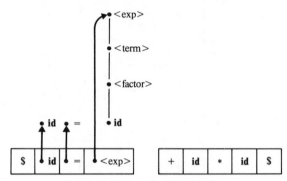

Fig. 8.17 Seventh configuration.

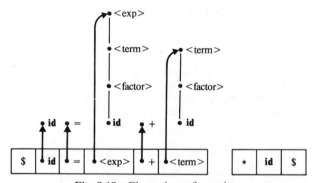

Fig. 8.18 Eleventh configuration.

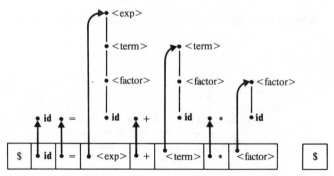

Fig. 8.19 Fourteenth configuration.

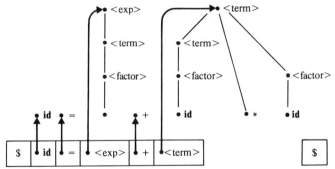

Fig. 8.20   Fifteenth configuration.

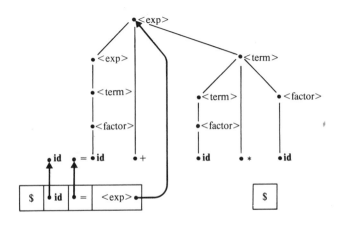

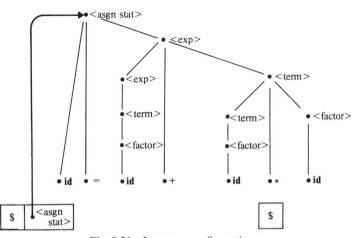

Fig. 8.21   Last two configurations.

the tree than the expressions surrounding + (**id** on the left and **id** * **id** on the right). Thus, the parse tree correctly groups operators and operands, under the assumption that * is of higher precedence than +. Of course, the grammar was chosen to reflect that order of precedence, which is why we have to deal with factors, terms and expressions, rather than expressions alone. ∎

After each step of the parsing process we see a right sentential form surrounded by \$'s, if we read the stack from bottom to top (left to right, as shown) and then the input from top to bottom (again, left to right as shown). Moreover, the right sentential form either does not change (if the move is a shift) or becomes the one previous in the rightmost derivation of the original input (if the move is a reduction). At the end of the parse, we see only the distinguished variable (i.e., the first right sentential form) with two \$'s. The top record of the stack points to the root of the derivation tree of the input, which we have constructed by successive reductions.

8.7   CONSTRUCTING THE SHIFT-REDUCE TABLE

We now demonstrate how to construct the shift-reduce table from a grammar which happens to be a weak precedence grammar. A detailed justification for why the table should be constructed in this way is beyond the scope of this book, although we can give some intuitive hints. The rules for table construction are:

1. Place S (shift) in the row for X and column for Y if either:

i) there is a right side of a production having the form $\ldots XY \ldots$, i.e., X appears immediately to the left of Y, or

ii) there is a right side of the form $\ldots XA \ldots$ (i.e., anything with an X immediately to the left of an A), where A is a variable which derives[†] a string beginning with Y.

2. Place R (reduce) in the row for X and column for Y if there is a right side of the form $\ldots AB \ldots$, A derives a string ending in X and either B derives a string beginning with Y or B is Y.

3. In addition, the entry in the row for \$ and column for Y is S if there is a sentential form beginning with Y; there is an R in the row for X and column for \$ if there is a sentential form that ends with X.

Note that Y must be a terminal symbol in all cases above.

Example 8.14.   In Fig. 8.13, the entry in the row for ⟨exp⟩ and the column for + is S because of the right side ⟨exp⟩ + ⟨term⟩. That is, in rule (1i), X can be ⟨exp⟩ and Y can be +.

The entry in the row for left parenthesis and the column for **id** is S because of the right side (⟨exp⟩) and the derivation ⟨exp⟩ ⇒ ⟨term⟩ ⇒ ⟨factor⟩ ⇒ **id**, among others. That is, in rule (1ii), X is the left parenthesis, A is ⟨exp⟩ and Y is **id**.

[†] Technically, we have only discussed derivations that begin with the distinguished variable, however, the notion that a derivation (sequence of replacements of left sides of productions by their right sides) can begin with another variable should not be hard to swallow.

The entry in the row for ⟨factor⟩ and the column for + is R, because of the right side ⟨exp⟩ + ⟨term⟩ and the derivation ⟨exp⟩ ⇒ ⟨exp⟩ + ⟨term⟩ ⇒ ⟨exp⟩ + ⟨factor⟩, among others. That is, in rule (2), A is ⟨exp⟩, X is ⟨factor⟩, and B and Y are both +. Note that the case $B = Y$ in rule 2 applies here. ∎

Why the table-constructing rules are the "right" ones is difficult to explain. Perhaps easiest to see is why we should shift terminal Y if X is on top of the stack and ... XY ... is a right side. Since the parser works by getting complete right sides on top of the stack, it "looks like" we must move Y, and possibly some more symbols onto the stack before we can complete this right side.

If rule (1ii) applies, that is, there is a right side ... XA ... and A derives something beginning with terminal Y, then it "looks like" we should shift Y onto the stack to begin a new right side. If rule (2) applies, then it "looks like" we have found the end of a right side and should reduce.

Of course, what the situation "looks like" and what is actually occurring may be quite different. However, we are relying on special properties of the grammar, as yet unstated, so that the table-constructing rules we have given will in fact work.

An algorithm to compute shift-reduce tables can be given by recursively defining two relations on the grammar symbols and $. These relations are indicated $\lessdot$ and $\gtrdot$.[†] They are related to the shift and reduce entries, in the sense that if $X \lessdot Y$ and Y is a terminal, then the shift-reduce entry for row X and column Y will be shift; if $X \gtrdot Y$, and Y is a terminal or $, then the entry will be reduce. However, we can have $X \lessdot Y$ or $X \gtrdot Y$ even when Y is a variable, while there will be no corresponding entry in the shift-reduce table. The rules for computing $\lessdot$ recursively are:

1. a) $\$ \lessdot A$, where A is the distinguished symbol of the given grammar.

   b) If there is a right side with X immediately to the left of Y, then $X \lessdot Y$.

2. If $X \lessdot Y$ and there is a production $Y \to Z_1 \ldots Z_n$, then $X \lessdot Z_1$.
   The rules for computing $\gtrdot$ are:

3. a) $A \gtrdot$, where A is the distinguished symbol.

   b) If $X \lessdot Y$ and there is a production $X \to Z_1 \ldots Z_n$, then $Z_n \gtrdot Y$.

4. a) If $X \gtrdot Y$ and there is a production $X \to Z_1 \ldots Z_n$, then $Z_n \gtrdot Y$.

   b) If $X \gtrdot Y$ and there is a production $Y \to Z_1 \ldots Z_n$, then $X \gtrdot Z_1$.

We compute the shift-reduce table for the grammar by making the entry in row X and column Y be shift if $X \lessdot Y$, reduce if $X \gtrdot Y$, and blank if neither $X \lessdot Y$ nor $X \gtrdot Y$ is true. Note that Y must be a terminal or $. Of course, if the grammar is weak precedence, we shall never have $X \gtrdot Y$ and $X \lessdot Y$ simultaneously.

[†] We should not think of these relations in the same way we regard $\leqslant$ and $>$ on numbers. $\lessdot$ and $\gtrdot$ do not have the same properties. For example, we can have $A \lessdot B$ and $B \lessdot C$, while $A \lessdot C$ will not be true. Or, in a grammar which was not a weak precedence grammar, we could have $A \lessdot B$ and $A \gtrdot B$ at the same time.

Example 8.15. Let us again take up the grammar of Example 8.11 and show how the shift-reduce matrix of Fig. 8.13 is constructed. We begin by computing $\lessdot$. (Note that we must compute $\lessdot$ before $\gtrdot$, because $\lessdot$ is needed in rule (3b). By rule (1a), $\$ \lessdot \langle \text{asgn stat} \rangle$, and by rule (1b), production $\langle \text{exp} \rangle \to \langle \text{exp} \rangle + \langle \text{term} \rangle$ gives us $\langle \text{exp} \rangle \lessdot +$, and $+ \lessdot \langle \text{term} \rangle$. Production $\langle \text{term} \rangle \to \langle \text{term} \rangle * \langle \text{factor} \rangle$ gives us $\langle \text{term} \rangle \lessdot *$ and $* \lessdot \langle \text{factor} \rangle$. Production $\langle \text{factor} \rangle \to (\langle \text{exp} \rangle)$ gives us $(\lessdot \langle \text{exp} \rangle$ and $\langle \text{exp} \rangle \lessdot)$. Production $\langle \text{asgn stat} \rangle \to \textbf{id} = \langle \text{exp} \rangle$ gives us $\textbf{id} \lessdot =$ and $= \lessdot \langle \text{exp} \rangle$.

We must now add relations $X \lessdot Z_1$ by rule 2. In Fig. 8.22 we list all pairs related by $\lessdot$, and if added by rule (2), we indicate which symbols played the roles of X, Y, and $Z_1 \ldots Z_n$.

		Rule	If by rule 2	
Pair		used	$X \lessdot Y$	$Y \to Z_1 \ldots Z_n$
$\$$	$\lessdot \langle \text{asgn stat} \rangle$	1a		
$\langle \text{exp} \rangle$	$\lessdot +$	1b		
$+$	$\lessdot \langle \text{term} \rangle$	1b		
$\langle \text{term} \rangle$	$\lessdot *$	1b		
$*$	$\lessdot \langle \text{factor} \rangle$	1b		
$($	$\lessdot \langle \text{exp} \rangle$	1b		
$\langle \text{exp} \rangle$	$\lessdot)$	1b		
$\textbf{id}$	$\lessdot =$	1b		
$=$	$\lessdot \langle \text{exp} \rangle$	1b		
$\$$	$\lessdot \textbf{id}$	2	$\$ \lessdot \langle \text{asgn stat} \rangle$	$\langle \text{asgn stat} \rangle \to \textbf{id} = \langle \text{exp} \rangle$
$+$	$\lessdot \langle \text{factor} \rangle$	2	$+ \lessdot \langle \text{term} \rangle$	$\langle \text{term} \rangle \to \langle \text{factor} \rangle$
$+$	$\lessdot \textbf{id}$	2	$+ \lessdot \langle \text{factor} \rangle$	$\langle \text{factor} \rangle \to \textbf{id}$
$+$	$\lessdot ($	2	$+ \lessdot \langle \text{factor} \rangle$	$\langle \text{factor} \rangle \to (\langle \text{exp} \rangle)$
$*$	$\lessdot \textbf{id}$	2	$* \lessdot \langle \text{factor} \rangle$	$\langle \text{factor} \rangle \to \textbf{id}$
$*$	$\lessdot ($	2	$* \lessdot \langle \text{factor} \rangle$	$\langle \text{factor} \rangle \to (\langle \text{exp} \rangle)$
$($	$\lessdot \langle \text{term} \rangle$	2	$(\lessdot \langle \text{exp} \rangle$	$\langle \text{exp} \rangle \to \langle \text{term} \rangle$
$($	$\lessdot \langle \text{factor} \rangle$	2	$(\lessdot \langle \text{term} \rangle$	$\langle \text{term} \rangle \to \langle \text{factor} \rangle$
$($	$\lessdot \textbf{id}$	2	$(\lessdot \langle \text{factor} \rangle$	$\langle \text{factor} \rangle \to \textbf{id}$
$($	$\lessdot ($	2	$(\lessdot \langle \text{factor} \rangle$	$\langle \text{factor} \rangle \to (\langle \text{exp} \rangle)$
$=$	$\lessdot \langle \text{term} \rangle$	2	$= \lessdot \langle \text{exp} \rangle$	$\langle \text{exp} \rangle \to \langle \text{term} \rangle$
$=$	$\lessdot \langle \text{factor} \rangle$	2	$= \lessdot \langle \text{term} \rangle$	$\langle \text{term} \rangle \to \langle \text{factor} \rangle$
$=$	$\lessdot \textbf{id}$	2	$= \lessdot \langle \text{factor} \rangle$	$\langle \text{factor} \rangle \to \textbf{id}$
$=$	$\lessdot ($	2	$= \lessdot \langle \text{factor} \rangle$	$\langle \text{factor} \rangle \to (\langle \text{exp} \rangle)$

Fig. 8.22   The pairs related by $\lessdot$.

Let us now turn to the computation of $\gtrdot$. The table of Fig. 8.23 summarizes the pairs produced by rule 3; that in Fig. 8.24 summarizes what can be added by rule (4a).

If by rule (3b)

Pair	Rule used	$X \lessdot Y$	$X \to Z_1 \ldots Z_n$
$\langle$asgn stat$\rangle \gtrdot \$$	3a		
$\langle$term$\rangle \gtrdot +$	3b	$\langle$exp$\rangle \lessdot +$	$\langle$exp$\rangle \to \langle$term$\rangle$†
$\langle$factor$\rangle \gtrdot *$	3b	$\langle$term$\rangle \lessdot *$	$\langle$term$\rangle \to \langle$factor$\rangle$
$\langle$term$\rangle \gtrdot)$	3b	$\langle$exp$\rangle \lessdot)$	$\langle$exp$\rangle \to \langle$term$\rangle$

Fig. 8.23 Pairs related by $\gtrdot$ according to rule (3).

Pair	$X \gtrdot Y$	$X \to Z_1 \ldots Z_n$
$\langle$exp$\rangle \gtrdot \$$	$\langle$asgn stat$\rangle \gtrdot \$$	$\langle$asgn stat$\rangle \to$ **id** $= \langle$exp$\rangle$
$\langle$term$\rangle \gtrdot \$$	$\langle$exp$\rangle \gtrdot \$$	$\langle$exp$\rangle \to \langle$term$\rangle$
$\langle$factor$\rangle \gtrdot \$$	$\langle$term$\rangle \gtrdot \$$	$\langle$term$\rangle \to \langle$factor$\rangle$
id $\gtrdot \$$	$\langle$factor$\rangle \gtrdot \$$	$\langle$factor$\rangle \to$ **id**
$) \gtrdot \$$	$\langle$factor$\rangle \gtrdot \$$	$\langle$factor$\rangle \to (\langle$exp$\rangle)$
$\langle$factor$\rangle \gtrdot +$	$\langle$term$\rangle \gtrdot +$	$\langle$term$\rangle \to \langle$factor$\rangle$
id $\gtrdot +$	$\langle$factor$\rangle \gtrdot +$	$\langle$factor$\rangle \to$ **id**
$) \gtrdot +$	$\langle$factor$\rangle \gtrdot +$	$\langle$factor$\rangle \to (\langle$exp$\rangle)$
id $\gtrdot *$	$\langle$factor$\rangle \gtrdot *$	$\langle$factor$\rangle \to$ **id**
$) \gtrdot *$	$\langle$factor$\rangle \gtrdot *$	$\langle$factor$\rangle \to (\langle$exp$\rangle)$
$\langle$factor$\rangle \gtrdot)$	$\langle$term$\rangle \gtrdot)$	$\langle$term$\rangle \to \langle$factor$\rangle$
id $\gtrdot)$	$\langle$factor$\rangle \gtrdot)$	$\langle$factor$\rangle \to$ **id**
$) \gtrdot)$	$\langle$factor$\rangle \gtrdot)$	$\langle$factor$\rangle \to (\langle$exp$\rangle)$

Fig. 8.24 Pairs related by $\gtrdot$ according to rule (4).

It turns out that nothing can be added by rule (4b), since an application of (4b) requires that we have $X \gtrdot Y$ and a production $Y \to Z_1 \ldots Z_n$, which implies that Y is a variable. As we have no such pair, (4b) cannot be applied.

If we delete all pairs $X \lessdot Y$ or $X \gtrdot Y$ where Y is a variable, we have the shift-reduce table of Fig. 8.13. Of course, in Fig. 8.13, S replaces $\lessdot$ and R replaces $\gtrdot$. ∎

We can now state precisely the conditions for a grammar to be a weak-precedence grammar. We have already mentioned the first rule.

1. No two productions have the same right side. The next rule has also been mentioned.

2. For no pair (X, Y) should the entry in the shift-reduce table for row X and column Y be both S and R.

The third rule is needed to guarantee that the choice of the longest right side in a reduction is correct.

---

† We could also use $\langle$exp$\rangle \to \langle$exp$\rangle + \langle$term$\rangle$ here. The next two entries and many subsequent ones could similarly be added by alternate means.

3. If $A \to X_1 \ldots X_n$ and $B \to X_i \ldots X_n$ are two productions, then we do not have $X_{i-1} \lessdot B$.

Example 8.16.   Let us again consider the grammar:

$$\langle \text{asgn stat} \rangle \to \mathbf{id} = \langle \text{exp} \rangle$$
$$\langle \text{exp} \rangle \to \langle \text{exp} \rangle + \langle \text{term} \rangle \mid \langle \text{term} \rangle$$
$$\langle \text{term} \rangle \to \langle \text{term} \rangle * \langle \text{factor} \rangle \mid \langle \text{factor} \rangle$$
$$\langle \text{factor} \rangle \to (\langle \text{exp} \rangle) \mid \mathbf{id}$$

By inspection, there are no duplicate right sides, so rule (1) holds. We have already seen that there are no conflicts in the shift-reduce matrix, Fig. 8.13. Thus, rule (2) is satisfied. Now consider rule (3). There are two pairs of right sides that could play the role of $A \to X_1 \ldots X_n$ and $B \to X_i \ldots X_n$. One such pair is $\langle \text{exp} \rangle \to \langle \text{exp} \rangle + \langle \text{term} \rangle$ and $\langle \text{exp} \rangle \to \langle \text{term} \rangle$. Here, $n = 3$, $i = 3$, $A = B = X_1 = \langle \text{exp} \rangle$, $X_2 = +$, and $X_3 = \langle \text{term} \rangle$. We must check that $X_2 \lessdot B$ is false, that is, we do not have $+ \lessdot \langle \text{exp} \rangle$. A check of Example 8.15 assures us that $+ \lessdot \langle \text{exp} \rangle$ is indeed false.

The other possible candidate for $A \to X_1 \ldots X_n$ and $B \to X_i \ldots X_n$ is $\langle \text{term} \rangle \to \langle \text{term} \rangle * \langle \text{factor} \rangle$ and $\langle \text{term} \rangle \to \langle \text{factor} \rangle$. A similar argument convinces us that no violation of rule (3) occurs, since $* \lessdot \langle \text{term} \rangle$ is false. We conclude that our grammar is in fact a weak-precedence grammar and that the parsing algorithm described will work for it.   ∎

8.8 AMBIGUOUS GRAMMARS

We have seen that a sentence may have many derivations in a given grammar. This situation is not a bad one, since it is only the parse tree which is of real importance. However, it is nice if a sentence has a unique parse tree, and we shall call a grammar *unambiguous* if all of its sentences have unique parse trees. If even one sentence of the grammar has more than one parse tree, we call the grammar *ambiguous*.

Our desire for unambiguity forces us to avoid certain styles of productions in grammars.

Example 8.17.   It might seem convenient to define binary integers by the grammar:

$$\langle \text{integer} \rangle \to \langle \text{integer} \rangle \langle \text{integer} \rangle \mid 0 \mid 1$$

However, this grammar has many parse trees for integers of length greater than two. For example, 101 has the two parse trees shown in Fig. 8.25. Thus the grammar is ambiguous.

One way of avoiding this ambiguity is to introduce a new variable $\langle \text{digit} \rangle$ and write the grammar as:

$$\langle \text{integer} \rangle \to \langle \text{integer} \rangle \langle \text{digit} \rangle \mid \langle \text{digit} \rangle$$
$$\langle \text{digit} \rangle \to 0 \mid 1$$

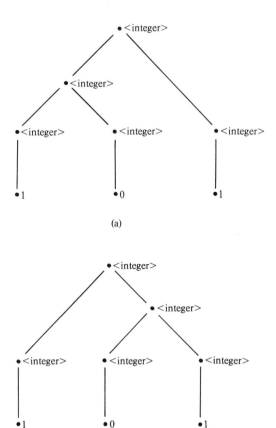

(a)

(b)

Fig. 8.25   Two parse trees.

The new grammar has only one parse tree for 101, the tree shaped like Fig. 8.25(a). Effectively, the new grammar groups digits from the left only, while the original grammar could group them many different ways. ∎

An interesting problem of ambiguity which comes up frequently in programming languages such as PL/I is known as the "dangling else."

Example 8.18.   Let **exp** and **as** be terminals standing for "expression" and "assignment statement," and consider the grammar:

⟨statement⟩ → **if exp then** ⟨statement⟩ **else** ⟨statement⟩ |
                if exp then ⟨statement⟩ |
          as

Consider the two derivation trees of Fig. 8.26. The yield of each is the sentence **if exp then if exp then as else as**. The two derivation trees reflect two different possible interpretations of statements of this form. Take a specific example with actual expressions substituted for **exp** and **as**:

$$\textbf{if } A < B \textbf{ then if } A < C \textbf{ then } X = 1 \textbf{ else } X = 2$$

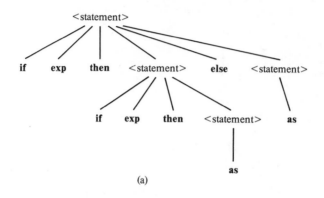

(a)

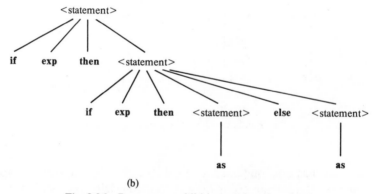

(b)

Fig. 8.26 Parse trees exhibiting a "dangling else."

If we believe the first tree, then the above sentence is of the form **if** $A < B$ **then** ⟨statement⟩ **else** $X = 2$, where the ⟨statement⟩ referred to is **if** $A < C$ **then** $X = 1$. According to this interpretation, we assign X the value 2 wherever $A \geqslant B$. If $A < B$, then we assign X the value 1 if $A < C$ and make no assignment to X if $A \geqslant C$.

If we believe the second tree, then the structure of the sentence is **if** $A < B$ **then** ⟨statement⟩, where ⟨statement⟩ refers to **if** $A < C$ **then** $X = 1$ **else** $X = 2$. Here, we make no assignment to X if $A \geqslant B$. We assign X the value 1 if $A < B$ and $A < C$ and the value 2 if $A < B$ but $A \geqslant C$.

The differences are summarized in Fig. 8.27.

Conditions		Tree of Fig. 8.26(a)	Tree of Fig. 8.26(b)
$A < B$	$A < C$	$X = 1$	$X = 1$
$A < B$	$A \geqslant C$	None	$X = 2$
$A \geqslant B$	$A < C$	$X = 2$	None
$A \geqslant B$	$A \geqslant C$	$X = 2$	None

Fig. 8.27 Assignment to X under various conditions.

In essence, the "dangling else" problem is: determine to which **then** the **else** is an alternative. The usual solution is to say that the **else** is an alternate to the preceding **then** which does not already have an **else**. That is, the tree of Fig. 8.26(b) is "correct," while that of Fig. 8.26(a) is not. ∎

8.9 PARSING AMBIGUOUS GRAMMARS

When we have an ambiguous grammar, we have a choice of either revising the grammar to make it unambiguous as we did in Example 8.17, or trying to write a parser for the ambiguous grammar that will produce one parse tree. The first alternative often requires that many new variables be introduced.

The second alternative is more attractive, but it requires that we use some intelligence in deciding which parse tree we really want and in deciding how to obtain the desired parse tree by simple means.

Example 8.19. In Example 8.18, we "resolved" ambiguities by saying that a dangling **else** belonged to the previous "un-**else**'d" **then**. It turns out that the grammar of Example 8.18 is not a weak-precedence grammar. Conditions (1) and (3) are easily seen to be satisfied, but condition (2) is not. That is, we have ⟨statement⟩ ⋖ **else** and ⟨statement⟩ ⋗ **else**. Thus, the shift-reduce matrix requires both S and R in the row for ⟨statement⟩ and the column for **else**.

It turns out that we can resolve this problem by choosing S for the (⟨statement⟩, **else**) entry.

Essentially, when we have **if exp then** ⟨statement⟩ in the four top stack records and **else** is the first input symbol, we could reduce **if exp then** ⟨statement⟩ to ⟨statement⟩ or we could shift the **else**, hoping to complete the right side **if exp then** ⟨statement⟩ **else** ⟨statement⟩. The rule that **else**'s are associated with the previous "un-**else**'d" **then** tells us to try for the latter right side. Shifting the **else** instead of reducing is thus required. ∎

In summary, the weak-precedence parsing algorithm and other "ready made" parsing algorithms require an unambiguous grammar, which is not too hard to find for most programming languages. However, if one is willing (and able) to be clever about it, one can often find a simple ambiguous grammar with a simple parsing algorithm which will select those parse trees which put the "right" structure on each sentence.

EXERCISES

8.1 Consider the context-free grammar:

$$\langle expression \rangle \rightarrow \langle expression \rangle + \langle term \rangle \mid \langle term \rangle$$
$$\langle term \rangle \rightarrow \langle term \rangle * \langle factor \rangle \mid \langle factor \rangle$$
$$\langle factor \rangle \rightarrow (\langle expression \rangle) \mid \textbf{id}$$

from Example 8.5. For this grammar, find (i) leftmost derivations, (ii) rightmost derivations, and (iii) derivations which are neither leftmost nor rightmost for the sentences:

a) **id** * **id** + **id**

b) (**id** + **id**) * (**id** + **id**)

c) ((**id** + **id**) * **id**) + **id**

8.2 Find parse trees for the sentences of Exercise 8.1.

8.3 Find context-free grammars generating the following sets of strings:

a) strings of exactly two letters,

b) strings of one or more letters,

c) strings consisting of a letter followed by up to five letters and/or digits.

* **8.4** Find a context-free grammar generating expressions whose (binary infix) operators are +, −, *, and / and whose "identifiers" are either **id** or strings of the form **id**($\langle expression \rangle$, $\langle expression \rangle, \ldots, \langle expression \rangle$) representing subscripted identifiers such as $A(B + C, 2)$.

** **8.5** Find a context-free grammar generating all and only the strings of balanced parentheses. That is, "(" and ")" are the only terminal symbols; a string is balanced if it has an equal number of each, and each prefix of the string has at least as many left as right parentheses.

8.6 Show the steps of the weak-precedence parser for the grammar of Example 8.11 (p. 235) when given the strings:

a) **id** = (**id** + **id**) * **id**

b) **id** = ((**id**)) + **id**

*c) **id** = ((**id** + **id**)) * **id**

* **8.7** Find the shift-reduce tables for the following weak-precedence grammars:

a) $\langle signed\ integer \rangle \rightarrow \langle sign \rangle \langle integer \rangle$
$\langle integer \rangle \rightarrow \langle integer \rangle \langle digit \rangle \mid \langle digit \rangle$
$\langle digit \rangle \rightarrow 0 \mid 1$
$\langle sign \rangle \rightarrow + \mid -$

b) $\langle statement \rangle \rightarrow$ **while** $\langle expression \rangle$ **do** $\langle statement \rangle \mid$
               if $\langle expression \rangle$ **then** $\langle statement \rangle$ **else** $\langle statement \rangle \mid$
               begin $\langle stat\ list \rangle$ **end** $\mid$
               stat
$\langle stat\ list \rangle \quad \rightarrow \langle stat\ list \rangle; \langle statement \rangle \mid$
                  $\langle statement \rangle$
$\langle expression \rangle \rightarrow$ **exp**

8.8 Verify that the grammars of Exercise 8.7 are indeed weak-precedence grammars.

8.9 Show the steps of the weak-precedence parser for the grammar of Exercise 8.7(a) when given +101 to parse.

8.10 Find an unambiguous grammar to generate strings of one or more letters.

*__8.11__ The following grammar is proposed to "solve" the dangling else problem:

$$\langle\text{statement}\rangle \rightarrow \textbf{if exp then } \langle\text{substat}\rangle \textbf{ else } \langle\text{statement}\rangle \mid$$
$$\textbf{if exp then } \langle\text{statement}\rangle \mid$$
$$\textbf{as}$$
$$\langle\text{substat}\rangle \rightarrow \textbf{if exp then } \langle\text{substat}\rangle \textbf{ else } \langle\text{statement}\rangle \mid$$
$$\textbf{as}$$

Show that the above grammar is, unfortunately, still ambiguous.

**__8.12__ Find an unambiguous grammar generating the same set of strings as those of Exercise 8.11 and Example 8.18.

Programming Exercise

8.13 Implement the weak-precedence parser for the grammar of Example 8.11. Your input should be a string of terminal symbols of the grammar with no intervening blanks. You may, for convenience, use *I* in place of **id**. Your output should be the sequence of moves made by the parser, using 0 for a shift and 1 to 7 for the seven productions of the grammar (choose any order you like).

FURTHER READING

More information about context-free grammars can be found in Ginsburg [1966], Hopcroft and Ullman [1969] or Salomaa [1973]. The origin of such grammars is traced to Chomsky [1956]. For more on parsing see Aho and Ullman [1972], Aho and Johnson [1974], or Lewis, Rosenkrantz, and Stearns [1975]. Weak-precedence grammars have been used in at least one compiler writing system (Ichbiah and Morse [1970]), and an early version of the XPL compiler writing system (McKeeman, Horning and Wortman [1970] used a generalization of the weak-precedence idea called "mixed strategy precedence."

Chapter 9

Compilers

In this chapter we shall discuss how programs written in a programming language are translated (*compiled*) into machine language. As programming languages possess considerably more structure than assembly languages, the algorithms used to compile a programming language are correspondingly more complex than the algorithms used in an assembler. Moreover, one finds more variety in the strategies used in compilers than in assemblers, so it is difficult to generalize about compilers. We shall therefore discuss only one strategy, "syntax directed" compilation, of which most compilers partake to at least a modest degree. In compilers of this design, the parser can be thought of as "directing" the action, calling upon a number of routines in turn. We shall introduce these routines in the next section.

9.1 A BRIEF OVERVIEW OF A COMPILER

We may partition a compiler into several subprocesses, called *phases*. The names which we give to the phases of a compiler are:

1. lexical analysis,
2. syntactic analysis (parsing),
3. intermediate code generation (translation),
4. code optimization,
5. code selection (object-code generation),
6. bookkeeping,
7. error recovery.

The notion of a phase is distinct from a pass as used in the discussion of assemblers. Recall that a "pass" in our assembler consists of a scan of the input (or the output of the previous pass) and some manipulation upon it. The phases of a compiler are logically distinct operations which may be done in separate passes (although not in the order shown above). More often, however, several phases are merged into one pass and are done simultaneously, with control alternating between several phases. Since there is no set grouping of phases into passes, nor is there one "best" number of passes for a compiler, we shall not discuss the matter of compiler passes further.

We proceed now to discuss each of the phases of the compiler and the links between them.

9.2 LEXICAL ANALYSIS

The input to the lexical analysis phase is the *source* program, that is, the string of characters which forms the writer's program. The lexical analyzer deletes blanks and groups the other characters into logical units, called *tokens*. Some common tokens are:

 i) identifiers,

 ii) keywords, such as DO, GOTO, etc.,

 iii) signs, e.g., + or =, which are tokens by themselves.

Often, it is straightforward to group characters into tokens. At other times, one may have to look far beyond the point of the token itself before one can group characters with assurance.

Example 9.1. Suppose we' are lexically analyzing FORTRAN, and find that DO10I = 1 are the first seven nonblank characters on a card. If the next character is a period, then we find that DO10I is an identifier, and we are working on an assignment statement, such as

$$\text{DO10I = 1.7 * XYZ.}^{\dagger}$$

If, on the other hand, the eighth character is a comma, then we have a DO statement, such as DO 10 I = 1, 40. Here the tokens are the keyword DO, the statement number 10, the identifier *I*, the equal sign, the identifiers 1 and 40, and the comma. ∎

The output of the lexical analyzer is a sequence of symbols (typically binary integers) standing for the various tokens. One token, representing any identifier (or several tokens, if we distinguish classes of identifiers, such as constants or statement labels) must be treated specially. Along with each identifier token there must be a pointer to the *symbol table*. For each different identifier there must be an entry in the symbol table giving its name in the source program and any other information we have about it. For example, we might store in the symbol table the fact that ABC was a real array of dimension 10×20 and that it was stored in the blank COMMON block, starting 150 words from the beginning of the block. The maintenance of the symbol table is called *bookkeeping*.

---

† Recall that FORTRAN ignores blanks. We have shown blanks to allow the reader to group tokens by eye, but the blanks provide no clue to the lexical analyzer.

Example 9.2. The FORTRAN statement

$$101 \quad \text{IF(A.EQ.B)} \quad A = A + C$$

would be translated by the lexical analyzer into a sequence of tokens[†] such as

lab$_1$ **if lp id**$_1$ **eq id**$_2$ **rp id**$_1$ **as id**$_1$ **pl id**$_3$

The token **lab** stands for a statement label, and we have subscripted it to indicate a pointer to a place in the symbol table (or, more likely, a separate table for labels) for 101. The token **if** stands for the keyword IF; **lp** stands for the left parenthesis; **id** stands for any identifier, and we have subscripted each instance of **id** to indicate a pointer to the symbol table for the particular instance of that token **id**. Continuing, **eq** stands for .EQ., **rp** for the right parenthesis, **as** for the assignment symbol ($=$) and **pl** for the plus sign. Identifiers 1, 2 and 3 are A, B, and C, respectively. ∎

9.3 PARSING AND SYNTAX-DIRECTED TRANSLATION

The output of the lexical analyzer is a stream of tokens. This stream is treated by the parser as a sentence of the context-free grammar which defines the syntax of the programming language.[‡] We can think of the role of the parser as the construction of a parse tree for the input. In the previous chapter, one method (weak-precedence) of building parse trees for some grammars was discussed. There are other methods of course.

In practice, the parse tree might be built in a figurative sense only. For example, the parser might only step through a rightmost derivation, in reverse. Every time the parser did a reduction, it would call a subroutine to generate some output. We shall consider this special form of syntax-directed translation in Section 9.10. However, we shall for the time being assume that a data structure representing the parse tree has actually been built by the parser. The next phase of the compiler uses this parse tree to generate intermediate code.

Let us digress to a philosophical point for a moment. One might naturally ask why the parse tree should be an aid to compiling programming languages. Part of the answer concerns the way programming languages are designed. It is easy for language designers to view programming languages as composed of a hierarchy of certain entities (variables of a grammar). The entities themselves are composed of smaller entities, and so on. Thus grammars, putting a natural hierarchical structure on the sentences they generate, are useful in defining these entities. It is also natural to view these entities as having a "meaning" of their own; normally the "meaning" is part of a machine language program. Finally, we often find it convenient to express

---

[†] We show the tokens as boldface strings of letters. In a compiler, the tokens would be coded by integers and subscripted tokens by pairs of integers of the form (token type, subscript).

[‡] Of course, if there is a programmer error the output of the lexical analyzer may not be generated by the grammar, or the lexical analyzer may be unable to break its input into tokens. We shall discuss how the compiler handles errors, subsequently.

the meaning of a variable in terms of the way it is built from constituent variables (i.e., the production used to expand the variable) and the meaning of these constituents.

Let us now discuss the translation phase briefly. A typical *syntax-directed translation* technique is to define one or more "translations" for each node of the parse tree. Each translation is a function of:

1. the production used at the node,[†] and
2. the translations of the children of the node.

We shall give examples of appropriate translation formulas subsequently. In general, choosing the proper translation formulas is a creative task, in the sense that programming in general is creative.

The output of the translation phase is usually an assembly-like language, which we shall refer to as *intermediate code*. Intermediate code has the property that each instruction corresponds to a limited number of machine instructions. In comparison, programming-language statements such as assignment statements do not, in principle, have any limit on the number of machine instructions required to execute a single statement. On the other hand, assembly-language statements often are restricted to one machine instruction per assembly statement, while intermediate-code statements may generate a fixed number of instructions larger than one.

One example of an appropriate intermediate code is an assembly language. Another frequently used intermediate code is referred to as "three-address code."

The thing which distinguishes three-address code from assembly code is the former's lack of specificity as to where operations and tests actually occur in the machine and where data is stored. In the next example we shall consider a set of instructions that could be referred to as three-address code.

Example 9.3. The term "three-address code" actually refers to instructions which correspond to binary operations. We recall that binary machine operations generally specify three addresses—the addresses of the two operands and that of the result. However, in real machine languages, some of these addresses are constrained to be registers. The same three addresses are present in three-address code, but all addresses are symbolic; they are not tied to any particular register or memory location. When more than one of the addresses turn out to be in memory, the "three-address" instruction will require more than one machine instruction for implementation, but no more than three machine instructions of the usual type.

In addition to binary operations, three-address instructions include some which correspond roughly to the other types of machine instructions such as data motion, unary operations, tests, and control transfers. The formats of these instructions may involve more or fewer than three addresses, but each instruction takes a fixed number of addresses.

[†] Note that the way a parse tree is formed assures us that the labels of the children of a node form the right side of a production whose left side is the label of the node in question.

Let us design some typical three-address instructions. Suppose $+$, $-$, $*$, and $\div$ stand for the fixed-point versions of the obvious operations. To denote floating-point, we shall circle the operators. Then $+(A, B, C)$ means: "Add A and B in fixed-point and call the result C." The other seven operators mentioned can substitute for $+$, with an obvious change in the meaning. Let **as** (A, B) mean "Assign the value of B to A."[†]

Then the FORTRAN assignment statement:

$$\text{COST} = (1. + \text{RATE*PERIOD})*\text{COST}$$

can be translated to the three-address code:

$$\circledast(\text{RATE, PERIOD, TEMP1})$$
$$\oplus(1. , \text{TEMP1, TEMP2})$$
$$\circledast(\text{TEMP2, COST, TEMP3})$$
$$\textbf{as } (\text{COST, TEMP3})$$

Here, we have observed that the first calculation which must be performed is RATE $*$ PERIOD. The value of this product is assigned to the name TEMP1 by the compiler.[‡] Next, we must compute 1. + RATE $*$ PERIOD, that is, 1. + TEMP1. This is accomplished by the second instruction, and the name TEMP2 is used for this value. The third instruction computes TEMP2 $*$ COST, that is, the value of the expression on the right of the $=$ sign. TEMP3 is the name given to this value. The last instruction assigns the value of the expression to the variable on the left of the $=$ sign.[§] ∎

We should note that each instruction of three-address code takes a single operator. Thus, the more complex the expression, the longer the sequence of three-address instructions. Three-address code is therefore not a trivial rehash of assignment statements, but gives explicitly something important which is only implicit in arithmetic expressions, namely, the order in which operators are to be applied.

Three-address code includes more than instructions for applying operators. We shall next consider an example on the handling of loops. Here, we shall consider a few more typical three-address instructions.

Example 9.4.   The "three-address" instruction **goto**(A) is an unconditional transfer to A, where A is the name of an instruction. Names of three-address instructions

---

[†] Note that this "three-address" instruction takes only two addresses.

[‡] The name is arbitrary. If the compiler is sophisticated, it will not use a different memory location for each temporary name, so the number of different names used is unimportant.

[§] Note that we could omit the last instruction if we used *COST* in place of *TEMP3* in the third instruction. We have not done so because the typical syntax-directed translation algorithms will generate intermediate code for the right side of an assignment without knowing that it is a complete right side—it could be a subexpression of the right side. When we study object-code generation and optimization, we shall see that it is not necessary to avoid the use of the **as** type instructions. Their presence does not adversely affect the speed of the machine-language program produced.

will be indicated by the name and a colon, prefixed to the instruction. The instruction **el**(A, B, C) tests if the value of A is equal to or less than the value of B, and transfers to the instruction named C if so. We assume A and B are fixed-point here, and use the operator **fel** if they are floating-point.

Thus, the portion of a FORTRAN program:

$$\begin{array}{ll}
\text{DO} \quad 10 \quad \text{I} = 1, \; 20 \\
10 \quad \text{K} = \text{K} + \text{I}
\end{array}$$

might be translated to:

$$\begin{array}{ll}
 & \textbf{as}(\text{I, 1}) \\
\text{INST1}: & +(\text{K, I, TEMP1}) \\
 & \textbf{as}(\text{K, TEMP1}) \\
 & +(\text{I, 1, TEMP2}) \\
 & \textbf{as}(\text{I, TEMP2}) \\
 & \textbf{el}\,(\text{I, 20, INST1}) \quad \blacksquare
\end{array}$$

Syntax-directed translation will be covered in much greater detail in Sections 9.9 through 9.11.

9.4 CODE SELECTION AND OPTIMIZATION

In the final two phases, the intermediate code is optimized and converted to machine code. One job of the code-selection phase is the creation of memory locations for all the identifiers in the symbol table. The amount of memory assigned to an identifier and the initial value of this memory is a function of the type (real, pointer, etc.) of identifier at hand (See Section 6.2). Type information is stored in the symbol table when declarations are encountered in the source program, and the information can be used in code selection.

The second job in the code-selection phase is the conversion of intermediate code to machine code. If intermediate code is of the three-address type, then it can be converted instruction by instruction to assembly code and then assembled.

Example 9.5. We shall convert the three-address code of Example 9.4 to our assembly language. The rules which we shall use are quite naive. In particular, they do not take advantage of the fact that our computer has seven registers; all computation is done in register 1. Neither do our rules "remember" what is left in register 1 by the previous instruction. Some improvement in the generated machine code can be made in a code-optimization phase, either preceding, along with, or following code selection. Our rules are the following:

1. Convert **as**(A, B) to

$$\begin{array}{ll}
\text{LOAD} & \text{B} \\
\text{STORE} & \text{A}
\end{array}$$

2. Convert "op"(A, B, C) to

$$\begin{array}{ll}
\text{LOAD} & \text{A} \\
\text{"op"} & \text{B} \\
\text{STORE} & \text{C}
\end{array}$$

where "op" stands for any of the eight arithmetic operations we have used and also for the obviously corresponding mnemonic.

3. Convert **el**(A, B, C) to

```
LOAD    B
SUB     A
JPLUS   C
```

and **fel**(A, B, C) to the same, with SUBFL instead of SUB.

4. Convert **goto**(A) to

```
JUMP    A
```

If any of the above arguments are constants rather than variables, then we must prefix them by an = sign or, if feasible, use immediate address modification.

Thus, we may convert the code for the loop in the previous example to the code of Fig. 9.1. ▮

```
                LOAD    1(IMMED)  ⎫ from as(I, 1)
                STORE   I         ⎭
        INST1:  LOAD    K         ⎫
                ADD     I         ⎬ from + (K, I, TEMP1)
                STORE   TEMP1     ⎭
                LOAD    TEMP1     ⎫ from as(K, TEMP1)
                STORE   K         ⎭
                LOAD    I         ⎫
                ADD     1(IMMED)  ⎬ from + (I, 1, TEMP2)
                STORE   TEMP2     ⎭
                LOAD    TEMP2     ⎫ from as(I, TEMP2)
                STORE   I         ⎭
                LOAD    20(IMMED) ⎫
                SUB     I         ⎬ from el(I, 20, INST1)
                JPLUS   INST1     ⎭
```

Fig. 9.1　Assembly code.

A quick perusal of the code of Fig. 9.1 tells us that it is hardly efficient. Most compilers will "optimize" the code they generate, either by transforming assembly code or by exercising considerably more care than we have when translating three-address code into assembly or machine code.

We shall consider code optimization more extensively in Section 9.8. However, let us consider here one example of the need for care in selecting code.

Example 9.6:　Whenever we see the sequence

```
STORE   A
LOAD    A
```

and there is no jump to the second instruction anywhere in the program, then that
instruction is superfluous, since it loads register 1 with the same value it had before
the load. If we have generated the assembly code from our hypothetical three-
address code, then transfers may occur only to assembly instructions with names.
Thus, in Fig. 9.1, LOAD TEMP1 and LOAD TEMP2 are both redundant, and we
can replace that program by the program of Fig. 9.2.

```
              LOAD    1(IMMED)
              STORE   I
      INST1:  LOAD    K
              ADD     I
              STORE   TEMP1
              STORE   K
              LOAD    I
              ADD     1(IMMED)
              STORE   TEMP2
              STORE   I
              LOAD    20(IMMED)
              SUB     I
              JPLUS   INST1
```

Fig. 9.2   Improved assembly code.

It is now possible that the instructions STORE TEMP1 and STORE TEMP2
are useless, in the sense that TEMP1 and TEMP2 either figure in no other instructions of the program or are stored into before any subsequent instruction loads
them into a register. (Recall that we are looking at only a piece of a program, not
the entire program.) If such is the case, and we delete these two instructions, we are
left with the program of Fig. 9.3. Note that the code of Fig. 9.3 is the same we would
have obtained had we been more sophisticated in generation of three address code
in Example 9.4. There, we could have used K in place of TEMP1 and I in place of
TEMP2, doing away with the assignments of steps 3 and 5.   ∎

```
              LOAD    1(IMMED)
              STORE   I
      INST1:  LOAD    K
              ADD     I
              STORE   K
              LOAD    I
              ADD     1(IMMED)
              STORE   I
              LOAD    20(IMMED)
              SUB     I
              JPLUS   INST1
```

Fig. 9.3   Second improvement.

A more sophisticated form of code optimization attempts to utilize registers to best advantage. For example, we could attempt to keep in registers those variables that are manipulated in a loop.

Example 9.7. In the above example, I and K are candid.tes for being kept in registers, and we shall use registers 1 and 2, respectively, for this purpose. We must bring these variables to registers before entering the loop for the first time (or in the case of I, initialize it in register 1 directly). Then, we must follow the loop with instructions to store the values in the locations reserved for I and K.[†] Such a modification could produce the code of Fig. 9.4. Note that the loop of Fig. 9.4, where the code spends most of its time, has five instructions compared with nine in the loop of Fig. 9.3. Thus the code of Fig. 9.4 will take about 5/9 the time taken by that of Fig. 9.3. ∎

```
          LOAD1  1(IMMED)    /*  INITIALIZE I IN REGISTER 1   */

          LOAD2  K           /*  BRING K TO REGISTER 2        */

INST1:    ADD21              /*  K=K+I                        */

          ADD1   1(IMMED)    /*  I=I+1                        */

          LOAD3  20(IMMED)   /*  TEST IF I ≤ 20               */
          SUB31
          JPLUS3 INST1

          STORE1 I           /*  AFTER THE LOOP, STORE        */
          STORE2 K           /*  THE VARIABLES                */
```

Fig. 9.4 Code taking advantage of several registers.

9.5 BOOKKEEPING

During the phases mentioned above, namely lexical analysis, parsing, translation, code generation, and optimization, there are two phases, bookkeeping and error handling, which interact with these periodically. We shall discuss bookkeeping here and error handling in the next section.

As we have previously mentioned, the compiler keeps a symbol table for the identifiers used in the program. The symbol table of a compiler is really no different from the symbol table of an assembler except:

1. considerably more information is associated with the identifiers in a compiler than in an assembler, and

---

[†] It is likely that the variable I will not be used outside its DO loop. If so, we need not store it.

2. the symbol table of a compiler may be several separate tables. For example, we could have special tables for those identifiers representing labels and those representing subroutine names.

Since the techniques used to implement compiler symbol tables (e.g., hashing) are the same as for assemblers, we shall not discuss the matter here. Rather, we shall discuss what information goes into a symbol table, how it is determined, and how it is used.

Let us recall from Section 6.2 the discussion of the types of attributes appearing in declarations of a typical programming language. For each identifier, an entry in the symbol table must tell which of the possible attributes apply. If the identifier represents data (rather than a label or a subroutine), then the attributes are typically either:

1. mode information, (Is the identifier fixed- or floating-point, is it double precision, is it an array?) or

2. storage-location information. (Is it dynamically or statically allocated; is it in COMMON?)

Certain attributes also require parameters, in addition to a bit indicating their presence. For example, a FORTRAN array name requires, in its symbol-table entry, the number of dimensions, and the length along each dimension. We shall now give a simple example of a record format for a symbol table.

Example 9.8. Let us suppose that we are dealing with a language whose variable names may only have the following attributes:

1. the mode—either fixed-point, floating-point, or Boolean;

2. the precision—either single or double;

3. the structure—either simple (no structure) or array. An array can have up to three dimensions; each dimension can have length up to $2^{12} - 1$.†

Identifiers may be declared to have any of these attributes, and the default condition, in the absence of declarations to the contrary, will be floating-point, single-precision, and simple. Identifiers may be up to five characters in length.

Fig. 9.5 shows a possible format for the records of the symbol table for variable names. The portions *A*, *B*, and *C* have the following uses.

A—The mode. Two bits are needed, and the following code is used:

> 00   floating
> 01   fixed
> 10   Boolean

B—The precision. One bit is used, with 0 standing for single and 1 for double precision.

---

† It may not be obvious that a compiler has a limit on the size of an array. Try compiling a FORTRAN program with a 1,000,000 × 2 array.

C—The structure. Two bits are used. 00 stands for simple, 01, 10, and 11 stand for 1-, 2-, and 3-dimensional arrays, respectively. The lengths along these dimensions are indicated in the 12-bit fields named *dim*1, *dim*2, and *dim*3, as needed.

Note that the default conditions may all be indicated by 0's. Thus, we may at the outset fill all records with 0's and change the various fields as needed. ∎

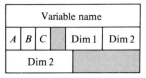

Fig. 9.5   Record of symbol table. Variable name is needed if we are using a hash table.

Information for the symbol table is gathered primarily in the lexical, parsing, and translation phases. In the lexical phase, the various identifiers used by the program are detected, and symbol table entries for them are created. Certain attributes may also be detected and entered into the table. For example, FORTRAN has a convention regarding first letters of variable names that gives each name either fixed or floating mode. This information may be entered into the symbol table as soon as the name is encountered. Of course, if the first occurrence of a name is in a declaration statement, the conventional mode may be immediately overruled.

Other attributes may be entered into the symbol table as a result of translation.

Example 9.9.   In Fig. 9.6, we see a portion of a parse tree in a hypothetical grammar for FORTRAN. A DIMENSION statement is parsed here; **dim** is the token for the keyword DIMENSION.

The translation of the node labeled ⟨dim stat⟩ in Fig. 9.6 could be an instruction to the compiler to enter into the symbol table the information that the particular variable name represented by **id** is a two dimensional array whose size is given by the integers represented by the two tokens **const**. ∎

Symbol table information is used during the generation of intermediate code and code selection. Obviously, many or all of the attributes of a variable must be known before storage can be allocated to it. Attribute information is also necessary for the generation of intermediate code.

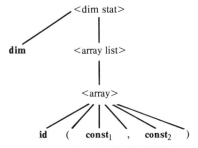

Fig. 9.6   Parse tree for a DIMENSION statement.

Example 9.10. $A = B * C$ in some programming language might be translated to three address code as:

$$\text{"op" (B, C, TEMP)}$$
$$\textbf{as} \quad \text{(A, TEMP)}$$

However, "op" could stand for fixed-point or floating-point multiplication or logical "and," depending on the mode of A, B, and C, and the generated machine code would be different in each case. If B and C were of different modes, we would have to insert a conversion routine in the machine code. If B and C were, say triple precision, the machine code generated would be a long sequence of machine instructions or subroutine call for most computers.   ∎

9.6 ERROR CORRECTION

One of the important functions of a compiler is the detection of errors in the program. Furthermore, when an error is detected, the compiler must perform "error correction," that is, take a guess as to what the programmer meant. It is not really important whether the compiler guesses right or not, since the object program being generated will probably never be executed. What is important is that the compiler be able to pick up the thread of the (presumably) correctly written program following the error. Only in this way will the compiler be able to scan for additional errors in the source program.

As we mentioned before, errors can be detected in various ways, such as the following.

1. In the lexical phase, we could reach a point where no token could be found. For example, in FORTRAN, if we search for a token and find .Z as the next two nonblank characters, no token is present.

2. While parsing, we could reach a point where the parser can make no legal move. For example, suppose a programmer intended to write $A = (B + C) * D$ but accidentally omitted the left parenthesis. If we were parsing, say according to the grammar of Example 8.11 (p. 235) we could not process the corresponding token string $\textbf{id} = \textbf{id} + \textbf{id}) * \textbf{id}$. The reader should attempt the (weak-precedence) parse and observe that error is detected immediately after the right parenthesis is shifted onto the stack and a reduction called for.

3. While generating intermediate code, we could detect an attempt to apply an operator (e.g., logical "and") to operands (e.g., integers, which are not of permissible type for the operator). (What is permissible depends on the programming language being compiled, of course.)

4. While entering information in the symbol table, we could discover that an identifier has been given two contradictory attributes, e.g., real and integer.

5. While optimizing code, we could discover that certain portions of the program cannot be reached. This situation most likely indicates some sort of programmer error.

The last three situations require only that the compiler give a diagnostic message telling what rule of the programming language has been violated. On the other hand, lexical and syntactic errors require that some alteration be made to the source program or the stream of tokens. Some possible alterations are the following.

1. Look for a misspelling of a keyword. If a keyword is misspelled, the lexical analyzer may have "recognized" an identifier. Replacing an identifier by a similarly spelled keyword may allow processing to proceed normally.

2. Attempt to make a small change in the sequence of tokens. Some simple changes are:

a) insert a token

b) delete a token

c) change one token

d) interchange the order of two tokens.

For example, a common FORTRAN error is the insertion of a comma after 10 in a statement like

```
DO   10   I = 1,20
```

The error correction phase could successfully remove the token **comma**. Conversely, a comma can "disappear" due to a miscounted Hollerith field. For example, a token **comma** should be inserted into the stream that comes from:

```
FORMAT(10HANSWER IS, I10)
```

3. If all else fails, the parser and/or lexical analyzer can skip to a point where it can be reasonably sure of being able to pick up the thread of the program. For example, a FORTRAN compiler could skip to the beginning of the next card (not a continuation card, though). An ALGOL or PL/I compiler could look for the next semicolon.

9.7 INTERACTION OF THE PHASES

We have pictured the phases of lexical analysis, parsing, intermediate code generation, optimization, and code selection as coming sequentially in that order. Actually, we often find that at least the first three phases operate simultaneously.

For example, we may think of the parser as being "in control." When the parser needs another token on its input list (right after a shift, if the parser is a weak-precedence parser), it calls the lexical analyzer as a subroutine. The lexical analyzer can then scan the source program, find the next token, place it on the parser's input list and return control to the parser.

When the parser performs a reduction and constructs a node of the parse tree, the parser calls the syntax-directed translator, which constructs the translations associated with the node just added to the parse tree. Thus, the three phases may operate at essentially the same time. It is often convenient to use one pass for lexical analysis, parsing, and intermediate code generation, together with their interactions with bookkeeping and error correction.

9.8   MORE ABOUT CODE OPTIMIZATION

Having had an overview of a compiler and studied the parser in detail (in Chapter 8), we shall now examine two other parts in detail. In this section we shall revisit the code optimization phase, and in the next three sections, we shall consider syntax-directed translation.

It is not necessary that a compiler produce "good" code if the object program is to be run only a few times. That is, the time saved when the program runs may be considerably less than the time the compiler spent improving the object code. However, for each language, a compiler which produces highly efficient code should be available when we compile the "final" version of a program that is to be run many times.

While there are many optimizations[†] that may be performed, the following three are probably the most important.

1. Clean up inner loops to make them run faster. Take loop-independent computations out of the loop and allocate registers to hold variables needed in the loop whenever possible.

2. Replace recursive subroutines by nonrecursive ones if possible.[‡] Also, expand nonrecursive subroutines "in line," as if they were macro uses, when possible. These transformations are difficult and generally not implemented in optimizing compilers, but they have great potential for speeding up programs.

3. In very large programs (those which do not conveniently fit into main memory), one can attempt to reduce the size of the program considerably by condensing certain infrequently executed portions (Not inner loops!). The chief technique is to create one subroutine that can be used several times to replace several similar sequences of instructions. Although this may increase run time slightly, it can greatly decrease the size of the program.[§]

The next example exhibits some of the techniques which may be used to optimize three-address intermediate code. We introduce "indexing" three-address instruction **asi**(A, B, I) which sets the location I words beyond B to the value of A.

[†] The term "optimization" is a misnomer, since there is no guarantee that any program is the best possible for the job. What so called "optimizing compilers" do is to improve the code generated, compared with what would be generated by "obvious" methods.

[‡] This remark should not be construed as applying to the programmer; it is the compiler that should eliminate the recursion, not the programmer. Recursion often helps the programmer write concise, well-structured programs.

[§] (1) and (3) are not contradictory. (1) applies where a negligible increase in program size yields a significant decrease in running time. (3) applies when a negligible increase in running time produces a considerable decrease in size. Since a program may well spend 90% of the time in 5% of the instructions, (1) applies to the frequently executed 5% and (3) applies to the other 95%.

Example 9.11.   Consider the three address code which might be generated from the
FORTRAN DO Loops:

```
        DO   10   I = 1,10
        DO   10   J = 1,20
   10   A(I,J) = I + J
```

operating on a 10 × 20 array stored in row major form. The type of code to be
generated for arrays was discussed in Section 6.3. One possible intermediate program is shown in Fig. 9.7.

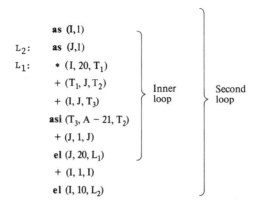

L_2:   **as** (J,1)
L_1:   * (I, 20, T_1)
          + (T_1, J, T_2)
          + (I, J, T_3)
          asi (T_3, A − 21, T_2)
          + (J, 1, J)
          el (J, 20, L_1)
          + (I, 1, I)
          el (I, 10, L_2)

Fig. 9.7   Intermediate program. Note A − 1 stands for a location which can be determined by the
compiler. No code to perform the subtraction is needed, nor will be generated, so we have not
violated our three-address ground rules.

We must first attempt to optimize the inner loop. We notice that I is never
changed as long as we remain within the inner loop. Thus, the statement *(I, 20, T_1)
is *loop invariant*, that is, it produces the same result each time through the loop.
We may bring it out of the loop by the simple expedient of moving the label L_1
down to the statement +(T_1, J, T_2) as shown in Fig. 9.8.

While the overall length of the program has not changed, the inner loop has
been reduced from six instructions to five, and we may expect the generated machine
code to be sped up almost proportionally, since the inner loop instructions are
executed 20 times as frequently as second loop instructions.   ∎

The next "optimization," the elimination of recursion is not nearly as easy to
implement by computer as is detection of loop-invariant instructions or other loop-
improving transformations. However, it can be just as useful, if not more so.

The third suggestion, introduction of subroutines into infrequently executed
regions of code applies to large programs, such as systems programs.

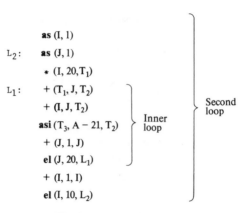

Fig. 9.8   Revised program.

Example 9.12.   A compiler is a large program which can be shortened by introduction of subroutines. For example, the lexical analyzer may be called upon to
test for the presence of various keywords in the input stream. We could write a
separate piece of code for each keyword, or we could write one subroutine which
would take two arguments:

1. the current place in the input stream, and

2. the sequence of characters in the desired keyword.

While we must pay the price of transmitting data to and from the subroutine,
we have replaced many (perhaps a hundred) pieces of code by an equal number of
calling sequences and one subroutine. ∎

9.9   SYNTAX-DIRECTED TRANSLATION

We shall now take up in detail the notion of a syntax-directed translation, which is a
convenient strategy for generating intermediate code from a parse tree. We shall
give some examples of the generation of three-address code, which is relatively easy,
and also of the generation of assembly code, which is harder.

Recall that a *syntax-directed translation scheme* consists of the following elements.

1. There exist several (possibly only one) *translations* associated with each variable
A. Each of these translations has a value at each of those nodes of the parse tree
which are labeled A. If A is the distinguished variable, it has at least one *distinguished
translation*, and possibly others.

2. For each production, say $A \rightarrow X_1 \ldots X_n$, there is a set of *translation rules*, one
for each translation of A, that express the translations of A in terms of symbols for
the translations of $X_1, \ldots, X_n$. At a particular node labeled A, the translations of A
are found by substituting, for each translation symbol in the translation rules, the
value of the corresponding translation found at the appropriate child of A.

3. To compute the translation of a sentence from its parse tree, compute all translations at all the nodes of the tree (except the leaves, which have no translation). The desired translation is the distinguished translation at the root.

Because of the way translations are to be computed, the translations at a node must be computed after the translations at its children. Therefore, we must choose a "bottom-up" order in which to compute the translations. A perfect choice is the order in which the weak-precedence parser creates nodes of the parse tree. Thus, translations can be computed every time a reduction is called for.

Let us proceed directly to some examples of how to design syntax-directed translation schemes.

Example 9.13. Our first example will produce our computer's assembly code from the grammar for assignment statements first introduced in Example 8.11, on the assumption that all operands are fixed-point numbers. The philosophy of the translation scheme is to associate assembly code to compute a certain value in register 1 with each node in the parse tree labeled $\langle exp \rangle$, $\langle term \rangle$, or $\langle factor \rangle$. The desired value is the value of the expression formed by reading, from the left, the leaves of the portion of the parse tree dangling from the node in question. The translation associated with $\langle asgn\ stat \rangle$ will be code that performs the assignment statement.

To help us, we shall make use of two functions. The first, which we call NEWTEMP( ), has no argument. It produces a new name for a temporary storage location each time it is invoked. We shall assume that the compiler keeps an integer stored, and each time we want a new name, we refer to NEWTEMP( ), which gives us the string TEMP concatenated with that integer and then increases the integer by one.[†]

The second function, NAME(id_i) takes as argument an identifier token with a pointer (the subscript i) to the symbol-table entry corresponding to that identifier. (Recall that the lexical analyser produces a pointer to the symbol table with every token **id** that it finds.) The value of NAME(id_i) is the actual variable name represented by that **id** token, or "$= \alpha$" if that **id** represents the constant α.

Let us now consider, one by one, the productions and design translation rules for them that will be consistent with the intuitive meaning of the translation (code to compute a value in register 1). The translations of $\langle exp \rangle$, $\langle term \rangle$, $\langle factor \rangle$, and $\langle asgn\ stat \rangle$ will be denoted E, T, F, and A, respectively.

1. $\langle factor \rangle \rightarrow$ **id**. The expression dangling from the node labeled $\langle factor \rangle$ is here a single identifier. The way to compute the value of this expression is to bring the value of the identifier to register 1. We therefore say that F, the translation of $\langle factor \rangle \rightarrow$ **id** is 'LOAD' NAME(id_i), where the subscript i indicates a particular identifier. The quotes around LOAD indicate that it is to be taken literally. The absence of quotes around NAME(id_i) indicate that the value of the function is meant. This is a general

---

[†] It would be convenient to reset the integer to 1 after each statement so as not to use too many different temporaries.

rule—quotes indicate strings to be taken literally; unquoted objects are to have their value substituted where they appear.

2. $\langle factor \rangle \rightarrow (\langle exp \rangle)$. The parentheses do not affect the value of the $\langle exp \rangle$, so code to compute the value of the $\langle exp \rangle$ will also compute the value of the $\langle factor \rangle$. Thus, the translation rule for this production is just $F = E$, meaning that the translation of the node labeled $\langle factor \rangle$ is equal to the translation of its child labeled $\langle exp \rangle$.[†]

3. and 4. Similarly, the productions $\langle term \rangle \rightarrow \langle factor \rangle$ and $\langle exp \rangle \rightarrow \langle term \rangle$ have translation rules $T = F$ and $E = T$, respectively, meaning that the translation of the variable on the right (parent in the tree) is the same as the translation of the variable on the left (the child).

5. $\langle exp \rangle \rightarrow \langle exp \rangle + \langle term \rangle$. Here we have an $\langle exp \rangle$ which is the sum of a smaller $\langle exp \rangle$ and a $\langle term \rangle$. The latter two variables correspond to nodes which are children of the node for the complete expression, i.e., we see the situation of Fig. 9.9.

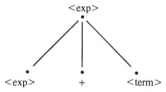

Fig. 9.9   Part of a parse tree.

Since translations are computed bottom up, we may suppose that translations of the children exist. These translations compute the value of the smaller $\langle exp \rangle$ and the $\langle term \rangle$ in register 1. One way to compute the value of the complete $\langle exp \rangle$ is to:

i) compute the value of the $\langle term \rangle$,

ii) store it in a temporary storage location,

iii) compute the value of the smaller $\langle exp \rangle$, and

iv) add the value in the temporary storage location (the value of the $\langle term \rangle$) to register 1.

In this way, we have correctly stated a formula for computing the value of an $\langle exp \rangle$ which is the sum of an $\langle exp \rangle$ and a $\langle term \rangle$. We shall state the translation rule

---

[†] Often, before translating, the parse tree is collapsed somewhat, into a tree called a *syntax tree*. The syntax tree is formed from the parse tree by combining a node N with one of its children, if the translations of N are identical to the translations of that child. Thus, in the grammar under discussion, a node labeled $\langle factor \rangle$ having children labeled $(\langle exp \rangle)$ could be combined with the child labeled $\langle exp \rangle$, and the nodes labeled with parentheses could be deleted. Then, we would not have to bother computing translations for a node such as N. This simplification will also apply to the pairs of nodes reflecting reductions by $\langle exp \rangle \rightarrow \langle term \rangle$ or $\langle term \rangle \rightarrow \langle factor \rangle$, as we shall see.

for the production $\langle exp \rangle \rightarrow \langle exp \rangle + \langle term \rangle$ by means of a little program (*semantic routine*):

$$
\begin{aligned}
&X = NEWTEMP(\ ) \\
&E = T \ ';STORE' \ X \ ';' \ E \ ';ADD' \ X^{\dagger}
\end{aligned}
\qquad (9.1)
$$

In words, the first statement says to make X be a new temporary name. The second statement says that the translation of an $\langle exp \rangle$ formed by the production $\langle exp \rangle \rightarrow \langle exp \rangle + \langle term \rangle$ begins by taking the translation of the $\langle term \rangle$ (code to compute the term) and following it by: an instruction to store register 1 in the location named by X, code to compute the smaller $\langle exp \rangle$, and an instruction to add the two values. Thus E and T on the right side of the $=$ sign in translation rules are symbols for the translations at the children of the node whose translation is being computed. The E on the left of the $=$ sign is the symbol for the translation at the node itself.

The intention is that when we wish to compute the translation of a node labeled $\langle exp \rangle$ whose children are labeled with $\langle exp \rangle$, $+$, and $\langle term \rangle$, we will execute the program (9.1). To evaluate the right side of the second assignment, we must substitute for the symbols E and T the strings for which they stand, namely the translations of the children having those labels. Having made the substitution, we concatenate the various strings and obtain a sequence of assembly instructions separated by semicolons.

6. $\langle term \rangle \rightarrow \langle term \rangle * \langle factor \rangle$. We handle this production exactly like the one above. Its semantic routine is:

$$
\begin{aligned}
&X = NEWTEMP(\ ) \\
&T = F \ ';STORE' \ X \ ';' \ T \ ';MULT' \ X
\end{aligned}
$$

7. $\langle asgn \ stat \rangle \rightarrow id_i = \langle exp \rangle$. The translation of the assignment statement should logically be code to compute the expression and store it in the location for id_i. This can be expressed by the one statement program:

$$
A = E \ ';STORE' \ NAME \ (id_i)
$$

For example, let us compute the translations of the nodes of the parse tree of Fig. 9.10.‡

Let NAME(id_i) be, respectively, ABC, XYZ, R, and Q for $i = 1, 2, 3, 4$. We shall compute the translations of the nonleaf nodes in the order $n_1, n_2, \ldots, n_{12}$, which is the order in which a weak-precedence parser would construct them.

By translation rule (1), the translation of n_1 is 'LOAD' NAME(id_2), which is LOAD ABC. By rule (3), the translation of n_2 is the same.

By rule (1), the translation of n_3 is LOAD R, and by rules (3) and (4), the translations of n_4 and n_5 are the same.

Similarly, the translations of n_6 and n_7 are each LOAD Q.

---

† We use semicolons to separate assembly statements.

‡ The reader should be reminded that in practice, there are usually more efficient ways to compute translations than a node-by-node evaluation.

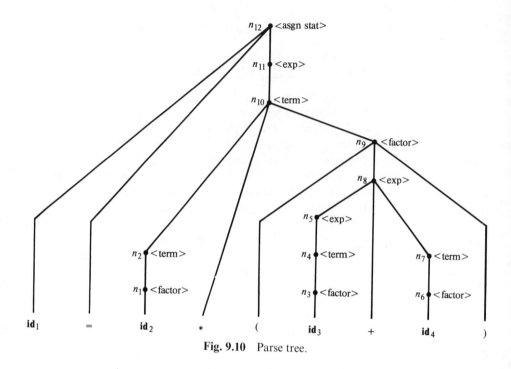

Fig. 9.10   Parse tree.

By rule (5) the translation of n_8 is computed by first setting X to be a new temporary location, which we may assume to be TEMP1. Then we compute the translation at n_8 to be the translation of n_7 followed by ;STORE TEMP1; followed by the translation of n_5 and ;ADD TEMP1. Substituting for the translations of n_5 and n_7, we find the translation of n_8 to be LOAD Q; STORE TEMP1; LOAD R; ADD TEMP1, or displayed as a normal assembly program, without the semicolons:

```
LOAD    Q
STORE   TEMP1
LOAD    R
ADD     TEMP1
```

We can verify that this program does in fact compute the value of the expression $R + Q$, which "dangles from" n_8. However, it does so in a sloppy way. There is no sense in moving the value of Q to TEMP1.

```
LOAD    R
ADD     Q
```

would have done just as well. Some instances of poor code can be "ironed out" in a code-optimization phase, or one can use a more complicated syntax-directed translation scheme to avoid generating them in the first place.

Proceeding up the tree, n_9 has the same translation as n_8 by rule (2). Then, by rule (6) we compute the translation of n_{10}. First, we set X to a new temporary, say TEMP2. Then we compute the translation of n_{10} to be the translation of n_9 followed by ;STORE TEMP2; followed by the translation of n_2 and ;MULT TEMP2. Making the substitution, we find the translation of n_{10} to be (with semicolons removed):

```
LOAD    Q
STORE   TEMP1
LOAD    R
ADD     TEMP1
STORE   TEMP2
LOAD    XYZ
MULT    TEMP2
```

By rule (4), the above is also the translation of n_{11}. We compute the translation of n_{12} by taking the translation of n_{11} and following it by STORE ABC. The translation of n_{12}, and hence of the entire statement is (with semicolons removed):

```
LOAD    Q
STORE   TEMP1
LOAD    R
ADD     TEMP1
STORE   TEMP2
LOAD    XYZ
MULT    TEMP2
STORE   ABC
```

It can be verified that the above code is equivalent to the assignment statement ABC = XYZ $*$ (R + Q), although it is not efficient code. ∎

Example 9.14.   Let us take the same grammar as above and use it to generate three-address code. The three-address statements $+(A, B, C)$ and $*(A, B, C)$ will have their obvious meanings. In practice, the parentheses and commas would not be generated, leaving only "quadruples" consisting of an operator symbol and three variable names. The generated quadruples could be stored in an array of records with four fields each or in four arrays, as discussed in Section 3.1.

Three-address code does not determine a place (register or memory location) where the value of an ⟨exp⟩, ⟨term⟩, or ⟨factor⟩ is to be computed. Thus, each ⟨exp⟩, etc., must be computed "in" a temporary name, which will be attached to the appropriate node as a translation (E_2, T_2, or F_2 in what follows). A second translation (E_1, T_1, or F_1) will be the sequence of three-address instructions which actually compute the value in that temporary. We shall thus have two translations of ⟨exp⟩, which we call E_1 and E_2, two translations of ⟨term⟩, T_1 and T_2, and two of ⟨factor⟩, F_1 and F_2; ⟨asgn stat⟩ has a single translation A, which forms the complete translation of a sentence when defined at the root of its parse tree. The following rules are used to compute the various translations.

1. $\langle\text{factor}\rangle \rightarrow \textbf{id}_i$. The appropriate name to hold the value of the $\langle\text{factor}\rangle$ is the name of the identifier. Thus, we have the rule

$$F_2 = \text{NAME}(\textbf{id}_i)$$

No code at all is needed to compute the value of the expression $\text{NAME}(\textbf{id}_i)$, since that value is presumably available in a location reserved for the ith identifier. Thus, we have the rule:

$$F_1 = \textbf{null}^{\,\dagger}$$

2., 3., and 4. The rules for the productions $\langle\text{factor}\rangle \rightarrow (\langle\text{exp}\rangle)$, $\langle\text{term}\rangle \rightarrow \langle\text{factor}\rangle$, and $\langle\text{exp}\rangle \rightarrow \langle\text{term}\rangle$ are, respectively:

$$F_1 = E_1 ; F_2 = E_2$$
$$T_1 = F_1 ; T_2 = F_2$$
$$E_1 = T_1 ; E_2 = T_2$$

That is to say, when these productions are used at a node, translations propagate upward, unchanged.

5. $\langle\text{exp}\rangle \rightarrow \langle\text{exp}\rangle + \langle\text{term}\rangle$. To compute the $\langle\text{exp}\rangle$ on the left, we must compute the $\langle\text{exp}\rangle$ and $\langle\text{term}\rangle$ on the right and then add the results. The translations E_2 and T_2 on the right (i.e., at the children) give the names for the results. If X is a new name, used for the value of the $\langle\text{exp}\rangle$ on the left, then code to compute the desired value is E_1 (the first translation of the $\langle\text{exp}\rangle$ on the right) followed by T_1 followed by the statement $+(E_2, T_2, X)$. The semantic routine to compute the translations of the $\langle\text{exp}\rangle$ on the left is:

```
X   = NEWTEMP()
E_2 = X
E_1 = E_1 T_1 '+(' E_2 ',' T_2 ',' X ')'
```

6. $\langle\text{term}\rangle \rightarrow \langle\text{term}\rangle * \langle\text{factor}\rangle$. In analogy with (5), the semantic routine for this production can be expressed:

```
X   = NEWTEMP()
T_2 = X
T_1 = T_1 F_1 '*(' T_2 ',' F_2 ',' X ')'
```

7. $\langle\text{asgn stat}\rangle \rightarrow \textbf{id}_i = \langle\text{exp}\rangle$. The translation of the assignment statement should be code which computes the expression and then assigns that value to the name represented by $\textbf{id}_i$. Thus the rule for this production is:

```
A = E_1 ' as (' NAME( id_i ) ',' E_2 ')'
```

Consider the parse tree of the previous example (Fig. 9.10), with $\textbf{id}_1, \ldots, \textbf{id}_4$ standing for ABC, XYZ, R, and Q again.

The translations at the various nodes are shown in Fig. 9.11.

---

† Let us use **null** to indicate the empty string, that is, the string that is zero characters long.

Node	Rule	$E_2, T_2,$ or F_2	E_1, T_1, F_1 or A
n_1	(1)	XYZ	**null**
n_2	(3)	XYZ	**null**
n_3	(1)	R	**null**
n_4	(3)	R	**null**
n_5	(4)	R	**null**
n_6	(1)	Q	**null**
n_7	(3)	Q	**null**
n_8	(5)	TEMP1	+(R, Q, TEMP1)
n_9	(2)	TEMP1	+(R, Q, TEMP1)
n_{10}	(6)	TEMP2	+(R, Q, TEMP1) * (XYZ, TEMP1, TEMP2)
n_{11}	(4)	TEMP2	+(R, Q, TEMP1) * (XYZ, TEMP1, TEMP2)
n_{12}	(7)	—	+(R, Q, TEMP1) * (XYZ, TEMP1, TEMP2)**as**(ABC, TEMP2)

Fig. 9.11 Translations.

Thus, the three-address code for the aforementioned tree is translation A at node n:

$$+(R, Q, TEMP1)$$
$$* (XYZ, TEMP1, TEMP2)$$
$$\textbf{as}(ABC, TEMP2)$$ ∎

Example 9.15.   Now let us write part of the translation to assembly code for the gotoless programs defined partially by the following productions.

⟨statement⟩ → **if** ⟨exp⟩ **then** ⟨statement⟩ **else** ⟨statement⟩ |
           while ⟨exp⟩ **do** ⟨statement⟩ |
           begin ⟨statement list⟩ **end**
⟨statement list⟩ → ⟨statement list⟩ ; ⟨statement⟩ |
           ⟨statement⟩

Presumably, there are productions defining ⟨exp⟩, but we shall not list these. We only assume that there is a translation E of ⟨exp⟩ which is code to evaluate the (presumably Boolean-valued) expression in register 1.[†] There are also additional productions for ⟨statement⟩ which define assignment, declaration and input/output statements.

The selection of translating rules we have made here is not generally considered best, but it is perhaps the easiest method to explain. We assume that ⟨statement⟩ has two translations S_1 and S_2. We let S_2 be the name assumed for the assembly instruction to be executed after the ⟨statement⟩ to which it is attached. S_1 is code to execute the ⟨statement⟩.[‡] Two translations L_1 and L_2 play the identical role for

---

[†] Let 1 denote the Boolean value **true** and 0 denote **false** in what follows.
[‡] If the ⟨statement⟩ is a declaration, then S_1 will be the empty string. A declaration statement should have another translation which is composed of instructions to the bookkeeping mechanism. Such a translation must be immediately executed by the compiler when we construct the node ⟨statement⟩ representing the declaration.

⟨statement list⟩. It is assumed that for the unseen productions for ⟨exp⟩ and ⟨statement⟩, rules to compute E, S_1, and S_2 have been correctly specified.

When we try to handle the matter of the "name of the assembly statement to be executed next," we find that we may be using two different names for the same assembly statement. For example, in the production ⟨statement⟩ → **if** ⟨exp⟩ **then** ⟨statement⟩ **else** ⟨statement⟩, the two ⟨statement⟩'s on the right each have a translation S_2 telling the name of the assembly statement to be executed next. But obviously control goes to the same place after either of these ⟨statement⟩'s, so both these names must be forced to be the same.

One solution is to introduce a new pseudo-operation into our assembly language (one which is typically present in assembly languages, anyway) which causes two symbolic names to refer to the same memory location. We will use

$$\text{EQUAL } \alpha, \beta$$

to mean that symbolic name α is to refer to the location named β.

Such a pseudo-operation is not hard to implement in pass 1 of the assembler. Upon encountering such an instruction, entries for α and β in the symbol table are created if they are not already present, and in the data for α is placed a pointer to the symbol table entry for β and a notation that the location for α can be found by examining the entry for β. Note that β in turn may be set equal to some other name, but that if the assembly program is legal, we can follow a sequence of pointers until we eventually reach a name that has a location of its own. Also, note that if the location of α is defined by an EQUAL pseudo-operation, then it may not also name an instruction, just as it is illegal for α to name two instructions.

We shall now give some of the productions and translation rules that translate gotoless programs into our assembly language.

1. ⟨statement list⟩ → ⟨statement⟩. Obviously the assembly code for the ⟨statement list⟩ is the same as the code for the ⟨statement⟩ and the names of the next executable statements are likewise the same. Thus, we have rules

$$L_1 = S_1$$
$$L_2 = S_2$$

2. ⟨statement list⟩ → ⟨statement list⟩; ⟨statement⟩. Now, the code to execute the ⟨statement list⟩ on the left is formed by concatenating the code for the ⟨statement list⟩ on the right and the code for the ⟨statement⟩. We observe that in this situation, the code for ⟨statement⟩ is the code which is executed immediately after the code for ⟨statement list⟩ on the right. Thus, the name L_2, which that ⟨statement list⟩ expects will be given to the next assembly statement to be executed, must be prefixed to the code for ⟨statement⟩ and followed by a colon. Thus, the rule for L_1 on the left is:

$$L_1 = L_1 \; ';' \; L_2 \; ':' \; S_1$$

For a name of the next instruction to be executed, we logically take the name that the ⟨statement⟩ expects. Thus, the rule for L_2 is:

$$L_2 = S_2$$

3. $\langle\text{statement}\rangle \rightarrow$ **begin** $\langle\text{statement list}\rangle$ **end**. Translations simply propagate up the tree. Thus, we have the rules:

$$S_1 = L_1$$
$$S_2 = L_2$$

4. $\langle\text{statement}\rangle \rightarrow$ **while** $\langle\text{exp}\rangle$ **do** $\langle\text{statement}\rangle$.

To begin explaining the translation rules for this production, we observe that code to execute it must first consist of code to evaluate the $\langle\text{exp}\rangle$, which we assume leaves a Boolean value, in register 1. If the value is 1 (i.e., the $\langle\text{exp}\rangle$ has value **true**), then we execute code for the $\langle\text{statement}\rangle$. If the value is 0 (**false**) we transfer to the first instruction following the code for this **while . . . do** statement.[†] Thus, we need a new name to give the code following, and the rule for S_2 must be:

$$X = \text{NEWTEMP}()$$
$$S_2 = X$$

After the code for the $\langle\text{statement}\rangle$ on the right is executed, we must return to the code which evaluates the $\langle\text{exp}\rangle$. Thus, the code for the $\langle\text{exp}\rangle$ must be given the name which is the translation S_2 of the $\langle\text{statement}\rangle$ on the right. The completion of the rule for this production is:

$$S_1 = S_2 \text{ ':' } E \text{ ';JZERO' } X \text{ ';' } S_1 \text{ ';JUMP' } S_2$$

Recall that S_2 on the right side of the line above refers to the second translation of the statement following **do**, not to X. That is, code for the **while . . . do** statement is:

i) code to evaluate the expression, the first instruction of which is given the name which the $\langle\text{statement}\rangle$ on the right expects will follow its own code;

ii) an instruction JZERO, causing a jump to the statement presumed to follow **while . . . do** if the value of the expression is **false**;

iii) code for the $\langle\text{statement}\rangle$; and

iv) a transfer to the code for the expression.

It should be pointed out that if the $\langle\text{statement}\rangle$ on the right is, say, a simple assignment statement, then the last transfer is needed, as there will be no transfer to S_2 "built into" the code S_1. If, however, the $\langle\text{statement}\rangle$ on the right is another **while . . . do** statement, then there will be such a transfer (JZERO X in the above rule), and the additional transfer is superfluous. Since these translation rules do not allow us to tell which case pertains, we must put in the JUMP instruction "just in case."

It is possible to delete unnecessary JUMP instructions in the code optimization phase, since it will be apparent that such an instruction could never be executed. Alternatively, we could create an additional translation of $\langle\text{statement}\rangle$ having a Boolean value and indicating whether or not the final JUMP instruction should be there.

[†] A more efficient approach would be to have the code for $\langle\text{exp}\rangle$ itself make the jump to this statement, but to do so would introduce more complications into this example.

5. ⟨statement⟩ → **if** ⟨exp⟩ **then** ⟨statement⟩ **else** ⟨statement⟩. Code for this statement must evaluate the expression and execute the appropriate ⟨statement⟩ on the left. Whichever statement must be executed, the instruction to be executed next is the same. Thus, the S_2 translations of the two ⟨statement⟩'s on the right must be set equal, and the translation S_2 of the ⟨statement⟩ on the left will be the same as these two. We shall use superscript (1) to indicate translations of ⟨statement⟩ following **then** and superscript (2) to indicate the ⟨statement⟩ following **else**. Thus, the following semantic routine can be used to define the desired translations.

$$X = \text{NEWTEMP}()$$
$$S_2 = S_2^{(2)}$$
$$S_1 = \text{'EQUAL'}\ S_2^{(1)}\ \text{','}\ S_2^{(2)}\ \text{';'}\ E$$
$$\quad\text{';JZERO'}\ X\ \text{';'}\ S_1^{(1)}$$
$$\quad\text{';JUMP'}\ S_2^{(2)}\ \text{';'}$$
$$\quad X\ \text{':'}\ S_1^{(2)\dagger}$$

The constituents of the code S_1 for the ⟨statement⟩ are:

i) an instruction to equate $S_2^{(1)}$ and $S_2^{(2)}$, the two names for the instruction which should be executed after the **if** ... **then** ... **else** statement whose code we are generating;

ii) code to evaluate the expression and skip to $S_1^{(2)}$, the code for the **else** portion, if the expression has value **false**,

iii) code to execute the **then** portion, that is, $S_1^{(1)}$ and then transfer to the instruction to be executed after this **if** ... **then** ... **else** statement, and

iv) code to execute the **else** portion, $S_1^{(2)}$.

Consider the program of Fig. 9.12, whose parse tree is shown in Fig. 9.13.

> **begin**
> **while** $\mathscr{E}_1$ **do**
>   **if** $\mathscr{E}_2$ **then** $\mathscr{S}_1$
>   **else**
>   **while** $\mathscr{E}_3$ **do** $\mathscr{S}_2$;
> $\mathscr{S}_3$
> **end**

Fig. 9.12 Sample Program.

---

† Note that $S_1^{(2)}$ may already have a name for its first assembly instruction, for example, if the ⟨statement⟩ following **else** were a **while** ... **do** statement. Thus, certain assembly statements may have more than one name. Handling of this situation should not present any great difficulties for the writer of the assembler. Alternatively, we could indulge in the subterfuge of replacing X ':' $S_1^{(2)}$ by X ':BLOCK 0;' $S_1^{(2)}$. This would set up a dummy statement BLOCK 0 having name X, but generating zero words. Thus, the location for X would be the same as the location for the first instruction of $S_1^{(2)}$.

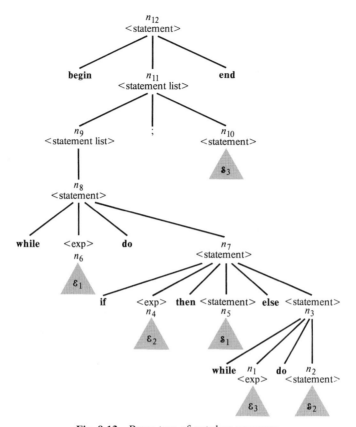

Fig. 9.13   Parse tree of gotoless program.

Let us refer to the translation E of an $\langle\text{exp}\rangle$ as "code for $\mathscr{E}_i$." Likewise, S_1 at nodes n_5, n_2, and n_{10} will be "code for $\mathscr{S}_1$," etc., and S_2 at these nodes will be TEMP1, TEMP2, and TEMP3, respectively. This symbology reflects the idea that translations at these nodes are computed by a mechanism involving productions which we have chosen, for simplicity, not to discuss at this point.

We begin by computing translations at n_3. By rule (4) we have (with semicolons removed):

$$S_2 = \text{TEMP4}$$
$$S_1 = \text{TEMP2: code for } \mathscr{E}_3$$
$$\qquad\qquad \text{JZERO TEMP4}$$
$$\qquad\qquad \text{code for } \mathscr{S}_2$$
$$\qquad\qquad \text{JUMP TEMP2}$$

We presume that TEMP4 is the next name generated by NEWTEMP( ) and that subsequent calls to NEWTEMP( ) produce TEMP5, TEMP6, ...

Next, we use rule (5) to create code for n_7:

$$S_2 = \text{TEMP5}$$
$$S_1 = \text{EQUAL TEMP1, TEMP4}$$

    code for $\mathscr{E}_2$
    JZERO TEMP5
    code for $\mathscr{S}_1$
    JUMP TEMP4
TEMP5: TEMP2: code for $\mathscr{E}_3$
    JZERO TEMP4
    code for $\mathscr{S}_2$
    JUMP TEMP2

By rule (4) again, the translations of node n_8 are $S_2 = \text{TEMP6}$ and S_1 is formed by prefixing:

TEMP4: code for $\mathscr{E}_1$
    JZERO TEMP6

to the code for S_2 at n_7 and following it by:

JUMP TEMP4

The translations at n_9 are the same as at n_8, but they are called L_1 and L_2 instead of S_1 and S_2. At n_{11} we compute by rule (2):

$$L_2 = \text{TEMP3}$$
$$L_1 = \text{TEMP4: code for } \mathscr{E}_1$$
        JZERO TEMP6
        EQUAL TEMP1, TEMP4
        code for $\mathscr{E}_2$
        JZERO TEMP5
        code for $\mathscr{S}_1$
        JUMP TEMP4
TEMP5: TEMP2: code for $\mathscr{E}_3$
        JZERO TEMP4
        code for $\mathscr{S}_2$
        JUMP TEMP2
        JUMP TEMP4
TEMP6: code for $\mathscr{S}_3$

By rule (3), these translations apply to n_{12}, the root, as well. To be strictly correct, we should take into account the possibility that there are transfers to TEMP3 within the code for $\mathscr{S}_3$, although none are shown explicitly. One way to do this is to recognize that a ⟨program⟩ is different from a ⟨statement⟩ in that the former has to have an end to its computation, such as a HALT instruction (or better, a call to the operating system that would allow the system to begin work on another program without halting).

We could, for example, have an additional production $\langle program \rangle \rightarrow \langle statement \rangle$, with one translation P and rule:

$$P = S_1 \ \text{';'} \ S_2 \ \text{':HALT'}$$

$\langle program \rangle$ then becomes the distinguished variable, and the translation of the example program would be S_1 above, followed by TEMP3: HALT. ∎

9.10   A SIMPLE IMPLEMENTATION FOR SOME SYNTAX-DIRECTED TRANSLATION SCHEMES

In the previous section, we described translation schemes in which strings were defined at all the interior nodes of a parse tree. In practice, these translations are not physically constructed by the compiler, and to do so would use more time than we are willing to spend. In this section we shall describe a simple way to implement certain specific translation schemes. In the next section, a general implementation method will be described.

We may begin by observing that in the three previous examples there was one translation at each node which was three-address or assembly code. This translation is a string whose length increases as we go up the parse tree. The computation of this translation would be time consuming if we computed it by copying as we went up the tree.

On the other hand, the other translations, such as the temporary name used in Example 9.14 and the name for the next assembly instruction used in Example 9.15 do not grow in size as we go up the parse tree.[†] Let us call the one translation, if there is only one, whose length increases significantly as we go up the tree the *main* translation, and the others *auxiliary* translations.

In many cases, it is possible to construct the main translation at the root by adding characters to the right end of a string every time a reduction is called for by the parser. The values of the main translation at the various nodes of the parse tree need not be computed separately, and, in fact, the parse tree itself can often be dispensed with. That is, when we use a parser, such as a weak-precedence parser, which works by tracing through a rightmost derivation in reverse, each variable placed on the stack corresponds to some node of the parse tree (the one which was created when a reduction caused that variable to be placed on the stack). The records of the stack can hold the values of the auxiliary translations.

Example 9.1.   Let us consider the translation into three-address code of Example 9.14. Since the stack may be implemented as a table, no pointers between records are needed. There is one auxiliary translation, denoted E_2, T_2, or F_2, which is the location where the main translation E_1, T_1, or F_1, (a three-address program) leaves the result

---

[†] Strictly speaking, a translation of the form TEMPi does grow as more and more digits are required for i. However, this growth is obviously so slow we can ignore it.

of its computation. The value of E_2, T_2, or F_2 is either:

1. a source program variable, which we may represent by a pointer to the symbol table, or
2. a temporary name TEMPi, which we can represent by the integer i.

Fig. 9.14   Stack record.

Grammar symbol	Octal representation
=	00
(	01
)	02
+	03
*	04
id	05
⟨exp⟩	06
⟨term⟩	07
⟨factor⟩	10
⟨asgn stat⟩	11

Fig. 9.15   Code for grammar symbols.

Thus, we may use one word per stack record, divided into fields as shown in Fig. 9.14. The fields have the following interpretations:

A is a six bit code for the grammar symbol represented. The code in Fig. 9.15 could be used.

B is a bit which indicates whether the auxiliary translation is a source program name $(B = 0)$ or a temporary $(B = 1)$. B will only be examined if A is ⟨exp⟩, ⟨term⟩, or ⟨factor⟩.

If A is ⟨exp⟩, ⟨term⟩, or ⟨factor⟩, then C is a 12-bit pointer to the symbol table if $B = 0$ and C is the 12-bit binary representation for i if $B = 1$ and the auxiliary translation is TEMPi.

Note that no pointer to the parse tree is present in the record. As we shall see, there is no need for a parse tree in the implementation of the translation of Example 9.14   ∎

The conditions under which it is possible to produce the main translation of the root of the parse tree by generation of characters after each reduction are the following.

1. There must be a main translation (possibly with auxiliaries) at each node of the parse tree.

2. The main translation at the root must be the distinguished translation.

3. The formulas for the main translation at each node must consist of the main translation at each of its children, in left-to-right order, followed by some additional

symbols (which we call the *tail*). The tail is composed only of fixed characters and the auxiliary translations of the children. In many cases the tail will be the empty string.

4. The formulas for auxiliary translations may not involve the main translation.[†]

Example 9.17.   The translation of Example 9.14 meets the above requirements. The main translations are E_1, T_1, F_1, and A. The formula for E_1 associated with production $\langle exp \rangle \rightarrow \langle exp \rangle + \langle term \rangle$ is

$$E_1 \, T_1 \, `+(' \, E_2 \, `,' \, T_2 \, `,' \, X \, `)'$$

This formula begins with the main translations of the variables on the right side of the production, that is, E_1 and T_1. The tail is '$+(' \, E_2 \, `,' \, T_2 \, `,' \, X \, `)'$. This string is composed of fixed characters, the plus sign, commas, and parentheses, with auxiliary translations E_2 and T_2 and the symbol X, which is the name of a newly generated temporary. It may not be clear whether we should consider the value of X to be "fixed characters," but clearly, after generating the new temporary, it is no harder to list that name than to list characters such as $+$. It is convenient; therefore, to permit such symbols in the tail of a rule.   ∎

The method for producing the main translation when the translation scheme meets the above requirements is to parse bottom up. Each time a reduction by some production $A \rightarrow X_1 \ldots X_n$ is called for, append the tail of the rule for the main translation associated with $A \rightarrow X_1 \ldots X_n$ to what has already been generated.

Example 9.18.   Let us consider Example 9.14 again. The productions, their rules for auxiliary translations, and the tails of their rules for main translations are listed in Fig. 9.16.

Production	Auxiliary rules	Tail
$\langle factor \rangle \rightarrow \mathbf{id}_i$	$F_2 = NAME(\mathbf{id}_i)$	**null**
$\langle factor \rangle \rightarrow (\langle exp \rangle)$	$F_2 = E_2$	**null**
$\langle term \rangle \rightarrow \langle factor \rangle$	$T_2 = F_2$	**null**
$\langle exp \rangle \rightarrow \langle term \rangle$	$E_2 = T_2$	**null**
$\langle exp \rangle \rightarrow$	$X = NEWTEMP()$	'$+(' \, E_2 \, `,' \, T_2 \, `,' \, X \, `)'$
$\quad \langle exp \rangle + \langle term \rangle$	$E_2 = X$	
$\langle term \rangle \rightarrow$	$X = NEWTEMP()$	'$*(' \, T_2 \, `,' \, F_2 \, `,' \, X \, `)'$
$\quad \langle term \rangle * \langle factor \rangle$	$T_2 = X$	
$\langle asgn \, stat \rangle \rightarrow$	none	'$\mathbf{as}(' \, NAME(\mathbf{id}_i) \, `,' \, E_2 \, `)'$
$\quad \mathbf{id}_i = \langle exp \rangle$		

Fig. 9.16   Translation rules.

Let us imagine a weak-precedence parser processing the statement ABC = XYZ ∗ (R + Q) as in Example 9.14, where ABC, XYZ, R, and Q are represented by tokens $\mathbf{id}_1$ through $\mathbf{id}_4$. We shall denote a stack record containing the code for

---

[†] This virtually follows by definition. If an auxiliary translation had the main translation as part of itself, it would grow in length and not be "auxiliary" as we have defined the term.

	Stack	Remaining input	Output so far
1.	—	$id_1 = id_2 * (id_3 + id_4)_4$	—
2.	$[id_1]$	$= id_2 * (id_3 + id_4)$	—
3.	$[id_1] [=]$	$id_2 * (id_3 + id_4)$	—
4.	$[id_1] [=] [id_2]$	$* (id_3 + id_4)$	—
5.	$[id_1] [=] [\langle factor \rangle, XYZ]$	$* (id_3 + id_4)$	—
6.	$[id_1] [=] [\langle term \rangle, XYZ]$	$* (id_3 + id_4)$	—
7.	$[id_1] [=] [\langle term \rangle, XYZ] [*]$	$(id_3 + id_4)$	—
8.	$[id_1] [=] [\langle term \rangle, XYZ] [*] [(]$	$id_3 + id_4$	—
9.	$[id_1] [=] [\langle term \rangle, XYZ] [*] [(] [id_3]$	$+ id_4$	—
10.	$[id_1] [=] [\langle term \rangle, XYZ] [*] [(] [\langle factor \rangle, R]$	$+ id_4$	—
11.	$[id_1] [=] [\langle term \rangle, XYZ] [*] [(] [\langle term \rangle, R]$	$+ id_4$	—
12.	$[id_1] [=] [\langle term \rangle, XYZ] [*] [(] [\langle exp \rangle, R]$	$+ id_4$	—
13.	$[id_1] [=] [\langle term \rangle, XYZ] [*] [(] [\langle exp \rangle, R] [+]$	id_4	—
14.	$[id_1] [=] [\langle term \rangle, XYZ] [*] [(] [\langle exp \rangle, R] [+] [id_4]$	$)$	—
15.	$[id_1] [=] [\langle term \rangle, XYZ] [*] [(] [\langle exp \rangle, R] [+] [\langle factor \rangle, Q]$	$)$	—
16.	$[id_1] [=] [\langle term \rangle, XYZ] [*] [(] [\langle exp \rangle, R] [+] [\langle term \rangle, Q]$	$)$	$+(R, Q, TEMP1)$
17.	$[id_1] [=] [\langle term \rangle, XYZ] [*] [(] [\langle exp \rangle, TEMP1]$	$)$	$+(R, Q, TEMP1)$
18.	$[id_1] [=] [\langle term \rangle, XYZ] [*] [(] [\langle exp \rangle, TEMP1] [)]$	—	$+(R, Q, TEMP1)$
19.	$[id_1] [=] [\langle term \rangle, XYZ] [*] [\langle factor \rangle, TEMP1]$	—	$+(R, Q, TEMP1)$
20.	$[id_1] [=] [\langle term \rangle, TEMP2]$	—	$+(R, Q, TEMP1) * (XYZ, TEMP1, TEMP2)$
21.	$[id_1] [=] [] [\langle exp \rangle, TEMP2]$	—	$+(R, Q, TEMP1) * (XYZ, TEMP1, TEMP2)$
22.	$[\langle asgn\ stat \rangle]$	—	$+(R, Q, TEMP1) * (XYZ, TEMP1, TEMP2)las(ABC, TEMP2)$

Fig. 9.17 Sequence of configurations for parser-translator.

grammar symbol X and auxiliary translation Y by $[X, Y]$. If X is not $\langle \exp \rangle$, $\langle \text{term} \rangle$, or $\langle \text{factor} \rangle$ we indicate the record by $[X]$. The sequence of stack contents which the parser goes through is shown in Fig. 9.17. We also indicate the remaining input and the translation constructed so far.

For example, at the fifth line, **id** is reduced to $\langle \text{factor} \rangle$. The auxiliary translation F_2 gets value XYZ, and that name is placed on the stack along with $\langle \text{factor} \rangle$. The tail of the rule for the main translation of $\langle \text{factor} \rangle$ is the empty string, so no translation is printed at the moment. At the 17th line, $\langle \exp \rangle + \langle \text{term} \rangle$ is reduced to $\langle \exp \rangle$. The auxiliary translation for $\langle \exp \rangle$ is TEMP1. The tail is formed from the auxiliary translations (R and Q), associated with the stack records replaced, and the symbol X, which represents the temporary (TEMP1 in this case) created for the new stack record. This tail is appended to the generated code. ∎

9.11   IMPLEMENTATION OF GENERAL TRANSLATION SCHEMES

Of those realistic translation schemes which fail to meet the four conditions mentioned in the previous section, most violate condition (3). That is, we can identify a main translation and auxiliaries, but we cannot express the formula for the main translation at a node as the main translations at its children, in order, followed by a tail. Examples 9.13 and 9.15 are examples of such a situation. Thus, in Example 9.13 the rule for the lone (and hence main) translation of $\langle \exp \rangle$ associated with production $\langle \exp \rangle \rightarrow \langle \exp \rangle + \langle \text{term} \rangle$ is

$$E = T \text{ ';STORE'} X \text{ ';'} E \text{ ';ADD'} X$$

In the above rule, the main translations at each of the children appears exactly once, but they are in the wrong order, and other characters, namely ';STORE' X ';', intervene.

We may replace condition (3) of the previous section by: (3'). In the formula for the main translation at each node, the main translation at each child appears exactly once.

If we do, we are able to produce the desired translation by handling auxiliary translations as in the previous section. The main translation at the root of the parse tree is constructed by building an *output* tree whose leaves have labels which, when read from left to right, form the desired translation. The output tree can be built in lieu of the parse tree.

A scheme in which we build a tree whose yield is the desired output and then walk the tree to produce the output itself is often referred to as *two-pass compiling*. The scheme of the previous section, where output is produced directly and no tree is actually built, can be called *one-pass compiling*, of course, other phases such as code selection or optimization may add to the total number of passes, and we must take the terms "one pass" and "two pass" with a grain of salt.

Of the two schemes, the one-pass scheme is generally preferable. The two-pass scheme may require us to move pieces of the parse and output trees between main and secondary memory several times, if a large program is being compiled. Often, three-address code, rather than assembly code, is selected as the intermediate code specifically to avoid the two pass arrangement.

Let us now discuss the construction of an output tree. Suppose a parser reduces by some production $A \rightarrow X_1 \ldots X_m$ and the rule for the main translation associated with this production is $T = \alpha_1 S_1 \alpha_2 S_2 \ldots \alpha_n S_n \alpha_{n+1}$, where the α's are strings of "fixed characters" and the S's are symbols for the main translations of the variables among $X_1 \ldots X_m$. There will be a tree for each variable on the stack, and a pointer will link the stack records for the variables to the roots of corresponding trees. (This arrangement is similar to the construction of parse trees discussed in Chapter 8.)

When we reduce by $A \rightarrow X_1 \ldots X_m$, we create a new node whose children are the roots of the trees for the variables among $X_1 \ldots X_n$ in the order in which their translation symbols appear. Interspersed with these are newly created leaves labeled by the α's. After reducing $X_1 \ldots X_m$ to A, we place a pointer in the record for A to the newly created root.

Example 9.19. Let us use the above mechanism to produce a translation for XYZ = ABC * (R + Q) according to the translation scheme of Example 9.13. The sequence of steps taken by the parser is the same as that of Example 9.18. There will, however, be no auxiliary translations on the stack, as Example 9.13 uses only one translation for each variable. Instead, along with each ⟨exp⟩, ⟨term⟩, ⟨factor⟩, or ⟨asgn stat⟩ on the stack will be a pointer to the root of an associated output tree.

Referring to the steps of the parser in Example 9.18 we see that the first reduction occurs at step (5), where id_2 is reduced to ⟨factor⟩. The rule in Example 9.13 associated with the production ⟨factor⟩ → id_i is

$$F = \text{'LOAD' NAME}(id_i).$$

There are no translation symbols on the right side of the = sign, so we simply create a root associated with this ⟨factor⟩ and give it one child, a leaf labeled LOAD ABC [i.e., NAME(id_2)]. The configuration of the stack and output tree is shown in Fig. 9.18.[†]

At the next step, ⟨factor⟩ is reduced to ⟨term⟩. The associated rule is $T = F$. We therefore create a new root and give it one child namely the root of the tree in Fig. 9.18. The resulting configuration is shown in Fig. 9.19,[‡]

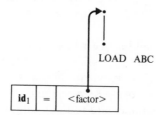

Fig. 9.18   Configuration after first reduction.

[†] It should be obvious that nodes with single children can be combined with the child. The tree of Fig. 9.18 could therefore be replaced by a single node labeled LOAD *ABC*.

[‡] As in Fig. 9.18 the three nodes of Fig. 9.19 can be combined into one.

Similar reductions occur at steps 10, 11, 12, 15, and 16. The configuration after step 16 is shown in Fig. 9.20.

At this point, $\langle exp \rangle + \langle term \rangle$ is reduced to $\langle exp \rangle$. The associated rule is

$$E = T ';STORE' X ';' E ';ADD' X$$

where X stands for a new temporary, say TEMP1. We create a new node with four children.

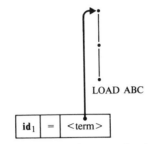

Fig. 9.19   Configuration after second reduction.

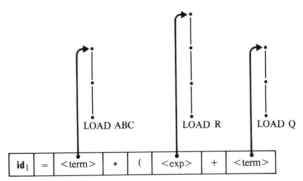

Fig. 9.20   Configuration after step 16.

In order from the left, the children are:

1. the node pointed to by the rightmost $\langle term \rangle$ in Fig. 9.20;
2. a newly created leaf labeled ;STORE TEMP1;
3. the node pointed to by the $\langle exp \rangle$ in Fig. 9.20; and
4. a newly created leaf labeled ;ADD TEMP1.

The configuration after the reduction is shown in Fig. 9.21. Note that LOAD Q appears to the left of LOAD R in Fig. 9.21 (and in the desired output), even though R appeared before Q in the source program XYZ = ABC $*$ (R + Q). It is inversions of this type that require us to use the two-pass scheme rather than the simpler scheme of the previous section.

The tree after the final reduction is shown in Fig. 9.22. ∎

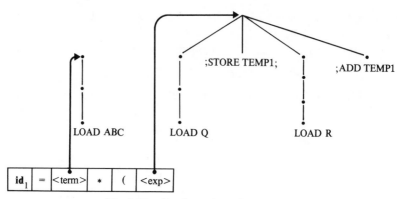

Fig. 9.21   Configuration after step 17.

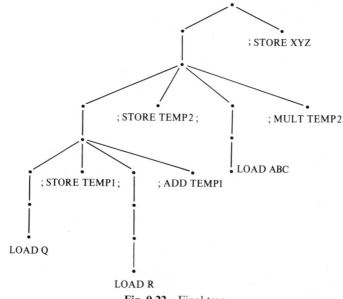

Fig. 9.22   Final tree.

In order to visit each leaf in order from the left, we may place in the record for each node three pointers, to the

1. leftmost child,
2. right sibling, and
3. parent.

We may then visit all the nodes of the tree and print the leaves from the left by executing the following procedure, beginning at the root of the tree.

1. Suppose we are at node N. Then:
   a) If N is a leaf, print the label of N. Then execute step (2) at N.
   b) If N is not a leaf, execute step (1) at the leftmost child of N.
2. Suppose we are at node N. If N has a right sibling, next execute step (1) there. If N has no right siblings, next execute step (2) at the parent of N, or halt if N is the root.

The above procedure is flowcharted in Fig. 9.23.

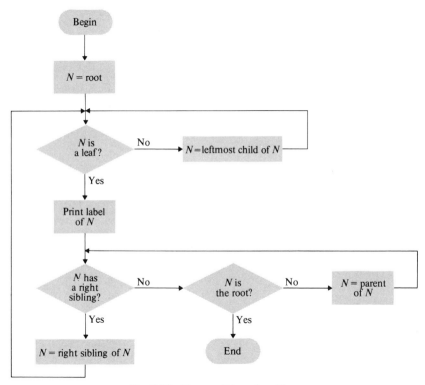

Fig. 9.23   Tree-walking algorithm.

Example 9.20.   In Fig. 9.24 we see the simplified version of Fig. 9.22, where nodes have been merged with their children, if they have exactly one child.

We begin by applying step (1) at n_1. Case (b) applies so we execute step (1) at n_2. Twice more, case (b) applies, as we are told to execute step (1) at n_3 and n_4. When we reach n_4, case (a) applies, so we print 'LOAD Q' and execute step (2) at n_4. We thus move to n_4's right sibling, n_5, and execute step (1a). We print ';STORE TEMP1;', move to the right sibling, n_6, print 'LOAD R', move again to the right sibling, n_7, and execute step (1a) there. We print ';ADD TEMP1' and, since n_7 has no right sibling, execute step (2) at n_3.

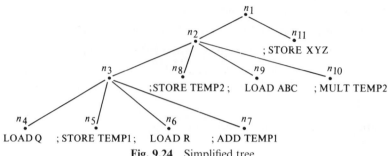

Fig. 9.24   Simplified tree.

Next, we repeatedly move to right siblings n_8, n_9, and n_{10}, printing their labels. When we execute step (2) at n_{10}, we move to n_2 and execute step (2) there. We thus move to n_{10}'s right sibling n_{11}, and execute step (1) there by printing 'STORE XYZ'. When we execute step (2) at n_{11} we move to n_1. Step (2) applied to n_1 causes a halt since n_1 is the root. Note that we have printed the label of each leaf in order from the left.

9.12   EXTENSIBLE LANGUAGES

Just as assembly languages can be extended by macros, some programming languages have the capability of defining within their programs new kinds of statements or new uses for old ones.

Extensibility creates a new problem for the compiler writer, and we shall discuss one partial solution to this problem subsequently. While the notation used to define language extensions varies greatly, two features are always present.

1. a way to use the new facility,[†] and
2. a meaning for the new facility (e.g., the macro body in the assembler case).

The kinds of language extensions permitted also varies, but we can identify two general types:

i) additional program structures, such as new types of statements or new operators, and

ii) new data types. (Often these are accompanied by the definition of new meanings for old operators on these data types.)

To define additional program structures, we must allow the programmer to add to the set of productions of the grammar defining the language. Then we must provide a translation rule for the new production. One way to do so is to give a program in the original language that "means the same" and translate the equivalent program every time the new structure is used.

[†] In the case of a macro this was quite simple—we had only to give the name of the macro and the proper number of arguments.

Example 9.21. Let us consider gotoless programs as in Example 9.15, with an additional statement type that is essentially a macro definition. The form of this statement will be

$$\langle \text{production} \rangle \textbf{ means } \langle \text{statement} \rangle$$

where ⟨production⟩ stands for any production with ⟨statement⟩ on the left of the arrow, involving terminal symbols and the variables[†] of the underlying grammar.

For example, suppose we wished to have a type of statement which allowed us to loop while an index counted by 1's from its current value to some specified value. We might write:

$$\langle \text{statement} \rangle \rightarrow \textbf{loop id}^{(1)}, \textbf{id}^{(2)} \textbf{ do } \langle \text{statement} \rangle$$
$$\textbf{means}^{\ddagger} \textbf{ while id}^{(1)} \leqslant \textbf{id}^{(2)} \textbf{ do}$$
$$\textbf{begin}$$
$$\langle \text{statement} \rangle;$$
$$\textbf{id}^{(1)} = \textbf{id}^{(1)} + 1$$
$$\textbf{end}$$

We have used superscripts to indicate the two instances of the token **id**. A means for such distinction needs to be part of every extension facility. ∎

Now let us consider the matter of how the compiler is to go about translating uses of the newly defined structure. We must assume first that the lexical analyzer, parser, and translator work in a *table-driven* way. That is, we assume the parser to have tables, such as the shift-reduce table of a weak-precedence parser, or a table listing all the productions of the grammar. The translator would have a table listing the translation rules for each production.

A table-driven compiler consists of routines which examine these tables to make the parsing and translating decisions. Thus, in a sense, the compiler works independently of the contents of the table. When the compiler encounters a statement that defines a new structure, it enters new productions into the parse table and possibly, new keywords (e.g., **loop** in Example 9.21) into a table for the lexical analyzer.

Unless the structure violates the conditions under which the parser may work (e.g., the additional production changes the grammar from weak precedence, if we are using a weak-precedence parser), the compiler will continue to parse its source program, essentially unaware that its tables have changed.

Obviously there are certain disadvantages to the table-driven approach (in a nonextensible language) over the writing of ad-hoc code for the particular grammar. Especially, it is possible to write faster code in an ad-hoc way. However, the advantages of table-driven compiling predominate, so that even for nonextensible languages, almost all compilers are table-driven to some extent. These advantages include ease

---

[†] We only showed two such variables—⟨statement list⟩ and ⟨statement⟩, but presumably there are others needed to define ⟨exp⟩, etc.

Note that we might have some problems if **means** could be part of the new production. Let us assume it cannot.

of writing and debugging and smaller space requirements. Example 9.12 (p. 270) shows the advantage of a "table-driven" lexical analyzer. Instead of passing a keyword to the subroutine mentioned in that example, we could give it a pointer to a record in a table where the desired keyword would be found.

Let us now continue the previous example to see one way in which an extension might be entered into parsing and translating tables.

Example 9.22. Suppose we are using a weak-precedence parser to parse gotoless programs with an extension feature. Suppose further that the particular program being compiled has the extension statement of Example 9.21. The "translation" of such a statement is an entry in the parsing and translation tables. The parse table receives some entries in the shift-reduce table as well as a new production, but what do we place in the translation table?

Reasoning in analogy with the macro, once we have detected the right side of the new production

$$\textbf{loop id}^{(1)}, \textbf{id}^{(2)} \textbf{ do } \langle \text{statement} \rangle$$

on the stack, we have an instance of the "macro use." We may replace this by the "macro body," which is

$$
\begin{aligned}
&\textbf{while id}^{(1)} \leqslant \textbf{id}^{(2)} \\
&\quad \textbf{begin} \\
&\qquad \langle \text{statement} \rangle; \\
&\qquad \textbf{id}^{(1)} = \textbf{id}^{(1)} + 1 \\
&\quad \textbf{end}
\end{aligned}
\tag{9.2}
$$

This sequence of grammar symbols must be partially parsed. (The tokens which were reduced to ⟨statement⟩ have already been parsed, and presumably the translation of ⟨statement⟩ is available.) To do this parsing, we should throw the "body," Expression (9.2) above, onto the input stream, after substituting the actual values for $\textbf{id}^{(1)}$ and $\textbf{id}^{(2)}$. This operation is analogous to an assembler placing a macro body onto its input.

Since a variable ⟨statement⟩ appears on the input, we must expand the shift-reduce table of a weak-precedence parser to include a column for ⟨statement⟩. Since the translation of ⟨statement⟩ has already been computed, we may treat it essentially as a terminal symbol.

Thus, if we find a statement such as

$$
\begin{aligned}
&\textbf{loop I, J do} \\
&\quad \textbf{begin} \\
&\qquad X(I) = I; \\
&\qquad Y(I) = I \\
&\quad \textbf{end}
\end{aligned}
$$

We shall shift it onto the stack token by token, reducing

$$\textbf{begin } X(I) = I; \quad Y(I) = I \textbf{ end}$$

to ⟨statement⟩ and producing the translation of ⟨statement⟩ as we go. When we get

$$\textbf{loop } I, J \textbf{ do } \langle statement \rangle$$

on top of the stack,[†] we remove it from the stack and place

$$\textbf{while } I \leqslant J \textbf{ do begin } \langle statement \rangle; I = I + 1 \textbf{ end}$$

on the input. This sequence of tokens will be shifted onto the stack and reduced ultimately to ⟨statement⟩. ∎

Another example of an extension, which we shall not consider in detail, is the definition of some new data types, for example, 3×3 matrices. In a given program we would define a new kind of declaration statement, say

$$\langle declaration \rangle \rightarrow \textbf{3 by 3 matrix } \langle identifier\ list \rangle$$

so that if we later encountered the statement

$$\textbf{3 by 3 matrix } A, B$$

we would give the appropriate attribute to A and B in the symbol table. (Thus, the symbol table also has to be "table driven" to an extent, since it must be able to store an arbitrary collection of attributes.

We could then appropriately define $+$ and $*$ for the case where their arguments are 3 by 3 matrices. Their meanings could be programs in the programming language or calls to subroutines that would perform the matrix addition or multiplication. In the portion of the program that followed the definition of the 3 by 3 matrix declaration and the definition of $+$ and $*$ for data of this type, variables could be declared to be 3 by 3 matrices and manipulated in statements that looked like ordinary arithmetic statements.

EXERCISES

9.1 Give three-address code equivalent to the following statements.[‡]

a) **for** I = 1 **to** 20 **do**
     A(I) = A(I − 1) + A(I − 2)

b) **for** I = 1 **to** 20 **do**
     for J = 1 **to** 20 **do**
       begin
         C(I, J) = 0. ;
         for K = 1 **to** 20 **do**
           C(I, J) = C(I, J) + A(I, K) * B(K, J)
       end

[†] Instances of token **id**, namely *I* and *J*, are shown as themselves, rather than as a subscripted **id**.
[‡] Make up your own three-address statements with arguments X, Y, and Z to assign the value of $X(Y)$ to Z. Recall the **asi**(X, Y, Z) instruction assigns the value of X to $Y(Z)$.

9.2 Convert your programs of Exercise 9.1 to assembly code using the simple conversion scheme of Example 9.5 (p. 260).

* **9.3** "Optimize" your answer to Exercise 9.2 by:

 a) eliminating redundant LOAD's and STORE's,

 b) making use of the fact that our computer has seven registers.

** **9.4** Improve your three-address programs of Exercise 9.1 by eliminating loop-invariant computations from loops and combining two or more computations of the same value whenever possible.

9.5 Write your best

 a) recursive

 b) nonrecursive

assembly language programs to compute N^2 by summing $1 + 3 + 5 + \ldots + (2N - 1)$. How do your programs compare in length and running time (as a function of N?)

9.6 Compute the translation of $\mathbf{id}_1 = (\mathbf{id}_2 + \mathbf{id}_3) * \mathbf{id}_2 + \mathbf{id}_1$ according to the translation schemes of

 a) Example 9.13 (p. 271)

 b) Example 9.14 (p. 275).

Assume $\mathbf{id}_1$, $\mathbf{id}_2$, and $\mathbf{id}_3$ are A, B, and C, respectively.

9.7 Show the output of the translation scheme of Example 9.15 when presented with the input:

> **begin**
> > **if** $\mathscr{E}_1$ **then**
> > > **while** $\mathscr{E}_2$ **do** $\mathscr{S}_1$
> >
> > **else**
> > > **begin**
> > > > $\mathscr{S}_2$;
> > > > $\mathscr{S}_3$;
> > >
> > > **end**;
> >
> > **while** $\mathscr{E}_3$ **do**
> > > **if** $\mathscr{E}_4$ **then** $\mathscr{S}_4$ **else** $\mathscr{S}_5$
> >
> **end**

Use "code for $\mathscr{E}_1$" etc. to represent the translations of the expressions and simple statements.

9.8 Example 9.14 (p. 275), which translated assignment statements into three-address code can be extended in various ways. Modify the translation scheme of that example to do the following.

 a) Accept binary $-$ and $/$ as operators.

* b) Generate fixed- or floating-point code depending on the mode of the operands. Assume there is a function MODE($\mathbf{id}_i$) which returns FIXED or FLOAT, depending on the mode of the ith identifier. MODE is a function which presumably looks up information in the symbol table. You need not generate code for mixed mode expressions. *Hint:* Introduce a new auxiliary translation for $\langle\text{exp}\rangle$, $\langle\text{term}\rangle$, and $\langle\text{factor}\rangle$ which indicates the mode of the expression represented by each variable. Also, use branching statements in your semantic routines.

c) Do the same as (b), but allow mode conversion by a "three-address" instruction $\mathbf{fl}(X)$ which changes the value of X from fixed to floating point.

** **9.9** Generate "optimal" assembly code by modifying the scheme of Example 9.13 (p. 271). The case where one or both arguments are single identifiers requires special treatment; that is, we must avoid loading and storing into a temporary location in situations such as the treatment of identifier Q in Example 9.13. Do not forget to take advantage of the commutativity of $+$ and $*$. That is, the code to be generated from Fig. 9.10 (p. 274) is

```
LOAD    R
ADD     Q
MULT    XYZ
STORE   ABC
```

*9.10 Which of the translations of Exercises 9.8 and 9.9 can be implemented by the one-pass method of Section 9.10, and which require the two-pass method of Section 9.11? In each case, describe an implementation, giving a format for stack records and describing the action to be taken by the translator for each reduction made by the parser.

9.11 The translation scheme of Fig. 9.25 computes the derivative of expressions involving $+$, $*$, variable X, and constant C; that is, E_2, T_2, and F_2 are the undifferentiated expressions and E_1, T_1, and F_1 are the differentiated expressions.

a) Use this scheme to find the derivative of $C * (X + C) * X$.

* b) Suggest an efficient implementation for the scheme.

** c) Are the parentheses around T_1 in the rules for the production $\langle\text{term}\rangle \rightarrow \langle\text{term}\rangle * \langle\text{factor}\rangle$ really necessary?

Production	Rules
$\langle\text{ex}\rangle \rightarrow \langle\text{exp}\rangle + \langle\text{term}\rangle$	$E_1 = E_1 \text{ '+' } T_1$
	$E_2 = E_2 \text{ '+' } T_2$
$\langle\text{exp}\rangle \rightarrow \langle\text{term}\rangle$	$E_1 = T_1$
	$E_2 = T_2$
$\langle\text{term}\rangle \rightarrow \langle\text{term}\rangle * \langle\text{factor}\rangle$	$T_1 = T_2 \text{ '*' } F_1 \text{ '+(' } T_1 \text{ ')*' } F_2$
	$T_2 = T_2 * F_2$
$\langle\text{term}\rangle \rightarrow \langle\text{factor}\rangle$	$T_1 = F_1$
	$T_2 = F_2$
$\langle\text{factor}\rangle \rightarrow (\langle\text{exp}\rangle)$	$F_1 = \text{ '(' } E_1 \text{ ')' }$
	$F_2 = \text{ '(' } E_2 \text{ ')' }$
$\langle\text{factor}\rangle \rightarrow X$	$F_1 = 1$
	$F_2 = X$
$\langle\text{factor}\rangle \rightarrow C$	$F_1 = 0$
	$F_2 = C$

Fig. 9.25 Syntax-directed translation scheme to take derivatives.

*9.12 Find a syntax-directed translation scheme to translate binary integers with no leading 0's into octal. *Hint:* Think carefully about the grammar you use to generate the binary integers.

*9.13 Use the extension facility of Example 9.21 (p. 293) to introduce the following kinds of statements

a) **if** . . . **then** . . . (no **else** clause) with the obvious meaning.

b) **repeat** . . . **until** . . . as in Section 0.4. Using these definitions, show how the translator would process:

$$\begin{aligned}&\textbf{repeat}\\&\quad \textbf{if } I > 0 \textbf{ then } I = I - 1\\&\textbf{until}\\&\quad I \text{ .EQ. } 0\end{aligned}$$

Programming Exercises

9.14 Implement the one-pass translation of Example 9.14 (p. 275).

9.15 Implement the two-pass translation of Example 9.13 (p. 271).

9.16 Build a "syntax-directed desk calculator" whose input is an expression involving whatever set of operators you wish to handle and operands which are all constants. The output should be the value of the expression, of course. Note that, while we have only considered syntax-directed translators whose translations were string valued, there is no reason to be so restrictive. Here, it is most useful to have translations with numerical values and translation rules involving arithmetic calculation.

9.17 The ambitious reader will probably want to build a compiler. To make the job as simple as possible, we suggest any or all of the following restrictions.

1. Use our gotoless language from Section 0.3 as the basic language. Use our assembly language as the object language (you may use another intermediate language).

2. Restrict simple statements to be either assignments or of the forms READ α or WRITE α. Do not permit declarations or subroutine calls.

3. Make all variables be single letters and be of integer type; make all constants be integers.

4. Permit arithmetic expressions to have only binary operators $+$, $-$, $*$ and $/$.

5. Permit FORTRAN logical expressions only of the form **id** $\langle$rel$\rangle$ **id**, where $\langle$rel$\rangle$ stands for any of the six FORTRAN relational operators, .EQ., etc.

6. Do not attempt to recover from errors. Simply print a message that an error has occurred.

7. Attempt no code optimization; generate the code that is most convenient.

FURTHER READING

Lewis, Rosenkrantz, and Stearns [1975], Gries [1971], and McKeeman, Horning, and Wortman [1970] cover the fundamentals of compiling more extensively than we have done here. Aho and Ullman [1972, 1973] gives a more mathematical treatment of the subject. The notion of syntax-directed translation is generally attributed to Irons [1961]. Lewis and Stearns [1968] and Knuth [1968] are worthwhile papers on the subject. For more on code optimization see Schaefer [1973] or Hecht [1975]. The notion of extensibility treated in Section 9.12 is from Leavenworth [1966].

Chapter 10

Proving Programs Correct

In this, the last chapter of the book, we shall take up the subject of proving that a program works as intended, or *program verification*. First we introduce the fundamental notion of an *assertion*, a statement about what we believe holds at a given point in a program. We show how assertions may be used to prove a program correct and give some hints on how to construct such proofs. We then discuss how the concept may be utilized by the programmer to write more reliable programs without actually getting involved in detailed mathematical proofs.

10.1 WHY STUDY PROGRAM VERIFICATION?

There is no doubt that the motivation for studying proofs of program correctness is less clear than for the other topics covered in this book. We can, however, make five separate arguments in favor of such study. First, it is, in principle at least, possible to design automatic or semiautomatic program verifiers. These are programs which aid the programmer in debugging his programs by helping to prove their correctness. The programmer makes assertions about his program, and the verifier attempts to prove their truth.

At the time of this writing, such verifiers do not have the capability of handling long programs, and there are often severe limits on the kinds of data structures that programs may use if the verifier is to be able to prove them correct. Nonetheless, it is hoped that further development will produce verifying systems that can be regarded as practical.

A second argument for studying program verification is the possibility that the concept may help the programmer write his programs with less debugging than usual. That is not to say that the programmer should write a complete proof of his program's correctness. Rather, as he writes his program, he should think a bit about how such a proof would go. If he is familiar with program verification techniques, yet cannot see even roughly how a proof could be formulated, then he might suspect that there was a mistake somewhere. Moreover, if his failure to see a proof can be traced to one area of his program, he has possibly localized the problem without even running the program.

The third argument is that assertions at key points in the program are an excellent form of documentation. Fourth, assertions can be checked while the program is running, forming a useful debugging tool. Several experimental compilers now have the facility for the programmer to make whatever assertions he likes about his program. Each assertion is compiled into code which tests its validity each time the point in the program to which the assertion applies is reached. Should the assertion prove false at some time, a warning is printed. We expect that such facilities will become widespread in the future.

Finally, the fifth argument is that there is really no other way to be sure a program works. Test runs on sample data are a help in checking out programs, but we can never be sure that some data on which the program was not tested will not expose a "bug." There are some programs such as antiballistic missile systems for which complete testing is simply not possible under any circumstances.

Before beginning to describe verification techniques, we should mention the need for a formal system in which to write proofs. Without such a formal system, usually "predicate calculus," we are subject to arguments over whether a given sequence of statements really is a proof or not. More important, automatic verifiers need precise statements in a precise notation, or we cannot hope for them to help find proofs.[†]

We shall not, however, define a notation such as predicate calculus here. Thus, our "proofs" will be informal ones only. Nevertheless, it is hoped the reader will be able to develop some appreciation for the techniques which we use for verification.

10.2 INDUCTIVE ASSERTIONS

The basic technique for proving programs correct, known as the *inductive-assertions* method, is to attach to each point in the program an *assertion*. The latter is a statement of what we believe true about the values of the various identifiers at that point. Presumably, one assertion is that the output, when computed, bears the intended relation to the input.

By methods we shall describe later, we shall attempt to prove that the truth of the assertion at each point follows from the truth of the assertions at all points previous to it in the program. Thus, all assertions will be proven true.[‡] For the time being, we shall content ourselves with an example.

Example 10.1. Figure 10.1 shows a flowchart of a program to compute $M = N!$ for $N \geqslant 0$. An assertion has been attached to the entrance of each block. We use n_0

[†] This situation is analogous to the situation in programming language design. Computers cannot be expected to compile programs written in an informal way. Every known programming language has syntactic and semantic rules which are very restrictive compared with those for English.

[‡] There is a small problem, in that the inductive assertions method does not tell us about infinite loops. Thus, if we prove a set of assertions, one of which is that the output is the desired function of the input, we have only shown the program either to be correct, or not to give any output at all. We shall fix this problem subsequently in Section 10.5.

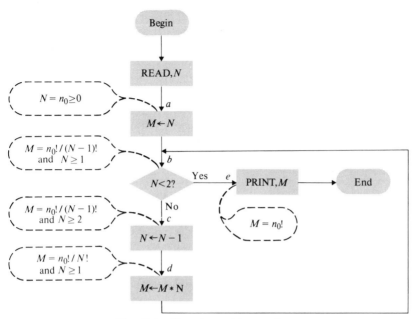

Fig. 10.1   Flowchart with assertions.

for the value of N when it is read and N for the current value of N. Also, we use $\leftarrow$ for the assignment symbol to avoid confusion with the equal sign, asserting that two quantities are equal.

We shall not yet attempt to prove all the assertions in Fig. 10.1. Let us suppose, however, that the assertion at point (c) holds. That is, $M = n_0!/(N - 1)!$[†] and $N \geqslant 2$ before executing the statement $N \leftarrow N - 1$. If $N \geqslant 2$ before subtracting one from N, surely $N \geqslant 1$ will hold afterwards. Thus, the second part of the assertion at (d) will hold.

The first part of the assertion at point (d) is $M = n_0!/N!$. Let us see if it follows from the assertion at (c). Suppose n is the value of N at point (c). Then M at that point has the value $n_0!/(n - 1)!$ After doing $N \leftarrow N - 1$, we see the value of N at point (d) is $n - 1$. The value of M at (d) has not changed, so it is still $n_0!/(n - 1)!$ Thus, $M = n_0!/N!$ holds at point (d), since $N = n - 1$ is true. ∎

10.3 PROVING ASSERTIONS

Let us now learn a few of the "tricks" that make proofs of certain assertions easy. First, suppose we have an assignment statement as shown in Fig. 10.2. Identifier X is assigned the value of expression $\mathscr{E}$, and assertions A_1 and A_2 are made before and after the assignment. The easiest way to prove that A_1 and the statement $X \leftarrow \mathscr{E}$ implies A_2 is to substitute $\mathscr{E}$ for X in A_2. If a statement that is A_1, or is implied by

---

[†] Note $n_0!/(N - 1)!$ is the product of the integers from n_0 through N, inclusive.

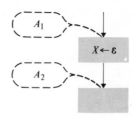

Fig. 10.2   Assignment statement with assertions.

A_1, results, then we know that A_2 follows from A_1 and the effects of the assignment $X \leftarrow \mathscr{E}$. A certain amount of algebraic manipulation may be necessary after substitution. When doing this manipulation, one should be careful to use only algebraic laws which hold generally. Especially, when dividing by some quantity Y, we should be sure that the assertion A_1 is sufficient to imply that $Y \neq 0$.

Example 10.2.   Let $X \leftarrow \mathscr{E}$ be $N \leftarrow N - 1$ in Fig. 10.1. Then assertion A_1 is:

$$M = n_0!/(N - 1)! \text{ and } N \geqslant 2 \tag{10.1}$$

and assertion A_2 is:

$$M = n_0!/N! \text{ and } N \geqslant 1 \tag{10.2}$$

If we substitute $N - 1$ for N in (10.2), we get:

$$M = n_0!/(N - 1)! \text{ and } N - 1 \geqslant 1 \tag{10.3}$$

When we use algebraic manipulation to change $N - 1 \geqslant 1$ into $N \geqslant 2$, Expression (10.3) becomes Expression (10.1) exactly. That is, A_2 with $N - 1$ in place of N has become A_1.

For a more complicated example, consider $M \leftarrow M * N$, also from Fig. 10.1. There, A_1 is:

$$M = n_0!/N! \text{ and } N \geqslant 1 \tag{10.4}$$

and A_2 is:

$$M = n_0!/(N - 1)! \text{ and } N \geqslant 1, \tag{10.5}$$

the assertion at point (*b*). We substitute $M * N$ for M in Expression (10.5) to obtain:

$$M * N = n_0!/(N - 1)! \text{ and } N \geqslant 1 \tag{10.6}$$

Surely, $N \geqslant 1$ in (10.6) is implied by $N \geqslant 1$ in A_1, i.e., Expression (10.4), so that part of A_2 is proven. We must now prove the first part of Expression (10.6), namely that $M * N = n_0!/(N - 1)!$, given Expression (10.4). Since Expression (10.4) asserts $M = n_0!/N!$, we may multiply both sides by N to get:

$$M * N = n_0! * N/N! \tag{10.7}$$

Since Expression (10.4) also asserts $N \geqslant 1$, we have that $N/N! = 1/(N - 1)!$. Thus Expression (10.4) implies Expression (10.7), which implies the first part of Expression

(10.6). We have now shown that A_1 plus the effect of assignment $M \leftarrow M * N$ does imply A_2. ∎

The next "trick" concerns branches. Figure 10.3 shows a branch which tests some condition $\mathscr{P}$. We may use both A_1 and the fact that $\mathscr{P}$ is true to prove A_2; we may use A_1 and the falsehood of $\mathscr{P}$ to show A_3.

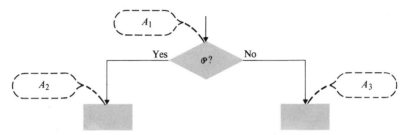

Fig. 10.3   Branching statement with assertions.

Example 10.3.   Referring again to Fig. 10.1 (p. 301), we may let $\mathscr{P}$ be $N < 2$, and let A_1 be the assertion:

$$M = n_0!/(N - 1)! \text{ and } N \geqslant 1 \tag{10.8}$$

at point (*b*). Then A_3 is:

$$M = n_0!/(N - 1)! \text{ and } N \geqslant 2$$

If $\mathscr{P}$ is false, then $N \geqslant 2$. The latter is just the second part of A_3. The first parts of A_1 and A_3 are the same, so A_3 follows from A_1 and the fact that $N < 2$ is false.

Next, A_2 is the assertion at point (*e*), namely:

$$M = n_0!$$

Let us show that $M = n_0!$ follows from Eq. (10.8), i.e., from A_1 and the truth of $N < 2$. Since part of Eq. (10.8) is $N \geqslant 1$, and N is of integer type[†], we may conclude that $N = 1$. Thus, $(N - 1)! = 0! = 1$, and $M = n_0!/(N - 1)! = n_0!$. We have thus proven $M = n_0!$ from Eq. (10.8) and $N < 2$. ∎

To make a complete proof that a program works correctly, we must select assertions for each point in the program. One of these assertions must state that the output bears the correct relation to the input. Then, for each pair of points x and y such that y can be reached from x after a single step, we must show that the assertion at x, together with the action at the step between x and y, implies the assertion at y.

When we have done the above, we have almost proven the program correct. What we have actually shown is that if the program makes an output, then it is the correct output. In order to have a complete proof, we also need to prove that the

---

[†] Technically, the types of variables should be part of the assertions if necessary. We have assumed that the knowledge of types was implicit here to simplify the assertions.

program *terminates*, i.e., does not loop indefinitely. Then, provided that the structure is such that it cannot halt without making an output, we shall have completed the proof of the program's correctness.[†]

The subject of proving termination will be taken up subsequently. Now, let us complete the example concerning Fig. 10.1 (p. 301).

Example 10.4.   In order to prove the correctness of the flowchart of Fig. 10.1 subject to the condition that it terminates (which in fact it does), we must show the claims about the assertions indicated in Fig. 10.4.

	The assertion at	With the action	Implies the assertion at
(1)	**begin**	READ, N	(a)
(2)	(a)	$M \leftarrow N$	(b)
(3)	(b)	$N < 2$ is false	(c)
(4)	(b)	$N < 2$ is true	(e)
(5)	(c)	$N \leftarrow N - 1$	(d)
(6)	(d)	$M \leftarrow M * N$	(b)

Fig. 10.4   Claims needed to prove the correctness of Fig. 10.1.

For (1), there is no assertion at the beginning, or rather, nothing is asserted before the program begins. The assertion at (a) is that $N = n_0$ and $n_0 \geq 0$. The condition $N = n_0$ is obvious, since by definition, n_0 is the value read. The condition $n_0 \geq 0$ is not implied by the read statement. Rather, its presence stems from the fact that we are only asserting that the program computes $n_0!$ when $n_0 \geq 0$.

Parts (5) and (6) were proven in Example 10.2, and (3) and (4) were shown in Example 10.3. This leaves only (2). We must show that $N = n_0$ together with $M \leftarrow N$ implies:

$$M = n_0!/(N - 1)! \text{ and } N \geq 1 \tag{10.9}$$

The first part of Expression (10.9) does follow, since when $N = n_0$ we have $n_0!/(N - 1)! = n_0$. As we assigned M the value n_0, we surely have $M = n_0!/(N - 1)!$

However, $N \geq 1$, the second part of Eq. (10.9), does not follow. For in fact, if $n_0 = 0$, we can have the assertion $N = n_0 \geq 0$ satisfied at point (a), yet still not satisfy Eq. (10.9) at point (b). If we reconsider Fig. 10.1 we see that there is a mistake. When 0 is read, the program prints 0 instead of 1. This flaw can be remedied in various ways. One correct flowchart, together with its assertions, is shown in Fig. 10.5. A proof that each of its assertions imply succeeding assertions is left for an exercise. ∎

[†] Clearly there are programs that do not have this structure. There may be more than one place at which output is produced, and the number of outputs may be different for different inputs. One solution in this case is to attach an assertion to each halt statement to the effect that the output is the correct function of the input.

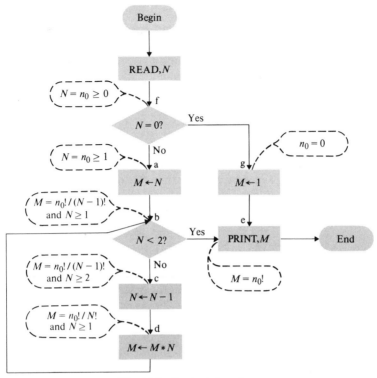

Fig. 10.5   Revised flowchart.

By now, we should have some idea about how to prove that correctly chosen assertions imply one another. However, it is reasonable to ask how one goes about selecting the correct assertions. To begin, one should have a rough idea of the important relationships between the values of identifiers at each point in the program. These make a natural first approximation to the assertion at that point. Then, we attempt to show that each assertion follows from its predecessors.

Quite possibly, we shall find a point whose assertion we cannot prove from one of its predecessor points. Then, we must assert enough new conditions at the predecessor point to make the proof possible. Of course, it only makes sense to assert conditions we believe true. Having augmented the assertion at one point, we may find it necessary to augment assertions at its predecessors, and so on. Hopefully, we shall eventually assert enough so that all assertions follow from these predecessors.

Example 10.5.   Let us reconsider points (b), (c) and (d) of Fig. 10.5, (or equivalently, of Fig. 10.1). It is quite possible that we would see the necessity of asserting $M = n_0!/N!$ at (d) and $M = n_0!/(N-1)!$ at (b) and (c). However, it might not be so apparent that $N \geqslant 2$ was needed at (c) or $N \geqslant 1$ at (d). However, when we try to prove

$N = n_0!/(N - 1)!$ at (b), we discover that $N \geqslant 1$ is needed at (d) (see Example 10.2 on p. 302 for the argument). Then, we need to augment the assertion at (c) by adding $N \geqslant 2$, so we can prove $N \geqslant 1$ at (d).

Note that $N \geqslant 2$ at (c) needs no change at (b), since $N \geqslant 2$ is implied by the fact that $N < 2$ is false whenever the branch from (b) to (c) is taken. We need $N \geqslant 1$ at (b) so that, together with $M = n_0!/(N - 1)$ at (b) and the truth of $N < 2$, we can show $M = n_0!$ at (e).   ∎

It should be emphasized that the method described here is not guaranteed to work, even if the program is correct. It is possible that we shall continue forever augmenting assertions. In fact, we can say more. There is no method of finding assertions, or of proving programs correct in any other way, that will work for all correct programs. Thus, proving programs correct is and will remain an intellectual challenge—and a useful one at that.

10.4   PROVING CORRECTNESS OF RECURSIVE PROGRAMS

Suppose we are given a main program and a collection of subroutines, perhaps recursive ones. We can attach assertions to both the beginning and end of each subroutine. Each time we call a subroutine we must show its beginning assertion holds at the point of call. Using its final assertion we must prove the assertion at each point to which return could go.

In making such proofs we may have to deal carefully with questions of what data has or has not changed during the call. If the subroutine manipulates pointer variables the question of exactly what gets changed is subtle. However, in simple cases it is possible, by paying careful attention to the linkage convention used, to make the essential inferences about identifiers whose values do not change. These ideas are perhaps best illustrated with an example.

Example 10.6.   Let us consider the recursive subroutine FACT(N, M) which sets M to $N!$ as in Fig. 10.6(a). Suppose FACT is called by the program of Fig. 10.6(b), and assume for specificity that the call of FACT is by reference. Fig. 10.7 shows flowcharts of the programs in Fig. 10.6 with assertions made and the points named.

Let us begin by proving the assertions in Fig. 10.7(b). Except for the transition from (h) to (i), all implications should be easy for the reader to prove using the techniques of the previous section. The assertion at (h) is sufficient to show the assertion at (a), the beginning of FACT. They are identical, since actual parameter K in the call of FACT is the same as formal parameter N in the body of FACT.

The final assertion of FACT, at (e) is $M = N!$. It is easy to check that, under the rules of call-by-reference, the M in each call of FACT is the local identifier L belonging to the calling routine of Fig. 10.6(b). Thus N at (e) is the same as K at (i) when FACT returns to the calling routine, and similarly, M at (e) is L at (i). Thus the assertion at (e) is identical to, and hence implies the assertion at i.

Now let us turn to the assertions of FACT itself. All the transitions except that from (c) to (d) are again easy to show, using the techniques of Section 10.3. We leave

```
begin
    if N .LE. 1 then
        M = 1
    else
        begin
            CALL FACT(N − 1, M);
            M = N * M
        end;
    RETURN
end
```

(a)

```
begin
    READ, K;
    if K .GE. 1 then
        begin
            CALL FACT(K, L);
            PRINT, L
        end
end
```

(b)

Fig. 10.6   Program to compute factorials: a) FACT (N, M); b) Calling routine.

these to the reader. We must show that the assertion at (c) implies that at (a). Let N have value n at (c). Then actual parameter $N − 1$ in the call of FACT$(N − 1, M)$ has value $n − 1$ and thus so does formal parameter N at (a). Hence the assertion $N \geqslant 2$ at (c) implies $n \geqslant 2$, which implies $n − 1 \geqslant 1$, which proves $N \geqslant 1$ at (a). Thus, the assertion at (a) is shown.

Finally, we must show that the assertion at (e) implies the assertion at (d). We argued above that all references at M are to the same datum. We have already argued that the actual parameter $N − 1$ in the call has the same value as the formal parameter N when FACT$(N − 1, M)$ is called. Since no assignments to N are made, this relation holds at the end of FACT. Thus $N!$ at (e) has the same value as $(N − 1)!$ at (d). We may conclude that $M = N!$ at (e) implies $M = (N − 1)!$ at (d). In addition, since N does not change, $N \geqslant 2$ at (c) implies $N \geqslant 2$ at (d). We have completed the transition from (c) to (d) and completed the proof of correctness for the program of Fig. 10.6. ∎

It should be noted that there is no paradox in Example 10.6 where we apparently used the correctness of FACT to prove the correctness of FACT. What we really did was show that if FACT works correctly when called with first parameter having value $n − 1$, then the same was true when called with parameter n. That is, the transition from (c) to (d) assumes FACT works correctly when called with first argument $N − 1$. The fact that the transition from (c) to (d) is correct is the key step in

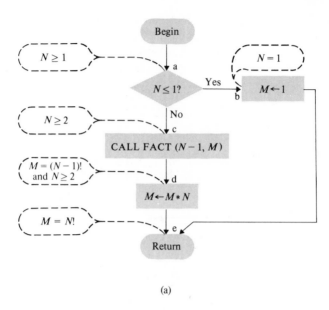

(a)

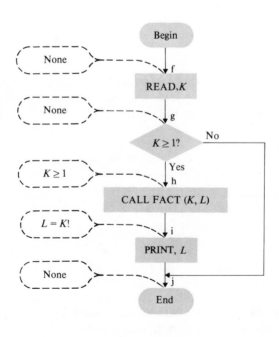

(b)

Fig. 10.7 Flowcharts of programs in Fig. 10.6: a) Flowchart of FACT (N, M); b) Flowchart of calling routine.

showing that Fig. 10.7(a) is correct, and knowing Fig. 10.7(a) is correct we know FACT is correct with first argument N. Thus the proof of the correctness of FACT(N, M) is really by mathematical induction on the value of N.

It should also be noted that Example 10.6 has proven correctness for the program in Fig. 10.6 only under the assumption that calls to FACT eventually terminate (which they do).

10.5 PROVING TERMINATION

Now, let us consider how to check or prove that a program does terminate. As we have mentioned several times, such a proof is technically necessary if we are to prove that a program is "correct," i.e., that it computes the function we say it computes. The matter of detecting and avoiding infinite loops is, of course, important in its own right as well.

The basic method of proving that a program without recursion terminates is the following:

1. identify all the loops of the program;
2. for each loop, find a function f of the values possessed by some program variables such that:
    i) each time around the loop, f decreases by at least 1, and
    ii) exit from the loop occurs when f reaches 0 or below.

Example 10.7. Consider the flowchart of Fig. 10.5 (p. 305). It should be obvious that the only loop is from (b) to (c) to (d) and back to (b) again. A suitable function f is $f = N - 1$. Since N decreases by 1 each time around the loop, so does f. When $N - 1$ reaches 0, i.e., $N = 1$, the loop terminates, as the YES branch is taken from (b). ∎

It should not be imagined that loops are uniformly easy to identify in programs or flowcharts. However, in structured programming languages, such as our language of Chapter 0, loops are indicated by loop forming constructs. For example, our language used the **while** . . . **do** . . . , **repeat** . . . **until**, and **for** . . . constructs, and nothing else, to form loops.

We should also realize that selecting the decreasing function f is not as easy in all cases as it was in Example 10.7. However, it is fair to state that if the programmer cannot find such a function, either he has an infinite loop, or he was being more clever when he wrote the program than when he tried to prove that it terminated.

The second need when proving termination is some way of dealing with recursive programs. In addition to showing the absence of infinite loops, we also need to show that there are no infinite recursions. Put another way, for each possible input, we must show that there is an upper limit on the length of the stack used for implementation as in Section 7.2. The bounds on stack length need not be the same for all inputs, of course.

One strategy is to find a function f to associate with each call of a subroutine, such that:

   i) f decreases by at least one each time a subroutine is called, and

   ii) no calls are made if f is 0 or below.

Example 10.8. The appropriate f for FACT of Fig. 10.6(a) (p. 307) is again $f = N - 1$. A recursive call to FACT only occurs if $N - 1 > 0$, i.e., $N \geqslant 2$.

The appropriate f for COMB(N, M, P), the recursive routine discussed in Example 7.5 (p. 202) is more subtle. We suggest $f = N + M - 2$. We note that f decreases by 1 when COMB(N $-$ 1, M, P1) is called and by 2 when COMB(N $-$ 1, M $-$ 1, P2) is called. Thus condition (i) is satisfied. When $f \leqslant 0$, we have $N + M \leqslant 2$. Since $0 \leqslant M \leqslant N$, we can only have $M = 0$ or $M = N = 1$. In neither case is a recursive call of COMB made. Thus condition (ii) is satisfied. ∎

10.6 APPLICATIONS OF CORRECTNESS PROOFS

As mentioned in the chapter preface, the techniques of this chapter can help the programmer in various ways, even though he is unlikely ever to write formal proofs that his programs are correct, as we have done here. The first simplification of the ideas of this chapter is that the important inductive assertions are:

1. the assertions at the beginning (*entry point*) of loops such as point (*b*) in Fig. 10.5 (p. 305). As mentioned in Section 10.5, the loops are easy to identify if a structured programming language is used. If a language with goto's is used, the loops may not even have unique entry points, and we can make no promise about the success of the simplified technique described here.

2. the entries of subroutines.

If we have correct assertions at the loop or subroutine entry points, we can if we wish, deduce the assertions at the other points in the program. But in fact, the "other points" in the program, having no loops or subroutine calls, are usually fairly easy to understand and check without the aid of inductive assertions.

Example 10.9. The crucial assertion in Fig. 10.5 (p. 305) is at (*b*), where we assert

$$M = n_0!/(N - 1)! \text{ and } N \geqslant 1. \tag{10.10}$$

That is, M is the product of integers from n_0 to the current value of N. From Expression (10.10) we can deduce the assertions at (*c*) and (*d*) as follows. Recall from p. 303 our rule for proving assertions across a branching statement as in Fig. 10.3. There A_1 would be Expression (10.10) and the proposition $\mathscr{P}$ would be $N < 2$. A_3 would be the proposition at (*c*) in Fig. 10.5. We were told in Section 10.3 to try to prove A_3 using A_1 and the falsehood of $\mathscr{P}$. Thus if we choose A_3 to be $A_1 \vee \neg \mathscr{P}$ (i.e., A_1 is true and $\mathscr{P}$ is false), we shall have no trouble proving A_3. This reasoning tells us to assert:

$$M = n_0!/(N - 1)! \text{ and } N \geqslant 1 \text{ and } N \geqslant 2$$

or more simply:

$$M = n_0!/(N - 1)! \text{ and } N \geqslant 2 \tag{10.11}$$

Note that (10.11) is the assertion at (c) in Fig. 10.4.

Now let us consider the assertion at (d). We go from (c) to (d) through the assignment $N \leftarrow N - 1$. The rule for assignments suggested by Fig. 10.2 is to substitute the right side $\mathscr{E}$ of the assignment for the left side X in A_2 of Fig. 10.2 and try to prove the resulting proposition from A_1. Putting the idea in reverse, if we know A_1, the assertion A_2 which we know we can prove is A_1 with X substituted for $\mathscr{E}$. For example, A_1 could be Expression (10.11) at (c) in Fig. 10.4. There the assignment is $N \leftarrow N - 1$, so we must substitute N for $N - 1$, or equivalently $N + 1$ for N. If we do so in (10.11) we get

$$M = n_0!/N! \text{ and } N \geqslant 1$$

which is the assertion at (d) in Fig. 10.4. ∎

In Example 10.9, we saw rules for going around a loop and checking a correct assertion at the beginning of the loop. One additional rule is necessary when paths come together inside a loop as at point (a) in Fig. 10.8. The rule is to compute the assertions A_1 and A_2 which would follow blocks B_1 and B_2 at points (b) and (c), using the rule for assignments (or branches if B_1 or B_2 were a test) just described in Example 10.9. Then, to get the assertion at point (a), take the logical "or" of A_1 and A_2, i.e., $A_1 \vee A_2$.

Although filling in the assertions around a loop is easy; once we have a correct assertion at the loop entry, there is no "easy" way to get correct assertions for the loop entries. The programmer must use his understanding of this program he has just written to tell what those assertions must be.

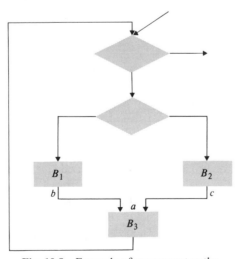

Fig. 10.8 Example of convergent paths.

Example 10.10.   Let us return to the factorial flowchart of Fig. 10.5. If the programmer has just written a program from which that program is derived, presumably he knows that his strategy was to set M to n_0 and multiply M by each of $n_0 - 1$, $n_0 - 2, \ldots, 1$ in turn. Moreover each time through point (b), N takes on the values $n_0, n_0 - 1, \ldots, 2$. Thus it should not be hard for him to deduce that any time (b) is reached, $M = n_0 *(n_0 - 1) * \cdots * N$, that is, $M = n_0!/(N - 1)!$.

Unfortunately, $M = n_0!/(N - 1)!$ is not enough to assert. We must also assert $N \geq 1$ at (b), or we shall not be able to prove the assertion $M = n_0!$ at (e) from (b) and the fact that $N < 2$ is true. This last detail can only be discovered if and when the programmer works out a complete proof of his program.   ∎

There is another important application of assertions, especially the ones at loop entries and the beginning and end of subroutines. This application is in documenting programs. For example, for the routine COMB(N, M, P) of Fig. 7.5 (p. 201), the crucial comment is that $P = \binom{N}{M}$ at the end, provided $0 \leq M \leq N$ and $N \geq 1$ at the beginning. With these assertions at the beginning and end, plus the algebraic identities from Expression (7.1), the program becomes easy to understand; without them the program is virtually impossible to understand. For a more subtle example, let us consider the following.

Example 10.11.   A *graph* is a collection of nodes and edges from one node to another (as discussed for trees in Section 3.5). One way to represent a graph is to number the nodes $1, 2, \ldots, N$ for some N, and represent the edges by an $N \times N$ Boolean array $G(I, J)$, where $G(I, J) =$ **true** if there is an edge from node I to node J and $G(I, J) =$ **false** if not. For example, the graph G of Fig. 10.9(a) has the array representation in Fig. 10.9(b), where $1 =$ **true** and $0 =$ **false**.

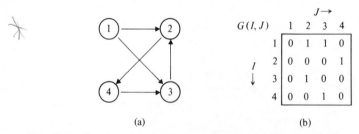

(a)   (b)

Fig. 10.9   Graph and its array representation: a) Graph; b) Array representation.

Sometimes we are interested in which nodes are connected by a path. We say there is a *path from node I to node J* if there is an edge from I to J or a sequence of nodes $K_1, K_2, \ldots, K_m$ such that there are edges from I to K_1, from K_1 to $K_2, \ldots,$ from K_{m-1} to K_m, and from K_m to J. For example, there is a path from 1 to 2 in Fig. 10.9(a), since there is an edge. There is a path from 2 to 3, via 4. That is, let $I = 2, J = 3, m = 1$, and $K_1 = 4$. Then there are edges from I to K_1 and K_1 to J. Finally, there is a path from 2 to 2. Let $I = J = 2, m = 2, K_1 = 4$, and $K_2 = 3$.

There is an algorithm, known as *Warshall's algorithm*, which constructs from an array G for a graph the *path matrix*, an $N \times N$ Boolean array $P(I, J)$ such that

$P(I, J) = $ **true** if and only if there is a path from I to J. We give this algorithm in Fig. 10.10.

Now it is fairly easy to see that lines (2) to (4) in Fig. 10.10 serve simply to copy G into P. A comment to this effect before line (2) would amply document this part. It is also evident that lines (5) to (7) set up a triple loop on indices L, I, and J, whose loop body is statement (8). However, it is not at all obvious that the algorithm works, and the reader should decide now whether or not he is being led down a "primrose path" as he was in the "proof of correctness" of the incorrect algorithm in Fig. 10.1. Moreover, a comment about line (8) such as "if $P(I, J)$ is **false** but $P(I, L)$ and $P(L, J)$ are both **true** then make $P(I, J)$ **true**" is really no help in explaining how the algorithm works, or even, in fact, if it does work.

```
(1) begin
(2)     for I = 1 to N do
(3)         for J = 1 to N do
(4)             P(I, J) = G(I, J);
(5)     for L = 1 to N do
(6)         for I = 1 to N do
(7)             for J = 1 to N do
(8)                 P(I, J) = P(I, J) .OR. (P(I, L) .AND. P(L, J))
(9) end
```

Fig. 10.10 Warshall's algorithm.

It turns out that Warshall's algorithm is hardly an obvious one, but it does work and is quite fast compared with other ways of computing the path matrix. Moreover, once we see the correct inductive assertion at the beginning of the outer loop, lines (5) to (8), we shall understand how the algorithm works. To begin the statement of the inductive assertion, we say that a path from I_1 to I_2 to ... to I_r *goes through* I_2, $I_3, \ldots, I_{r-1}$, that is, it goes through all but the endpoints. For example, in Fig. 10.9(a) the path 2 to 4 to 3 goes through 4 (but not 2 or 3). The path from 2 to 4 to 3 to 2 goes through 3 and 4. The path from 1 to 2 goes through nothing. Then the inductive assertion true just before we commence lines (6) to (8) for a fixed value of L is:

$$P(I, J) = \textbf{true} \text{ if and only if there is a path from} \qquad (10.12)$$
$$I \text{ to } J \text{ that goes through no node } L \text{ or higher.}$$

For $L = 1$ Expression (10.12) says $P(I, J) = $ **true** if and only if there is a path from I to J that goes through no node at all. That is, there is an edge from I to J. Since lines (2) to (4) have just copied the edges from G into P, we see that Expression (10.12) holds just before executing lines (6) to (8) for $L = 1$.

To see that Expression (10.12) continues to hold after we step L to $L + 1$, note that lines (6) to (7) cause line (8) to be done for all I and J. There is a path from I to J that goes through no node $L + 1$ or higher if one of the following two cases holds:

i) there is a path from I to J that goes through no node L or higher, or

ii) there is a path from I to L and a path from L to J, neither of which goes through a node L or higher. In case (i), $P(I, J)$ is already **true** when we execute (8) for I, J, and L. In case (ii), $P(I, L)$ and $P(L, J)$ are both already **true**, so we set $P(I, J)$ to **true**.

The above argument shows that Expression (10.12) continues to hold as L is increased. Now consider what Expression (10.12) says after L is increased to $N + 1$ and the loop terminates. It says $P(I, J) =$ **true** if and only if there is a path from I to J that goes through no node higher than N. But there are no higher nodes than N, so Expression (10.12) for $L = N + 1$ says $P(I, J) =$ **true** if and only if there is any path at all from I to J. ∎

Even with the inductive assertion Expression (10.12), we still had some work to do to understand this clever algorithm. But Expression (10.12) did give us the clue we needed; without it there was very little chance of our understanding the code of Fig. 10.10. Put another way, if we were given this program to understand and modify, we could expect to eventually understand it if it were documented to the extent of the assertion in Expression (10.12). If the only documentation were trivial restatements of what lines (4) and (8) did, we might very well not comprehend it even after considerable thought. The moral of Example 10.11 is that the inductive assertions at loop entries are often good, even essential pieces of documentation.

EXERCISES

10.1 Figure 10.11 shows a flowchart for computing $N ** M$, together with assertions. Prove that the flowchart program prints $(n_0)^{m_0}$ on the assumption that the values n_0 and m_0 of N and M, respectively, are read in as integers and satisfy $n_0 \geqslant 1$ and $m_0 \geqslant 1$.

*10.2 The flowchart of Fig. 10.12 computes N^2 by summing $1 + 3 + 5 + \cdots + 2N - 1$. That is, the ith term of the series is $2i - 1$. Place assertions at the various points and prove that the program computes $(n_0)^2$ if integer $n_0 \geqslant 1$ is read in. *Hint:* After $M \leftarrow M + 2 * N - 1$, the value of M is $n_0^2 - (N - 1)^2 + 1$.

**10.3 Prove that if real number $X \geqslant 1$ is read in, then the program of Fig. 10.13 computes the characteristic of the base 2 logarithm of X.[†]

*10.4 Fig. 10.14 shows a recursive program to compute $M = N^2$, for $N \geqslant 1$ essentially by summing the series given in Exercise 10.2.

    a) Draw a flowchart for the routine SQUARE.

    b) Prove its correctness by using inductive assertions. Assume call-by-reference.

**10.5 Is SQUARE of Fig. 10.14 correct if the call is

    a) by copy-restore

    b) by name?

*10.6 Prove the termination of the following programs.

    a) Fig. 10.11

    b) Fig. 10.12

[†] The *characteristic of the base 2 logarithm of* X is the largest integer i such that $2^i \leqslant X$.

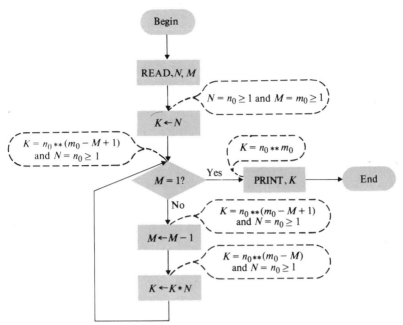

Fig. 10.11   Flowchart to compute N∗∗M.

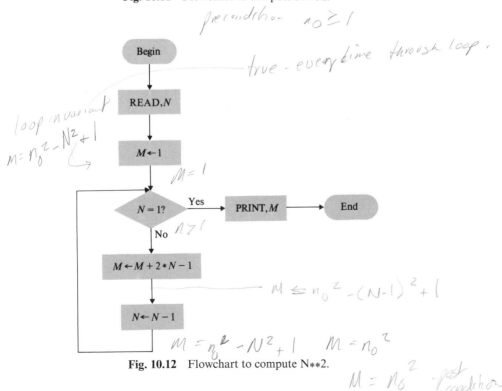

Fig. 10.12   Flowchart to compute N∗∗2.

c) Fig. 10.13

d) Fig. 10.14

**10.7 Exercise 7.4 (p. 218) gave two mutually recursive subroutines that computed squares and triangular numbers. Prove that they terminate and are correct.

10.8 The program of Exercise 0.1(b) plays the following "game." We generate a sequence of numbers $a_1, a_2, \ldots$ by the following rules. Assume we have just found a_i for some $i \geq 1$.

i) If $a_i = 1$, then stop.

ii) If a_i is even, let a_{i+1} be $a_i/2$.

iii) If a_i is odd, let a_{i+1} be $3a_i + 1$.

For example, if we choose $a_1 = 19$, we have the sequence 19, 58, 29, 88, 44, 22, 11, 34, 17, 52, 26, 13, 40, 20, 10, 5, 16, 8, 4, 2, 1. It is an open problem whether such sequences can go on forever, or whether for any positive integer a_1, the number 1 must eventually appear in the sequence. However, you may, as an exercise, prove that if the PRINT statement is reached, N has the value 1. Can you prove termination? If you can, you have solved a very tough problem.

```
begin
    READ, X;
    I = 0;
    while X .GE. 2. do
        begin
            I = I + 1;
            X = X/2.
        end;
    PRINT, I
end
```

Fig. 10.13   Program to compute characteristic of base-2 logarithm of X.

```
if N .EQ. 1 then
    M = 1
else
    begin
        CALL SQUARE(N − 1, M);
        M = M + 2 * N − 1
    end
```

Fig. 10.14   The recursive subroutine SQUARE (N, M).

FURTHER READING

The origin of the inductive assertions idea is with Floyd [1967]. Hoare [1969] is another fundamental paper on the subject. Much of the research developing the concept can be found in ACM [1972]. Elspas, Levitt, Waldinger, and Waksman [1972] is a good survey of the subject.

Warshall's algorithm, mentioned in Example 10.11, is from Warshall [1962].

Bibliography

ACM (1972) *Proceedings of an ACM Conference on Proving Assertions about Programs*, ACM, New York.

Aho, A. V., J. E. Hopcroft, and J. D. Ullman (1974) *The Design and Analysis of Computer Algorithms*, Addison-Wesley, Reading, Mass.

Aho, A. V., and S. C. Johnson (1974) "LR parsing," *Computing Surveys*, **6**:2, pp. 99–124.

Aho, A. V., and J. D. Ullman (1972) *The Theory of Parsing, Translation and Compiling, Vol. I—Parsing*, Prentice Hall, Englewood Cliffs, N. J.

Aho, A. V., and J. D. Ullman (1973) *The Theory of Parsing, Translation and Compiling, Vol. II—Compiling*, Prentice Hall, Englewood Cliffs, N. J.

Barron, D. W. (1969) *Assemblers and Loaders*, MacDonald-Elsevier, New York.

Bell, C. G., and A. Newell (1971) *Computer Structures*, McGraw-Hill, New York.

Berztiss, A. T. (1971) *Data Structures: Theory and Practice*, Academic Press, New York.

Bohm, C., and G. Jacopini (1966) "Flow diagrams, Turing machines and languages with only two formation rules," *CACM*, **9**:5, pp. 366–371.

Booth, T. L. (1971) *Digital Networks and Computer Systems*, Wiley, New York.

Brinch-Hansen, P. (1973) *Operating Systems Principles*, Prentice Hall, Englewood Cliffs, N. J.

Bruno, J. L., and K. Steiglitz (1972) "The expression of algorithms by charts," *JACM*, **19**:3, pp. 517–525.

Chomsky, N. (1956) "Three models for the description of language," *IRE Trans. on Information Theory*, **2**:3, pp. 113–124.

Coffman, Jr., E. G., and P. J. Denning (1973) *Operating Systems Theory*, Prentice Hall, Englewood Cliffs, N. J.

Denning, P. J. (1971) "Third generation computer systems," *Computing Surveys*, **3**:4, pp. 175–216.

Dijkstra, E. W. (1960) "Recursive programming," *Numerische Math.*, **2**, pp. 312–318. Reprinted in Rosen [1967].

Dijkstra, E. W. (1968) "Goto statement considered harmful," *CACM*, **11**:3, pp. 147–148.

Donovan, J. J. (1972) *Systems Programming*, McGraw-Hill, New York.

Elson, M. (1973) *Concepts of Programming Languages*, Science Research Associates, Palo Alto, Calif.

Elspas, B., K. N. Levitt, R. J. Waldinger, and A. Waksman (1972) "An assessment of techniques for proving program correctness," *Computing Surveys*, **4**:2, pp. 97–147.

Flores, I. (1963) *The Logic of Computer Arithmetic*, Prentice Hall, Englewood Cliffs, N. J.

Floyd, R. W. (1967) "Assigning meanings to programs," *Proc. Symposia in Applied Math.*, Vol. 19, pp. 19–32, AMS, Providence, R. I.

Galler, B. A., and A. J. Perlis (1970) *A View of Programming Languages*, Addison-Wesley, Reading, Mass.

Gear, C. W. (1974) *Computer Organization and Programming*, McGraw-Hill, New York.

Ginsburg, S., *The Mathematical Theory of Context Free Languages*, McGraw-Hill, New York.

Gries, D. (1971) *Compiler Construction for Digital Computers*, Wiley, New York.

Harrison, M. C. (1973) *Data Structures and Programming*, Scott, Foresman, Glenview, Ill.

Hecht, M. S. (1975) *A Theoretical Foundation for Global Program Improvement*, American Elsevier, New York.

Hoare, C. A. R. (1969) "An axiomatic basis for computer programming," *CACM*, **12**:10, pp. 576–580.

Hoare, C. A. R., O. J. Dahl, and E. W. Dijkstra (1972) *Structured Programming*, Academic Press, New York.

Hopcroft, J. E., and J. D. Ullman (1969) *Formal Languages and Their Relation to Automata*, Addison-Wesley, Reading, Mass.

Ichbiah, J. D., and S. P. Morse (1970) "A technique for generating almost optimal Floyd-Evans productions," *CACM* **13**:8, pp. 501–508.

Ingerman, P. Z. (1961) "Thunks," *CACM*, **4**:1, pp. 55–58.

Irons, E. T. (1961) "A syntax directed compiler for ALGOL 60," *CACM*, **4**:1, pp. 51–55. Reprinted in Rosen [1967].

Kernighan, B. W., and P. J. Plauger (1974) *The Elements of Programming Style*, McGraw-Hill, New York.

Knuth, D. E. (1968a) *The Art of Computer Programming, Vol. I, Fundamental Algorithms*, Addison-Wesley, Reading, Mass.

Knuth, D. E. (1968b) "Semantics of context free languages," *Math. Syst. Theory*, **2**:2, pp. 127–146.

Knuth, D. E. (1969) *The Art of Computer Programming, Vol. II, Seminumerical Algorithms*, Addison-Wesley, Reading, Mass.

Knuth, D. E. (1973) *The Art of Computer Programming, Vol. III, Sorting and Searching*, Addison-Wesley, Reading, Mass.

Kohavi, Z. (1970) *Switching and Finite Automata Theory*, McGraw-Hill, New York.

Leavenworth, B. M. (1966) "Syntax macros and extended translation," *CACM*, **9**:11, pp. 790–793.

Lewis II, P. M., D. J. Rosenkrantz, and R. E. Stearns (1975) *Compiler Design Theory*, Addison-Wesley, Reading, Mass.

Lewis II, P. M., and R. E. Stearns (1968) "Syntax directed transduction," *JACM*, **15**:3, pp. 464–488.

Lo, A. W. (1968) *Introduction to Digital Electronics*, Addison-Wesley, Reading, Mass.

McIlroy, M. D. (1960) "Macro instruction extensions of compiler languages," *CACM*, **3**:4, pp. 414–420. Reprinted in Rosen [1967].

McKeeman, W. M., J. J. Horning, and D. B. Wortman (1970) *A Compiler Generator*, Prentice Hall, Englewood Cliffs, N. J.

Morris, R. (1968) "Scatter storage techniques," *CACM*, **11**:1, pp. 35–44.

Nievergelt, J., J. C. Farrar, and E. M. Reingold (1974) *Computer Approaches to Mathematical Problems*, Prentice Hall, Englewood Cliffs, N. J.

Peterson, W. W. (1974) *Introduction to Programming Languages*, Prentice Hall, Englewood Cliffs, N. J.

Pratt, T. W. (1975) *Programming Language Design and Implementation*, Prentice Hall, Englewood Cliffs, N. J.

Presser, L., and J. R. White (1972) "Linkers and loaders," *Computing Surveys*, **4**:3, pp. 149–168.

Randell, B., and L. J. Russell (1964) *ALGOL 60 Implementation*, Academic Press, New York.

Richards, M. (1969) "BCPL: a tool for compiler writing and system programming," *Proc. Spring Joint Computer Conference*, Vol. 34, pp. 557–566, AFIPS Press, Montvale, N. J.

Rosen, S. (1967) *Programming Systems and Languages*, McGraw-Hill, New York.

Salomaa, A. (1973) *Formal Languages*, Academic Press, New York.

Sammet, J. E. (1969) *Programming Languages: History and Fundamentals*, Prentice Hall, Englewood Cliffs, N. J.

Schaefer, M. (1973) *A Mathematical Theory of Global Program Optimization*, Prentice Hall, Englewood Cliffs, N. J.

Stone, H. S. (1972) *Introduction to Computer Organization and Data Structures*, McGraw-Hill, New York.

Stone, H. S. (1973) *Discrete Mathematical Structures*, Science Research Associates, Palo Alto, Calif.

Warshall, S. (1962) "A theorem on Boolean matrices," *JACM*, **9**:1, pp. 1–12.

Wegner, P. (1968) *Programming Languages, Information Structures and Machine Organization*, McGraw-Hill, New York.

Wirth, N. (1973) *Systematic Programming: An Introduction*, Prentice Hall, Englewood Cliffs, N. J.

Wulf, W. S., D. B. Russell, and A. N. Habermann (1971) "BLISS: a language for systems programming," *CACM*, **14**:12, pp. 780–790.

Appendix

1. INSTRUCTIONS FOR OUR COMPUTER

Octal code—bits 1 to 6	Mnemonic	Meaning	Page reference
00	HALT	Halt.	
01	COPY	Move register to register.	p. 62
	LOAD	Move memory to register.	
	STORE	Move register to memory.	
02	ADD	Add in fixed-point.	p. 63
03	ADDFL	Add in floating-point.	p. 63
04	SUB	Subtract in fixed-point.	p. 63
05	SUBFL	Subtract in floating-point.	p. 63
06	MULT	Multiply in fixed-point.	p. 63
07	MULTFL	Multiply in floating-point.	p. 63
10	DIV	Divide in fixed-point.	p. 63
11	DIVFL	Divide in floating-point.	p. 63
12	AND	Logical "and."	p. 64
13	OR	Logical "or."	p. 64
14	XOR	Logical "exclusive or."	p. 64
15	NOT	Logical "not."	p. 65
16	COMP	Complement (negate).	p. 65
17	SHIFTL	Shift left.	p. 65
20	SHIFTR	Shift right.	p. 65
21	JUMP	Unconditional transfer.	p. 67

22	JPLUS	Transfer if plus sign in register.	p. 67
23	JMINUS	Transfer if minus sign in register.	p. 67
24	JZERO	Transfer if register holds zero.	p. 67
25	JNONZ	Transfer if register does not hold zero.	p. 67
26	JDIS	Transfer on "disaster."	p. 67
27	READ	Read.	p. 72
30	WRITE	Write.	p. 72

2. ADDRESS MODIFIER

Bits 13 to 15	Mnemonic	Meaning	Page reference
1	IMML	Left immediate	p. 74
2	IMMED	Right immediate	p. 74
3	INDL	Left indirect	p. 75
4	IND	Right indirect	p. 75
5	CH	Character handling	p. 78
Bits 16 to 18			
i	Xi	Index by register i, for $1 \leqslant i \leqslant 7$	p. 76

3. I/O DEVICE CODES

Bits 7 to 12 of READ/WRITE instructions	Device
00	Printer
01	Card reader
02	Card punch
03	Disk

4. CHARACTER CODES

Character	Code (octal)
0 through 9	00 through 11, respectively.
A through Z	12 through 43, respectively.
blank (ƀ)	44

Index

absolute address; *see* offset
abstract meaning, 162–163
activation record, 197–199, 201, 210–217
actual parameter, 134; *see also* parameter passing
addition, 27–28, 32–33, 37–38
address, 52, 61, 83, 91, 126
address modification, 74–80, 82
address register; *see* memory address register
Aho, A. V., 49, 119, 253, 298
ALGOL, 170, 181–182, 209
ALLOCATE statement, 170
ambiguous grammar, 248–251
ancestor, 101
and (logical), 64
APL, 170, 182
argument; *see* actual parameter, formal parameter, parameter passing
arithmetic expression, 130–131, 174–178, 222, 271–277
arithmetic operation, 56, 63–64
arithmetic unit, 51, 56
array, 167–169, 177–178, 210
ASCII, 44
assembler, 121–143
assembly language, 80–84
assertion, 300–314
assignment statement, 9, 162, 178–179, 301–302
associative law, 31, 46, 175
associative memory, 104
associative structure, 103–114, 162, 170

attribute, 164
automatic identifier, 170
auxiliary translation, 283
available space, 94–95, 171

Barron, D. W., 143, 160
base; *see* radix
base register, 85, 149–152
BCD, 44
BCPL, 20, 80
Bell, C. G., 88
Berztiss, A. T., 119
best fit, 192
binary number, 21, 26
binary operator, 174–176
binary search tree, 105–108
binding, of identifier, 179–183
bit, 30
bit string, 165
blank, 43
BLISS, 20, 80
block, 8, 162, 213
BNF, 223
Bohm, C., 20
bookkeeping, 255–256, 263–266
Boolean variable, 165–166
Booth, T. L., 88
bounding register, 85
BREAK statement, 15
Brinch-Hansen, P., 88
Bruno, J. L., 20